THE CHALLENGE

Other Books by
Phyllis Bottome

The Challenge

by

PHYLLIS BOTTOME

HARCOURT, BRACE AND COMPANY
NEW YORK

COPYRIGHT, 1953, BY
PHYLLIS BOTTOME

first American edition

LIBRARY OF CONGRESS CATALOG CARD NUMBER: 52-11350

PRINTED IN THE UNITED STATES OF AMERICA

33338

To

MY HUSBAND

" Thought's the slave of life, and life's time's fool ;
And time, who takes survey of all the world,
Must have a stop."

—SHAKESPEARE

PREFACE

It is not difficult to write the history of childhood in old age. Those who knew us best and who are responsible for revealing life to us are already dead. We can therefore write of them without bitterness or illusion. Nor need we seek to idealize, for defensive purposes, the facts themselves, since in these first years of innocence we are not seriously concerned by the impression we make upon ourselves or upon others.

The years from adolescence to the early thirties are a far more difficult and dubious business. Here there is a real danger of becoming

> *Like one*
> *Who into truth, by telling of it,*
> *Makes such a sinner of the memory,*
> *To credit his own lie.*

These are the years of challenge in which we must expose those hidden aims we have been choosing, and upon which we have built our life-plan, from our earliest childhood.

It is the foreknowledge of this inevitable exposure far more than our growth into sexual maturity that makes adolescence so difficult a time for the young. Facts have begun to bite into our fairyland, and our future usefulness and reliability depend on the amount of unreality we are prepared to throw overboard in our search for truth.

There is a still greater difficulty. Our contemporaries may have survived, and as memory is largely individual their interpretation of what once took place may differ widely from our own.

Adler believed that we choose our memories, so that what has happened to us is less important to us—and even less true—than what we have accepted from the impact of our individualities upon events.

9

In writing of my broken engagement I am now certain that, good as were the reasons for breaking it, those reasons need never have arisen, nor proved so painful to us, had I shown less determination to remain in a fairyland contradicted by facts.

To have accepted the absence of joy with patience, and to have taken the long up-hill climb into normal health alone, by suspending our engagement until circumstances warranted marriage, would have solved our chief problem.

Tuberculosis is a mysterious illness, not unallied with discouragement; and the guilt sense, so often discussed in modern psychology, and which in my own case accompanied it, cannot be altogether separated from psychic responsibility.

Nietzsche claims that "remorse is always dishonest", but its dishonesty may arise, not because there is nothing wrong with the stricken soul, but because we often use our remorse as a screen between ourselves and the *real* cause of our misfortune; and sometimes even as an excuse for not remedying the misfortune itself. "Courage", Adler wrote, "is the health of the soul", and "the best education for a child is an education towards courage."

For psychological reasons I have written rather more fully about these years of frustration and ill-health than many people may think desirable. I have done this purposely because these years—and there were ten of them between seventeen and twenty-seven— were a major part of the challenge which is the subject of this volume; and also because I now believe that my illness could have been considerably shortened, if not avoided altogether, had my childhood not been based upon the fears of my self-tortured mother.

Human relationships have always had first claim upon my heart and mind; and for this reason I feel unable to separate the training I gave myself as a writer from the training I received through my human relationships.

This has not meant that my actual writing has not been of absorbing and increasing interest to me. For fifty years I have written with the wind or against it. Real life is the only material upon which a writer has to draw for the material of fiction. An extrovert by nature, my novels have been largely based on excursions into the lives of others, built up by observation, out of experience.

For thirty years I lived in six countries other than my own, so that what I missed by living without the strengthening society of my professional contemporaries and our English critics, I may perhaps have gained from the variety of my adventures into other lands and among other nationalities.

In writing *The Challenge* I have tried not only, as in my earlier memoir *Search for a Soul,* to deal faithfully with my main relationships, but also to avoid interfering with my friends' rights to their private interpretations of our contacts. I have only used complete freedom of delineation where, as in *From the Life*, I knew my subjects were dead, and could not suffer from any strictures I made upon them.

In dealing with people whom I know to be still alive I have tried to limit myself to events—and my own reactions to them. With slighter relationships lost in time, I have either avoided criticism altogether or, in case these few persons survive without my knowledge and might by chance recognize long-distance portraits of themselves, while objecting to the likeness, I have invented names which I hope place them beyond the reach of recognition.

The three unacceptable admirers of my youth—Herbert, Paul and the "Black Adder" are no more, and therefore I feel free to write of them without disguise though under different names; but "Sylvia" I hope is still alive, and—since I have no certain knowledge of the fact—I have taken the liberty of re-christening her. Her name was *not* "Sylvia", though "all her swains commended her".

There is one more fact I should like my readers to bear in mind. I had not met Adler nor heard of Individual Psychology until several years after this period of "challenge" ended. My interest in psychology has been life-long, but it came from instinct and thorough observation. It could not therefore be of value to me personally in handling the problems of this part of my life. Christian in *Pilgrim's Progress* was unable to escape from Giant Despair's Castle. Not even the friendship of Faithful, nor his own belief in prayer, came to his rescue until he put his hand into his own breast and drew out a key which alone could unlock the many doors standing between him and the Castle of Deliverance.

I

The first death in a family is always a terrifying, sometimes a disruptive event. It is a test of the family's cohesion: either such a death draws the members together into a more devoted and conscious whole, or else it can, as it did in my own family, widen gulfs already there, and scatter its members further apart.

After the death of our eldest sister Wilmett at twenty-three, except for a few scattered months, our whole family never lived together again.

Wilmett had been the "flower" of the family. She was beautiful to look at, courageous and talented. Perhaps we should now describe her as "a dictator type"; for she had a driving will, though unlike that of most dictators it was attached to a generous passion for service. Wilmett carried all her family's burdens, she nursed us, advised us in season and particularly out of season, ordered us about and fought us, while valiantly fighting for us, when we had any other opponent than herself.

She met every emergency head on, and at any crisis of our mercurial lives she was her family's main support and best representative.

Now after two years' heroic struggle against a cruel disease Wilmett was no more; and we all looked at each other—taking stock of our moral poverty—as if for the first time. Who was now going to shoulder burdens, and meet lions in the path? Not my father since although he was a man full of ardour, humour and congeniality, he had never wholly grown up. My mother had always presented him to us (and it should never be forgotten that most children see the world through their mother's eyes for the first few crucial years) as an anxiety rather than as a protection. We could indeed, as I had already found out, count on his deep affection and his generous sympathy; but not upon his strength. He was a man who dumped burdens, generally on the nearest child's shoulders; and after Wilmett's death, I realized that I was the nearest child.

Mary, the sister next in age to Wilmett, had had the initiative crushed out of her early in life by our eldest sister's determined and energetic will. My mother for some strange reason—perhaps because she did not want a second child so soon after the first and had been too ill to nurse Mary—never showed her the love and understanding she gave to the rest of her children. Mary was therefore definitely out of the picture as a mainstay, although she had many of a mainstay's best characteristics including the good will; but even a mainstay requires an audience. Too early in life Mary had lost her audience. George, our only boy, was at a Public School— his career was to be normal; and normal children are not put in control of their elders' problems. It seemed therefore at eighteen that I was the best fitted to carry on Wilmett's responsibilities.

Nursing my mother was a congenial task to me, for I was devoted to her; and as for being my father's perpetual, unpaid but free-handed curate, nothing could have pleased me better. I had already for the last two years carried out most of these duties. In spite of the fact that I was unequipped for life, without training of any useful kind and, except for reading, uneducated, it never seemed to occur to my parents or myself that I was unsuited to teach others.

I had been too absorbed in my mother's health, and parish problems, to be more than intermittently aware of Wilmett's approaching doom; but when she came home, four months before her death, she became my chief preoccupation. At last I saw, in these final months of her silent heroism, what she was; and gave her what help I could. When her life ended I found my own life curiously empty. I had lost the person I had noticed most. Faced by her problems, without her courage or her wisdom, I knew that I had always admired her more than I hated her.

A few weeks after Wilmett's death I had an attack of influenza. I went to bed for it but refused a doctor. I saw no one but Mary who devotely read aloud to me for hours together; and kind Nelly, the housemaid, who brought up my meals.

I was sure I was going to get well at once, and determined to carry out my plans. I didn't get well at once; and at last very unwillingly consented to see a doctor whom I loathed. Dr. T. was new to us—and indeed disliked by us all; but he was nearer and considerably cheaper than the Gravesend doctor we had had before. He was happily an exceptional medical type. Dr. T. liked to exaggerate; boast; reveal the private affairs of his patients; and carry excitement and alarm wherever he called.

When therefore he told me that both my lungs were seriously affected by T.B. caught from nursing my sister, I did not believe him. I was indeed extremely angry—a rare occurrence—and I forced him to promise that he would tell nobody of his suspicions until I returned from a visit to the sea. He could easily order my mother to the sea and she would certainly take me with her; there I privately thought I should get perfectly well and no more need be said about the matter. To terrify my parents within six weeks of Wilmett's death would be a dastardly performance. "If you do tell them," I said with grim determination, "you may take it from me that I will never let you come into this house again!" This was certainly not the way to talk to doctors much older than myself, however venal and pushing; but it was the way in which I quelled Dr. T. and my parents had at least a few weeks' respite.

It was hard enough to have to leave my father and the parish for six weeks. Fortunately my father had Mary; but to leave my boys' club felt to me like signing away my soul. What would my bad boys do if they lost their jobs, and had no one to plead for them? What would become of all my parish duties? And of all the multifarious odds and ends of human relationships which fanned out from these duties? I resorted to prayer, but leaving such important things to an unknown Deity seemed a little precarious.

In a week my mother and I found ourselves in a much more comfortable hotel at Southbourne than was our usual custom. We had a south room, a sunny garden and good food.

It was early March when we left our gloomy, smoke-invested slum, and found ourselves in brilliant sunshine on the Bournemouth cliffs. Perhaps it was the sharpness of new grief that made the world so beautiful, and life so dear. Perhaps it was the faint shadow in the back of my mind that perhaps even a stupid doctor might be right; and that this might be the last of my springs. The daffodils shone as I had never seen them shine, the gorse was out over the dunes and under the pines. There was a golden light upon the cliffs; and all the distances were blue. My heart danced with the rough, boisterous wind; and any sea-gull I saw balancing his silver wings in tireless flight upon the sunny air carried a part of me with him.

I was prepared for sadness, and for imparting ceaseless sympathy; but my mother did not seem to be sad; it was as if she too had relaxed into security from a torture chamber.

How much of this shared felicity was camouflage on her part to save my feelings I am not now sure, but I was never easy to deceive where her emotions were concerned—they seemed an extension of my own; and I felt then wholly convinced of her happiness. Perhaps the intense relief of Wilmett's end, having been without pain or horror, was such an escape for my mother's imagination that she was not till later fully aware of her loss. She only knew that her responsibility was now at an end. Wilmett was safe, and she who had been the loving victim of Wilmett's supremest tyranny may also have felt a sense of her own release. When a neurotic relationship is brought to a sudden end, however dear or intimate it may have been, there is always a sense of escape; until those qualities which brought it about in the first place attach themselves to a new victim.

We were seldom free to be together without hindrance or anxiety. The relationship between my father and mother made everything painful to a child who loved them both. These swift weeks of solitude and sunshine alone with my mother, had all the happy amazement of a honeymoon.

We both loved out-door beauty, we shared a passion for the sea, we read with avidity and sympathy—discussing by the hour—the same books. God—people—ideas—politics—national fervour—all moved in our minds in the same direction and at the same tempo.

Wilmett had been our only difference of opinion; and now this difference was solved. Not even my mother could think of Wilmett with more admiration than I did now that she was removed from my path. We talked of her constantly, and vied with each other in remembering her successes and perfections.

It seems curious in the light of the present day to remember how fully employed we felt doing nothing; and how deep our contentment was without any amusements beyond each other's companionship. I believe that my father must at this crisis have treated my mother with such tenderness and generosity as to break down for the time being her stores of resentment against him, for not once can I remember hearing her complain of him throughout these halcyon weeks, although complaints against him formed the greater part of her usual conversation.

This absence of criticism greatly added to my happiness, for though I was still drugged and blinded into acquiescence in my mother's judgments however harsh they might be, it cut me like a knife to hear my father blamed.

I could—and did—imagine him far other than he ought to be; but I loved him with a long, irritated ache, against any detraction from qualities in him which I instinctively felt were greater than his faults.

In a curious sense, which had to do with my very blood, I belonged to my father and to his side of the family. My relationship with him was incomplete, yet it was the deepest thing in me. I remember once looking at his hands and feeling as if they were my own. This separation from my mother, soon after his agonizing loss, must have cost him a great deal, but he had risen generously to meet the sacrifice and urged us to stay on longer.

As an off-set to our unharassed days, I had terrible nights. Dreams of ghastly vividness and horror pursued me through sleep till I waked in a storm of tears.

I relived every aspect of my sister's long hopeless fight. I carried on the act of death a hundred times, the grave and all its physical horrors painted themselves against my eyelids.

When I woke, no matter what endless stretches of darkness lay before me, I would force myself to keep awake that I might not sink back into that pit of horror.

17

When the day came my heart rose with it, and I was once more happy as a child can be. I never mentioned these dreams, I carefully hid the temperature chart on which I had been told to record my daily temperatures, and took them twice a day behind a locked door.

I felt a great deal better. I was only a little tired in the morning, and a little hot and excited in the afternoon; the clear smokeless air relieved my cough, but the unsteady mercury in the thermometer did not go back to normal.

All of the other guests in the hotel were old, my mother was a child by comparison. The oldest of them all was a General Baker. One day I was left alone with him, and we began to talk about the revolt of India which was called the Indian Mutiny.

He found that I knew every famous name and incident by heart. This unlocked his memory and he told me the story of his own landing in India when he was nineteen years old.

Within a few days he had found himself caught up into the sudden storm of bitter hatred and misunderstanding. The sepoys of his regiment murdered all their officers but him. A few faithful men clung to this boy officer and when he set off alone to try to join up with Havelock's forces they went with him. They hid him by day and marched with him by night. They brought him food which he often feared might be poisoned. He knew no word of their language, they only a few uncertain words of his. Often they brought him cruel news of the overthrow of the British forces, till he believed himself to be the only white man left in the whole of India.

He wandered through plains and jungles for hundreds of miles, speechless, footsore and bereft, always shadowed and protected by this dwindling band of dark brothers, till at length he reached Cawnpore a few days after the massacre. There was still smoke in the air, and on the ground children's empty shoes, and the long golden hair of women lay in dust and blood. Wells were filled with hacked and mutilated bodies. He said the terror and the desolation in that hot light were beyond description. No living person was visible, only the heavy birds; the smoke and the awful stench of death hung in the air.

When Havelock's men found him he did not believe they were real. They had to catch hold of him and shake him before he could accept that they were not a mirage or a cruel dream.

My mother came in to find me sitting on a foot-stool at the General's feet, shaking with sobs. The tears streamed down the General's cheeks as well as mine.

To my astonishment my mother could not seem to understand the emotion that held us both alike in so fierce a grip. She had always expressed such intense interest in the uprising before—the revolution broke out the year she was born—and now she seemed shocked that we even minded. Yet this *was* the "Indian Mutiny"! This old man had been that lonely boy, who was first on the scene of the massacre. She drew me aside and lovingly, but with the utmost firmness, told me never to talk with the General about the Indian Mutiny again.

She was to give me one more surprise of an even more painful nature during those short weeks. All the old people in the hotel had been extraordinarily kind to me and perhaps the kindest of all had been an elderly widower, who had lately lost a consumptive wife. He could not do enough for us both; he brought us chairs to sit in the garden, and constantly presented us with chocolates and flowers. He must have been older than my mother; and was bald.

We were told he was a retired chemist and very well off.

One day my mother said to me, "I am sure Mr. So-and-So likes you very much. I believe you could marry him if you wanted to—and there is no doubt Bournemouth would be a much better place for you than Swanscombe!"

My horror was so profound I nearly fell off the borrowed chair. Why on earth should I marry him? What disgusting exploit had she placed before me—and for what reason?

I daresay I had never really got over my thirteen-year-old romance with an extremely handsome young soldier. Harry's image was still the only portrait in the otherwise empty gallery of my heart; and anyone less like Harry than this hairless old chemist could not be imagined.

I stared at my mother in such angry and complete bewilderment that she hastily retreated from her suggestion. But the harm was

19

done. I am afraid I extended my fury to the kind and harmless chemist, for I refused all his subsequent offerings, and never willingly spoke to him again.

There were, I reluctantly admitted to myself, actually things—and even important things—upon which my mother and myself could not agree.

2

The last few days of our Southbourne reprieve were black with my secret anxiety. An adolescent does not readily perceive moderate alternatives; his sharp set mind, unpadded by experience, has only a raw edge to present against the unknown. I saw my future swinging between Heaven and Hell; and it was not (if it should prove to be Hell) one that I could even tackle alone; I should have to drag my parents into it with me. I could not be certain that Dr. T. was as stupid as he was tactless; I was still losing weight, nor had the figures on that aggravating little thermometer ceased their see-saw-like proclivities. I tried hard to prevent our London visit to our beloved friend and physician Dr. Schacht from taking place; but my mother was naturally against this unreasonable block to our plans. She had not seen Dr. Schacht since Wilmett's death, and she wanted fresh advice for the future. Surely I, who had such a poor opinion of our local doctor, would be the last person to wish her to depend solely on him? Besides, we both loved London, and our old lodgings on Campden Hill were free. We could enjoy a week there without great expense; buy our summer clothes; and go to our favourite church on Sunday. I couldn't tell her that I had concealed a danger from her—a danger that might materialize and have to be admitted —in London. Whereas I felt that at home—with only Dr. T. to contrive against—I could wriggle out of doctors' verdicts; and postpone, if not "defy" auguries.

We went to London as we had arranged; and Dr. Schacht received us as usual, with extreme kindness, flurried by an unaccustomed gravity. He too had loved Wilmett—and lost her. He was a childless man of middle age, who took the deepest and most benevolent interest in his young patients. As a family he knew us, as nobody else knew us, with an individual thoroughness that was only un-terrifying because he was so kind. He was a big, blond creature of German extraction, too tall to appear stout, with a golden-brown beard of great splendour, and blue eyes that sparkled easily. He liked *chosen* fun, and talked exactly like the booming old hypocrite in Bernard Shaw's *Doctor's Dilemma*. Only I am quite sure Dr. Schacht was *not* a hypocrite. He merely had a gift for booming. I gazed at him with gimlet eyes trying to discover what, if anything, Dr. T. had told him about my lungs, while he kept assuring us how well we were both looking.

We got through this preliminary geniality in time; and I remained alone with volumes of *Punch* in a dusty, velvety room overlooking the more opulent portion of the Earl's Court Road.

It was a much quieter road then than now, and the trees gave it a more pastoral look. I found plenty to look at; though it seemed that I was looking at it for a long time, before my mother and Dr. Schacht returned.

My mother looked composed and smiling. "Dr. Schacht," she said, as if it were rather a joke, "says he would like to see *you*, now." So I went with him, to that room where I had been so often before with my sister Wilmett.

We had been fellow conspirators over her. I had been as deep in Dr. Schacht's confidence as he had been in mine. It was quite useless, I thought, for him to try to dodge behind that lovely, golden-bearded manner with me. "Have you heard from Dr. T.?" I instantly demanded. "He says there's something the matter with my lungs, I haven't told mother." "Well, I have said nothing to her either about what Dr. T. wrote to me," he admitted with bland unconcern, "but you see I don't suppose there's anything to tell! When *he* saw you you'd got influenza, and I don't suppose he even knew you'd had pneumonia sixteen months ago. You look very well indeed now—and I quite expect that I shall find nothing wrong with you at all!" I saw that I was not to be a fellow conspirator any more. I was to be instead, the new victim of that old conspiracy. "There," he said, when he had finished with me. "Just as I thought. Nothing! Well—to be on the safe side, shall we say *next* to nothing the matter with your lungs! Very good thing Dr. T. sent you to the sea-side though, and it might not be a bad thing if you were to go again for a short time. Didn't your mother say you were to be a week in London now?" I admitted that she had, and it turned out that this was another good thing. Good things were mounting up in a most alarming manner; a friend of Dr. Schacht's, a very big man indeed, Sir Douglas Powell, just happened to be free tomorrow morning. Dr. Schacht was to see him about another patient, and he could take a look at me at the same time. There couldn't be a better man to confirm his own opinion that there was nothing wrong with me and to allay my mother's anxiety if she should be anxious. "Very natural indeed," Dr. Schacht boomed defiantly meeting my watchful eyes, "under the circumstances. Very natural indeed!" I didn't say anything. I continued to look at Dr. Schacht; and he at me. I think he saw the game was up. "It's my mother I mind about," I explained. "Can you tell her, if she *has* to be told— without upsetting her?" "There's nothing to upset her about!" he said testily. "Wait here till I come back!" and then he went, to upset her, while I waited.

When he came back, he looked I thought rather puzzled. "She's *not* upset!" he assured me quickly. "She was surprised, of course, but she was not even as upset as I had expected, though of course fortunately there's nothing for anyone to be upset about! You'll just have to be a little more careful than usual, till you get quite strong. You can go to her now and see for yourself!" I went at once, and found out that what he had said was true. My mother was not upset.

I doubt if any doctors like Sir Douglas Powell exist at the present day. Like Rossetti's "Blessed Damozel" he had reached "the gold bar of Heaven", and from its celestial height he could look down at Science and watch it "spin like a fretful midge".

His house was in the exact spot in the West End where the socially great in those dazzling Edwardian days glued themselves together to do their shining.

I remember well, the lovely airy hall, with its spiral staircase leading into mysterious regions airier still, and a good deal lighter, where drawing-rooms and boudoirs flourished.

There was no vulgar waiting room. A magnificent butler noise-lessly introduced us into a circular hall. Sir Douglas himself made a swift appearance from a side door dressed in riding breeches and carrying a crop in his hand. Ours was an early appointment and I think a graciously informal concession to Dr. Schacht, an old but obviously obscure, friend.

Sir Douglas Powell was quite one of the handsomest men I have ever seen. His expression was grave with his own importance; his eyes like splintered ice-bergs; his features were the kind known as "chiselled". He was not pompous unless pomposity can be congealed. Dr. Schacht in spite of his size and expansive manner was frost-bitten into silence by him. He and my mother sat huddled together, at the end of a vast room, the size of a field with dim horizons (it was Sir Douglas's consulting room, disguised as a library) while I went through the medical drill to which I had become vicariously accustomed. It seemed funny to be undressing myself, instead of helping to undress Wilmett.

No doubt Sir Douglas Powell had been told my family history; he knew what two obscure medical men thought of my con-dition; and after a silent twenty minutes' examination, he made up his own mind—and to Dr. Schacht's evident horror—spoke it.

"There is a slight, a very slight tubercular infection, at the apex of your right lung," he said to me, with severe precision. "But there is no reason why you should not get well. Yours is a very early stage of lung trouble. It might even be that in a few months these symptoms will clear up, but I must warn you that anything the matter with the lungs, however slight, can become serious if it is neglected. You must be prepared to do exactly what you are told, whether you like it or not. Will you?"

I suddenly realized that this was a skilled man. I believed what he said; and I felt as if he was prepared to believe my answer.

These moments of mutual respect and confidence, which flash between doctor and patient, are, I believe, part of the secret of cure. Yet it was a long and solemn moment before I could bring myself to say, "Yes, I will do what you tell me!"

The icy grey eyes looking into mine for a brief moment became

24

the eyes of a friend. With his back to the others, Sir Douglas gave me his succinct and clearly worded orders.

Perhaps what makes a great doctor is that he knows by instinct what he can afford to say to each individual patient as well as what is the matter with him.

Such a doctor sums up the human being who is behind the illness and finds out what he can count on, in the way of wholeness. He has to decide just how much strength there is in that beating heart, how much fortitude to bear necessary pain, how much desire to accept life however hard the cost!

I could see, as we left the two doctors together, that my mother was impressed and pleased by so much dignity and importance. I was myself impressed, but I was also secretly dismayed. There was more, I somehow felt, up the capacious sleeve of Time, than I was at all prepared to pull down.

Sir Douglas Powell strolled back, after an interval, with Dr. Schacht and invited my mother to sit in the hall for a few minutes to talk over our plans with Dr. Schacht; then he turned to me and said, "I should like to see you again in three months' time," and left us.

I watched him walking up the shallow staircase with wrought-iron railings, into a home of unimaginable splendour where I felt sure some enamoured and exquisite woman must naturally await him. I was for the moment far more interested in what kind of a life Sir Douglas lived, when he wasn't a great doctor, than of what might be going to happen to me, because he was. However I came back to my own affairs with a jerk, when I heard Dr. Schacht saying, "Although of course you understand there is very little wrong with her chest—if indeed anything—yet Swanscombe with all that smoke—is quite out of the question for her! Sir Douglas agrees with me—it is simply impossible!" My mother and I stared at each other in complete bewilderment and consternation. They might just as well have asked us to walk over a precipice or sit down under the nearest bus.

We had always been together. At this time in my life I had only three interests: my mother—my boys' club—and my father's parish. Exile from these three interests meant exile from life itself.

"But Dr. Schacht," I said accusingly, "Mother can't leave father and I can't leave her! Swanscombe is my home."

Suddenly he was angry, he was really angry, but I somehow felt that though he spoke to me, it was not altogether I who had made him so angry. "No, you mustn't stay at home!" he fiercely roared. "I've come to the conclusion that you're very bad for each other! You worry too much about each other's health! You'll be a great deal better apart—and as for you—you'll have to make up your mind to go wherever you are sent!" Then he added the most astonishing and the most crushing thing he could possibly have said, perhaps the only one that could have insured my instant obedience. He said, "Your mother agrees with me: she's quite willing for you to go away! She's just told me so!" My mother did not deny it. She sat there with her beautiful blue eyes full of tears, while I cried out appalled, "But we're so happy together! Surely there's nothing in the world so bad for us—as to be apart?" And then suddenly I knew that this *wasn't* what she wanted! Dr. Schacht was right. Hadn't it always been the same through Wilmett's long ordeal? Mother could never bear to be with her, though Wilmett was the core of her heart; and now she couldn't bear to be with me in my ordeal either. It was no use asking it of her. It was the way she loved us. How could I dream of demanding any further effort from her, only three months after Wilmett's death?

I capitulated. "I'll go—anywhere," I agreed, "only I don't quite know where to go." My mother, to my astonishment, had the solution ready. "Elena!" she said triumphantly. "Elena will be sure to take you!"

My friend, Miss Ellen Mary Gurney, was a single woman of private means, ten years older than my mother. She had been our next door neighbour for six months in a beautiful country village a year before my father finally accepted Swanscombe, and we had seen a great deal of her. Elena had been highly educated, she was deeply religious and a solitary, or at least a very secluded person. I loved her dearly, but how could I expect her—even if she returned my affection—to take me on such prolonged and rather exacting terms? On this uncertain issue however my mother proved to be right.

Elena *did* want to have me, indefinitely and accepting the conditions that I was a semi-invalid and had to be most of my time out-doors. When told of the Swanscombe dilemma she did not even wait to be asked, she instantly offered to take me, as we called it— till I was well.

As it was only April, and Elena, whose immediate plans were already made, would not be ready for me before June, I was to carry out Sir Douglas's preliminary suggestion and go to the East Coast. My mother thought I could quite well manage in lodgings by myself, if we could find a nice landlady. It was obvious that what she wanted now was to go home immediately and alone, but my father wouldn't hear of it. As soon as he had heard the result of our visits to the doctors, he came up to town, my mother thought most unnecessarily, but I was somehow very glad to see him. His occasional explosions of rage shook me very little—in between he was exaggeratedly kind to me; and the plans that he insisted upon were a good deal less lonely. We would go to Sheringham together where there was a splendid golf links; and Elena's cousins, the Augustine Birrells, already had a house. She herself was coming there on a visit later on, so that we could talk over all our plans. Father would join mother and myself, going back to Swanscombe for week-ends; and Mary would go to our grandmother in Tunbridge Wells. Under the barrage of these magnificent prospects, I discovered that my father was a good deal more upset about my health than my mother had been.

I laid myself out to re-assure him. Firmly I upheld the fiction— and improved upon it—of how little there was the matter with me —how much better I felt already, and how perfectly well I was soon going to be. About not going back to Swanscombe nothing however could be done except suffer. My father and I could not bear to speak of it to each other, but I think we well knew what each of us felt. It had been my parish because it was his—and now the grip of my young hands on it were to be unfastened—and the full weight of it left upon his own.

The great thing was—my father now declared—that I was going to be a writer. He had always wanted to be a novelist himself. Perhaps we might one day write a book together? Whatever those "kid-gloved Blizzards", the doctors, had shorn off my back, that particular piece of wool still adhered to it. How fortunate that I was going to meet Augustine Birrell, who was not only a Cabinet Minister, but one of the acknowledged heads of the kingdom of letters! My father saw my bright fortune as already made and spurred me encouragingly forward towards it. I was at the moment writing the worst book I ever wrote. It was called *The Master Hope*. It was to be very properly refused by Longmans and Green, my first distinguished publisher, and strangely, accepted shortly afterwards by Hurst and Blackett. In the fifty years of my writing life none of my books were ever refused final publication, and only twice have I had to try the verdict of a second publisher; but this was hardly owing to their merit. The standard of novels fifty years ago was extremely low, and I doubt if my first half a dozen novels even reached that standard. My first two long novels paid for their typing and brought me in about three pounds each. My third novel, appropriately entitled *The Imperfect Gift*, was commercially more of a success since it went into three editions, but at the time of my father's castles in the air such prospects as paying my own expenses were too lavish for my sceptical mind to envisage.

My parents and my home were my chief possessions; and I very fully realized that they were both going to be taken away from me. The idea of death didn't occur to me. It was the idea of life, made out of completely new materials at a moment's notice, that I thought a trifle disconcerting.

3

Sheringham was viciously cold in April and my out-door treatment, which consisted in sitting among wind-swept dunes on a small square of waterproof, was a gloomy affair. There was nothing else but a golf-links, a few beach cottages, and a small and uninteresting village a mile away. Whether you liked it or not you heard all day and night

> *The scream of a madden'd beach*
> *Dragged down by the wave.*

The only advantage that Sheringham possessed was the presence of the Birrells.

The Augustine Birrells were distant cousins of Elena's, and at a word from her, with that disinterested and lavish kindness which no longer has time to exist, they procured good lodgings for perfect strangers, and invited us to tea.

Not Boswell, panting to sit at the feet of Johnson, nor Hazlitt, on that immortal walk with Coleridge under the winter moon, can have been filled with greater excitement than I was by this happy introduction.

I very well knew how unsubstantial was my own claim to literature. I had no foundation of learning, my untrained imagination, filling and emptying with its intensities of observation and deduction, was not so much a power as a liability.

I had no skills, except my prodigious memory; and I longed to meet someone who could point out to me the way to develop my urge for self-expression.

I had read with delight Augustine Birrell's two urbane and

scholarly books: *Obiter Dicta* and *Res Judicatae*. I knew him for a man who loved Lamb, and had Dr. Johnson in his blood. Few girls of my age had read more of eighteenth-century writers than I had, and Mr. Birrell was the essence of the eighteenth century. Would he not use the key of his fine mind to unlock the door of executive literature and let me in?

The tea party was a great success. I had long been accustomed to the entertainment value of my father's conversation, but to my surprise and delight it was on this occasion my mother who shone. Mr. Birrell afterwards said of her, "That is the wittiest clergyman's wife I ever met!" Their taste in books matched, banter flew between them. Biblical texts were quoted in unusual contexts. My mother's knowledge of the Scriptures matched Mr. Birrell's own, and was as apposite. The hours flew past like minutes. Mr. Birrell looked as I had expected him to look; and was as kind. He had a great brow, eyes alive with humour; and sometimes with irascibility.

Mrs. Birrell I saw through a haze of poetry. Had she not been the widow of Lionel Tennyson—son of the poet? And was she not the daughter of Locker-Lampson?

She was not beautiful, yet I find it hard to describe her without using the word "beauty". She had a fastidious gentleness that was the perfection of good manners. She appeared to be everybody's friend while being nobody's adherent. She did not talk much herself, but like a great dressmaker, whose touch on the simplest material brings out a hidden line, she evoked the separate flavour of every person in her company.

This first tea party was the stepping stone to frequent talks with her. I told her of my ambitions, and she promised to tell Mr. Birrell about them. "He is quite sure to want to talk to you about writing," she told me. "He likes to help young people and I shall arrange a special opportunity for it."

The cold, grim days slipped by and I was invited to dinner. I went alone, my mother refusing to dine out and my father being at Swanscombe. I was highly excited, and as usual at that time in the evening, feverish. Probably my clothes were unsuitable. I was glad to think that Helen, Elena's niece and my own age, was to be there as well.

30

I had never been to a dinner party before, and this was, though on a small scale, a real dinner party. The food and wine were of a kind I had never tasted, the conversation was even more heady than the wine. The two Tennyson sons, Alfred and Charles, were down from Cambridge. The Birrells were not opulent or spectacular people; but they were financially as well off as they were intellectually.

The dinner party itself went very well indeed, and for what happened afterwards no one was directly responsible, except perhaps the Japanese.

Mr. Birrell became—and remained throughout the rest of the evening—extremely angry. Perhaps before the talk began the clever stepsons had roused some slight spirit of aggression in him, or else his intense annoyance may have been the echo of some Cabinet discussion in which he had been over-borne, but the topic of the new Japanese alliance acted upon him like gunpowder.

The occasion which had promised to be halcyon became suddenly extremely sinister. None of us knew much, and we cared less, about the Japanese alliance. Why then was he so angry? What hidden depths floated below this social occasion? What were the Japanese to us—or we to them? Mrs. Birrell, with delicate and unobtrusive skill, slowly drew Mr. Birrell away from this offensive people; but nobody—not even Mrs. Birrell—could float the rest of the evening into essential harmony. It remained a truncated occasion; and under its shadow, the two sons, Alfred and Charles, escorted Helen and myself to our respective roofs.

I had never met clever young men before, and they both made, particularly Charles, who was not only clever but good-looking, a very happy impression upon me; but I do not think it was reciprocated, for I never saw either of them again.

Mrs. Birrell met me once afterwards on the inhospitable Sheringham shore, and spoke with her lovely kindness unwithdrawn; but no further invitation fell from her lips; and my introduction to the art of writing through Mr. Birrell never materialized.

I slowly became conscious with a surprise as sharp as my dismay that this lovely light had vanished. I know now that writers are not made or destroyed by the absence of advice from their elders. No doubt then I exaggerated the importance of my loss. I puzzled a good deal about the reason. Were my clothes irretrievably wrong for a dinner party? Were my manners too enthusiastic? I was, I realized at this time, a good deal more American than English. But however inexpert my behaviour, I was the same girl to whom they had all been previously so kind. Elena was to tell me later that an outside intervention *had* taken place.

A connection by marriage of Elena's had appeared upon the scene, who suspected us of having the gloomiest designs upon Elena's fortune. I was, she felt sure, about to rob her daughter Helen of her natural heritage; and the Birrells loved Helen, who was as nice as any girl could well be.

I do not know how much the Birrells believed of this alarming story—and I was always glad to know that Mrs. Birrell told Elena sometime afterwards that she, specifically, could *not* agree that I was a designing person; but they had yielded to family pressure, and decided to drop what had after all been to them only an insignificant acquaintance.

I had already met Elena's niece, Helen Gurney, the daughter of Edmund Gurney, the scientific explorer of life after death—and with F. W. Myers joint founder of the Psychical Society.

Although we might very well have been rivals for Elena's favour I don't think either of us ever felt that we were. The greater magnanimity was, of course, Helen's. Hers was the prior claim, and the tie of blood relationship; but Helen was a generous, good-natured girl of great common sense and far more intelligence than I think her aunt had ever given her credit for. She had already suffered a good deal from Elena's trying to turn her into something that she wasn't, and I think that she was not altogether sorry to share her aunt's affectionate vigilance with me. She stayed with Elena as often as she ever had, and for as long; and we often timed our visits to overlap so that we might see more of each other. Elena's fortune never strayed beyond its original intention, though she did once anxiously suggest leaving me a sum of money as a safe-guard for my precarious health. I indignantly refused it—for was I not on the verge of earning my own living? And besides as I pointed out to her, when my English grandmother died my mother would automatically inherit her share of a not inconsiderable fortune. I even refused to be left a pearl necklace, since I disapproved of jewels at that period, a refusal I afterwards regretted; but I agreed that if Elena were to die before me I would value a Rossetti drawing of Fiametta, which now hangs over my bed.

Looking back on the actual history of this long, innocent and happy friendship I can now understand that Helen's relatives might well have taken a gloomy view of such an intimacy. Although Elena never ceased to be staunchly loyal to her brother's child, she did practically adopt me, for the time being, "Until I get well," we always called it; but alas, Elena died long before that happened!

In some ways as a companion I suited Elena far better than Helen suited her.

I found Elena perfectly easy to live with—but no doubt she was exceptionally indulgent to me on account of my ill-health. She had no preconceived idea as to what she wanted me to become; and both of us at that time wanted what the other had to give. Later on, the advancing freedom of my opinions was to be a source of dismay to Elena, but at the moment I went to church with gusto, whenever she did, and even consented once to go to her Father Confessor— a very celebrated and sought-after one, whom she had procured for me with some difficulty—and who did not take my sins as seriously as I had hoped and expected.

Whatever Elena loved with thrift and austerity, I loved recklessly and with ecstasy. My repudiations were more shallow than her own, but a good deal more spectacular.

Elena's life was one of great simplicity and self-suppression. She expected far too much of herself; and sometimes she expected a little too much of others—especially of those she loved most; but she had a serene integrity of life and purpose, which were infinitely restful to a wilful adolescent.

Elena was wholly without vanity or self-assertion; what she had accepted, she practised. She seldom spoke of religion yet it was innate in her attitude towards every other subject. She was much more than a good woman, she was very nearly a saint; and as far as I was concerned, for the next five years of my life (until her death), she was my mainstay and my refuge.

33

4

From the moment the gates of Berry Head House swung behind me, I entered Paradise.

Most of my life had been spent in ugly surroundings on the low marshy plains of Long Island, or in the back slum, walled in by smoke from cement works, between Dartford and Gravesend. I had not resented this degraded earth; so deeply had the excitement of living possessed me, that I doubt if I knew I was surrounded by ugliness. I would detach a red sail on the river from the smoke stacks to delight in, or find the spire of a church driving its arrowy flight above the mean houses that defied the faith it promised. But except for the nine country months we had once spent in the mere prettiness of Surrey, I had never breathed deeply of pure air, or rested my eyes on uninterrupted beauty. This summer on Berry Head was an extension of living. I fell in love with the earth and sky and with the air which tasted of honeysuckle and the saltness of the sea.

I could not take my eyes from the silver lightnings of gulls' wings above red rocks under pale summer skies. A spell was on me which never lifted all summer long. The old eagerness to be at home still burned in me; I wrote lavishly to my sister Mary and to my parents. I planned and remembered and took part in all the activities of my home. But behind them, and beyond them, stretched this new vision of beauty. Whether I waked into the silent night or into the grey dawn stirring with a wind from the sea, and soon pre-occupied with the voices of bird after waking bird, I no longer felt frightened or alone. Dawn and sunset, the birds and the flowers, released the grip of my remorse. I had been haunted by sorrow, as only those can be who have not done justice to those they loved until death took them out of their hampered reach. Now it was as if a veil was drawn between me and the sharpness of death. I did not have to see Wilmett's suffering with raw eyes, or feel the impact of it on my senses. It was already more a dream than a fact to me that Wilmett was dead.

Berry Head House itself was far from beautiful. It had been built for a public hospital, but it was found that the windows were too high and narrow for this purpose and so it had been sold to a private owner. The two great wings, connected by a centre building, jutted out onto a gravel terrace with deep fuchsia hedges, facing the sea. Once we had passed the front door, however, this grim façade became forgotten. Elena and I had nothing to do with the gravel terrace or the grey unfriendly exterior; we had a wing to ourselves, and our doors were french windows, leading to a hidden lawn. An enchanting little ravine ran downwards to the sea. It was called "the happy valley".

In March daffodils danced down to the rocks' edge, and the stream that ran through it was banked by primroses. Above our lawn, terrace after terrace of flowers rose up the cliff's side, to a gate in the wall that led on to the springy turf of the Head. The gardening had been inspired and directed by the lady of the house who never left her room. She had a strong will, great botanical knowledge, and an ardour that both led, and daunted, the most inflexible of gardeners. In her early youth she had made the garden and she knew exactly what she could get from it. Every fault or failure of her well-directed plans was probed to its roots. Even Nature obeyed her. It was she who knew how to present a bed of Madonna lilies—like the hanging gardens of Babylon—between the blueness of the sea and the sky.

A lower terrace, filled with columbines of every shade and colour, made an intricate and exquisite pattern like a ballet.

There were roses everywhere; and great herbaceous borders in a walled garden that protected fruit and flower from the severity of winds and cornered every gleam of sun.

The 'Invisible Lady' knew where each flower grew, and specimens of its blooms were constantly carried in for her inspection.

35

There was a malmaison carnation of stupendous size, and the most exquisite shell pink; and when something went wrong with it, the whole garden shuddered. I never heard her voice—but not a flower escaped it.

It was my greatest summer privilege, after a series of carefully devised but secret tests (for I never guessed that I was under these examinations) to be promoted to "do" the flowers of the house.

It was an easy and ecstatic performance. Gardeners brought the flowers in on trays and put them in the pantry. Housemaids filled and emptied vases. I had only to choose which flowers, and persuade the blossoms to arrange themselves.

There was a rhythm and a ritual, about everything that went on in Berry Head House. The arrangement between Miss Gurney and the invisible owner was strict and ceremonious, but carried out, upon either side, with infinite grace. Each had her own wing, her own privately ordered meals, her own visitors, and was waited upon by special servants. A cook housekeeper supervised the entire affair, and took her orders equally from both. The visitors, Elena told me, did not meet each other socially, except by some special arrangement agreed upon by both ladies. Should they appear at the same place in the garden, at the same moment, it would of course be suitable to bow and exchange a polite greeting; but more was not expected—or desired.

It was pointed out to visitors which part of the garden belonged to which wing. If there were no other visitors, the whole garden was at our disposal.

The rocks, and the way down to them, were neutral territory. A gate in the garden wall led on to the Head itself; and the Head as far as it belonged to anybody, was occupied almost exclusively by sea-gulls.

We walked there every evening after tea on the short smooth turf, starred with yellow ladies' slippers, thyme and white clover. The sky was full of shining wings, and indignant protestations.

Once a week we drove into Brixham to an early service at the Parish Church; otherwise we never left the Head. It was more than enough for me. I never wanted to look at anything else, or to speak to any other human being than Elena. I was a thrall to beauty

36

"and, though her gaze struck awe, I drew it in as simply as my breath".

Elena had seen Dr. Schacht in London, and one of his suggestions had been a long garden chair, so that I no longer had to perch in the low notches of trees, or spread my waterproof square on unyielding stone walls.

No Princess could have been more comfortable than I was, lying out from dawn to dusk wrapped in rugs, supported by cushions, with every sense I had at work upon the garden.

I watched birds for hours, I drew leaves and flowers. I wrote my extremely bad novel with fresh gusto, while Elena painted. She had once been a pupil of Ruskin's.

Elena was a good flower painter and liked to draw a minute and accurate copy of her subject, but unconsciously she added to her skilled precision the entire flavour of her personality. All her paintings had an extraordinary spiritual quality. You could not associate them with earth, roots or wire worms. Her flowers seemed to float ethereally in the blue air, and you could easily imagine them to be, as Newman somewhere suggests, the thoughts of angels and under their direction.

We never had an idle or a restless moment. Elena began her day long before I did, with religious exercises. I don't know how long they took, but they were followed by household orderings, and she seldom came out to paint before I was deep in my morning's book excursions.

If it rained, or was cold, she wrote indoors, and I would see her lovely, medieval head bent over the writing table, where she wrote innumerable letters in her meticulous handwriting, as easy to read as print, while I would have been shepherded, chair and all, by a kindly gardener to the shelter of the summer-house roof.

We worked steadily till lunch; and then for a strict hour "rested", then Elena would bring out her Italian books, and we would read Dante in Italian, of which I knew nothing and Elena not a great deal, but mercifully there was a translation on the opposite page from the original. I learned practically no Italian from this exercise but I slowly grew into an appreciation of Dante.

We had tea in the garden, and took our walk after it, in all weathers. Elena had valvular heart trouble, but this never was allowed to interfere with her Spartan existence. She lived by rule, and her heart had to accommodate itself to it.

Our supper could be as late as ever we liked. It was laid in the dining-room, with soup to be warmed up over a silver spirit lamp when we came in.

The meals seemed to me nicer than anything I had ever eaten, and this concession to time—so that we were enabled to have a full free evening—was such a happy break in regularity, that we never missed one of the beauties of those long, summer days melting into moonlit nights.

Elena was deeply disappointed at my impatient incapacity to draw, but agreeably surprised by a talent I managed to produce for illuminating. This much more pernickety, and exact art was for some reason more accessible to my inexact and careless nature. I took endless pains over it, I clung to rulers, and exulted when I reached brushes and was allowed colours; and in the end produced some quite creditable results.

I was always happy with Elena. Both of us had escaped into a relationship which we equally needed. Elena told me once that I had fulfilled her frustrated longing for motherhood, while she gave me, even though at nineteen I thought myself long past the age for it, a sense of the irresponsibility of childhood which I had always missed.

I had no wish to rebel against her gentle control. For the first time in my life I felt secure, and much more than physically secure, morally secure. I was living with someone who moved towards what she wanted. Even then I realized that I couldn't *share* what she wanted. I could barely touch the fringe of Elena's deep religious life. She lived for God. She may have been mistaken in what she supposed God wanted of her, but she was utterly sincere. To live with her was to feel inspired—not by her ideals, but by her oneness with them. She *was* what she believed. Whenever she reproved me, and she never pampered or gave way to the objects of her affection, I felt convinced she was right. I never forgot a reproof she gave me; it entered like iron into my soul and mine was a soul which needed a good deal of iron.

Of the invisible lady, Elena saw very little, and I saw nothing. Elena visited her for a short interval once every twenty-four hours, and I think it seemed to Elena that her friend *was* strong enough to see me for a few minutes; but I cannot remember that she ever did, though we constantly exchanged courteous and even affectionate messages. She read almost nothing but Jane Austen from end to end; and could manage to do some very fine Church embroidery.

Elena had no other house visitors from the outer world during this summer; but one of the Baring-Goulds, who was the Vicar of Brixham, called comparatively often, and told us interesting stories about the Brixham fishermen, and the history of the country round us. He was a celibate High Church parson with an over-sweet manner. I don't think we either of us cared for him very much, though Elena would rather have died than admit it.

Elena walked (a mile and a half) to early service on Thursdays, or on a Saint's day whenever there was one. She never spoke before, nor until some hours after, she had received her Communion. She regularly visited the sick and carried out—though with some natural reluctance if it were social—any duty laid upon her by her parish priest.

She had never had the care of an ill person before, but I think her understanding of our situation was deep. We never spoke about my health unless some new feature occurred; she respected, and, within commonsense limits, encouraged, my passionate desire not to be considered an invalid.

Our summer solitude had only two slight interruptions. One day Elena told me that a boat-building boy was to stay with our hostess, his aunt. He was about my age, and Elena thought it would be polite, and not against his aunt's wishes, if we were to be introduced. We need see no more of each other than that, but it would be a little awkward if we met without this preliminary warning.

The boat-building boy was entirely concentrated on his task, and worked away in a garden shed from morning till night. He was a flaxen-haired giant with a pair of most engaging blue eyes; and I liked to hear him whistling away in the distance, like a blackbird with an Albert Hall voice.

We went to the shed in order to meet him. He was extremely shy, in fact we both were, and Elena, hovering in a benevolent but restraining manner beside us, was shyer than either of us, so that the introduction did not carry us very far.

A few days later, when I came in to the library to take shelter from a shower of rain, I rather surprisingly—for it was our wing of the house—found him there. He asked me if I liked Omar Khayyam and was shocked to find that I had never read him. He found a copy, put it into my hands and left me.

I was of course carried away by this great poem, and spent the next week learning it by heart. Elena was extremely annoyed by this incident. She did not like Omar Khayyam at all. The Persian poet's attraction to wine, his one-sided view of women, and his repudiation of the Deity were all equally anathema to her. She was still more displeased when one evening the boat-building boy joined me on the rocks and we spent an hour together in amicable discussion upon this equivocal poem.

The invisible lady was equally displeased, and it was gently but firmly decided that we were not to meet again. If we did nevertheless meet by force of circumstance we were to pass each other like shadows—not like ships—for we were *not* "to speak to each other in passing". I don't know what his aunt said to the boat-building boy; but we never *did* meet again. I don't think either of us really minded, but had we lived fifty, or even twenty years later, I think we should have put up a fight.

The sad last I heard of him several years later was that a modern-minded doctor, called in during the absence of her usual physician, was shocked to find that there was nothing whatever the matter with the invisible lady. He took her nephew into his confidence and begged him to persuade his aunt to give up her invalid life. The boat-building boy adored his aunt; but he was not tactful in his approach to her upon this delicate subject. He blurted out the truth, which roused both her pride and her temper. She took no precautions, but at once dressed, got up, and without assistance or practice walked into the garden, where she died of heart failure, the walls of her heart being weakened too greatly during her bed-ridden existence to withstand the sudden pressure of unpractised activity. I could never bear to think what a shadow his well-meant and courageous action must have cast over his life.

The other two visitors who appeared in the course of the summer were of less interest to me, but I saw considerably more of them.

They were the two disapproved-of daughters of an extremely worldly and tyrannical mother. Indeed even Elena thought both their parents quite wicked.

The elder of the two, once very pretty, had fallen in love with a curate. Of course this was trampled upon with the utmost ferocity; and on her steady refusal to make a more profitable marriage, her parents had actually turned her out of the house. "I can't have you under my roof," her mother had stated, "spoiling your sister's chances. If you won't marry there's nothing left for you but to go and work in the slums."

Agnes had gone into the nearest slum and worked there ever since. She was at thirty-four quite definitely an old maid, but she was not as unhappy as I should have liked to think she was. She had quite got over the curate; and liked living in a Settlement and working in the slums.

The younger daughter was still only thirty-one and she had not lost her looks, though she had refused in season and out of season the good matches her mother pressed upon her. She had golden hair, a briar-rose complexion, a long pointed chin and the figure of a goddess.

She was to be sent to stay with a married brother who lived in South Africa, since there was nothing to be done with her in London.

Something, her mother hoped, might come of South Africa; and something did. On her way across the ocean Margaret met an elderly widower neither rich nor of noble birth, and incontinently married him.

The sisters' fate, at the time, seemed to me hideous; and it is a comfort to realize that now no such completely helpless, unwanted, unskilled, perfectly healthy young women are quite so wasted, simply because they happen to have been born women, and can live without working for their bread.

We were allowed their company. They sometimes, when not on

excursions by boat and carriage in which they never invited us to join, took meals with us. We often had tea together in the large drawing-room full of chintz-covered chairs, sofas and pale water-colours, overlooking the sea—which we never otherwise used.

Elena did not care very greatly for either of these young women, though she was extremely sorry for them. I think she privately thought that if they had had more character they would have become missionaries.

Their clothes, their rather curious ways and their beautiful manners alike fascinated me. When I was alone with them (which rarely occurred) I tried to find out what, if anything, they were up to, but I never did. Still I was not sorry when they went. Elena and I both preferred our dual solitude. We had more fun by ourselves; and the garden grew smaller and yet somehow less intimate when it was shared.

5

Early in September my mother wrote that George, now about fifteen, had to have an aggravated tonsil operation, which involved ten days' nursing, and would I like to combine this task with my consultation visit to Sir Douglas Powell? I agreed enthusiastically for it was long since I had had the chance of intimate contact with my beloved little brother—now as big as I was—and, severed as I felt, for such long intervals from my family, I hailed with delight this opportunity to be once more an integral part of it; but to my pained astonishment, Elena did not share my enthusiasm. She was frankly horrified, and not until I had shown her my mother's letter did she—returning it to me in grim silence—relax her opposition to the plan.

Health is bound to assume a far larger part in an old-time memoir than in our modern days. For it was then a home-made affair: illnesses were protracted, little understood, and inefficiently handled. George, for instance, was to be operated on in the bedroom of his London lodging, conscious, sitting on a backless chair under a window. He had a local anaesthetic, which was more than I had had for the same operation at two years old, standing between the doctor's knees; but the operating instrument was much the same, a kind of miniature guillotine, snapping off what could be seen and handled by the surgeon—not, in Dr. Schacht's case, a very expert surgeon. I remained till the last moment with George, and then slipped into the next room with the door open, so that I might supply Dr. Schacht with anything he needed.

As soon as the doctor and anaesthetist got George back to bed Dr. Schacht gave me full directions, as to what to do if anything

43

went wrong (there was no telephone of course) and then we were left to each other. George had to lie still without speaking and suck ice, while I read aloud to him. He had already told me that he wanted a momentarily popular book, on vampire bats, which I had procured for him, and which he obviously found soothing.

My father came up a day or two later for a few hours to see how we were getting on; and was extremely angry with me for not having provided chicken for lunch. George came to my rescue by declaring in a whisper that as soon as he had stopped sucking ice, he had wanted—and received—chops; but my father associated any kind of ill-health with chicken, and felt that I had failed as a nurse. Stung to the core by this accusation I then confessed that the money at my disposal could not possibly run to chickens, even though extended by the single pound I had myself possessed. My father was horrified at the smallness of the sum allowed to me, and lavishly added to our store. I particularly remember this incident, because George having expressed a fancy for cold salmon, I was shocked to discover, when I bought it, that it was three and sixpence a pound. No doubt I should have been incredulous, as well as shocked, had I been told that forty years later it was to cost thirteen and six the pound; and often to be unprocurable at any price.

It was always an awkward problem to please my father and mother simultaneously, and I often received secret instructions from both, to do the opposite of what the other had suggested.

As soon as George had reached the stage when he could be safely left to himself with his favourite literature, I went off for an hour or two, on her evenings off, with a friend of mine who was training to become a hospital nurse. When we had shared George's supper, and made him comfortable for the night, we would sally forth together on the top of a bus. Perched up, in the misty September air, above the horses' heads, often in the seat nearest a friendly and jocular driver, we would see the whole of gas-lit London—silver and blue—spread itself out before us. In spite of coal fires I believe the air was purer then than the petrol-soaked stuff we breathe to-day; certainly it was sweeter, for I can remember hay carts passing us by in Maida Vale, and whiffs of scented clover. We were young to be out by ourselves in days when good young

44

girls stayed at home in the evenings or went out with their elders. But the London we had chosen, on the tops of buses, surrounded by working people, was an innocent place, and we met with nothing but good fellowship. Nobody could, however, have felt more adventurous and even dissipated than we did on these harmless excursions. We went far afield, to out-lying districts of which we liked the names. We followed the river beyond Chiswick, we went into the city and crossed the Thames below Westminster to visit the Elephant and Castle.

We hunted up the Angel at Islington. Not Captain Cook landing for the first time on a tropical island, or Livingstone in darkest Africa could have felt a keener edge to the unknown than we felt.

When we had got safely back to Campden Grove and entered our darkened lodgings, with the novel rapture of a latch key, we crept upstairs, to peep at the calmly sleeping George, and made ourselves a parting cup of cocoa on a gas-ring.

This early friendship was a violent delight—and had a violent ending.

I first met K. on a football field with a curate, all three of us took to each other and watched our rival teams with mutual sympathy. The curate I never saw again; but I found that K. lived within reach near Swanscombe. During the long harrowing months of Wilmett's last illness, to be able to run out and meet K. by the river side, was a relief so intense and glittering, that I never realized how I exaggerated my feeling for her, or how unfair to anyone of her nature, self-restrained, shy and introspective, this assault upon her feelings could become. We had nothing but our youth in common. My interests began where hers left off; even her home and her habits, when I came to know them, were so wholly unlike my own, that we had to build ourselves an unreal world in which to meet at all. I was only too capable of this form of romantic construction; but unreal worlds do not last. Elena suddenly awakened me to this unpleasant fact.

"This," she told me with stern gentleness, "is what the Church rightly calls, 'inordinate affection', and you must bring it to an immediate end. It is harmful to both your characters. You do not really love this girl as much as you have led her to believe. I doubt if you really love her at all. You must write and tell her that all these endearments and excitements must cease; and that if your friendship is to be conducted at all, it must be conducted upon quite a different basis."

If the rebel in me, seldom a passive partner, did not spring into instant activity under this spiritual discipline, it must partly have been because I had a shrewd suspicion that Elena was in the right. This unequal friendship was already a strain on my emotional resources, and threatened to become a burden. Besides, sceptic as I was, my confidence in Elena was by now complete. I felt certain she would not put this atrocious task of abrupt renunciation upon us without due cause.

I wrote from Berry Head, to warn K. that our friendship must slow down. I explained at some length all that Elena had told me about "inordinate affection"; but to no purpose whatever.

K. had not enjoyed a long summer at Berry Head with a near-saint. She saw no reason why our friendship should not follow the impulses of our hearts. She suspected me (as I had already begun to suspect myself) of basic treachery. She hated the thought of Elena.

The breach between us did not immediately take place. When she saw me in London she was so concerned over my state of health that she never even referred to it.

George returned, at the end of a fortnight, to his public school, and I was sent very reluctantly to visit my English grandmother at Tunbridge Wells till Christmas.

Rocklands was a large suburban villa, with a garden chiefly composed of broad gravel paths and rhododendron bushes. My step-grandfather had recently, through unwise speculation, lost a very large fortune; he would, I think, have had to be declared bankrupt, had my grandmother and the whole Pease connection not come to his rescue. My grandparents were at this time suddenly reduced, from an income of fifteen thousand a year, to what they considered the actual penury of three thousand a year. My grandmother had sacrificed nearly half her fortune to save her husband, and would gladly have sacrificed the whole, had it not been tied up in the stiff Quaker fashion for her descendants. As my step-grandfather was almost wholly pre-occupied with money during a long life-time—only faintly flavoured with religion—gloom now settled upon the household. Gloom—plunged in what I felt to be comfort of a restrictive kind—was not the atmosphere which best suited me. The very air seemed thick with sofa cushions.

My grandfather's heart was seriously affected; there were less than half the servants the household had been used to in Grosvenor Square; and the six servants who remained had to work much harder. Anything amusing was said "No" to, on the score of expense. There was no entertaining except an occasional single guest to tea, generally a Low Church clergyman. Beyond the fact that I had to behave properly and hold my tongue, I was very kindly treated. My step-uncle, who went to town every day, gave me the use of his big library-sitting room to work in; and when it was fine, which that autumn was very seldom, I was allowed a long chair to lie out in, under a big chestnut tree on the lawn.

The worst thing I had to face at Tunbridge Wells was the break with K.

Elena had not let the matter rest. She now demanded to know what restrictions had taken place in our friendship. I had to confess that there had been tears and recriminations, but so far no restrictions. Elena was deeply grieved and very stern. She told me I must act with finality and courage, to put an end to a situation which I now knew to be wrong.

K. insisted that I must not do this by letter, and that she must at least be able to spend her next long day's leave with me at Tunbridge Wells. No doubt I exaggerated everything that K. felt, and that I myself felt about her. But our friendship need never have come to so abrupt an end if I had not counterfeited an ardour which was without foundation in understanding or respect. When I heard a few years later that K. was happily married, it was as if a dead albatross had fallen off my neck.

I was increasingly ill all the while I was at Tunbridge Wells, and no doubt all that happened to me—through those dull months—had a peculiarly lurid gleam. It was in Kennie's still and beautiful library, with the rain beating relentlessly against the window panes, that I first read Galsworthy's *Forsyte Saga*.

It was the first book dealing intimately with the fact of sex that I had ever taken in, for though I had read Hardy's *Tess* and *Jude the Obscure* much earlier, their impact upon me had been, though intense, of quite a different nature. It was the tragedy of human misunderstanding that had sucked me down into the depths when I read them. Sex was incidental, it was the core of the shaken heart that mattered. I had never felt—as I now felt—mortally outraged by the act of Soames. Here at last, in its stark and indisputable ferocity, was sex in the home—and in a home almost incredibly resembling the home I was actually in! James *was* my step-grandfather—the step-uncles—always excepting Kennie—might each have been a Soames. Behind all those cold baths, school ties and Harris tweeds stood the brute aggressor. Curiously enough, I did not at first realize, in my flurried passion of distaste, that Galsworthy was on my side. I knew that Soames was my mortal enemy, but I had not the sense to understand that this exposure of Soames was the best, in fact the only efficacious, weapon against him.

Soames crashed through Edwardian homes like a thunderbolt. People were forced to think as they had never thought before. Silent victims found a voice, triumphant tyrants lost theirs.

The Forsyte Saga was a book through which society was forced to see exposed for the first time the full hollowness of a world where property was earnestly worshipped under the guise of Christianity. I knew that under the roof which sheltered me, my step-grandfather, a publicly religious man, was dying of a broken heart because he had lost his money; not all his money either—but all that had made him famous, his—"property".

Eventually I recognized Galsworthy's contribution to life—as well as to literature, but my immediate reaction to *The Forsyte Saga* was indignant horror. My chief quarrel with the author was that Irene didn't hit back. I felt that Charlotte Corday and Judith would never have been so supine.

Uncle Kennie tried to calm me. He pointed out that there weren't many Soameses and perhaps even fewer Irenes; but I remained maddened and inconsolable for several weeks.

My grandmother greatly disliked the increasing friendship between Uncle Kennie and myself. He insisted—an extravagant act of courage on his part—on my having a fire in the library to work by; and sat and talked to me under the chestnut tree whenever it was fine. My grandmother felt it very unsuitable for us to indulge in such long conversations on the lawn in full view of the drawing-room window. She had accepted her unmarried step-son as part of her home, but she had never liked him. He had ill-health, and a sense of humour, both of which things my grandmother preferred men to be without. She liked them strong, romantic and stupid.

Thomas Mackenzie Fowler, as his full name was, remained all his life a delicate bachelor with a genius for kindness. He was that rare combination, a man of the world with a heart. Though he loved society as it then was, he loved as well art, literature and music. He was a High Churchman and in spite of his love for this world, kept his eyes serenely on the next. He disliked intimacy or excitement; but he resigned himself to my dramatic spirit, laughed at my jokes and helped to direct my taste in every possible direction.

He could not have liked my clothes, nor felt wholly secure as to my opinions, yet later on in our friendship when occasion arose he bravely introduced me to two of his most prized friends, Lilian Beit and Marguerite Carter; and never showed a spark of jealousy when they in turn became even more intimate friends of my own.

Rocklands, although I am bound to admit it did nothing else for me—for I left it considerably worse than when I had arrived—gave me twenty years of one of the best and happiest friendships of my life.

6

The first Christmas after my sister Wilmett's death was the last I spent under my parents' roof. We were all desperately anxious to make it as easy as we could for each other; but determined cheerfulness has an awkward way of hanging fire.

Poor George, who was the youngest, had, I fear, most of this attempted jollity thrust upon him. Anything we could manage in the way of presents, special privileges or exotic foodstuffs were dedicated to his never very enthusiastic appetite. My father even demanded a Christmas tree especially for George; but this was bitterly repudiated by George himself. He was not at an age when he could afford to be considered young; and he had no use for Christmas trees.

I doubt if any of us could have got through this household ceremony without a breakdown remembering that a year before at Wilmett's wish we had decorated a little glittering tree to put by her bedside, while we stood round it, accepting her long-thought-out presents till she grew too tired for the weight of pleasure.

Fortunately a clergyman's house at Christmas is not much forced in upon itself. There were the sick, the young and the old to be planned for, so that everyone was rushing here and there with parcels and on errands, decorating the church and taking round gifts, while none of us had time for reflection except my quiet mother. I could not help noticing how withdrawn my mother was from all that took place round her. More than anyone I have ever known she lived exclusively along the avenues of her deep affections, and the deepest of all her affections had been her love for this brilliant firstborn. None of us had so dragged her out of herself, and launched her on the wide currents of the world, as my sister Wilmett had succeeded in doing. In Wilmett my mother was young again; melted down by her ardour; thrilled by her quick vision and constantly finding herself challenged by the dramatic incidents of Wilmett's swift career. Her own beautiful voice, far better trained, was born again in Wilmett; and her love of music was set free through Wilmett's flying fingers.

When Wilmett died my mother had refused all natural grief. She had neither cried nor mourned; but what she could not refuse was the withdrawal of life itself. My father, after his stormy grief, was exactly the same person, generous, impatient, passionate and responsive to every wind that blew. But my mother had not so much aged as frozen. Quite half of her had ceased to live, she was no longer accessible to outside interests. I was conscious of the tremendous difference in her whole attitude. She was not less tender to me, but she was far more remote.

I could not reach her, with my new experiences and excitements; and I soon realized that she did not even want to be reached. It was strange, but not so terrible as it might have been if I had not realized the depth of her love, and how intermingled it was through every strand with fear; I saw that my mother would be glad to have me go away again—out of sight and sound.

For the last three years I had been her physical mainstay. Now that I was incapacitated from giving her what she needed, the sight of me only increased her deep anxiety. Instead of being her support and consolation I was now the source of new and unendurable pain.

I did not feel that she was any the less the core of my heart; but I began to understand as never before my father's unanswered needs; and my love for him deepened. When I left Swanscombe, it was leaving my father and his work that was the bitterest wrench. We had long shared a special joviality of outlook and interests, which I knew could not for either of us be replaced. I loved his brilliant mind, and was proud, with passion, when on his visits to his friends, I could watch his wit flash out and vivify any society in which he found himself.

Between us, by exchanging our day's experiences with dramatic intensity, we could even break down the walls of my mother's solitude. I comforted myself with thinking that Mary was going to remain at home and share his work; but I knew at what a cost she gave up her independence and freedom for my mother's searing criticisms. My parting from Mary was less complete because of our intimate and continuous correspondence. In one sense of the word we never were really parted. Still, the separation in our daily lives, though it never lessened our intimacy, was bound to increase her loneliness. George, except for holidays, was never at Swanscombe. I should therefore see just as much of him or just as little as usual. The long summer holidays we always spent together at some golfing seaside resort. It was Swanscombe that I was now to part from with the truest finality, Swanscombe that perversely I loved with all its ugliness, its littered mean streets, its dusty highway leading into an uglier Northfleet, the little church with its firm outline and squat tower on the hill-side, the daily fellowship of work for or with my father—and hardest of all, what I believed to be my mission in life, the boys' club, where each individual boy burned in my imagination with all the difficulties and dangers of his unenlivened existence. These boys leaving school at thirteen years of age had most of them to enter by force of economic pressure, the "death factory" or else to work long heavy hours as dockers upon the riverside.

I remember a barge-boy called Jim—a wit and a thinker—once saying to me, when I reproached him for getting drunk, "Yer see, Miss Phyllis, it's like this—yer kin 'ave football till you're twenty but arter that there ain't nothink *but* the Public 'Ouse an' girls—so I might as well get used to gettin' drunk, before I got ter! Nah! I don't want no girls! 'Stan's ter reason yer carn't keep a fambly on a pahnd a week can yer? So I 'as ter git drunk!"

Fifty years ago a pound a week was the peak of an unskilled labourer's wages; and unless a boy's parents could afford to apprentice him, or to do without the quick cul-de-sac earnings of his first after school years, he had to remain an unskilled labourer. There was secondary education even then, but to attend night schools entailed great personal efforts and sacrifices. Few children were so exceptional or so fortunate as to be able to avail themselves of any further education. They left school intelligent and eager youngsters able to read and write, and interested in acquiring further knowledge, but by twenty they could no longer read easily enough to entertain themselves, and had lost all love of knowledge. Funerals were the greatest and pleasantest excitements of the Swanscombe workers' lives. They saved for the "Death Club" as people now save for a great football event.

I felt that God could hardly be so obdurate or so short-sighted as to remove me from the boys' club when they needed me so badly. I clamoured at the Gate of Heaven for a cure at least by next autumn, so that I could return in time to open the club. I had what I supposed was faith, and woke each morning with the thought, "Today I shall begin to get well!"

It never occurred to me that practically speaking since I had no money, no influence, and no power to remove the difficulties in the boys' lives, that God might have other—rather better—plans both for them and for me.

I tied the Deity down to my own desires as most petitioners do; and when finally torn away from Swanscombe against my faith as well as against my will, I felt that somehow or other a great break had taken place in the whole scheme of things.

Elena had taken a house in Stoke D'Abernon in Surrey, as she had found Berry Head, in spite of its beauty, too wild and lonely in winter, as well as too remote from her relations and London friends.

In the early nineties, Stoke D'Abernon was a pretty country village, pleasantly surrounded by bracken and gorse covered commons, now snapped up into building lots and suburban villa gardens.

Elena's new home was two or three miles away from favourite cousins, and within—or so she had supposed—easy reach of London; but nothing turned out as favourably as she had expected. Stoke D'Abernon was just too far away to make London visits convenient, and favourite cousins who come to visit you once a year in your own surroundings and at your own time are quite different and somehow more charming than neighbours whom you must see at their times, and in their surroundings. Elena saw much less than she had expected to see of these cousins, and she cared less for what she saw. They expected her to start, at short notice, a career resembling as much as possible their own. They were bustling, active women considerably younger and stronger than Elena; and they had groups of slum women and children down to stay with them, whom they invigorated physically and morally.

Elena was a solitary, and had neither the desire nor the capacity to invigorate slum families. She was fifty-seven, delicate and very highly cultured, and she was not without good deeds of her own. Besides her care of myself, she invited for long week-ends, once a month, over-worked nurses from a London hospital, who were too far off from their homes, to get the rest and relaxation that they needed. She even took nurses recovering from illnesses for longer periods. She did not care much for the society of these women, since she particularly disliked any reference to diseases; and their conversation was mainly made up of such references, but she saw they had all they needed physically and put herself out for them considerably both financially and physically.

Neither of us liked the house at Stoke D'Abernon nor, as time went on, the neighbourhood. The house was old without being historic, and gloomy without being romantic. Its small garden was charmless and unenterprising; and nobody called. Country neighbourhoods are always slow to expand for strangers. Elena was neither so aristocratic as to bring the County to her gates, nor so rich as to support local activities; and she took not the least interest in games or in any form of sport. Elena's cousins were self-absorbed women, and as conductors to the social life of the neighbourhood (which they had promised her would be freely open to her) they simply did not work.

The church was Elena's one stand-by. She had seen to that before she took the house. It was a beautiful old church—perhaps the oldest in Surrey, with fine windows of old Flemish glass, and quite High enough in its ministrations for Elena's taste. She liked the young clergyman who was acting for the Vicar (abroad on a lengthened holiday) although she admitted his sermons were far from interesting.

It was perhaps not surprising that I found the house haunted. Whether it really was haunted or not I shall never know—for I have never been able to decide on the origin of haunts; but the room I occupied rather than slept in, certainly roused and troubled most of those to whom it was given. It was the best spare room; and Elena had put me into it because it was opposite her own. She had refrained from telling me, until I ventured to complain, that she herself had heard strange and unaccountable noises in the room, and on more than one occasion left her own room to investigate—in vain—what might be the cause.

We never did find out. It may have been owls, cracks in furniture on frosty nights, or restless denizens of unimaginable spheres intent on somewhat inconsiderate returns. But although I never "saw" anything, I would lie awake for hours, my heart thumping with terror, certain that I had felt the touch of a cold hand on my shoulder; or I would hear the definite sound of footsteps crossing the floor close to my bed. Still more sharp and dire noises would stab me awake out of deep slumber. I was soon removed to a second spare room in which no such sounds occurred, and visiting nurses had to stand the pressure of this disturbing room instead of me. They were never forewarned, but most of them complained. One of them, who possessed a highly religious nature, spoke of being awakened by a procession of great beauty, complete with lights, singing and incense, and was enchanted with her vision. She was, however, the only one who really enjoyed these interventions of the unseen.

At Berry Head I had seemed to lose the sharpest of my remorse and grief over Wilmett's death, but now that the first anniversary drew nearer I once more relived her illness every night and was terrified by heart-rending dreams. If I could have thought the unseen presence in the haunted room was hers, I should, I think, have been deeply re-assured, since I wanted nothing so much as to be able to believe that Wilmett was still alive; but I never associated her familiar spirit with these strange and indiscriminate sounds. My dreams and my remorse were unchanged wherever I found myself.

In spite of the cold January weather which kept us house-bound Elena and I were never bored. We had finished both the Inferno and the Purgatorio, and were now deep in Paradise with Beatrice.

Elena hired a pony cart and in fine weather we explored the blue-edged commons. When it was wet Elena read aloud while I did some extremely rudimentary embroidery.

Our walks were restricted by my decreasing strength, and it occurred to Elena that to ride on a pony might be better than any walks at all.

Neither of us realized that learning to ride is rather an arduous way of evading exercise.

It was the same pony that in the cart I had felt to be a singularly mild and trustworthy animal. I gave it sugar when I saw it—and was under the impression that it returned my affection; but when I mounted it in a long flowing habit of Elena's, assuming, as I was told to assume, what seemed to me the position of a crab without the benefit of its claws, the creature's whole nature changed.

Whatever I expected it to do, that pony did the opposite. Not only had I no control over it, but I had no control over myself either.

I was always in the air when I had meant to be upon the pony's back and when I ultimately descended, by force of gravity, I found its back as hard as a mill-stone. I never actually fell off the pony but neither could I affirm that I was ever actually on it; and we soon decided that even quite long walks were less physically exhausting than this cup and ball form of exercise.

I was much interested to find that one of Elena's nearest neighbours was the sister of one of my father's younger friends. She was a very pretty girl, like a highly idealized fox—with perhaps a faintly vixenish expression in her lovely hazel eyes, and I was soon to find, with thrilled horror, that her husband was another "Soames". If less brutally masterful than Galsworthy's repulsive hero, he certainly had the expression of a big contented bully—though I rather overlooked the fact, in the excitement of my discovery, that unlike Irene my new friend had freely chosen to marry him against the wishes of her family—and had unaccountably, once at least, wished to live with him. Now she complained of him bitterly and when we met her two babies in a pram and I stopped to admire them, she turned away shuddering, and said, "How can you? They look exactly like my husband!" The babies were of the type described by Thomas Mann as "Henry the VIII babies". They were huge, pink and white creatures with splendid blue eyes and double chins, while their mother was pale and sylph-like; still as babies go there was a good deal to be said for them. I retailed with horror to Elena the sufferings of my new friend, and was astonished at her reaction to them. She showed no sympathy whatever for this wronged wife, and declared that I must have nothing more to do with her. Young, unmarried girls, she said, should never be told the unhappy secrets of married women. This was the only time Elena and I sharply differed. I refused to give up my friend—Elena told me that as her guest I could not carry on such a relationship against her wishes. It looked like a deadlock. In the end we compromised. I was allowed to write to my friend, and explain my momentary withdrawal which was only to extend until my visit to Elena was over; but I did withdraw my visits, and reluctantly gave up the prospect of helping my new friend to disrupt her marriage immediately. I am bound to admit that she had already shown a reluctance to put her distaste to so drastic a test, and it may be that the kind and understanding reply she sent me expressed some slight sense of relief. Nor did we ever meet again, as I had planned, against another background, in order to carry out her release.

One cold spring Sunday Elena came back from church touched with pleased excitement. The nice young clergyman, on hearing my name, declared that he already knew me! Did I not remember him? I hadn't remembered him, but it suddenly flashed through my mind that his name *was* familiar.

Some years before I had had a short but warm friendship with the daughter of one of my father's golf-playing parsons. I now remembered that my friend's pretty elder sister had been engaged to a tall young clergyman of the curate's name. My father's friend had been deeply shocked by my recitations, which he had declared were highly dangerous for young men, and he had implored me to give them up. Perhaps Mr. C. was one of the young men whose moral nature had been threatened by Kipling's *Barrack Room*

Ballads. However Mr. C. wished to meet me again and he was duly invited to tea. He came to tea several times in quick succession, and on one occasion we went for a walk alone together. He then told me of how his long engagement had come to be broken off. He had had to have a serious but radical operation, and his future father-in-law would not accept the risk for Dolly, in spite of the surgeon's verdict that marriage was perfectly safe. Mr. B. had refused a father's blessing, and not even a good living offered to Mr. C. in New Zealand had softened his refusal. Obviously they could not marry without a parent's blessing.

I stopped to get my breath in the middle of a field and turned upon him in a fury of bewildered sympathy and rage—more rage, I fear—than sympathy. I had always disliked his potential father-in-law but never as much as I did now, and I expressed my feelings in no uncertain terms. I besought the young man to overlook so trivial an asset as Mr. B.'s blessing. Ten years of cruel frustration—and now this! I well remembered Dolly. I was thirteen when I knew the sisters and Dolly was already twenty-six. She must by now have passed the tremendous (for in those days it *was* tremendous) milestone of thirty. My companion was a little startled at the active strength of my sympathy. He said that Dolly was now a semi-invalid with a delicate heart and he thought that their marriage was out of the question. I told him that Dolly's ill health didn't matter at all—anyone engaged all that time could have any sort of upset heart.

All this would be set right if he would but act with decision, marry Dolly and take her out to New Zealand at once! I reminded him of the Brownings. Elizabeth was far more delicate than Dolly, as well as older, yet the Brownings' had been the most perfect marriage in the world. The father in the Brownings' case too had acted in just the same paltry fashion; but *they* had had the sense and the pluck to repudiate his blessing!

Mr. C. looked considerably shaken by my eloquence, but he did not seem to see his way to carry out the Brownings' adventure.

Once more he came to tea. Elena saw him afterwards alone at his request. They seemed to have a good deal to talk about, pacing to and fro over the little lawn while I watched them, a little impatiently, from the window sill.

At last Elena, looking very grave and unaccountably flustered, came in alone. She asked me if I liked Mr. C. I answered that I should like him better if he would give up his nonsense about Mr. B.'s blessing and marry Dolly. Elena sat down beside me looking graver and graver. She told me that the engagement to Dolly had come to a natural end and that this decision could not possibly be reversed. Mr. C. had now quite other ideas. He wanted to marry me. His stipend in New Zealand would be sufficient and his doctor had assured him that he was cured; Elena liked him very much. It was true that he was thirty-six and I was only nineteen, yet such a disparity of age, she felt, in my case need not be unsuitable. New Zealand was exactly the right climate for my health. Mr. C. liked me. He thought I had shown great kindness and sympathy over his late troubles, and he hoped I would let him know through Elena if he might see me with a view to marriage. He did not expect my immediate consent, but he wanted to be allowed the opportunity to win it. I was not only astonished, I was shocked and indignant! What—this man whose only interest to me was that poor Dolly had loved him for so long and so unavailingly, actually thought *I* would consent to marry him? He must be mad! Mr. C. I explained to Elena, was in my eyes far *worse* than married already. Besides I didn't even like him—I thought that if he had possessed an ounce of spirit he would have carried Dolly off, and let the blessing rip!

I was rather shocked with Elena too. Surely she knew me better than to expect I should do such a thing? Elena apologized profusely. I think it was always easier for her to sympathize with a young woman refusing marriage than with a young woman accepting it; but it had, she thought, been her duty to lay his proposal before me; and she rather shame-facedly promised that I need never see him again.

She wouldn't, she admitted, have considered his offer so seriously herself if it had not been for the beneficial climate of New Zealand.

She added very gently that since I had felt no interest in him it would surely have been wiser to have expressed less sympathy about his broken engagement?

I failed to grasp this point, but I accepted her apology, though it was a long time before I could get over my indignation for the devoted Dolly.

This incident was one more nail in the coffin of Stoke D'Abernon. I did not like the place, and if anything happened at all, it seemed to me, it was bound to be disagreeable.

I was glad to find that Elena agreed with me, and had determined to seek another home.

7

After a visit to Stoke D'Abernon Mary was very disheartened by my condition. She had found me considerably worse than she had expected.

With great courage and initiative she thought out a way of meeting the emergency; and I think that this action of Mary's probably saved my life.

She made a secret appointment with Dr. Schacht and went up to London to meet him. Mary asked him point blank what my chances were. He replied that Sir Douglas Powell and he had both thought them good at first, had I been sent, as they advised, to the Swiss mountains the previous winter; now they thought them lessened and that unless I could be sent to Davos or St. Moritz this next winter they were both obliged to take a much graver view of my case. Dr. Schacht had done his utmost to persuade my parents to send me abroad, but since they said they could not possibly afford the expense, he felt it would be cruel to press them further.

Mary then produced the exact figures of their income for his consideration; and added that if he thought this was not enough she felt sure my English grandmother, who was quite rich enough and very fond of me, would provide more.

Dr. Schacht was meticulously old-fashioned and I am sure he must have been both astonished and shocked at this well-informed and forthright statement; but he was a doctor first and a moralist afterwards, so that he was even more relieved. "Thank God," he exclaimed, "that you have told me the facts! I am free now to tell your parents that I consider it a matter of life or death!" Under this direct pressure my parents immediately gave way.

It must be understood that they had never loved their ducats better than their daughter; it was merely that neither of them knew very much about either money or health; and that the judgments of both were weakened by long anxiety and grief. My father's resistance to my going abroad had, I am sure, nothing to do with expense. It was based on the tenderness of his heart, inflated by his boundless optimism. How could he bear to send me away, ill and lonely, perhaps to die, among strangers? At the same time he managed no doubt to believe that I might get perfectly well nearer home. My mother's resistance was a more complex affair. She had been brought up in extreme wealth and had married into what seemed to her extreme poverty. She was still far too much of a Quaker not to believe in cutting her coat exactly to her cloth. She did not believe she could keep her household going on less than she had. Added to her morbid horror of debt, she thought my father far more extravagant and irresponsible than he really was. My father belonged to a family that spent what it had; and made more. My mother belonged to one that saved what it had; and spent less. Besides, my mother was both a determined and a broken-hearted pessimist. She had probably by now trained herself into believing that Heaven was the best place for all of us. Was not Wilmett already there?

But this harsh statement of medical fact crashed through all their fears and alibis. Neither of my parents was willing to accept the responsibility of keeping me at home against such a decisive medical verdict.

Elena, informed of all that had taken place, immediately stepped forward with an intermediate and helpful plan. I need not go abroad by myself. In September she would take me to Switzerland and the Italian lakes for two months at her own expense. She would see me off in November from Chiavenna at the head of Lake Como; and I could drive up the Maloja Pass to St. Moritz. She could not accompany me for the winter as the altitude was too high for her heart; but it was found that I could board quite cheaply with two British ladies in St. Moritz, who ran simultaneously a small pension and a teashop.

This would be quite respectable for a young girl without a

chaperone, as well as inexpensive. I should be on my own, and yet there would be, if I needed it, someone to fall back on.

Kennie Fowler always spent part of each winter at the Kulm in St. Moritz and could report to the family on my condition. I would be under the care of his own doctor and great personal friend, Dr. Holland, and no doubt Dr. Holland's charming wife would act as my social sponsor. These promises looked fool-proof at the time. My father's patron came forward and offered him fifty pounds towards my expenses. I am ashamed to say that false pride made me implore my parents to refuse this useful gift; fortunately I was overborne, and the money was accepted. I had no right to such an expensive type of self-respect since *The Master Hope* had brought me in nothing and it was some time before I could pull my weight or contribute at all substantially towards my parents' burden.

Meanwhile I was so wildly delighted to be going abroad with Elena and to see Italy, that I almost overlooked the fact that my prayers to return to the boys' club in the autumn had remained unanswered.

Miss Hardy and Miss Dyble, my two teacher friends, with unfailing self-sacrifice and courage, agreed to run the club by themselves till my return.

My mother and I were to spend the intervening months at Eastbourne, joined for the summer holidays by the rest of the family.

Everything, except my health, appeared to be going well. I should of course recover immediately, I told myself, at St. Moritz, Meanwhile my father chose this moment to present me with my heart's desire—a brindle bull pup. Bill was two and a half months old, and if you prodded him suddenly with one finger he rolled over. He was wrinkled, heavy-browed and bandy-legged. Sturdy and active as a cricket ball in flight, he swung into my affections with imperturbable good humour. He was, I think, the gayest and steadiest dog that I have ever possessed. His courage was such that he would have challenged a bulldozer. He shared every thought of his heart with me; and was of so generous and unsuspicious a nature that even his bones—after his first attack upon them—were gingerly shoved in my direction.

As for his bread and milk, he would turn round from his morning bowl, his jowl crested with white foam, and persist in returning thanks, by burrowing his head in my lap.

My mother was horrified by what she thought his illtimed advent; and watched with great anxiety his swiftly unfolding strength.

It was, she thought, highly unsuitable for me to have a dog to train at the very moment in which it had been decided to send me abroad; especially so large and powerful a dog. But invalids do not thrive on precautions alone; and I am inclined to think that a bull pup at this juncture of my life was better than any tonic. We took Bill to Eastbourne with us where he played an exciting part in a small badly run pension. He ate half of one of the disagreeable land-lady's blouses; and had he not made bosom friends with Polly, the young cook, our stay would, I am sure, have been shortened.

I used to hear her crooning softly to him in the narrow strip of kitchen garden when she was hanging out the wash. "Such a 'andsome face 'e 'as! An' 'e *knows* 'e 'as a 'andsome face 'e does!" While Bill, uglier than any gargoyle, leered sardonically up at her.

George never cared for Bill as much as I did. His school-boy sense of what was proper shrank from Bill's youthful *faux pas.* Still, I think even George would have admitted that Bill's presence greatly assisted the holiday spirit.

I found George at fifteen extremely hard to understand. He was more silent than ever; deeply conventional and, though I think completely master of his own world, a stranger in mine. His world— as far as I was concerned—consisted of foreign matter; and I have no doubt that he was equally bewildered by the nature of mine.

I was already a woman. George was no longer a child; but neither was he a young man. He was a fast-developing human being faced by new responsibilities and powers, only partially under-stood. In his family of almost overpowering feminine influence— with an erratic male parent (for to an English Public School boy our impulsive American father must have seemed erratic)—he stood baffled—and alone. The one person—girl that she was—who had understood him best and perhaps loved him most, was now dead;

64

and her recent loss must have added greatly to his adolescent sense of insecurity.

My mother told me that George had reached the age when I, as his nearest sister, must act as his protector from marauding females.

Since my father and Mary had not yet joined us it was essential that if George wanted to go out in the evening I should go with him.

There was a certain conflict between George's morals and my health; and I think it often worried my mother that she had to spur me on to exertions far beyond my strength; but at the time it seemed to both of us that George's immortal soul required all that we could possibly do for it—whether he liked it or not—or whatever its consequences might be for others.

Eastbourne was not yet the expert and fashionable place that it was to become; and the Tennis Tournament week, in its earliest stages, was inexpensive for onlookers; so George and I joined the Eastbourne Club and watched for days on end the best tennis in the world.

White balls leaped against my eye-lids while I said my prayers at night; and through the long hours of darkness; but by day I was as full of excitement and enjoyment as my brother.

The artist in me was perfectly satisfied to watch the lovely leaps of the Doherty brothers, and the mad rhythm with which rackets swung—as it sometimes seemed unaided—to meet balls.

The evening strolls however were rather beyond my powers. We compromised, for George was a most humane companion, by sitting most of the time on the pier, listening to comic songs.

Ever since those evenings the first chord of a song intended to be humorous—or even the first rasp of a comedian's voice—sounds more ominous in my ears than a funeral dirge. George too, I now fancy, must have found those interminable summer evenings as great a strain as I did. People may make many cogent objections to cinemas; but they replace some forms of amusement still more open to complaint.

Our landlady was a mean and bullying spinster, and the bane of our indoor existence, so that partly for Bill's sake and partly for our own we remained out doors as much as possible.

Miss B. had hired a villainous Italian waiter, provided by an agency which called itself a Christian Institution, though its Christianity consisted solely in presenting strayed and blackened sheep to any fold that wanted to pay considerably less than the market price for labour. This ill-paid brute attacked Polly. Miss B., a coward as well as a tyrant, fled, and finding me alone above stairs she implored my assistance. I took the stairs in a swallow flight, arriving, as Polly afterwards declared, in the nick of time to save her from criminal assault.

The Italian was so surprised at the speed and force of my eruption that he let go of Polly, who sprang to safety behind me on the stairs.

The waiter, wildly excited, drew a large knife from some portion of his person and waved it madly in my face; but I saw that he was far more frightened than frightening. A few words of Italian, picked up from Dante's Inferno, served to quiet him sufficiently for explanations. I told him he must go immediately or Polly would run for the police; and he told me that he *would* go, if he was given two shillings owed him by Miss B. Knowing Miss B.'s disposition I felt it probable that she *did* owe it to him and luckily found that I had two shillings in my pocket. Except for a spate of highly un-Christian language, after he received the two shillings, this ended the emergency. The waiter left by the back door; Polly fell into my arms and Miss B. descended from the top of the stairs and reproached me for having produced the two shillings. However she was in no position, after her rescue, to evict Bill, even if he ate the other half of her blouse.

Another uncomfortable way of accumulating money possessed by Miss B. was that she included among her pensionnaires what was known at that time as a "Nugget".

Nuggets were more usually found in doctors' families but they could easily stray into the hands of any determined and money-loving person; they were generally ladies of uncertain age and partial lack of intellect, whose relatives could no longer put up with their company.

I suffered a good deal from Miss B.'s "Nugget", who took a great fancy to me. She told me that she was often overwhelmed by fears in the night, and begged that she might come to my room

66

whenever this occurred, and share her terrors with me. I foolishly consented to this frightening and yet flattering arrangement. The lady must have been twice my age; and I felt pleased to imagine that I could dispose of her fears even while I added to my own. She did not come every night, but every night I would lie awake for hours, listening for the sound of creeping footsteps. When she came she would sit on the edge of my bed for hours, with her poor bony fingers twisting my hands, while she poured out her terrifying delusions by the light of one candle. I did not confide these nocturnal visitations to my family as I felt they might not feel that listening to this poor creature was a work of mercy incumbent on me; but I told Elena about them later on, and was hurt to find that she did not agree with me.

My father's arrival with Mary, not only gave me the easy companionship I loved, but greatly relieved my protective exertions. George had now two sisters to stand between him and the Eastbourne sirens.

From this sharply menaced time I can only recall one other vivid experience.

George and I had somehow managed to reach the top of Beachy Head together.

There was a strong wind blowing and even the gulls found themselves flung pell mell about the sky.

We had to lie flat on our faces, digging our hands into the short turf, to prevent ourselves from being carried over the edge of the cliff.

I can well remember the strange exultation that swept over my weakness, and took control of it.

All my difficulties would vanish if I let go.

I had wanted to be the prop and stay of my parents, and I was now only a burden. I had wanted to protect George; and I must now desert him. I had longed to make life easier for the working boys at Swanscombe; and this too had been denied me. What was the sense of my survival? I could hear George's voice shouting above the loud song of the wind. "Hold on like grim death, Parpa!" He did not know, I thought to myself, how much more grim a task it was to hold on to life.

I had only to let go, and the wind would take me as it took the gulls. The breath would be shaken out of me long before I reached the hard rocks beneath.

I wish I could say that it was the thought of George that restrained me from this act of cowardice; but it was a still older affection that gave me courage to hold on. There have been moments since when I found life far more difficult than in those exhausting, menaced weeks at Eastbourne, but I have never reached the point when I did not love life more than I feared it.

My fingers dug deeper into the short grasses; and slowly and cautiously, between the fierce rushes of the gale, George and I slithered back, from the cliff's edge into safety.

8

When I was young, going abroad was a far rarer, more independent and adventurous act, than it is now. Anything might happen in a world where you were free to go anywhere, without passport or identity papers, with no control beyond your own wishes and what you had in your pockets to pay for them.

Each European country had its private intelligence; and you were free to share it. Hotels were *not* the same everywhere. There was no Anglo-Saxon smear of hygiene and no attempt to copy—or even to produce for sale—the products of other richer lands. Architecture was as individual as speech; and what was in the shops was what the people of each country had had the skill to put there.

We left Victoria Station, from a platform isolated and catering solely for boat trains. It was the beginning of the Continent. My father and his patron, Mr. Fred White, saw us off.

Elena, calm outwardly and collected inwardly as she always was, whether she felt calm or not, awaited us with everything settled and arranged.

I then made one of those social slips which haunt the mind of youth like crimes.

How, I asked myself, could I best show Mr. White the gratitude I ought to feel for his generous gift to my parents? Nor was he merely generous, or he would not have broken into his busy morning with this further act of kindness. Surely to see off a chit like myself was a sign of affection? I must show him—on my side— some symbolic act of gratitude.

He was a pompous and terrifying figure, perhaps sixty years old, and I did not want to kiss him, but kiss him I would, in all the

69

glaring publicity of the crowded platform—and kiss him I—desperately—did. It was well within my power as I was rather taller than he was; but I instantly saw, by the horror in his eyes, how terrible had been my blunder. Elena, too, had seen it, and was a little vexed; but she realised my good intentions and tried to comfort me about it afterwards. My father was oblivious—the journey enchanted him —in his imagination he had practically reached Italy. He ran along beside the moving train, his eyes sparkling with fellow feeling and if he could have thrown his heart into the carriage after me, he would have thrown it. "Remember," he called out. "Don't try to save the world! and above all, never laugh!" My laughter was in youth much too loud and I think now too frequent, though my father always shared it. As to the former part of his advice, it was the best he could have given me, had I but known how to take it.

Elena must have spent a great deal of preliminary trouble over all our many journeys, for I can never remember any of them going wrong. We never failed to arrive at our pre-determined destination without losing luggage, and with what punctuality trains permitted.

Elena could make herself understood in at least three languages. She was just in all her dealings; and not easily fooled. She tipped in this spirit, and though never lavish, her tips were always accepted with respect. I think she was formidable in her quiet way and would have known how to check neglect or insolence had any been shown her. Although I deeply respected her I was myself perfectly at ease with Elena; and believed that she shared all her problems with me, as if I were as grown-up as I felt. There was a point, however, I now think on which she kept some of these problems to herself; but she must have shown infinite tact as well as self control to have left me feeling so unhampered, and spiritually free, as I did throughout all our long intervals of companionship.

Elena was not a good sailor and she insisted that we should descend into the rather gruesome ladies' cabin, where we both lay out flat like crusaders on their marble slabs, surrounded by other suffering women. It was hard to bear, but we both shut our eyes, and hardened our ears, for those terrible two hours, in which much happened round us—but nothing actually to us.

Cold and shaky we came up on deck, where even if I had been

70

sick, I should certainly have kept my eyes open. It was unbelievable that this pale strip of turbulent water between us and our home should have been wide enough to hold the differences between France and England.

The approaching cliffs had been sundered from our own; but they were nothing like our own. Not even the gulls scurrying out from Boulogne Harbour had the same light on their tireless wings as our sea-gulls. They looked to me stouter and more primeval.

The stumpy cathedral, a dark blue grey in the trough of the low divided cliffs, had a definitely less religious and a more mundane and frequented look.

The French trees had a sparse elegance and none of our trees' homely density. Boulogne itself, though I doubt if it was ever a beautiful city, had an interesting way of tumbling down its cliff sides onto the quay, as if it was in a hurry to get there and extremely concentrated on whatever may have been its purpose—which it seems now to have lost.

As for the French people, when we landed in their midst, so great was their visible and audible difference that they might have been denizens of another star. Nobody looked good-natured or at a loose end—perhaps there were no loose ends in France—and nobody was quiet or kept still for an instant.

The Boulogne porters—unleashed by some hidden signal—rushed upon us like wolves. Even to this day they are furious and insistent people, but some of their jungle habits have dropped off them. No tip satisfied them then, nor did they look as if anything had ever satisfied them. Heaven, as Robert Louis Stevenson said of Matthew Arnold, wouldn't have been able to please them if there had ever been any chance of any of them getting there.

We were to stop at Boulogne for the night, and this annoyed them beyond the power of profanity to assuage—they wanted to put us and everything we had on the Paris train—nobody, they shrieked at us, coming by this boat, ever stopped the night at Boulogne. The more they cursed and shrieked and even leapt into the air to deflect our purpose, the quieter Elena got, and the more firmly and gently she told them to take us and our luggage—which they ultimately did—to the Hôtel Cristal et Bristol. I thought we should never survive the final scene, in the far from secluded glass-covered hall, when they received their tips. It gave infinite pleasure to a group of Amazonian fisher-women with stout bunchy skirts, legs as solid as cathedral pillars, and marvellously expressive faces pressed as close against the glass as they could get. I never saw or heard such women. They shouted as if the very air had no other significance than to act as a medium for their clarion voices. They were not women, they were portents, extravagant, exhilarating portents. They held up their slippery silver fish for us to see, they pointed gleeful fingers at the baffled porters and grinned at me most engagingly through the glass. I grinned at them back, though I felt a trifle awed by their turbulence, their strength, and their breezy sociability. I could not help thinking of other baskets which were filled with heads, not fishes, under the shadow of guillotines not, as history goes, so very long ago.

The rain fell in heavy sheets, but they cared nothing for it under their oilskin hoods. The town ran together, a glimmering slate grey. The quay was full of sound and most of it human sound. The muffled peace of Folkestone or Dover was a thing unknown and undesired in Boulogne.

Here everyone spoke all day long with vigour and passion about everything. To me it was a delicious, racy clamour and I longed to be out on the wet cobblestones, taking part in it. Inside, the Hotel was full of spiky furniture covered with crimson plush, which gave it a misleading air of softness; and I had never seen so many gilt-framed mirrors in my life. From all sides of us—and at short intervals up the stairs—a tall pale lady, drooping a little after the alarming battle of the porters had been brought to its bravely successful finish, followed by a gaunt and spectral girl with shining eyes and wildly untidy hair, flashed back upon us with a disconcerting familiarity. Was it really us? Were we—triumphantly—*there*? Was this "abroad"?

It seemed so more than ever, when an hour later we sat in the glass-faced hall (there was no other sitting room) at a table in a window niche, gazing out once more at the vigorous wet turmoil. We were both hungry as well as tired; but I was oblivious of the good French food. I ate and drank the street scenery.

Women with long golden rolls tucked beneath their arms flashed by, shawled and hatless, under extravagantly large green umbrellas. Sprinkled through the crowds—and on any bare space of the quay—like confetti at a wedding—were small blue and red *gendarmes*. I suppose they were keeping order, but a good deal of it seemed to have escaped them. Horses' heads gingerly pushed their way through gaps in pedestrians.

Even the trains, with their engines so much larger than ours and their couplings so much looser, were obliged to stop and shriek at intervals—almost between the elbows of my friends, the fisher-women. It was as if the Marseillaise sprang out of the very air. Our bedrooms, though in many ways pleasantly exotic, managed to combine stuffiness with cold. I do not think they had ever been swept or dusted though the sheets were clean. We realised why the porters had told us no one ever slept there—though I think they did quite well to eat—at the Hôtel Cristal et Bristol.

I did not want to sleep. I listened to the night, and to the even noisier dawn.

I felt it sad to leave the friendly, jostling town, even for the un-folding of the fields of France.

The long day's journey stands clear at the gate of memory.

I never saw the grey, steep, secret-looking houses so plainly on later journeys; each rich, late September field might well have been a cloth of gold, spread for the meeting of kings. The church spires were narrower and more insistent than our own, they seemed always in the exact centre of every village, and were often sur-rounded by manure heaps. The new thin light made everything I looked at shine as if under water. Light in England is soft and penetrates what it rests on; but in France light keeps to its own sphere and is content with shining.

I thought of Mellie Darius—my French friend and teacher. "It is our light," she used to tell me, "that makes our minds clear." Shakespeare, she had impatiently informed me, "was often clumsy and bungled his meaning, but Racine never! He sharpened his way through words like a good knife!"

I felt that Mellie herself was now more comprehensible. I could accept her swift decisions, which had often seemed unkind, because

73

however much they hurt her or myself, she could not fumble or hesitate. "Les situations nettes" were for her the only possible conclusions. I remembered without bitterness her passionate possessiveness, her fiery jealousy and the drive of her aggressive spirit.

It was out of this clear French light that her unshrinking self-respect must have been born. She was without self-pity, and had no pity, either, for the weaknesses of others. But she had integrity and a tremendous sense—when she trusted—of obligation.

We travelled as Elena had told me we should, "like two princesses", but like the princess in a poem of Christina Rossetti. We were to use—and not give way to—our royalty.

As often as we could, we travelled by day, but when night journeys were compulsory we never indulged in sleepers. We hired pillows from central stations and hoped to find (and in those spacious days often did) an empty first-class carriage where each could stretch out at length. In the day time, on long journeys we travelled second; and on short journeys or for excursions, third. We saved our extra breakfast rolls, and what was left over from the hot milk (how I hated the skin on it!) and took these unpalatable forms of nourishment if Elena thought the intervals too long between meals.

We arrived at Basle jaded and crumpled after our first night journey and had our souls and bodies put together by its rolls and coffee. It seemed a singularly large and quiet place, and was very cold. Noise is not necessarily a spur to contact, yet the silence of Switzerland after the impassioned voice of France was of a slightly grim and repellent kind.

It was as if there were suddenly very much less to talk about.

It was still raining when we arrived at Lucerne. The mountains were shrouded, but I felt their bulky grey presences lurking behind the thick curtain of rain.

We were to spend two nights at Lucerne. Elena would hardly have felt justified in staying at so important a hotel as the Hôtel des Balances if it had not been out of season and practically empty. Memory of her own early travels dragged her back; and she wanted to share with me the great windows and balconies on the lake, overlooking the milky green river crossed by its dark covered bridges. I felt as if I had lifted the cardboard lid of a Swiss toy village. Lucerne, empty under the hopeless rain, looked like a dark reproduction on a larger scale of one of these models. They had always enchanted me when I was a child, but toys reminding one of architecture are somehow more enthralling than architecture reminding one of toys.

Yet the long, sunless day we spent rambling about the town under the misty bastions of invisible mountains has a remembered charm. My taste was quite untrained, and it was the clumsily carved bears and wooden swallows that filled me most with rapture. I wanted to buy them all. Elena did nothing to repress or correct my ignorant enchantment, but she gently reminded me not to spend too much on these exotic presents lest I should find later on things I should prize more and not be able to afford.

Lucerne, she told me, was only a gateway and indeed it was only as a rather empty gateway that I was content to accept it.

The St. Gotthard railway had not long been opened, and Elena's memory of driving across this splendid pass was hardly confirmed by its modern equivalent. The actual journey was for us both an unmitigated disappointment. We were even before we started extremely tired; and it rained all day long harder than ever. Were these rubbish heaps of lumpy black ice mixed with decaying vegetation the sunny "pleasure domes of ice", I had expected?

Elena was vexed at my not being able to thrill my imagination from her memories of past loveliness. She looked sad; and I felt thwarted all the way to Lugano.

We arrived in the rain but it was a different kind of rain. There was a stealthy softening in the darkened day. My eyes caught their first glimpse of old stone walls with roofs of slanting terracotta tiles—the neat Swiss chalets were no more. Instead there were towers, and rough stone houses clinging together like shells, the loggias under their pink tiled eaves, hung with golden maize; and a new sense of beauty came into my heart, a new form which had the quality of music. Even in the darkened sky these hills sprang up like tulips. Here and there a tall black cypress struck its question mark

75

against a hill-side; or a group of them, spectacular as pilgrims, skirted a cemetery.

I knew, long before the train jerked itself into the dark station trying to be tidy and pretending it was still Switzerland, that this was Italy.

Our hotel was a gloomy but stately villa visited by Elena in her early youth, set in a garden by the lake side.

We had only one hushed, velvety night, and one adventurous morning to enjoy its splendours. While Elena was still saying her prayers I was in the garden gazing at the mountains through a veil of purple mist. These stately presences blocking up the sky—with the dark green floor of the lake spread at their feet—were really mountains. They did not need glaciers. They were covered with soft brown fur, and there was no apparent interval between their brown and purple heights and the deep Italian sky. Great yellow leaves fell from a magnolia tree into a fountain basin, and church bells sounded desultory but continuous greetings from a hundred towers.

The Cathedral was close to our great iron gates. The glowing gentleness of Luini's immense Crucifixion was its altar piece. This was Luini's *paese* and he had given it the best he had.

I had never before seen a picture stretch itself so widely into space, to let one mingle with its life-sized figures. Elena knew a great deal about pictures and she began my education, with inspiration and without insistence, that morning before Luini's master-piece, and carried it on by books and through practical illustrations for the next three years. I held on to the excitement of this first morning with all the strength I could, but by the afternoon illness had broken down even my eagerness. A gloomy young doctor appeared, and removed us almost instantly into a bright, charmless Swiss hotel, inordinately clean, away from the lake side, the magnolia leaves and the little laughing town. I had to spend more than half of our allotted Lugano stay in bed, but I had the mountains to look at, and as soon as the sun came out I made up for this blank interval by the joy we packed into the other half.

I had already grown to love the single peak of San Salvatore, standing like a blue and silver sentinel behind the lake, but the day

I first came into actual collision with it, I saw what for a moment I took as the end of the world. The sky behind the peak, which I had supposed to be empty except for clouds, broke into a bevy of white flashing heads, like bands of surging angels, sparkling with gold. It was the Alps, unveiled after three weeks' rain.

Each Italian lake possesses its own particular hue. They may occasionally borrow from each other, but for the most part Como remains churned azure, Garda has a yet deeper if less dancing blue, Maggiore prefers pale amethyst and moonstone for its wide expanse, while little Orta harps on purple, varied by deep amethyst, or plain witches' cauldron black and white, when a mistral rushes down upon it; but Lugano—whenever I have seen it—(and for years all these lakes weaved themselves into my springs and autumns) remained green. The sun can do what it likes with green, and the shadows have a separate palette, so there is never any lack of variety on the surface of Lugano.

The first time I was allowed out on a golden day we took a little boat and rowed to Gandria. There was a wall along the lake side lost in a canopy of scarlet leaves. The little village—tower and terrace, leaf and stone—crept down into the water "quivering within the waves' intenser day". These double visions stared back and forth at each other, from the actual village above us, to where we gazed entranced into the imaged depth beneath. I could have dipped my hand into the stone and clung to the water—so closely did they match each other.

Morcote was a much longer and more enterprising excursion. I did not on this first occasion climb to its perpendicular heights. The village faced San Salvatore and was crowned by a towered monastery above a great flight of steps. Cypresses upon each side of the steps climbed with Morcote.

While our boat idled its slow way towards it, the whole village burst out upon the quay and down the steps like a scene in an opera.

We knew it was *not* a procession because the cassocked priest wore no surplice, and was unaccompanied by little white and scarlet boys with boats of incense. It was instead a small band of emigrants about to embark for America and being seen off by their whole *paese*.

Suddenly, in the mild peace of the golden afternoon, we found ourselves at the centre of a tragedy.

This little band thrust forth into the unknown were tasting the sharpness of death. These farewells were permanent. They were unlikely ever to see again their lake, Morcote, its accustomed cypresses, or their familiar guardian San Salvatore—and far worse even than the loss of their village—they were being torn by their roots away from fathers and mothers, sweethearts and familiar friends.

The women stood a little apart from the men, black-shawled figures, with only their eyes alive. I watched a father half laughing, half crying, fingering his son's shoulder in its new cheap suit with heart-breaking pride, while his son unashamedly wept upon his father's neck. The whole crowd laughed and wept together, pouring out wine and drinking toasts to each departing traveller in turn. A sea of bundles, suitcases, and even cages with birds, passed from hand to hand over the little steamer's side. She had crossed from the far side of the lake with an anxious agent in her counting over a list and trying to match each traveller to his printed name.

A girl moved slowly down the steps till she reached the ship's side. Just in front of the gangway the crowd parted and left a little space about her.

A young man plunged back across the gang plank and caught her in his arms. He gave a great cry as if someone had ripped the heart out of his breast. "Margherita!" he shouted again and yet again. "Margherita!" His father and the nervous agent pulled him forcibly back on to the boat. He was to go and Margherita was to stay. She stood there silent, and as if turned to stone. The steamer hooted, and moved off, once more across the widening water—and only held from plunging into it by the frantic arms of friends—the young man roared her name, "Margherita!" I could see her face, and if ever a heart moved out of a body to join its mate, her heart left Margherita. Her eyes clung to him while the boat grew smaller and smaller, disappearing at last behind the mountain's flank and even its smoke became just a white scarf, and then hardly a shadow, upon the nearest golden cloud.

What was to become of all that agony, we asked each other,

through the long years? Would he find her the home he had promised or would there, when at length the home was found, be another woman by its hearth called by a different name?

Elena thought it hardest for the old man who had lost his son; but I could not believe this was the sharpest pain. The old man had spent his life, his love was already grown into a human form; but these two were torn apart from each other in the passion of their youth, and were losing a life that they could never have.

9

When I first knew Baveno it still belonged to the late Victorians. Its mountain was Meredith's Mottarone. You could almost see the little cavalcade of conspirators setting forth on foot or on donkeys to take their separate ways to the summit, where their chief, Mazzini, was to meet them and give them the signal which was to release Milan.

On the slopes we walked over, Sandra Belloni had made her innocent betrayal of Mazzini's master-stroke to her English friends in league with the Austrian enemy.

All Meredith's most enchanting heroines deceive a little—themselves or their lovers. Only his awkward heroines are bluntly true. When they are true their lovers have to deceive them, for Meredith's betrayal by his own wife stirs at the heart of all his love stories.

We could not climb high enough to look down on the blue plain bounded by Alps, diamond bright with deep new snow, but our eyes swept the softness of light out of which soared Monte Boscero, and lingered over Piedmontese and the Swiss peaks. Unknowingly I saw the wooded hollow where Lake Orta hid, and where for three hundred years had stood an old stone villa which was to be my future home. We arrived out of the rain, into a clear sunset. Maggiore, vast as the sea, shone a luminous pink and lay so still that the mountains dipped unshaken into its amethyst mirror. Tethered between lake and sky floated the Borromean islands, light as drifting feathers.

Maggiore had been the early Victorian resort of distinguished English invalids. Traces of their sojourn still lingered, in large empty villas on small islands or spacious hotels specially designed for their convenience and dropped rather oddly at the edge of small, impecunious lake villages. It was for one of these hotels, strayed out of its period and filled by ghosts, that we were bound. There was a legend that Byron had stayed there. It would have been too respectable for Shelley. Rich industrialists from Milan in summer just kept its head above water now; but the season for them was over, and we were its last guests.

I think our happiest lake visit was at Baveno. The weather and I between us had spoiled Lugano; and at Como we were to part, but Maggiore was a tranquil breathing space—"sad with the whole of pleasure". Day after day slipped past us steeped in deep autumnal peace under that uninsistent amethystine light.

Even the two adventures that broke into our tranquillity, drained of their terror by memory, enhance the value of those serene and quiet days.

One evening Elena, who had gone for her daily walk (now strictly forbidden me by the gloomy young doctor of Lugano), did not come back for tea. It was her habit to go out at three and return punctually at four-thirty to find that I had frugally prepared our tea on the spirit lamp, and generally to give a more substantial air to it by producing cakes she had bought on her way home. The hour passed and dusk began to draw in. The clock struck six and the dark blotted out the lake. Terror drove me to seek our landlord, whom we did not like, and whom I liked still less when he told me sombrely that he had already warned the Signora not to take walks alone. Certainly Baveno was safe for English travellers—the whole lake district was safe at any hour of the day or night. But there were Neapolitans about at work on the new quarry and everyone knows what Neapolitans are like. Their own grandmothers wouldn't be safe with them. It was more than probable that the Signora had been at least murdered by one of those dogs. Did I know in which direction she was going? No? She hadn't told me? Then nothing could be done about it.

There must, I urged, be something we could do! Could we not ask the *guardia* to search for her? The landlord shrugged his shoulders. Such a search, he said, would cost a good deal of money. The porter, too, must be paid extra for fetching the *guardia*! I told him frantically that it didn't matter what it cost. That put a different complexion on it, the landlord explained, showing some interest for the first time, as long as money was forthcoming something could always be done.

He called the porter and I set forth with him, rehearsing in our two broken languages what description of Elena we could best impart to the *guardia*; but at the gate we met her hurrying figure. Nothing had happened to her but the dark. She had lost her way by taking a wrong path in the dusk, and turning up at a strange village, had been politely guided home. She was extremely annoyed with me for being frightened, and extremely frightened at being the source of my anxiety. When I ventured to chide her severely in my turn for disregarding the landlord's warnings, she gave me an answer which deeply impressed itself on me. "It is quite true," she admitted quietly. "Attacks upon lonely women do take place! As a young girl I was greatly afraid of such accidents, but I thought to myself, 'Perhaps I am to be alone all my life, am I to sacrifice beauty and experience, to the fear of what may never take place?' I made up my mind against such a sacrifice—and you see I have not yet been attacked by anyone."

Our second adventure was more formidable though I was a good deal less terrified by it. In retrospect it even seems to me funny.

We were in search of an eighth-century crucifix. We wound our way, by row-boat, through water-ways that led to another arm of the lake, where we reached our village. Unfortunately there was a *vino* by the water-side, and the church which housed the crucifix was invisible from it. The crucifix, a wild and archaic figure, stiff and slender and most curiously drooping away from its cross, we eventually found behind the High Altar, in a corner full of rubbish. The sacristan was astonished that we really wanted to see it instead of a very gaudy reproduction of the Stations of the Cross, given to the Church by an *Americano*, Italian by birth, of course, but one who had earned much money in America and returned to spend it in this profitable manner. The crucifix was *antico* he admitted, but *molto brutto*, and it was hidden away lest expectant mothers might be frightened by it.

Our boatman, when we returned, staggered out of the *vino*

looking rather red, and his rowing struck us as a little erratic. Suddenly he caught a crab and was shot out of the boat into the estuary. The water was deep and we retrieved him and his oar with some difficulty, only just escaping upsetting the boat in our efforts. His language was copious and frightful, but fortunately for us his wetting had completely sobered him, for this was not the end of our difficulties. We were crossing a wide part of Maggiore far from the shore when we saw that the boat had begun to leak. Each hid her knowledge from the other; but soon it became apparent to the boatman as well as to us. He wasted no time in excuses or even curses this time, but handed us an empty tin and told us to bale in turn for all we were worth. He then put his back into rowing. None of us could swim, no other boats were within hailing distance and we were too far from the shore to attract attention.

I do not know how that water-logged boat contrived to stay afloat, for it filled faster than we could empty it, and by the time we reached the nearest landing place we were wet up to the waist. If he had not been sober by then, what Elena said to that boatman in the most fluent Italian I ever heard her use, would certainly have sobered him. Neither of us suffered the least harm from our adventure, for as I have often found, physical danger has a stimulating effect upon the most delicate of invalids.

We loved all the Borromean Islands but our favourite was the Isola dei Pescatori. Elena painted it from a boat and I have the little picture now, the lake a trifle bluer than a moonstone, and the island lying like a russet leaf blown from the nearest promontory.

Elena's water colours were never very definite but they always carried with them what she saw.

The country people were extremely friendly to us on our small excursions. Pre-Mussolini Italy, especially in the North, was a land of exquisite sympathies and small excitements.

The pride and glory of the *Risorgimento* still lingered in the people's eyes and habits. Their country belonged to them; they were your courteous hosts, and wished you to carry away the handsomest of good impressions. All they asked of any foreigner was not to be a *tedesco*.

The *Mafia* had no grip in the North.

There was poverty but not misery in the lake district. The people were independent and hard working. There were a few able and chronic beggars in most villages; but they had a dignity of their own, and I think their needs were basically unavoidable, and that everyone round them knew it. I was once rebuked by an old lady to whom I had given what she thought was too much. "You must have forgotten who I am," she said reproachfully. "You gave to me already once this morning—and once a day is enough. Look out for me again tomorrow!"

Elena did not approve of giving indiscriminately to beggars, but we compromised in this as in other matters where we differed. Small change could be given but we must keep down the numbers to whom we gave it; and men, who looked strong enough to earn their livings, must never be helped at all.

I hated the idea of St. Moritz. Our last stop before the Pass was Cadenabbia on Lake Como, a place I have always disliked; and we found ourselves in a small, stuffy hotel full of English people. They were mostly old, and mostly ladies; but there was one young man— like an angel on a Christmas card—quite extraordinarily pretty and quite terribly ill.

The old ladies all adored him, and he adored showing off to them. It was a harmless—and it was to be a brief—exhibitionism; but I took an extremely adverse view of it.

Elena, too, disliked his conceit and particularly resented the public way in which he flaunted the disagreeable symptoms of his disease.

His room was next to mine, and one night I could tell from his fearful fits of coughing and other sounds of misery that he must be desperately ill. I ran across to Elena's room to borrow her sal volatile for him. "He must feel terribly faint," I explained, "between those paroxysms; and perhaps there is something else I could do for him as well." Elena, whom I had awakened (with dangerous suddenness considering her weak heart) said with the utmost severity, "You must do nothing of the kind! You mustn't go near his room—nor shall I. I don't believe it's in the least necessary!" She had never been angry with me before, though occasionally stern, but now she sat on the edge of her bed, very flushed and upset, and I felt astounded. "But he is dying!" I exclaimed. "I must go in and look after him!" "I have not much experience of illness myself," Elena said coldly, "but I think you exaggerate. I am almost sure that people are quieter when they are dying; and you certainly must *not* go to his room!"

It was a sharp cleavage but I had no doubt whatever that I was right. The young man's piteous groans still rang in my ears. Something must be done about him. I repeated with the utmost firmness, "Elena, I simply *must* take him the sal volatile!"

Elena sat, grieved and implacable, considering our dilemma. No doubt she resorted to prayer. At last she found a way. "Very well," she said. "I will let you do something. You can go and ask the land-lady to take it to him, if she thinks fit. She told me his mother had asked her to look after him. I will give you the sal volatile, and you must come back and tell me what she says. On no account must you go with her, if she decides that it is necessary to go to this young man at all."

The landlady, when at last aroused, was inclined to take Elena's view of the matter. However she yielded to my urgency and agreed to go and find out how he was; and she even took the sal volatile.

This greatly relieved me, whatever it may have done for the young man.

Mysteriously enough, he came downstairs next day, looking as pink and white as ever, with a fresh crop of horrible symptoms to relate to the old ladies.

Winter crept ominously down over the Como mountains. We could feel the breath of the approaching snows. Every day it rained below, and deepened the incredible purity of the peaks above; and every day we knew our parting was closer upon us.

Before the end came, we had one perfect day—a day that might have dropped from the heart of summer. We took a little steamer up the lake, puffing our zig-zag way between cohorts of gold and diamond mountains, over a brilliant azure floor. We stopped at Gravedona, where we had been told there was a church full of treasures.

We spent several hours there before the returning steamer hooted us away. I cannot remember what the treasures were, except one jewelled chalice that gleamed a little uncertainly under a heavy coating of dust. The sacristan told us it was never shown to ordinary tourists, an observation I refused to accept, feeling that this privilege was made "peculiar" to us merely to extract a larger offering. However, perhaps he spoke the truth after all, for I do not think there *was* much at Gravedona to tempt the ordinary tourist!

It was a tiny sleepy village, grass-grown, with a few rather pale children peeping cautiously out at us from their open doorways.

We sat under an olive tree a few yards from an over-grown cemetery and ate our lunch with rapture. Nothing else happened; but we were both so happy and the view was so beautiful, that we planned to return often together. I even foresaw an ultimate far-distant date, when I should be the age Elena was then and talk with someone else about her—perhaps a husband—and of this happy day, which we had spent here long ago.

But neither of us ever visited Gravedona again; though I once passed it with my husband on a steamer, which never stopped there.

10

I had expected a good deal from Chiavenna. The name sounded like music in my ears. Was it not an old Italian town beneath great mountains—the key to the most beautiful of passes?

> *What leaf-fringed legend haunts about thy shape*
> *Of deities or mortals, or of both,*
> *In Tempe or the dales of Arcady?*

was the question Elena and I naturally asked ourselves.

Besides, as long as we were in Chiavenna we should be together, one step beyond it and we should be separated.

Unfortunately Chiavenna had no shape, and if it had had beautiful architecture, instead of houses like clumsy stone coffins of the direst nineteenth-century conception, we could hardly have seen it, wrapt as it was in a dark, icy fog.

The hotel was cruelly unpleasant, a dingy cavern, haunted by gloomy mortals who hardly seemed to be Italians at all.

Scowls greeted our entrance; had Elena thought there was a better hotel to be found we should instantly have sought for it; but Baedeker had been inflexibly secretive in his description of Chiavenna, and had only recommended this one hotel as "suitable" for travellers. The Poste came and went from it, up and down the Maloja Pass. If travellers *had* to spend a night in Chiavenna this was where they spent it; but never more than one night was suggested; and we were going to spend two, with a day between. For us— there was no day between. What we spent was a mere extension of time, covered by the same black icy fog; and bad as it was inside the hotel, we decided that it would be worse outside.

Elena comforted herself with the thought of Mrs. Holland, the doctor's wife, and Uncle Kennie's devoted friend. We expected her all day long; she had asked us to hire an Extra Poste for her to share with me, and we were to start up the Pass at eight o'clock next morning. The torturing day dragged itself by, and evening lengthened, but no other traveller arrived. Mrs. Holland was expected, our host reluctantly admitted, her room was ordered. At nine o'clock Elena sent me to bed, and an hour later she crept inconsolably to her own.

Shortly afterwards, we gathered next morning from the landlord, Mrs. Holland and a friend of hers had arrived, slept in the room provided for them, and left by Extra Poste next morning for St. Moritz. There was a message left for us, to say that Mrs. Holland had unexpectedly met a friend with whom she was driving up, and would see me later on in St. Moritz. Elena was so overwhelmed with indignation and distress that it was all I could do to prevent her risking her life by driving up with me. We had to pay for Mrs. Holland's seat in my Extra Poste; but to Elena this was the least of her sense of grievance. She could not bear the thought of my taking this plunge into the unknown by myself. Perhaps she thought that not quite enough care had been taken to find out what awaited me; but had she thought I was going straight to an earthly paradise she belonged to an age when girls would not have gone to such a paradise unaccompanied.

At the last a calm despair engulfed her; and I left her standing in the doorway looking like a grieved Madonna, with her eyes fixed on the Cross.

There were bells on the harness of my Extra Poste; and I liked the look of my horse. We were part—(the tail-end part)—of a long line of sledges, and with great whip crackings and jinglings, we plunged into the icy darkness.

I was in a strange world, on my own, bound for a strange place, to live with unknown people. It was by no means an unpleasant sensation. I was twenty years old, and knew practically nothing; yet all my senses were lively and everything they fastened on responded to them in the most exhilarating manner.

As we climbed, the fog dropped beneath us. With splendid

88

clarity, the great snow peaks shot up into a pale blue sky—unending peaks—whiter than any snow that I had ever seen. The still air stung my cheeks with cold, like the light touch of a whip.

The drivers, wrapped in wool to their chins, were pleasant men, full of jokes and snatches of strange songs. To my surprise as we began to climb they leapt from their sledges, only the far-away leader remained upon his driver's seat. My driver tied the reins to a hook beneath his seat and nodding reassuringly, told me not to touch the reins; and joined the others. The men disappeared behind me—and the sledges in front. The horse and I were left alone together with the icy peaks.

The zig-zag path of snow edged close to precipices, sometimes a sharp corner hid the whole train from us, and all the confidence I had in life went into the habits of this strong unknown animal in front of me. I was frightened at first, but since the horse seemed to take the situation for granted and pushed steadily on, my fear soon changed into enchanted excitement. I liked knowing that no one knew where I was, or could be resorted to if I got into a difficulty. There we were, Life and I, alone together for the first time. Whatever happened I must meet it with my own resources. I did not know what they were but I enjoyed the feeling.

The separation from Elena hung apart from this new enthralment. I knew it was a tragedy for both of us, but I should have time enough to think about it (and think about it I did) all winter long. I doubt if many such relationships as ours exist today. In a world where there were no motors, aeroplanes, telephones, radio or cinemas there was a great deal of time for human relationships to grow into long and deep affections. People took trouble to learn how to entertain each other, and Elena had given me royal entertainment. Brought up in a highly privileged circle among the best thinkers and artists of her day, she united in herself the discipline of her old Quaker family with that of its remote French ancestry; and the very different discipline, with its enlargement into beauty, of the Tractarians' romantic medievalism.

If I had lived without those long months of intense companionship with Elena I think I should have plunged even more helplessly than I actually did plunge into the experiences that stretched before me. As it was Elena had given me a standard of comparison; she had trained my taste, by her integrity of living, so that vulgarity and the shams it is based on could not appeal to me. I was often deceived and perhaps more often still I may have deceived others; but at least my admirations moved in the right direction. I could not like bad art, bad literature or bad music, nor could I like bad company because I had so deeply liked Elena.

I had only a short interval in which to enjoy the glittering loveliness of the Pass before the Poste stopped at Vico Soprano. Here I saw an enraged young Englishman making a fool of himself, with the bewildered but controlled sledge drivers. He shouted into their bland perplexity that they were "bloody Kaffirs!" He did not try to listen to what they patiently reiterated in their own language, that since he had not ordered an Extra Poste beforehand, none had been provided for him. He must therefore either share an already overcrowded general Poste, or not ascend the Pass until tomorrow. It was impossible for him to believe that what he wanted could not be instantly produced, and fearing that he was about to break a blood-vessel or to resort to violence, in which he would certainly have been worsted—for even one driver was twice his size and he was shouting at half-a-dozen—I offered him the place reserved for Mrs. Holland. All his anger and abuse vanished. He became enchanting; he was enchanted; so were the porters. They swiftly packed him and his superlative leather suitcases into the back of my sleigh; and we drove off serenely into the golden light. As I had supposed from his recent language the young man had fought in the Boer War. He had already spent one winter at St. Moritz recovering from a severe chest wound, and was now well on his way towards a complete cure.

All his past adventures were spread before me. He gave me a graphic account of the amusements provided at St. Moritz; and enthusiastically suggested that we should enjoy them together. I listened with interest but without conviction. Something assured me that this ardent young man and I would not share these delectable entertainments.

Mountains, for instance, did he, I eventually demanded, *enjoy* them? Had he climbed any? No, he didn't care about mountains at

90

all—nor would he dream of climbing them, except to kill an animal at the top. He was that kind of young man. There was to be a dance at the Kulm next day, what dances would I keep for him? I told him that I wasn't going to the Kulm and shouldn't be at the dance. The pained surprise on his face enlightened me still further. But I must, he explained, I really must go to the Kulm—there wasn't anywhere else in St. Moritz fit to stay in. I was, I told him, going to a very small Pension run by English ladies, who kept a tea shop. Fortunately we arrived at St. Moritz almost immediately after this sad disclosure. The young man said "Goodbye" with nervous haste, and left me at the Poste Inn—where a sleigh from the Kulm awaited him—as if I were afflicted by some strange, and possibly catching, disease. No one met me and my driver dumped my things out on to the snow. It was between three and four o'clock in the afternoon and the thinnest and coldest of retreating sunshine spread over the little town. In those days there was only one village street in St. Moritz, a square where the Poste Inn was planted; and further up the hillside the Kulm bloomed in solitary glory opposite two Italian campanili—one belonging to the village church, and the other to the cemetery. These twin towers against the golden mountains, were to be my winter's chief companions. Even at my first glimpse of them they etched themselves into my heart.

I got hold of a porter from the Poste and explained where I wanted to go. It was just across the road, and he carried my luggage over for me, though even he looked rather contemptuously at me when I mentioned the name of my Pension. I was deeply thankful that neither my parents nor Elena could see my arrival.

We had all of us imagined a spacious, if simple chalet, surrounded by sunny balconies. The reality was a small, rather squalid little flat, cut off entirely from the sun by the Poste Inn. There was a kind of annexe with a small balcony attached to it, equally shadowed, devoted to the tea-room. Nor were the inhabitants of the gloomy Pension any more interesting than their immediate surroundings.

I got to like all of them in a queer detached way as time went on, but I knew from the first moment that I should never feel at home with any of them.

Two sisters, in their early thirties, ran the Pension and the tea-shop. The elder was an over-bearing, neurotic young woman, with red hair and bad manners. She had a good deal of determination and a fierce ambition, unlinked to common sense. The younger was a faded, passive, obstinate creature, hardworking and resentfully submissive. I think she might have been very pleasant if she had not been ordered about so much. They were quite respectable women, indeed I doubt if they had the gifts which would have tempted them to be otherwise, and any fears I might have held as to my social competence to deal with them, vanished at sight.

They had only two other regular boarders besides myself. One of these was a young photographer, who had been ill, but who, living up in the mountains all the year round and carrying on his profession, had now completely recovered; the other lodger was a woman, and once, I think, she must have been a very beautiful woman. She was now no longer young, and very ill. Her name was Ethel, and she ran a shop below the Pension. My room, to which the elder sister briskly led me, looked north; and was what in America is known as a "hall bedroom". The idea had been that I was to have a south room with a balcony. But it appeared there was no south room, except the double one shared by the sisters. Ethel had a more roomy west one, but it wouldn't do to turn her out of it, and Mr. Brown used what balcony there was above the tea-room staircase for his photography, and must never be disturbed.

I could have overlooked other short-comings, but about the balcony I was firm. There was only one small sitting room for all of us to sit in. Where could I write or cure, unless I had a balcony? I stated firmly that I could not stay unless one was provided.

The sisters were deeply concerned; but after a time they conceded that perhaps Mr. Brown would consent to my writing in a corner of *his* balcony, especially if I didn't talk. Mr. Brown, they explained, was most peculiar. He had said from the first that he didn't want to be a member of their household. He took his principal meal at the Poste, where he spent his evenings; and he worked from morning till night.

I dreaded sharing Mr. Brown's balcony; but in time he became my most valued ally. He consented to my long chair occupying half of his balcony, and came and went in companionable silence from his dark room, into the light, and back again. Neither of us spoke to each other beyond a greeting; but it became a more and more friendly greeting; and if he thought I was too far out of what little sun crept through, he even helped me move my chair. Sometimes he volunteered helpful advice about the climate or my hostesses and how to deal with difficulties, which he thought (rightly) might arise. I often took his advice and never failed to profit by it.

Ethel, the remaining guest, was a gay, vulgar, dying woman of thirty-five, plucky to the last ounce.

She was highly quarrelsome, indeed her wrangles with both the sisters took up much of their spare time and resounded throughout the flat. She had a bad reputation, but bad reputations in St. Moritz were easily acquired. It is true that she had had lovers and boasted of them; but even if her affairs had once been serious I did not believe that they could be so now.

She still had many men friends, and insisted on seeing them alone in her bedroom and never introducing them to the rest of us; but as her bedroom was the only room in which she could see any of her friends without an audience (and a hostile audience at that) I discounted the shocked suspicions of the sisters. I never quarrelled with Ethel myself, in spite of her perpetual railings, she had plenty of humour and I found her both a discerning and a kindly acquaintance. If she said to your face what you couldn't like, I am certain she said no worse behind your back. We did not see much of each other as Ethel had long hours in her shop, which she managed with great success, and the rest of the time she spent in her room, taking what repose was possible to her. She was a passionate snob and nothing so enraged her about me—as what she thought was my reckless disregard for social opportunities. "You at least have a chance," she told me. "You even have an uncle who stays at the Kulm. Why don't you dress up and make a bid for it? It's so damned silly of you to stay on here and play round with these frumps —you can only be young once!"

She died two years after I left St. Moritz, visited by her young men to the last, and trying to sing "Lead Kindly Light" while one of them held her hand.

Nobody I ever met at the Pension cared in the least for the things I cared for. There might have been no outside world at all. In my home we talked politics, religion, literature, the needs of the people round us and our own; interspersed with my father's parish and a little golf. The Pension talked about nothing but the Kulm and its scandals. I could not understand what interest they could possibly take in people whom they never knew, except by name. The tearoom, which they ran very well, was their only key to the life they never shared. It gave them the impression of great intimacy and understanding, and the scraps of conversation they overheard were an unending field for discussion.

I was told a great deal about Dr. Holland before I saw him; and none of it was to his advantage. He was much disliked by every member of the Pension, for different reasons. Uncle Kennie, however, had loved him dearly and it was with both a curious and a quaking heart that I awaited our first interview. Since this occasion I have known some forty or fifty medical men—some professionally —on my friends', as well as on my own account, and some unprofessionally; but I have only known three of them, whom I have not considered good—good in the sense that they genuinely tried to improve their patients' condition and generally *did* improve it. Dr. Holland was one of the three exceptions. But I did not think him bad for any of the reasons given to me by the Pension. I thought he was "too unhappy to be kind"; very pessimistic by nature; and careless—perhaps from some deep inner discouragement. He himself had had lung trouble, and had never completely recovered, nor did he believe in real recovery for his lung patients. Ours was a time before there was much that could be done about T.B., except sooner or later die of it. Still, in Davos there were constant attempts to discover cures; and there was a definite régime, which if carefully followed cured one out of every four slight cases; and often checked serious ones. I do not believe St. Moritz had any certain cures to its credit; all you could say for it (under Dr. Holland's sway, and he was its chief doctor for over thirty years) was that slight cases did not always get worse. It may or may not have been true that Dr. Holland connived with the hotel keepers in keeping St. Moritz as a sport centre rather than in cultivating its health facilities; but he certainly did nothing to cope seriously with the disease which it was his profession to cure.

I fancy that his main preoccupation was snobbery; but he was by no means ungenerous. He gave his services free to the Invalids' Home, which was run mainly on private charity; and I am sure that he did many acts of genuine and self-sacrificing kindness for his poorer patients. I found him gloomy and portentous; and the only really sound advice he ever gave me was to leave the Pension at once. Had I taken it I should have had a different, but not nearly so happy, life.

II

One Sunday morning, a fortnight after I had reached St. Moritz, Mrs. Holland called on me. She made no reference to having left me stranded at Chiavenna but she invited me to tea at the Kulm.

I had disliked her for the pain she had given Elena; and I did not like her any better when I saw her. Still she was Uncle Kennie's friend so that I felt bound to accept her invitation.

The whole Pension was extremely excited at this call. Mrs. Holland had never been inside it before. Nor had they believed I should ever meet her in the flesh.

They insisted I should wear my best clothes for the tea-party and do them as much credit as possible. Who knew what this single entry into paradise might not produce for them all?

It was a curious interview; and not at all like a tea-party. There was a good deal of coming and going in the hotel lounge, people in sports clothes carrying sports equipment. The whole place looked rather like a rabbit warren—low and dark—and far from being the brilliant spectacle I had anticipated.

Mrs. Holland received me in a small private sitting room. She did not get up from the piano stool on which she was sitting, as we shook hands; and she told me rather brusquely that she could only spare me half an hour.

She did provide me with tea but she lost no time in telling me that I must leave where I was staying at once, and come to the Kulm. If I accepted her advice, she would—for my uncle's sake—give me what chaperonage I needed, and introduce me to his friends. I told her that I was already an expense to my parents and could not ask them to allow me more; but she brushed this economic feather aside. Since I was her husband's patient, she explained, the Kulm manager could give me a remarkably cheap room on the ground floor—only thirteen francs a day—of course there would be extras. What was I paying now? Nine? Then my parents could easily manage so inconsiderable a difference. What surprised me was that since, from her manner, Mrs. Holland obviously didn't like me, she should suggest a transaction which implied seeing more of me. Hitherto I had supposed that you made no efforts to see people unless you liked them. Perhaps Uncle Kennie had put her under some deep obligation for which she felt bound to make some return? But somehow I did not think this likely. He had told me that she was a most charming woman and one of his greatest friends. In what did her charm consist? He couldn't, I thought, have really liked her, unless she had behaved very differently to him than she had behaved to me! Had people then two standards of behaviour? Kennie was a well-off bachelor and I was a poor young girl—could that be the explanation?

I thanked her for the tea; but I never seriously considered accepting her offer. I was quite sure that my parents couldn't afford the difference and I had no intention of asking them to make such an effort. I left within twenty minutes and never saw Mrs. Holland again.

I did not like the tea-room Pension and I was not happy with its inmates; nevertheless I felt convinced that I should like the Kulm and its company still less. At least where I was I had half a balcony on which to cure and write in peace, with no distractions.

The first serious incident of the winter happened soon after this, and made a great impression on me.

Our tea-room circle of acquaintance made up for its narrowness by the intensity of its observation. Nothing happened at the Invalids' Home that we did not share within twenty-four hours; and I expect that their knowledge of our Pension was equally searching.

This miniature Sanatorium with half-a-dozen guests, was run by an extremely disagreeable, high-handed matron. She took it upon herself to act like a pocket Hitler. What she thought the patients ought to do—they *must* do—or take the consequences of her offensive temper. If she liked them it was almost worse than if she disliked them, for she gave them no peace, and broke up what little privacy was possible for them. She was hand in glove with Dr. Holland, who thought the world of her; and through his support her word became law. Among the patients there was a very ill and rather pretty girl, and a man (I thought him middle-aged at the time, but I subsequently found out that he was twenty-nine), to whom the Matron had taken a violent fancy. Mr. White was a nice fellow, he had better manners, and was better bred than anyone else in the Home. His life, as well as this poor girl's, had been suddenly broken up—their illnesses had taken them unawares. They couldn't afford to live without working; and they couldn't afford to die unless they could die quickly. It was very unlikely indeed that either of them would get better soon enough to meet their economic necessities; and it was far from likely that they would die in time to be able to pay for their illnesses. Under these circumstances they sympathized very much with each other. They shared the same public balcony and exchanged histories. On one fatal occasion—when they found themselves alone together—the girl cried and Mr. White kissed her.

The Matron burst out of a French window on to the balcony and made a painful scene. Not satisfied with this vulgar exercise of her authority, she retailed the whole affair to Dr. Holland; and between them they decided to get rid of the girl.

Had Dr. Holland acted with tact and kindness (and he might well have done both if left to himself) no one would have blamed him for what followed. The girl had a weak heart, and this was a legitimate reason for sending her to a lower altitude. But she was sent down in a cloud of moral obloquy, roundly scolded by Dr. Holland, and cruelly insulted by the Matron. One of us went up to pack for her; and she begged very piteously that we would be kind to Mr. White, who had to remain behind to attempt his cure. How far the feeling between them had gone I never knew. They had only known each other for a week or two—but the girl died a few months later and I am quite sure that the ordeal she had gone through at St. Moritz hastened, if it did not cause, her death.

I was so horrified by what had happened that after a sleepless night I wrote to Mr. White vigorously expressing sympathy with them both, and offering him my company on our daily walks, if he cared to join me.

Had I been even a few years older I should not have acted with such precipitancy. I barely knew him by sight; and had no reason to suppose that the society of a strange girl would be of any particular comfort to him.

However, Mr. White was, I think now, a particularly kind and good-hearted young Englishman. He took my letter in the spirit in which it was written and cordially accepted my invitation. We took our daily walks together, in the serene and silent company of snow mountains, with the utmost regularity, for some long time. His only interests were cricket and his bank—both of which he had had to give up. In spite of my passionate sympathy with him, I found these daily conversations very heavy going. I always liked him. He was friendly, good-tempered and completely reliable; and I sometimes succeeded in making him laugh. I did not like to give up what I had begun with such passionate conviction; but it was a relief to me—and perhaps a greater relief to him—when our daily fellowship subsided.

I had already found that the incident with Miss R. was not the appalling catastrophe I had imagined it; nor was Mr. White permanently inconsolable.

On looking back over this uneven fellowship, the only thing I can now seriously regret is that I sometimes walked him off his feet, beyond the beaten track and into snow-drifts. "If only", he once said to me with a kindly smile, "you could remember that the way back is quite as long and twice as difficult as the way out."

12

The first part of the winter Hilda, our landlady-in-chief, was—or expressed herself as being—greatly attached to me. She told me all her troubles and explained all her feuds.

The tea-room plus the Pension was really too much for the sisters, both physically and financially, but Hilda had at last succeeded in getting a girl out from England who would undertake part-time work in return for half her Pension expenses. She was delicate but not actively tubercular, nineteen years old, and a doctor's daughter. Her name was Hope de Lisle Brock.

I was ill in bed when the new girl arrived; and Hilda gave me a very unpleasant account of her. She was sure I wouldn't like her. She was much more delicate than they had expected, made-up (a degrading practice at this period), common; and ineffectual.

One day when I was convalescing there was a knock at my door and Lislie, as her family called her, came into the room. The dullness of the long, speechless day suddenly lifted. It was as if spring had come into the room with her.

> She was a phantom of delight
> When first she gleamed upon my sight;
> A lovely apparition sent
> To be a moment's ornament.

Had she had health Lislie would have been a beauty. She had an inner liveliness and an extraordinary aptitude for joy that wrote themselves upon her countenance; and she had no vanity in her. Perhaps it was this lack which made her attractive to women as well as to men. It was as difficult not to like Lislie as not to like a flower or a bird.

She had just come in from a walk, and the icy air had whipped a lovely rose colour—which had nothing to do with cosmetics—into her cheeks. Lislie had large hazel eyes with very clear whites to them, under naturally arched eye-brows. These smooth brown arches gave her face a questioning look rather like a pansy's. She wore a short musquash coat, and fur cap, a shade lighter than her hair. She carried a copy of the *Spectator* under her arm, and held a bunch of scarlet and purple anemones in her hand which she had bought to give me. The tales I had heard of her receded. I had no voice to speak with and she left me very soon; but her gifts remained behind her.

Neither of us had the least idea that this short visit was to be the foundation of a friendship that would last till her death twenty years later; nor that the whole structure of our lives would be altered because we had met each other. This deep, harmonious, unimpassioned friendship was unlike any other I have known. It was more thorough and less possessive. What we each found in the other was confidence and understanding. We were both normal girls, not unattractive to men, and attracted by them. We wanted marriage and children; and we both of us knew that we stood only a bare chance of life at all. Fortunately we were attracted by different types of men. Lislie liked an aggressive, challenging type, men who were bold in their approach and difficult to handle. I liked quiet men, a little shy, who gave me the impression of force behind their shyness. I also preferred the kind that can amuse themselves and are not easily bored. Lislie did not mind in the least how difficult men were to amuse; and she did not care whether they bored themselves or not. Perhaps she was surer of their appreciation than I ever felt myself to be; and I think she trusted them more. Sex had never been the bugbear to her that it had been made to me. She enjoyed it and knew how to use it. Although men sometimes made advances to her which horrified her, this never shook her confidence in other men. Men never made advances that *could* horrify me—and yet I had no confidence that they wouldn't. I became engaged very soon after I met Lislie; but she, in spite of a long succession of what the French call *amitiés amoureuses*, did not fall in love till she was twenty-seven. She was easy to please a little; but very slow to be deeply and permanently pleased.

Whenever I think of Lislie I remember Donne's words:

> *She was so true*
> *She made dreams true*
> *And fables histories.*

I was never worthy of her friendship; and—in a sense—it harmed me; for she made me believe myself better and more honest than I actually was; but while Lislie lived, I gave her the response she expected. I even thought that the qualities which she believed that I possessed were natural to me; but after her death these virtues—which were but a pale reflection of her own—disintegrated; and I had at forty to re-make myself, and to learn with astonishment as well as pain how very far I was from being the person Lislie had for so long idealized—and supported.

Elena, though she approved of Lislie and personally liked her, warned me of this possibility. "Friendships such as yours and Lislie's", she told me, "are apt to be deceptive and even dangerous. You do not only think well of each other; but there is always the fear that you may think—because of the other's admiration—too well of yourselves."

Perhaps the hurried, multitudinous friendships of to-day with their group activities are wiser for human beings. But they cannot give such deep joy; and perhaps they do not even lead to such enduring and happy marriages.

I like to think our long and carefully built-up co-operation was not entirely wasted. We learned how to spare, as well as how to entertain. We were not selfish friends, we took it in turns as our needs arose to serve and nurse each other.

Lislie's wisdom (for she was an un-possessive, unpossessed spirit) brought me freedom; and curbed my swift compulsions. Lislie was never a partisan. Even where she loved most she was sternly critical. "Don't you think," she once said to me, "that it is a good plan after you've thought all the things you have to think against a person who has wronged you, to think of all the things you can say *for* them? It's no use *just* being wronged."

While she lived it would have been unbearable to me to be less fair or less reliable than she was determined to believe that I was.

I think I knew that I was not so brave as she believed—though I tried hard to be—and I knew I was never as gentle. What I missed—without knowing that I missed it—and what she possessed—was single-mindedness.

Our wits sharpened each other's. Lislie had a more critical but perhaps a less creative mind than mine. She saw what she was doing and how she was doing it, whereas I only felt things born in me, that I must bring out—at almost any cost.

I remember one criticism she gave me that I still think of importance to any artist. I was complaining that after perpetual efforts I could not get an incident in a novel the way I wanted it to be, and she said, "Isn't it perhaps because it oughtn't to be there?"

I almost always accepted Lislie's corrections; and I never resented them. Partly no doubt I found it easy to accept her criticisms because she admired my work and I knew that she only wanted to improve it, never to score off me. But also because her criticisms had an uncanny repercussion in my own mind.

Lislie always criticized what I had inwardly distrusted, but had hoped to get off from re-doing. I *knew* she was right; and after she exposed my blunder, I could not then afford to let my impatience or my dire facility, destroy my artist's integrity.

During my first winter at St. Moritz our friendship very slowly solidified.

Hilda was frantically jealous. Both sisters, and even Ethel, tried their hardest to put us against each other. The things I was told about Lislie and the things Lislie was told about me (when later on we compared notes) we found to be carefully chosen lies, hard to disbelieve.

As propaganda experts for dictator states both sisters would have done admirably. Yet we felt curiously uninfluenced by the fancy-dress monsters pushed forward to represent the relatively harmless young women beneath them.

Very slowly and gradually Lislie and I began to enjoy the taste of each other's minds. After all, we had no other minds to enjoy; and whatever shades of moral infamy we saw each other under, we could not help noticing that we always laughed at the same jokes.

I occasionally wondered how Lislie could have had time to practise all the bad qualities and habits so lavishly ascribed to her; and she may have had the same suspicion about the lengthy list of my flagrant crimes.

Mr. Brown helped to clear my mind of much of my distrust. We often now exchanged short observations, in the natural pauses of our work; and on one of these occasions I said to him, "I can't help thinking Lislie is much nicer than Hilda and Annie think she is!"

Mr. Brown was silent for a long moment, then he said slowly but with cautious conviction, "I wouldn't stay on here a single day if I could get a dark room as cheaply somewhere else! I wish you two girls would leave here. I should miss you, but I've often wanted to say this before. Get out of this Pension! It's bad for your health! As for Miss Brock she's young and pretty—that's all that's wrong with her in my opinion!" This made a very great impression on me, for I thought Mr. Brown a very observant man.

It had been planned that Lislie was to serve with Hilda in the tea-room itself; but Hilda soon put a stop to this lovely and lively child sharing her limelight; and so Lislie was placed instead in a black hole where the trays were prepared and handed out. Here she had to work from two to six daily, close to the heat of the kitchen fire. My attention however was for the time being diverted from Lislie's health by a sharper emergency.

Annie had agreed to accompany an invalid to some distant spot, settle her down and have a week's rest before her journey home.

Almost immediately after her departure I found Hilda, who had been out watching a bobsleigh race in intense cold, groaning on her bed. She was half unconscious and evidently in great pain. I took her temperature and found it 106°. Mr. Brown went, though unwillingly, for the doctor. Dr. Bernhardt, who looked after the whole Pension except myself, was both alarmed and alarming about Hilda's condition. He thought she was in for an attack of rheumatic fever, and he prescribed a medicine which must be given her every hour, without fail, night and day. There were no nurses to be got on account of an influenza epidemic, so that I nursed Hilda by night, and ran the tea-room in her place by day. I had never run a tea-room before, and having a trained memory I rather enjoyed the experience—on one day I had ninety orders to attend to single-handed. My only real difficulty was counting the change quickly enough. Lislie was engrossed preparing trays as fast as I ordered them; and we knew no one else who could help us. However an angel among the tea guests, whose name I never knew but I think from the set of his shoulders that he must have been a soldier, offered to take over this part of the business for me.

There was no difficulty in keeping awake at night for Hilda was most of the time delirious and it took all my strength to keep her in bed.

I thought, and I think Dr. Bernhardt thought, that Hilda was critically ill. We had sent for Annie but she could not arrive till the end of the week and by that time Hilda was out of danger.

Then I made a great mistake. I asked Dr. Bernhardt if I should not sit up one more night with Hilda, after her sister's arrival. Annie would probably be exhausted after a journey which had taken two nights and a day; and it was still necessary to give Hilda her medicine hourly. Dr. Bernhardt agreed whole-heartedly. It was most desirable, he said, that I should continue to nurse her: it would be a great mistake to change over too soon. Hilda might have a relapse and still needed careful watching. In another twenty-four hours he would see the sister and give her his orders, meanwhile I was to carry on as usual.

Annie arrived, terrified, aggrieved and very soon furious. I expect I was insufferable. She certainly thought that I was. She wanted to take over the nursing at once; and I refused to let her. We had a burning, blazing row. It was very quiet, for we were both quiet people; and we did not wish to disturb Hilda, but it was none the less deadly; and as I got the better of it, Annie never forgave me.

It seemed to me at the time that I was perfectly right; but I was soon to find, as I learned from Adler later on, that it is extremely dangerous to be too much in the right.

After making my patient's bed next morning I had a slight haemorrhage. Dr. Holland came to see me; and gave me the scolding of a life-time. Never had I been so berated. He told me, when he saw that he had sufficiently taken the stuffing out of me, that I had not only risked my life, but that I had risked it for nothing. Hilda was a violent hysteric. She had once been his patient, and had set up just such spells with high temperatures before. He had given up attending her because he had no time for such dangerous nonsense. "Now", he said, "you must get out of this place at once, and promise me never to nurse again, or take up—for whatever reason—other people's jobs while you are up here. If you won't I shall cable your parents immediately to come and take you home!"

As I was not allowed to speak I was unable at the moment to do more than agree to what he said. However when he came again, I begged him to let me stay on. Hilda's finances for the winter were largely based on my regular and relatively high payments. She wouldn't, in the middle of the season, easily find another guest to take my place. Dr. Holland partially relented. "I don't approve of your staying on," he told me, "but if she changes your room to the best she has—which gets *some* light and air—and if you promise to do exactly what I've told you, I'll let you stay; but I am going to talk to her first, and unless I'm satisfied in a week's time that you are getting the right attention, you'll have to leave—whatever her finances are. They're not my business, and I *am* your doctor." After this illness I felt more confidence in Dr. Holland than I had previously. I realized I had been unfair to my parents and foolish on my own account. I thought he had been unnecessarily brutal and autocratic but he had acted with most effective kindness. Hilda, having as I thought miraculously recovered, had failed to be in the least grateful. I had nursed her too long, I had done too much all round; the tea-room above all—her special sphere—had been far too much of a success in my inexperienced hands. She did not exactly say so, but I gathered she thought her sister Annie had a distinct case. However after Dr. Holland's talk with them, the attitude of both sisters wholly altered. They could not do enough for me. Annie, although she still hated me, apologized; and Hilda flung herself and her imaginary affections upon my mercy. I hesitated—I thought of Lislie—and I made terms. If I stayed on and they gave me Ethel's room, could Lislie be brought downstairs from her icy garret and given my room, which at any rate could be heated? Yes—that could be done. Most fortunately Ethel was going home for Christmas and not intending to return to the Pension. Her room should be fumigated and put at my disposal. Lislie should leave her icy attic and come downstairs.

I agreed to stay; but I was still unhappy. These outward triumphs did nothing to assuage my inward sense of failure.

Mr. White too upset me. While I had been kept in bed, Annie had told him her version of my brief dictatorship. I had expected, when we resumed our walks, praise and moral support, as well as advice. I only got the advice. Mr. White did not praise me. He had been greatly concerned about my health and he thought I might just as well have let Annie take over her sister's case immediately. It had upset her, he said, to be so useless, even if it was only for twenty-four hours, when she had given up her holiday and rushed back on purpose to look after her sister. I was horrified and aggrieved at this point of view; but I was not altogether able to confute it. I even slowly took it in. Mr. White was my friend, he would not say such things only to pain me.

I can see now, though I fear it did not occur to me at the time, that Mr. White did not only know about banking and cricket, he knew considerably more about life itself than I did. His friendship for Annie began at this time, and gradually mine was deflected by Uncle Kennie's arrival and by Lislie's increasing companionship. I was surprised that Mr. White should prefer Annie's companionship to mine; but I was not *greatly* aggrieved. We never stopped being friends, we simply drifted apart. Annie was devoted to Mr. White; and I think it did him good to be admired more than I had admired him. I did not realize then—or for many years afterwards—that most forms of unassimilated pity have arrogance at their core. The only sympathy that is of use to another human being is that founded upon respect. I had not given myself time to respect Mr. White before I flung myself into our untried companionship. I certainly did not respect the Pension sisters even while I was risking my life for them.

13

On New Year's Eve all St. Moritz was in the streets, every hotel —even our own little Pension—was empty; and every out-lying farm-house or distant mountain village joined the St. Moritz visitors, to listen to our bells ring in the New Year.

I was alone, strictly prohibited from speech or movement, but from an attic window, where I crouched in the dark, I could look into the heart of the festival. Red flares lit the campanile from within, and through its loggia arches the great bells swung out, above the newly fallen snow. I could see each individual bellringer on the high platform of the bell-room, clinging to his bell rope; and shooting backwards and forwards against the pull of the bell. The dark bee-like figures were as fixed in their rhythm as the notes of music in a fugue; their bodies were caught up into the bells, while the force of hidden music shot back into their bodies. Only the tower, and its leaping shadows, were visible; but I knew that the mountains were there—immovable presences—behind the black, heaving figures and the blood-red tower. All this human flurry and sound were held within the silent ramparts of their frozen cup.

As I sat entranced—watching the flying bells—I was suddenly aware, with all the intensity of youth, that this New Year rung in so gallantly, might be my last. I opened the window and leaned out into the icy, biting air. It shook and hummed with the music of the bells.

I do not think I was afraid of death. I simply felt like a child at a party, whose nurse comes to take him away too soon.

I did not feel the cold and I don't know how long I watched those swaying, tireless figures, and listened to the tremendous sounds reverberating against the hidden mountains down into the silent valleys; but when I closed the window the bitterness had slipped away from me and everything in my mind had changed. The energy of that unfettered music had got into my blood.

I think it was the 'turn' of my illness because I never again felt so entrapped by it. Nor did I fear—in the same way—the thought of travelling from light and laughter, away from the little group of beings whom I loved and knew—into the listening dark.

The rest of the winter was an easier and happier time. Uncle Kennie came out. He used to climb up to my balcony for a cigarette before lunch, or invite me to watch a curling match on the rink in the afternoon and take tea with him afterwards at the Kulm. He was a very good and precise curler—curling and bridge were his chief St. Moritz avocations; and though I did not share them, I thoroughly enjoyed his presence; and I felt very grown up to receive so old a man's visits on my balcony and to be able to introduce him to Mr. Brown, who took these additional interruptions with great magnanimity. A new friend, Julia Farrer, appeared at the Kulm, a friend, though not an intimate friend, of Elena's. At forty-two Julia seemed to be far too old to be so beautiful. She had lovely chestnut hair and large cool blue eyes, with clear-cut features; and a great deal of fierce and self-repressed character. Julia had been a nurse in many wars; and was to add three more to them. She was a heroic figure, and had even included in her youth the fiery experience of acting as secretary to Florence Nightingale.

It must have been difficult for her to avoid lovers; and the extreme austerity of her manner may have been due to the effort of warding them off.

She had once had a tragic heart-break; and had kept it as women did in those days, as a permanent obstruction to matrimony. Uncle Kennie, though he quite approved of her as a friend for me, was rather afraid of her; and begged me to manage to see her when he wasn't there.

Julia took greatly to both Lislie and me; she told me, long afterwards, that she had never known such gay and daring young creatures. We sparkled, with what seemed to be health and was certainly amusement.

Neither of us was allowed to take an active part in any of the winter sports, though I remember once on a moonlight night we succeeded in flying on a toboggan down a long snow run. Snow runs were not as fast or dangerous as ice runs, and as we did not fall off, no distinguishable harm followed. However, we looked on this sally as an immoral incident and did not repeat our adventure. Instead we enjoyed what we could vicariously of the St. Moritz sports, watching with particular ardour the Cresta Run, and hockey on the ice.

In those early days, the Swiss themselves led and joined in their visitors' sports. There were no professional or semi-professional experts to put their noses out of joint and so the people who lived, in conditions that involved skill in snow sports, and those who acquired their skill for fun, shared their excitements together.

Our two chief Cresta champions were a Swiss and an Englishman. The Swiss was the steadier and won more all round sporting events; but no one in my day rode the Cresta without breaking, except Captain Bott.

It was breathless ecstasy to watch him take Church Leap, and its two high corners, without a check—slide back into the straight with fearful momentum—shoot with increasing speed past the two smaller but deadly corners above the railway bridge, then disappear into the darkness of the bridge; to emerge—still travelling like a rocket—to spurt up the final hill and leap—toboggan and all —six feet into the air at the triumphant finish. In my day only three women rode the whole length of the Cresta. Mrs. Bott and her sister-in-law were the best of the three—young, intrepid and commonsense riders. A third woman nearly twice their age rode the Cresta with unflagging courage and appeared to be made of some tough variety of wood—but in spite of her terrific heart this elderly lady generally took Horse-shoe Corner much too fast and vanished in a cloud of snow at the top—only to reappear, eager as ever, for her second run.

Our ice-hockey heroes (equally admired by all the women in St. Moritz) were a lithe young Welshman—Gwynn-Evans—a first-class dancer and tennis star as well as a champion skater; and Captain Strutt—a Boer War hero—whose speed and language increased in intensity as the game advanced. When they played the Dutch, or in other international matches, these two heroes blended their individual skills together; but more usually they played as frank rivals. Gwynn-Evans was more at home on his skates than Captain Strutt but he appeared much less terrific in his approaches and had less driving force; although he must have had ankles made of steel, to fit into last moment passes, the resistless speed of his slide.

Captain Strutt was a far more formidable figure. He lifted up his skates and tore across the ice, breaking through his opponents like a battering ram—no one could withstand the ferocity of his rushes or the passionate, "Damn *everything*—pass that ball!" of his dramatic pleas to his own team. I never met either of these sports heroes in person; but we were all, from bell boys to Kulm beauties, deeply involved in their triumphs. If I were an artist I could still draw photographic likenesses of them, though I have not set eyes on them for forty years.

One snowy Sunday afternoon, a *Föhn* wind rose suddenly from the mountains, loosening up the newly fallen snow.

I forget how the news reached us, but we seemed to know with supernatural certainty that a party of St. Moritz skiers had been buried in an avalanche.

All St. Moritz turned out to look for them. The street filled with men on skis, with spades across their shoulders. We huddled together at our sitting room window watching and praying for their safe return. Digging for people in avalanche weather on a steep slope is rescue work of a most dangerous nature.

Hour after hour passed by—none of us moved from our window —no one could settle to anything. Excited messengers came to and fro with wild rumours. There was a chance! There was none! They were found! They were all dead! They were all alive! Finally as the last light failed the diggers came back. The buried skiers had been found. One out of the four was still alive.

Sport and its vicissitudes had a strange way of binding us all together. Language—race—class—money—all these insignificant differences were peeled away by mutual interest, leaving our essential selves solidly united against emergency. Everybody's house was open for a bobsleigh accident, everybody's coat to spare for a frozen child.

There were too few of us to become anonymous or robbed of personal responsibility by outside authority. The only authority generally recognized at St. Moritz was that of skill.

Lislie had far less opportunity to watch the sporting events than I had; but she shared Uncle Kennie with me; and he delighted in her company. She released his shyness and he never felt afraid—as he often did with older women—that she would want to marry him.

Lislie had other admirers, indeed most of the men she met became her admirers; but unfortunately she had little or no time for them. When she had finished her four hours' purgatory in the afternoon she was often too tired for further adventures. The unsuitable conditions under which she lived, and the standing for hours close to the kitchen stove, finally produced inevitable disaster.

Lislie became desperately ill. Her mother was sent for. Dr. Bernhardt dislocated the house—turned the sisters out of their double south room, for mother and daughter, and dashed in and out of the house once or twice daily, in his efforts to save Lislie. Lislie began to recover soon after her mother arrived. She had tremendous natural resiliency; and never spent any part of an illness that she could possibly avoid in being ill. Still, lung abscesses when they flare up take some little time to subside; and Dr. Bernhardt never let her out of her room until she left St. Moritz. The sisters resented Mrs. Brock's arrival and prepared to be as rude and obstructive as they could manage; but Mrs. Brock was more than equal to their combined efforts. She had good manners; and an extraordinarily gentle voice, yet the effect of her, when roused, was formidable. She was unchallengeably serene; and if she had a point to make, she knew exactly how to make it; and how to stick to it when made.

The sisters *did* contrive to be rude and mildly obstructive; but that was all they could manage.

Dr. Bernhardt and Carità (as she liked me to call her) presented a common front and had unbeatable weapons. The sisters did not want a death at the tea-rooms—above all not one that was demonstrably brought about by impossible working conditions. They gave in, when they had to—and they had to give in increasingly often.

Carità was full of character and charm. She enjoyed whatever came along and insisted on taking an active part in it. Lislie sent for me, before her mother's arrival, and begged me to show her St. Moritz and entertain her generally. She was far too ill for me to refuse any request she made, but though I undertook to do it, I felt reluctant for such a continuous companionship. I wrote and cured strictly all the morning; and this only left me an afternoon, curtailed by rest hours, to share with my other friends.

However I found Carità a most agreeable and easy-going companion; intensely interested in whatever was going on. The only hardship her society entailed was due to the fact that she was a great deal stronger than I was.

I soon discovered that Lislie's idea of being nursed by her mother was for her mother to be amused and entertained whenever there was any procurable entertainment. Nor did Carità dispute this arrangement. She adored her child, and it was this love that I think Lislie most needed; the little nursing she now required did nothing to detract from her mother's amusements.

Carità had many delightful qualities; besides her natural, lively charm, she had imperturbability and good humour. She was one of the most physically courageous human beings I ever met; but she had no imagination whatever. Anything could happen to her, or in her presence to others, without altering her cheerful calm. Unlike Queen Victoria, Carità was always amused even when things were not at all amusing. She was mercilessly optimistic. I don't think she was intellectual; she had, I imagine, a slight antipathy towards continuous thought. She liked to leap from subject to subject with curiosity but without conviction. Carità could not be easily convinced—even by facts.

Her attitude to Lislie was always difficult to understand. She had a son as well as a daughter and I think that she loved them both equally. Her son was in the Indian Army and she rarely saw him, while Lislie was her constant companion; but though she had always been prepared to make any personal sacrifice for her son, she seemed equally prepared to accept any sacrifice from her daughter. Perhaps she did not know that what Lislie so gaily and constantly offered to her *were* sacrifices, nor did she ever seem to grasp the precarious state of Lislie's health.

She was one of those mothers who "live the life of their daughters, as a hobby."

Carità expected as a matter of course that she should share whatever was meant for Lislie—her invitations—her friendships—as well as all her interests. Nor was she often disappointed, for Lislie expected it as well.

They were inseparable and good companions, pleasanter and more harmonious in their mother and daughter relationship than any others that I have ever known. Nevertheless Lislie had gifts, both of the heart and of the intellect, which were unshared and unsharable by her mother; and these had often to be thrust into the background so that her mother's tastes could be gratified.

I don't think it ever occurred to Carità that she was selfish; or that Lislie—apart from her—could enjoy a fuller and more satisfying life than she could enjoy with her.

Carità had been a great beauty and she had married young, a man who was whole-heartedly enslaved by her. Charles de Lisle Brock was a member of an old Guernsey family, who had been very well off; but by the time his parents died and their money had to be divided among a large number of children, Dr. Brock had barely enough to buy himself a small practice just outside of London. Mitcham was a pretty suburban place with hay fields stretching beyond his garden, and he had the kind of people to whom he was accustomed as patients. Their early life started in extreme happiness but alas, their home became—Tooting. Fidelè, my name for Dr. Brock, was quite unfitted to fight his way into the new claims of a working-class neighbourhood. He could not cope with patients who would not pay their debts; nor with his wife's unsatisfied social expectations. He had not earned sufficient money for a fresh start in a more suitable district; and Carità never became reconciled to anything but a social life.

I doubt if Fidelè liked his profession. He never willingly spoke of it; and very early in life he became deaf, which was an increasing professional handicap.

He loved reading and re-reading Charles Dickens; and talking politics. He always took the side of underdogs; and had a deep sympathy with all human suffering—including his own. Fidelè had had many devoted friends in his youth, but he was one of those men who lose their friends as they grow older; unless the friends refuse to be lost.

Lislie was a curious and advantageous mixture of her parents; she had her mother's equable temper and great courage; united to her father's imagination and deep sympathies. Both parents had humour—but of a different kind; Lislie had a share of each kind.

I saw very little of Lislie herself for the rest of the winter; but my promise to entertain her mother I indefatigably performed, although it involved seeing little or nothing of my other friends. In the spring we parted—Lislie as soon as she could be moved went with her mother to Thusis; and I was carefully shepherded—as all Dr. Holland's patients were shepherded—down the mountain to stay at the chief hotel in Ragatz.

14

Ragatz was an Englishman's Paradise. It suited all constitutions, the stronger patients could reach climbable mountains; and there was every form of sport, including—rare in those days—a golf course. Besides all these climatic and sports facilities, there was one great practical advantage, if you were one of Dr. Holland's poorer patients he would say a magic word to the hotel manager and you could get a room—not a very good room—in this first-class hotel —at a reduced price. The whole of Dr. Holland's flock went there for six weeks each spring, except a stray goat—like Uncle Kennie— who basely betrayed the trust of his faithful shepherd, and plunged into the wilderness of Italy.

There was nothing Uncle Kennie and I would have enjoyed more than to make this plunge together. He would have been an ideal guide, and I the most eager of pilgrims. But, as Uncle Kennie ruefully pointed out, I was not his real niece; and even if I were, the word "niece" was too often used (especially in Italy) as a courtesy title by young women who were anything *but* nieces. Grandmamma would be horrified. Such a scheme, too, would be financially impossible. I couldn't spend more than I had, and Kennie, though his father was both rich and devoted to his delicate son, would never allow him sufficient money for any freedom of choice. He would pay all his bills at expensive hotels, but he certainly wouldn't have paid both our expenses at a cheap hotel. Grandpapa Fowler always treated Kennie (who was over forty, and being both timid and deeply religious—untemptable) as if he were on the verge of becoming the prodigal son. So we reluctantly parted. Kennie went to Florence by himself, and I begged to be allowed to go to

Thusis—so that I might stay with Lislie and her mother. Dr. Holland was deeply shocked. Thusis was out of the question, it was far too damp. There was nothing for it but Ragatz; but it mattered less (except for my clothes which I knew wouldn't be suitable) since my mother had promised to join me in a month's time. Wherever my mother came would be Paradise.

I possessed a fortunate quality when I was young. I was unaware that I was unhappy in an unpleasant situation, so long as the situation lasted. It was not until the situation changed, and I was released into joy, that I became aware that I had been unhappy because of it. The whole winter at the tea-room Pension had been a long up-hill climb under adverse conditions; and it wound up with a third attack of influenza. From a lung point of view it was a much less serious attack than the two previous ones; but it was accompanied by an appalling sense of depression. Into this unusual state of mind dropped a letter from my mother to say that she could not keep her promise after all. My father would come out to me instead. Her health would not permit her to take the journey. Simultaneously I heard from my father and Mary that my mother was quite as well as usual and that the doctor thought a Swiss holiday would be just the thing for her.

I felt as if the earth had lost its orbit, and was plunging haphazard into empty space.

Perhaps from this moment the spiritual umbilical chord between my mother and myself was cut. I loved her as much as ever but like some deftly pushed-off bird there was no longer a nest beneath me; and I must now flap myself into security through the uncertain laws of the air.

Many girls learn this useful lesson much earlier than twenty; but the tie between my mother and myself had been inordinately strong; nor did I realise then that what my mother had written was quite true, she *could* not, rather than *would* not, join me.

She was defeated by that "invulnerable nothing" which lies at the core of all neurotic illnesses.

I turned my face to the wall and wept. I wept for hours; and what I wept away was my childish sense of security. No one but a mother can love us better than we love ourselves. Sooner or later we must accept the fact that the soul has to become its own master—or somebody else's slave. I should not have made a good slave; and I certainly had not yet learned how to be my own master; but I think that this sharp lesson first put me on the road to becoming a separate human being.

There was no difficulty in getting to Ragatz, the difficulty would have been to avoid it. The Hof was a large hotel and I thought it magnificent. It did not rain all the time, though it rained a great deal of it; and there were hours when the fog lifted.

I had a small room on the ground floor with one long French window, in which I sat, wet or fine, with a feeling of incredible freedom and well-being, scribbling away half a day at a time.

I was writing short stories. I don't think any of them were good —but they began to crystallise themselves into the shape of crucial instances, with some attempt at depicting character.

I had only one remaining anxiety. What was I to do with my father when he arrived? I loved him dearly; but he was not the kind of parent, as my mother undoubtedly was—with whom love was any kind of occupation. What he would want was golf; and Dr. Holland, the only person in the hotel whom I yet knew, was far too great a potentate to grant indiscriminate semi-social favours, pressed upon him by one of his poorer patients.

I only saw him at stated intervals—when he appeared bored, often cross, and always busy. I dared not say to him, "Please find me someone who can play golf with my father!" Nor did I dare say to my father, when he arrived, "I have not found anyone with whom you can play golf."

The Kulm taboos came with the Kulm guests. They walked through outsiders as if they were not only nonentities but invisible nonentities.

Thirty years later when I saw Robert Sherwood's play *The Idiot's Delight* I instantly recognised the helpless feeling of the anti-Nazis at the outbreak of war, for I had experienced precisely the same feeling at Ragatz in 1903. The Kulm world was composed of natural Nazis.

They all had separate tables; the best rooms were theirs; they were waited on by the best waiters; the smoking room and all sports facilities were certainly controlled by them.

The rest of us—consisting of Dr. Holland's poorer patients, besides people who came from places other than St. Moritz—sat together at a long table; and enjoyed whatever the Kulm guests didn't want.

Some of these outcasts were extremely entertaining; and I fancy we really had the best of the bargain—for we were a heterogeneous crowd and could do within reason what we liked. I found myself placed by the side of a Greek God—you could not have called the poor creature anything else. Shakespeare must have had him in mind when he described man as "The beauty of the world, the paragon of animals".

Dr. Andrews was six foot two, tough, slender and well proportioned. He had the features of a thinned-down Antinous, large clear grey eyes; and chestnut curls which he endeavoured to flatten. He was a distinguished member of the Alpine Club, and opposite me, on his other side, sat his plain, spectacled little wife of whom he took no notice whatever.

Dr. Andrews didn't believe in God, worshipped mountains, and liked arguments. He was by profession a research scientist, and I never saw him except at dinner, when we talked steadily for an hour every evening.

I had never met anyone before who quite pleasantly and contentedly didn't believe in God. I had read a great deal of theology and Newman was my guiding light, so it had seemed to me that my position was secure. Now I found I had no position at all. Newman's dialectical acrobatics were simply not arguments, since there was no scientific proof and no philosophical reason for the existence of a Deity at all, and indeed, from Dr. Andrews' point of view, no ground for any supernatural belief, except a desire for support, or a self-centred wish for more notice than was good for you. Dr. Andrews turned the whole universe against me. He seemed to know all its laws; and he was not only an extremely able and spectacular person, he was—as far as I was concerned—both kind and fair. He often gave me arguments—far better than my own—to bolster up a position which he was in the act of demolishing.

I don't believe he wanted to take away my faith; but he wanted to make me think; and he took a great deal of trouble over it.

I should certainly have fallen in love with him if he had only been a little nicer to his wife.

She adored him; and it was plain that she was concentrated upon nothing else but pleasing him; and equally obvious that she failed.

He gazed into the middle distance whenever she spoke to him; and he never answered one of her timid, tentative questions.

On one of his climbing days, when she was not well enough to accompany him, she asked me to tea in her room alone, and told me her whole romantic story.

They had lived in the same town since they were children; and she had loved him ever since she could remember; but he had not returned her schoolgirl adoration. She gave him up, but she thought and cared for no one else. Suddenly catastrophe engulfed her. After an attack of scarlet fever it was discovered that she was going blind. Dr. Andrews met her again by chance, and almost immediately proposed to her. He insisted on marrying her without delay, and set to work to save her sight. To a limited extent, he had succeeded. It was now considered improbable that she would go completely blind, although she had an incurable eye disease. She hated climbing but so as not to be deprived of her husband's society she went with him on any climb that he considered was not beyond her powers. He often praised her for her courage. She would spring over loose stones down a mountainside as if she were an antelope; and never complained of giddiness or fear of heights. The truth of the matter was she hated climbing and was terrified to the depths of her being. She could not see where she was going, and she hurried over the stones because they were invisible, and it was safer to hurry over them than to wobble. She was too delicate to have children but it didn't matter—she didn't want them. She had him. As far as a person who is frightened to death can be happy, Mrs. Andrews *was* happy. They left soon afterwards and I never met either of them again. But ten years later I came across a cousin of his, who told me quite a different story.

According to this version, Dr. Andrews (who had recently died of blood poisoning) was the victim of his wife—a neurotic demon who had tricked him into marrying her. She wasn't going blind; and she had ruined his career and embittered his life. But I was not at all sure that she had. I should like to have heard *his* version of the story; for he had struck me as a man who would not easily have been made into a victim. But all I ever had from him—and it was a good deal—was a book list. I was to read the chief works of Darwin and Herbert Spencer; Nietzsche, Schopenhauer and William James; and I spent the next three years of my life reading them.

Among the most interesting of the Kulm flock at Ragatz was a Mrs. Aubrey le Blond, who happened to be a friend of Uncle Kennie's, and on the look-out for me.

She too was a great mountain climber, perhaps the greatest woman climber of her day. We took to each other from the first and formed a real though intermittent friendship. Mrs. le Blond at sixty was far more active and physically at home in the world than I was; and spent most of her time in briskly carrying on one sport or another. Still we contrived to see a good deal of each other, and whenever there was a pause between games she would sit beside me in the garden and tell me thrilling tales of her mountain adventures. She had had three husbands. The first had been the famous Colonel Burnaby, who disguised as an Arab had penetrated to the shrine of Mecca. Her second husband had been an equally famous Professor Main, who had introduced her to mountain climbing before rather abruptly leaving her to finish her climbs by herself; and her third husband, Aubrey le Blond, who was still attached to her life, though I never saw them together, was twenty years younger than she was and an excellent skater. One of the most skilled of Mrs. le Blond's many skilled performances, was that while relating in a serial manner the adventures of her long career, she managed never to mention any of her husbands.

Mrs. le Blond was spare and lean, deeply bronzed by the sun; and had the dignified and hatchet features of a Red Indian. One day she came to me with a suggestion—a friend of hers, Victor Gibson, had written a diary of his experiences in the Boer War, and wanted to get it published. But the trouble was, though a dear good fellow and a capital sportsman, he didn't know how to write. Wouldn't I undertake to re-write his diary for him, putting into it as I wrote, wit and humour in order to make it more palatable? Otherwise his book would be too dull for anyone to read, and publishers mightn't like it. We could share the profits.

Everyone at St. Moritz—or Regatz—knew Victor Gibson. He was a younger son of a great family and came up regularly every winter to St. Moritz for sport. His elder brother Harry had come up still earlier for his health and had been one of the original makers of the Cresta Run, on which were lost whatever chances he might have had of recovery from his lung trouble.

Harry Gibson was now a walking skeleton, very near the grave. Both were staying with their parents and two sisters at Ragatz.

Mrs. le Blond did not say so but I knew that she considered this offer was a great honour; and that she expected me to jump at it. My whole soul recoiled from the prospect. I saw no possibility whatever of inserting wit into somebody else's book. "You see," I tried hard to explain, "if it's *his* book, he ought to have what could make it interesting in himself. His book must come out of his own mind—it's what *he* sees *his* adventures through; wit can't be spread on the top of it from another person's mind—like jam!"

But Mrs. le Blond was delighted with this simile. "Jam" was what —charming as dear Victor was—he hadn't got! He would even (when I had read the diary) consent to talk it over with me! I knew him well by sight and I liked the look of him. I saw there was nothing for it but to consent to reading his diary; though I read it without hope.

As practically every officer in the Boer War must have had the same experiences as Victor Gibson's, unless they had had even more exciting ones, I felt that he and Mrs. le Blond were right in supposing publishers would shrink from the MS. I saw no possibility whatever of inserting wit into this leaden record. Besides, if I had any wit it was of a kind that resisted the incidents of war, particularly the Boer War, towards which my mind had steadily receded from its first enthusiasm.

I did not agree with Kipling that it was a just war; and I had never thought it a funny one.

I had regretfully to tell Mrs. le Blond that the task was beyond me. Mrs. le Blond was loath to relinquish her idea, but she was a good sport and finally dropped it, without terminating our friendly relations.

Victor Gibson may have looked at me before, but he certainly never looked at me again. However I met several other members of his interesting family. His sister Violet and I talked a good deal together, sitting on garden benches in the sun. She was a very unhappy, white papery creature, cruelly crushed by the sternest of Victorian parents. Her father looked as if bullying had been the sole occupation of a long life. Her mother had escaped into Christian Science, in which she walked about as if it were a self-induced strait-jacket. No doubt it had been a much-needed support for her and she had been unable to resist pressing it with passion upon all her children. Harry had at last accepted it, when he was ill enough to have given up all hope in doctors. His sister Violet at length told me that she had a strange request to make to me. Harry was very sensitive to sounds; and he liked my voice. Would I permit him— and not think he meant to be impertinent—to sit on the same bench, while I was talking to other people? He would not of course listen, he did not even care to hear what people talked about, but he *did* happen to like the sound of certain voices. I begged to be allowed to talk to him direct, indeed he had often been on my mind and heart. He was so ill—so lonely—and so lost a human figure; but I had never dared. Violet said "No!" He was much too ill and nervous to talk; he just wanted to be quiet and listen.

I agreed of course, though with considerable reluctance, because it is not easy to produce sounds to order; and for some days the gaunt pathetic shadow of a man, like the archaic Christ Elena and I had visited on Maggiore, sat at the extreme end of any seat I happened to be on; then he suddenly vanished and Violet told me another terrible haemorrhage had laid him low. He went on with this grim business of dying for another year or two, until the tubercle reached his brain—or else he just got tired of how long it took to die—and drowned himself in the lake of Como.

Violet, too, had a tragic future. After Mussolini's rise to power she went to Rome. It is possible that Mussolini's intemperate grip of Italy reminded her of her own father's persistent tyranny; or else that she foresaw in her repressed but ardent soul the ruin Fascism would bring to the whole of Europe. She was one of the least conspicuous people I ever saw, and no one noticed her standing behind a pillar in a crowd listening to one of Mussolini's chin-thrusting speeches. Violet was a good shot; but the Devil who watches over dictators shifted Mussolini's head a split second too soon to save a world war, so that Violet's bullet which should have pierced his brain, only grazed the lobe of his ear.

It would have been difficult to imagine anyone who looked less likely to shoot dictators than Violet. She had a low, hesitant voice, downcast eyes, and appeared to apologise for the amount of chair she was obliged to sit on.

Another of my chance acquaintances was a society beauty with jaundice—a girl of about my own age—whom Dr. Holland asked me to visit. "She thinks you can make her laugh," Dr. Holland told me, "and if you can it will be a very good thing. Jaundice is a depressing disease." I found Monica in one of the luxury rooms of the Hof. She was a slender, listless, lovely creature; and I liked her much better than her elder sister, who had the face of a glorified sheep, but who had made the match of the St. Moritz season. Monica was distinctly less sheepish; and I had a feeling that perhaps the illness from which she suffered was not unsupported by personal defeat. The man who was to marry her sister had been constantly with both of them, and no one knew till the engagement was announced which was to be the more favoured sister. Monica led the life of a caged animal. All she had to do was to look nice all the time. She wasn't strong enough for sport, and although she danced every evening, it made her feel extremely ill. She had a feeling that she would like to do something a little more interesting, but she never quite knew what; and probably this was just as well, as she wouldn't have been allowed to do it. She asked me to come and see her daily and we often snatched occasions for meeting in the open air, during the following winter. There was very little indeed the matter with Monica's lungs, so Dr. Holland asserted, but she managed to die of what there was, plus discouragement, before she was twenty-one.

I must at this period have had rather an appetite for missions for Dr. Holland thrust another one upon me which I was unable to resist.

I had often noticed, with some distaste, a pale stout young man who looked extremely frightened. "That wretched boy!" Dr. Holland frowningly pointed out to me on the tennis court, "He has been put in my charge by his parents, who are immensely rich, for conduct into which I don't propose to go! What he needs is a healthy outlook! Perhaps you could do something to make him take a more normal line? He wants to be a writer—you might cheer him up. Laugh at him! Help him to get rid of his morbid decadent ideas! They must be stopped at all costs or he'll go mad—if he isn't mad already!" Dr. Holland glared at the unfortunate young man: and I had not the nerve to refuse the introduction before Dr. Holland beckoned him to join us.

A more miserable mistake than to have put such a young man in Dr. Holland's care could hardly have been made by any parents.

Christopher had been cruelly bullied and insulted all winter at the Kulm, thrown like a kitten into a pack of hounds by Dr. Holland; and frightened nearly out of his senses by the practical joking of his sporting contemporaries. I never liked Christopher but I was extremely sorry for him; and when he found that far from wishing to insult him he could command my sympathy and fellow feelings, we often companionated each other.

We had a common aversion for the same tyrant, and though we talked chiefly about Christopher's variegated sufferings, he also gave me real information about books. He had an informed literary standard and he quickly became quite a tyrant on his own account. He scolded me continually for liking the wrong things and especially for being pleased so often. "You cannot be an artist and you will never be a writer," he told me impressively, "until you learn to dislike more!" Still the fact remained that I had published two novels, and had the third on the way, whereas Christopher's poems remained unaccountably still unpublished. I have always been on the look out for his name in print, but unless he wrote under a nom de plume I think he must eventually have given up this form of self-expression.

Between us we concocted a letter of appeal to his parents to free him from the tyranny of Dr. Holland which was, I thought at the time, a masterpiece of subtlety and special pleading. Its results may have been favourable, for Christopher did not go to St. Moritz again the following winter.

One of the things of which Christopher most disapproved was the indiscriminate way in which I made friends. He practically gave me up when I refused to withstand the kindly advances of a large stout girl some years older than either of us, who had the features of the Sleeping Fury before she woke up.

Molly and her brother Herbert were not Kulm-ites; but they were nearly as good. They possessed a large new villa cheek by jowl with the mountain on whose slopes St. Moritz Dorf had climbed. Herbert was one of Dr. Holland's pets. He was also a "cure" in the sense that he never got any worse. He had a mouth like a snapping turtle, and contrived to be speechlessly shy and arrogantly rude, simultaneously. He had done rather well at Oxford, well enough at any rate to take pupils.

Their household was composed of boys and men, and his sister Molly who ran it for him felt lonely without another girl and invited me to join them in their villa next winter.

If I would accept her offer she promised me a south room with a private balcony for my writing; and I need pay no more than I had been paying at the tea-rooms. In return would I help her to take care of the boys if they were ill; and stay in on the evenings when she and Herbert were invited to the Kulm? The boys were quite young, and she was sure I could manage them. I saw no drawbacks whatever to her suggestion, except the bleakness of Herbert's trap-like countenance and long upper lip.

15

My father arrived, and I was transported with joy to see him. I knew I was changed—very much changed—and I wondered if he would notice it. I was grown up; I had paddled my own canoe; I was on the dizzy verge of becoming an agnostic. Would he mind if I became a hard and fast one, or would he help me not to be one at all? I had procured him a particularly nice single room (the flock was beginning to thin), and made safe arrangements for his golf. My father had thick prematurely whitened hair, large dancing brown eyes and a huge black military moustache. He looked more unlike a clergyman than anything else in the world.

You could never quite tell in advance how he would react to social life. He might dazzle everyone in the room with him; but not in an authoritative or overpowering manner, rather he released them by his direct and friendly approach into being more dazzling themselves than they had ever had a right to expect. On the other hand, after a hasty glance round him, he might be bored, make no effort at all to be nice to anybody, and move truculently away to smoke a pipe over a book.

I could never be sure what would happen but at first I thought all would be well. My father insisted on our having a separate table because, he said, he saw I was quite a new person, and he wanted to get to know me. He would not think of golf, beyond the game I had arranged for him with Herbert, and we would take long walks together every day. He was nice to Molly and approved of our arrangement for next winter; but we only took one of these walks.

Mr. and Mrs. Greek God had, perhaps rather fortunately, left Ragatz; but I had a lot of new friends and was adding to them day by day. I hoped that my father would think that for a stray girl I had done rather well for both of us.

However my father as an American saw no sense in the Kulm flock's exclusiveness; at first he thought I had shown bad judgement in my choice of friends, but when he himself came up against the frozen barbed wire that cut us off into our pen, he became enraged, and wished to leave the Hof at once and go off into some Swiss place by ourselves.

I had long cherished a secret hope that we might leave Ragatz together and join Lislie and her mother at Wesen. They had come down from Thusis with the expanding spring, and were now staying in what sounded a fairyland on the Wallensee—in a rambling simple hotel served by its own family with its garden running into the lake. It was very cheap and on the main line. There we should find the truest of friends living in absolute freedom, instead of dozens of mere acquaintances in a cast-iron cage. When it came to the point, however, my father shirked moving. Mrs. le Blond had put a hand through the barbed wire. She told me my father was the most entertaining clergyman she had ever met—and as a clergyman, the most unexpected; and she found him someone far more cheerful with whom to play golf than poor Herbert.

My father was greatly amused and gratified by a tremendous scene which rounded off the season between Dr. Holland and Hall Caine.

The Hall Caines were very rich indeed—though outcasts in a Kulm sense. They had the best table in the dining room to themselves, and the hotel manager bowed to their every whim. They had two monstrously greedy little boys, and platefuls of exotic food —off the usual menu—were borne to their places, consumed and replaced by still more exotic desserts. They had wild strawberries when nobody else had wild strawberries; and a great deal of cream. My father and I had a table not far off and rather enjoyed seeing these pampered piglets consume their Arabian Nights' entertainment. Their parents were very quiet, good-mannered people, and I have no doubt these orgies of youthful greed on the part of their offspring diminished with the years.

But Dr. Holland and his flock took a dim view of outsiders in their hotel eating large quantities of asparagus when they had none.

It seemed all wrong somehow, and I think that Dr. Holland was only waiting for an opportunity to prove that it *was* all wrong. He was not a man who liked brains, unless he was personally responsible for their owners, and could use the rather poor kind of distinction which he admitted attached to them as a feather in his own cap. Why was Hall Caine a guest at the Hof at all—if he was *not* one of Dr. Holland's patients?

One night Mrs. Hall Caine, in full evening dress, wanted the nearest window shut. It was pouring with rain.

Hall Caine asked the waiter to close the window. He closed it. Five minutes passed, then one of Dr. Holland's patients obligingly complained of lack of air.

Dr. Holland rose in his full majesty and crossed over to Hall Caine's table. No one ate or spoke; every knife and fork quivered into silence; the waiters were as paralysed as the guests; while Dr. Holland thundered. By this time half the room wanted the window open and the other half wanted it shut. Hall Caine was a small man and continued seated. Dr. Holland was a tall man and stood over him and shouted. The window, he said, *should* be open and *kept* open and his patients should *not* be allowed to suffer from the stuffy habits of unknown guests. He was very rude indeed and very noisy. Hall Caine let him speak; he did not bat an eyelid; but there was something in that small composed figure which was not defeatable. "Sir," he said quietly, when at last Dr. Holland's breath failed him. "I shall speak to you later—in the smoking room—not before ladies." Dr. Holland ordered the nearest waiter to open the window, waited to see his order carried out, and retired with a conquering swagger to his seat. Hall Caine got up, his head held high, and withdrew from the dining room, his wife and children following him in a steady line, like ducks across a field.

Hall Caine did not withdraw further than the smoking room, where my father promptly and sympathetically joined him.

I grieved that I could not be present, but I heard verbatim accounts of the scene that followed both from Christopher—an ecstatic witness—and my father.

Dr. Holland hastily finished his dinner and rushed towards his doom.

I doubt if the smoking room had ever been so full before, even the waiters thronged the corridor, while one of them obligingly held the door open for the passage of imaginary coffee cups.

Hall Caine sat in Dr. Holland's favourite chair in front of an open fire, looking more than ever like the bust of Shakespeare that he was said to resemble.

His eyes, like those of a cat that knows its business, pinned Dr. Holland in front of him.

"Sir," he said, "before taking up the question of your atrocious manners, I have one pertinent question to put to you. Are you financially responsible for the running of this hotel? If you are, my family and I will leave tomorrow morning and place before the public the manner in which the Hof Ragatz is run, by a bully and a snob, with no respect for the rights of his guests; or are you yourself merely a guest, in which case how dare you usurp the authority of a manager of this hotel?"

Dr. Holland, according to my father and Christopher, turned purple, stuttered an ineffectual retort, and retreated from the smoking room, never to return during the rest of Hall Caine's visit.

Hall Caine accepted my father's warm congratulations; and held the respect of all but the most enthralled of Dr. Holland's patients.

My father presented me to Hall Caine next morning, at the end of an avenue in the garden, close to a small column against which he leaned. He wore a cloak across his shoulders, and a hat that if it was not modelled on that of the portrait, was at least no one else's kind of hat.

I somehow doubt if Hall Caine looked like the *real* Shakespeare; but he certainly looked like the portrait.

I was too awed to speak. I bowed low over his out-stretched hand, while he murmured a few benevolent words about the profession of which at the moment he had some grounds for considering himself the head. He forgot me the moment I had timidly withdrawn from his tremendous presence, and never noticed me again. Nevertheless I felt the prouder for the introduction, and was relieved and still more exhilarated by the way in which Christopher reacted to the whole affair. Hitherto he had looked down on Hall Caine for being a popular novelist—now suddenly he changed hi tune. "After all," he said to me apologetically, "there must be something pretty magnificent about a fellow, when Dante Gabriel Rossetti *chooses* to die in his arms!" Never again did Christopher have to submit to the brutal bullying that had made his life a burden. He had only—and he had the wit to do it—to drop a casual reference to Hall Caine, to see Dr. Holland deflate like a punctured balloon.

I persuaded my father to take a day off from his golf to visit Carità and Lislie at Wesen; then if he were—as I hoped he would be—sufficiently impressed with Wesen we might give up Ragatz.

I know now that my father was deeply unhappy. He did not want to meet new people at all. He avoided walks with me because he had too much on his mind—which he dared not tell me. Forty-nine and twenty do not move to the same time sequence. I had got over Wilmett's death—my father, I now believe, never got over it. He had just been burdened by Dr. Holland with heavy anxiety about myself. He had a still worse tragedy threatening the family which he wanted and yet feared to make known to me. No doubt he did find me "grown up", but was I grown up enough to share his burdens? He did not try to find out, and I did not know how to help him to find out.

We went to Wesen together. It was an enchanting day. The lake shone like whipped forget-me-not. Carità and Lislie instantly loved my father. We got on wonderfully, as I thought, together; and enjoyed a meal more real than all the *tables d'hôte* of the Hof Ragatz put together—fresh home-made brown bread and butter, authentic honey and delicious coffee with whipped cream on the top, by the side of the lake and under the splendid shadow of an immediate gold and green mountain. But on the way back my father repudiated our joy. No, he did not care for the Brocks—Lislie looked too ill—her mother did not interest him. He thought Wesen no prettier than Ragatz. The mountains were just the same only nearer—you could not play golf on the lake. There was no one besides a few mountain-climbing Germans in the hotel, which wasn't in the same class as the Hof—and he thought we had wasted a fine day by spending four hours in a railway train for nothing.

I could not tell him what I had hoped, that if we had spent a few days together with Lislie and her mother we might have become really intimate friends. They would have helped us to get to know each other.

It is not enough for a parent or a child to trust to their natural affection. There must be, especially when adolescence changes to maturity, a new and careful approach. I think we both wanted to make this approach; but neither of us knew how to do it.

On our one and only walk next day we threw away our chance altogether; and it never came again. I could see that my father was in the blackest of moods. Something had gone wrong and he did not quite know how to put it to me. We had walked far beyond my powers, my father, like myself, always forgetting that there had to be a way back. I asked if we might sit down in a pine wood, above a stream, and rest. My father gloomily assented. Nothing suited him, he did not notice the lovely gleams of light on the pink pine stems, nor far below us the tossing amber of a mountain torrent. We were opposite strange and splendid peaks that we could not even see at Ragatz, bathed in the clear, fugitive light of spring.

At last however, in a burst of rage, some of his trouble came tumbling out. He had had a talk with Dr. Holland. Why had I told him I was perfectly well when I wasn't? Dr. Holland had told him that I had had setbacks and that now both my lungs were affected. Why should Dr. Holland—if I were really so much better—insist that I should stay above two thousand feet all summer? Did I really want to do such a thing? My father had taken a house at the seaside for us all for two months. He was bitterly disturbed and upset. I was as surprised as he had been, for Dr. Holland had said nothing at all to me about lungs or plans; and I had taken for granted that I was going home. But before I had time to say so, something worse followed. There was, my father told me, something wrong with Mary. He didn't exactly know what, but she was behaving in a most extraordinary and dreadful way with my mother. Here I stopped him; didn't he know, I reminded him, how unkind mother had always been to Mary? How could he be surprised if she sometimes answered back? But this wasn't just answering back, my father explained—it was something new and much worse. Mother was actually frightened—what was to be done about it if I didn't come

132

home? *Would* I come home? Didn't I think Dr. Holland was only out for money? Look how he had behaved to Hall Caine! Was such a man a doctor whose opinion anyone need bother about? Father glared at me, but I knew that his temper was only anxiety. His eyes were full of misery. He wanted me to take the responsibility of my own fate off his shoulders. He wanted me to decide for him—and with him. It was like offering alcohol to a drunkard. Of *course* I would decide for him! Of course I would go home! Of course I would undertake—not knowing in the least how to tackle such a problem—whatever was wrong between my mother and Mary!

But on the way back we definitely fell out over Mary. I would not accept his point of view nor he mine. Nevertheless the rest of our walk (except for extreme fatigue) was not wholly an unhappy one. My father was for the first time pleased with me for helping him make up his mind as he wished.

As for me, I was enchanted; I adored my family, and should have hated to stay alone in some Swiss pension. Everything was exactly as I wanted it to be.

I should visit Lislie, and my father promised she should visit us. He said he really had liked her very much, if she hadn't looked so ill. He understood that I mustn't be long at Swanscombe, but fortunately Elena had arranged for me to go to her, in her new home, under the spire of Salisbury Cathedral. I did not say anything about being an agnostic, because it did not seem a very good moment for opening up the subject. We talked instead about George Herbert.

16

My father and I travelled straight from spring in the mountains—clean as the first day of creation—to our dingy slum on the bare hillside, clogged with cement dust, under a pall of smoke from factory chimneys.

I think this was the first time I ever saw Swanscombe as it really was. Hitherto I had always accepted it, drugged with my own vitality, as a romantic quest. The parish was not only my father's life, it was a series of exciting problems for me to surmount, with him—or for him. Each life with whom I came in contact had its separate and thrilling values. It had not occurred to me before that people who lived there had nothing to do with beauty.

Poverty had seemed the one obstacle to happiness. But now I perceived that this chief product of Swanscombe, poverty, had less to do with money than I had once imagined. Cement workers and dockers, compared to agricultural labourers or even factory hands, were well off. The curse of Swanscombe was an inner poverty—its inhabitants had been cheated of a whole series of values. In this single street of mean, miserable little houses, thickly coated with cinders, what could men and women do but drink—or sin—or suffer?

On that stony hillside between Northfleet and Gravesend there was nothing physically—*but* darkness. A pall of it surrounded the house we lived in, as well as all the other houses. Money-making had corrupted living. Those who owned the factories had ignored the lives of those who worked in them. Neither education nor religion had discovered a solution.

I began to understand why my father so constantly escaped from

Swanscombe to golf links. My mother lived contentedly in a world of books, the constant pre-occupation of physical symptoms, her love for her children and her prayers. It was Mary who could never escape from it; because she had nowhere else to go. She was twenty-five; and there was not a single person of her own age and education within speaking distance of her—let alone a friend. I did not at first notice any great change in Mary. She was a good deal thinner; and when we were not alone together she was silent; but we talked, when we were alone together, as we had always talked, with complete intimacy and freedom.

More than ever I felt convinced that my version of Mary's troubles was the correct one. I knew nothing then about psychology; but it seemed to me that the circumstances of Mary's life were sufficient to produce uncontrollable misery in any human being.

When together we had enjoyed our Swanscombe life. We had done the work of two curates with considerable gusto, making up in ardour what we lacked in knowledge. But much of this ardour fell away from Mary when she found herself alone with exceedingly tough human problems, and no fellow traveller with whom to exchange counsel on the day's constant emergencies.

She had not been trained to any particular skill. Wilmett had had her music; I, my writing, but whatever interest Mary had shown had been checked in early youth. Father did not wish to hear about problems he could not solve; and mother never willingly listened to anything about the parish.

Mary's life had to function under a cloud of personal antagonism, directed by my mother's unconcealed scorn and impatience; and wholly without outside companionship.

No one dreamed of taking her to a theatre or finding her a friend. She had no relief and no outlet for her unexpressed powers or her adolescent emotions. She was not supposed—no girl of our period *was* supposed—to have such emotions. She had not even the work of the house to do, since this was efficiently done by two good servants. Mary was condemned to solitary confinement; with my mother as her jailor.

My mother had fallen in love with my father thinking that his tremendous charm and irresistible spirits could relieve her from all

135

her fears. But one cannot safely trust to the life-plans of others to release us from the snags in our own. My father slowly broke under this strain; and because Mary was incapable of the very faculties my mother had not got herself, my mother wanted—quite unconsciously—to get rid of her. Nothing could really have been wiser than that they *should* part. Nowadays daughters of five-and-twenty rarely live at home. But my parents, convinced that sentiments, backed by church practices, were enough for anybody, had overlooked providing Mary with a profession. Did she have to live at home or not, seemed to me the problem. Directly I was sent to see Dr. Schacht, I plunged into the subject of Mary. I knew that he had already seen her in my absence, and I was anxious that he should not be prejudiced by my parents' view of her. I told him what I felt were the real facts of the situation; and I begged him to realize that though I was personally wrapped up in my mother, this cruel threat of her attitude to Mary had run disastrously through all our lives. It was mitigated while I was at home, for Mary had me to fall back upon. Now she hadn't. What could be done to help her?

Dr. Schacht was cautious; he said he felt sure that something could be done to help Mary; and he agreed that she badly needed help. The next few years Mary's fate was to be in his hands; and without being a psychologist, simply by being a common-sense and very kindly human being, he saved her from extreme disaster. Nevertheless she had to suffer appalling fears, anxieties and depressions, which she could well have been spared had anyone dealing with her—including myself—known how to help her.

I think any psychologist would say now that Mary was partly suffering from delayed shock. She had been in America during Wilmett's illness and had not grasped its severity. She came back to find her dying. But her relationship to my mother was the core of her trouble. As long as they were under the same roof nothing could go right with Mary; nor had my mother any intention that it *should* go right.

Dr. Schacht's dilemma was that he knew all this as well as I did; but that he belonged to the Victorian era; and he believed that unmarried daughters should remain slaves to neurotic mothers. There was something sacred to him as a man in children being

136

subject to their parents—even when they were no longer children, and however unsuitable the parent. Boys might escape, but for girls there was no age limit to parental victimization.

"I don't think your mother understands Mary," Dr. Schacht at length admitted under bombardment, "and I will do my very best to help her; but I don't see my way—as things at present are—to removing her from home. After all, you will be all the summer with her; and perhaps she will recover her spirits before the autumn, being out of doors in a healthy place with a congenial companion is sure to be the best thing for her. Only I am going to ask you something you may find hard. Please do not sympathize with Mary about your mother. You will make things very much worse if you do! I want you to *minimize* your mother's part in this matter to your sister as much as possible!" This seemed to me surprisingly unkind; and indeed senseless, but I was accustomed to being influenced by Dr. Schacht, so I merely asked what good he thought that could do, when Mary's unhappiness was caused by my mother's attitude, and we both knew it. "Yes," he agreed, "I know it *is* a fact about your mother, nevertheless you must *not* stimulate your sister's unfortunate feeling against her, or you will make the trouble more serious than it actually is—and I must admit I do think it *very* serious."

It was not often that Dr. Schacht spoke so plainly and I was more alarmed than ever—and more anxious for some wise action to be at least planned immediately so that Mary might have some relief. "If she doesn't get better before the autumn," I demanded, "can't we decide on our being somewhere together, now? I can pay for nearly the whole of my next winter out of my short stories." Dr. Schacht had seemed so reasonably impressed with my recovery that I was quite unprepared for the extreme annoyance with which he tossed aside this suggestion. "No," he said, "you certainly can't! You must go back to St. Moritz alone, and complete your cure whatever happens! Leave your sister to me! I will promise to take care of her; but in return *you* must promise to follow my instructions!"

I promised; but I left him far from satisfied. I *did* carry out his instructions and I think largely owing to the dilution of my emphatic sympathy, Mary never really told me the depth of her insecurity. We skirted its surface, and I could not help showing sympathy with her state of mind as well as with her loneliness; but as far as I could I avoided implicating mother. Yet had we talked more fully and openly about her trouble than we did I doubt if anything I then knew (or could have gained for her through my knowledge) would have been of any use to her. Life is an expensive business. It demands the uttermost farthing for any mistakes in the art of living; and it is not always the person who is responsible for these mistakes who has to foot the bill.

17

When I first saw our summer home it was nothing but a ravine between high, white chalk cliffs. Now I believe it is part of a large seaside town. It was curiously sheltered, and foliage clung on both its sides, over the cliff's face and down to a few white-washed fishermen's cottages on the beach. A few more cottages, including one or two semi-detached, pill-box villas, stood at the top of the cliff, fronting an emerald rim of down. A mile of dusty white road between deep hedges connected the divided village with the main highway. The cliffs ran back into corn fields, under a featureless sky.

One of Keats' letters describes just such a landscape, where the green corn moves when the tide turns, so that you can tell by the bowing heads of corn the action of the invisible sea.

This was a good summer of long, blue and golden days; except for the bitter undercurrent of Mary's misery.

I used to wake to the sudden darkness of it when day broke; and when I fell asleep at night our beds were side by side, and I knew that Mary was not sleeping. But in the day-time the sun shone, I felt new health and everyone seemed smiling and kind. I was working too as I had never worked before. I was writing a book called "Raw Material" which was written out of my five years' experience of Swanscombe life. It was a study of my club boys' lives as dock-side and cement workers. Though I squirm today when I remember the hard shell of dogmatic religious ignorance that clings to it in patches, I still think that some kind of a live chicken pecked its way through the shell. I was much encouraged by a letter from John Murray himself, when I sent him the MS.; and T. P. O'Connor gave me a column and a half of signed review, full of keen perception and guidance—a real criticism such as no newspapers seem to have space for nowadays: even if our critics had the time or ability to do authors the courtesy of understanding what, as craftsmen, they are trying to say.

This writing gave me a deep joy, which was shared, and kindly prodded on, by the shrewd criticism of my friend Gerard Coleridge. This was our last summer holiday together before we each—simultaneously and suddenly—became engaged to someone else.

We used to read aloud every evening what we had written in the day-time, with Mary as our chief audience. Gerard wrote mainly poetry. I believed that he would become a great poet and develop into a second Samuel T. and I ardently spurred him towards this goal. But Gerard confessed to me with remorse that his best ideas always came when he hadn't got a pencil. This insuperable obstacle continued to thwart him throughout a long and useful life.

Gerard had been forced to introduce me, on the cliff's edge, to a fellow undergraduate of Cambridge, whom he intensely disliked. This young man we rather unkindly nicknamed "the Black Adder". He was staying at the only hotel the little village possessed; and it had a tennis court.

My brother George was now sixteen, a very good-looking, modest and kind-hearted boy, silent but companionable; and never either selfish or aggressive; but the kind of life which was natural at his age was at Swanscombe unprocurable for him. By accident I saw rather more of him than usual this summer.

The Black Adder immediately invited George to play tennis with him. Gerard warned me privately that this man was a belated offshoot of the already waning period of decadence started by Oscar Wilde. "Don't," Gerard warned me, "let *George* have anything to do with him!" But how could I stop George, whose holiday happiness hung on tennis from playing on the only court; and with the only person who was available for the purpose?

I *couldn't* "stop" George; my parents would have laughed at the bare idea; but I could share his dangers.

Nobody disliked the Black Adder more heartily than I did; but he did not know that I disliked him. Nothing pleased him better than to accept us both as companions on—or off—the tennis court. He was a clever young man, something of a pianist, a painter and a writer. He had not yet published anything and as I was the author of two books—both published—a pleasing halo hung about me, for him. Haloes might—I think he felt—be catching.

Our ideas differed. He was an atheist and despised morals. My belief that God existed became greatly strengthened by his arguments to the contrary; and my belief in morals had never yet been shaken.

The Black Adder invited me to judge which of his undoubted gifts was the greatest and should be made his profession. I listened to him playing; I studied his paintings; I read his MSS., and as I knew least about music I finally suggested that he should make music his career. However he told me he had something which he had shown to no one and which might change my verdict. It was the full length, typed MS. of a novel. He suggested that we should go together to a distant cove, where there would be complete solitude, and read this novel out loud. The cove was regularly cut off by the tide and there was a cave in it—grass grown, sea-bird haunted—ideal for our purpose. We should have five hours, if we timed the tide and ourselves carefully. He thought it was a very powerful novel but it was not a long one. When I showed signs of refusing this adventure the Black Adder rather deftly suggested taking George instead of me. After all, George was old enough to learn what life was like; and the Black Adder thought that his MS. would teach him. I hastily reconsidered my refusal, and we agreed to take our lunch, and the three of us went off together for the day.

We warned my mother not to expect us back till a late tea; and the tide suiting itself to our convenience we set off early one morning on a glorious September day.

We reached the cove and found the cave get-at-able by a little rock and cliff climbing. It was all that the Black Adder had claimed for it; and reassuringly grass grown.

I *did* go so far as to ask, "You're quite *sure* that the tide never comes up so high?" He *was* quite sure, he had spent days in the cave in former summers. We settled down to read, broke off to eat, returned to the MS. and watched the tide reach both corners of our

141

little cove until we were completely cut off. George and I—at this period of our lives—knew each other by heart. Until he went to boarding school I had been his nurse, champion, playfellow and friend. The turn of an eyelash told us what the other was feeling. Without exchanging a glance we now realized that both of us felt the book inordinately dull; and that neither of us liked the romping in of the tide.

It was late September, and half a gale blew in from the sea behind it.

The waves were already breaking over rocks which the Black Adder had told us they could never reach; and there was an hour to run before the tide would be high.

The cliff above us was sheer. No one knew where we were. No boats were on the sea; nor could they have put in to this rocky shore, had they been there, to note our predicament. For a long time we were too polite to say anything. George unobtrusively threw pebbles at chosen distances to test the rapidity of the incoming tide.

The Black Adder, white about the gills, stopped reading. "I don't like the look of this!" he informed us; nor did we. "But I know it's all right," he added in a shaky voice. "Look at the grass!" "Grass can grow in a year!" George said with aggravating accuracy.

One by one the high rocks we had climbed over to reach the cliff became submerged. There *was* grass growing on the one nearest to us. The sea broke over it. Foam splashed inside the cave's mouth. We retreated into the back of the cave. "It must be just on high tide now," George informed us reassuringly. But there was the wind behind the tide. Then the Black Adder made a suggestion that turned me into a tigress.

He suggested that George—six years younger than he was—should try to swim through those thundering seas and bring us help. My politeness vanished.

"If anyone tries to get back," I said firmly, "*you do*! You're responsible for this business! It would be certain death, but if you like to try, I shan't stop you. But I *shall* stop George—or go with him; and I don't advise either of you to try to stop me going with him either!"

I suppose the look I cast in turn on those two boys was the look with which a cat holds at bay large-sized dogs. I have felt no sympathy for cats since, for I was perfectly sure that I was competent to deal with either or both of them, even if they attempted force, and I knew that they wouldn't dare to attempt it!

George, who had already taken off his coat, put it on again.

I don't know what the others felt, but I was absorbed by rage and remorse—remorse for exposing my parents to fresh disaster, and rage with the Black Adder for trying to force George into solitary and certain death.

For the next few minutes, with the waves breaking at the cave's mouth, we faced a rather unpleasant and very watery form of end; but at least our risk was equal. We were drenched to the skin—huddled together at the back of the cave—clinging to its rocky ledges. After what seemed eternity we realized the waves were *not* coming any further in. It took at least another hour before the sea perceptibly retreated and even then an occasional monster soaked us with its spray; but at least we knew the tide had turned.

We still had several very unpleasant hours before us, which I employed in reading aloud the rest of the MS. It would have had to be a very powerful novel to have engaged our interest; and I think even the Black Adder felt that his was hardly powerful enough.. Our comments on it, when we had finished, were lack-lustre if not severe.

How could we be sure that the tide, which had been exceptional, would retreat sufficiently far to free the nearest corner? What if the sea decided to keep us cut off, and the tide turned back, a few hours later, with the rising gale's assistance, to finish the business? The tide was not going out in either a fast or regular manner. George and I consulted together as if the Black Adder was not there. We decided to make a try to round the corner even if it involved a bit of a risk, as soon as the waves retreated far enough to make it at all practicable. We paid no attention at all to the Black Adder's suggestion that it was safer to remain where we were. We scrambled down on to the wet beach, the Black Adder teeth-chattering behind us; and on reaching the corner we decided to make a dash for it. We took it hand in hand, and once a wave ran up to our waists and nearly sucked us out to sea; but we clung fast to each other, and the cliff's edge; and all three got round the corner safely.

We found that a sudden cessation of danger does nothing to relieve the nerves. We were all three very cross; and parted in extreme dudgeon. George and I got in the back way, swore our kind cook to silence, and succeeded in appearing calm and dry, only a little late for tea.

We had decided to conceal our adventure from our parents; but either the Black Adder could not refrain from relating it; or else the Coastguards (who had mysteriously spotted our dilemma and knowing they could do nothing to save us had written us off as a total loss) made it public, but the story got loose in the village somehow and the next morning we were told that we had all three been drowned. Fortunately by the time my parents heard that we were the victims of this drowning accident, they already knew that we were safe and had taken no harm; that I avoided catching cold I always put down to the warmth of my rage with the Black Adder.

There seemed, however, to be a general agreement that not even for the sake of tennis must we further cultivate his acquaintance.

For some perfectly unknown reason he and I found ourselves within reach of each other in church next Sunday. I had thought he never went; and I myself hardly ever attended Matins. He wrote in pencil on a piece torn out of a hymn book, "Am I to go my pathway through the world alone?" I wrote back, "Yes—you are!" And the curious part of it was that I had always thought he preferred George!

I met him once again thirty years later, in a London drawing room. I had by then made my name in America, and his was well known in England as a writer, so it seemed to me that we might safely be nice to each other. I greeted him heartily; but he was in an agony which I unintentionally heightened by saying, "It must be twenty years or more since we met!" "*Much much* more," he groaned. "Don't you *know* it's thirty?" He seemed so very aggravated by the change in our appearance, and the loss of our youth—his, I think, particularly—that I soon released him; when I heard of his death some years later, and read his many and admiring obituary notices, I realized that he had been—besides a success in the profession I had strongly advised him to avoid—a respected and popular human being. I do not know whether Gerard and I were too harsh in our judgement of him, or the obituary notices too flattering. Perhaps life itself does something to improve its material.

18

It was during the summer of 1904 that Lislie first stayed with us. Her visit cemented our friendship. My mother liked Lislie better than any friend of mine she had met; Mary grew to love her on her own account; George found her both congenial and attractive; my father's only criticism of her was that he preferred my choosing friends who had never been ill. Lislie became a part of my family circle as I soon became a part of hers.

I went to stay at Alstone Lawn that autumn on my way to Elena's "Corner Cupboard"; and it is impossible to express both how strange and how delightful I found Lislie's home. Alstone Lawn was set in the tawdry slum of Tooting, not even on the common, though near to it. Behind its jasmine-covered frontage it had a high-walled garden—a real country garden with a big lawn, in the centre of which was an ancient mulberry tree hanging its curtain of leaves to the ground, and making a summer house of itself. Behind the lawn, and deftly screened by hollyhocks and lilac bushes, lay a substantial kitchen garden; and Carità's chickens. There was a Skye terrier called Barny—a perfect gentleman of a dog, loving, considerate and rather dreamy in character, with occasional spurts of fiery mischief; and an affectionate, composed and self-willed cat.

Everyone was nice to everyone else, all the time. Dr. Brock adored both his wife and Lislie. He seldom left the house on his frequent errands without kissing one if not both of them, as if for a long parting.

He became, as the years passed, increasingly nervous, solitary and irritable; but when I first knew him he was a happy man with his heart filled with adoring love. He had extreme sympathy with the trials of others, and a great sense of humour. His only difficulties were financial ones. He had very little steady income from his profession. He was police doctor for the district and regular consultant and visiting doctor at a big mental hospital on Tooting Common; and these two appointments were his meagre mainstay. His private practice, never considerable, dwindled with the years. He had a curious kind of pride which prevented his telling anyone how little he made; so that he even paid income tax on an income he never possessed rather than acknowledge to the tax collector that he did not possess it.

Fidelè was never known to spend a penny on himself. Yet money slid away from him invisibly and without any apparent equivalent.

I do not know at this time how much income the family possessed, but it was—even at this peak of their prosperity—an incredibly small amount.

Yet they managed to do—and to possess—all the things that we, as a family, rigidly forwent. We never had any debts, nor any extraneous expenses beyond my father's golf and doctors' bills. We did no entertaining whatever and lived on the simplest food. The Brocks entertained every week-end; kept a good table and had a constant stream of interesting visitors. Carità and Lislie went up to London three or four times a week, to parties, theatres and social occasions. They wore, even though they often made and re-made them, enchanting and fashionable clothes.

They had a large circle of intimate relatives, one or two of whom were well off, and extremely generous to them. Yet how they managed, and managed so light-heartedly and well on so small an amount, always remained a mystery. They seldom mentioned money and never seemed put out by the lack of it. Occasionally disaster stared them in the face. Bills they had long forgotten broke over them like a hurricane, sometimes in these dire emergencies help came to them from relatives or friends; sometimes they gathered themselves together and took in a paying guest, or sold a household treasure. Then the high wind fell, the sun came out again, and no further precautions were taken.

Lislie often had to face—almost from childhood—long and painful interviews with their landlord. It was thought she was better at it than her parents. They held Alstone Lawn on a long unfurnished lease, and were very irregular in paying their rent; but to off-set this disability they made no demands on their landlord for repairs. Alstone Lawn during the nineteen years in which I knew it, gently disintegrated about their heads. When I knew it first, a haze of sunshine and happy living streamed through the house and out into the garden; and into the house from the garden, the stream returned, carrying flowers, vegetables and baskets full of eggs. Carità in her early fifties was still a strenuous gardener. She made her chickens pay. She was a good housekeeper, ingenious and far-seeing. In the days when it was easy and inexpensive to have servants they had one; and usually one who stayed for a long time.

Before pain, age and penury closed down on it, Alstone Lawn was a social paradise. At first I realized only its beauty. Here was a family like the MacCords of my long ago American days, who made amusements into a sort of exquisitely performed duty; who took and gave pleasure with regal regularity; and whose only regularity it was.

The Brocks were all three gentle, harmonious and generous people. What they could give they open-handedly gave. I never knew anybody who used a garden as generously as they used theirs. Every leaf, flower and vegetable was turned to good account; and what they gave, in one way or another was returned to them, full measure, pressed down and running over.

Patients, who never dreamed of paying Dr. Brock, often worked for him for nothing. Poor families given clothes to help out their wardrobes, or fresh eggs and vegetables during their difficult illnesses, returned these benefits by sending in one of their members to "char"—for the smallest of sums.

The Brocks never expected, or even wished, to be repaid by such generosities. They were simply the kind of people who inspired gratitude; but they rarely felt it. They had the sense not to over-estimate the value of money. They may have been a little too light-hearted about it but their seriousness was for life itself.

They never saved; they couldn't, I think, afford to; but they got their money's worth; and they gave *more* than their money's worth.

Brought up as I had been, and spending less than fifteen pounds a year on my clothes, I was at first shocked and even appalled at the amount of time and money which Lislie and her mother bestowed upon this matter; but it did me good to find that they were equally shocked at the time and money I didn't!

In my home everything and everybody—except my father, who was seldom there—worked by the clock. My mother's invalidism, her religious readings, meals and the ordering of her household were all punctual avocations; and as for Mary and myself we fitted our tasks into her routine, working steadily from breakfast to bedtime. People might come in, at any hour of the day, but they were seen for some purpose other than entertainment.

At Alstone Lawn entertainment was in itself a purpose and when people called everybody stopped whatever they were doing to help entertain them. Human beings, their pleasures, accidents or mere presences, broke through the day's tasks and stretched far on into the night in one continuous stream. There was an endless curiosity —mainly kindly, though with the salt of criticism—at every point at which any one of them touched life. The Brocks' visitors were often interesting in themselves. Fidelè's family was very large. Sir Charles and Lady Elliot were first cousins and near neighbours— besides a highly diverting Indian past and charming children, they possessed a bluebell wood. Sir Brian and Lady Donkin, with their Home Office background, were life-long friends, and came constantly for Sunday visits. The Harington cousins were perhaps the most stimulating of all their visitors. They were three daughters of an Anglo-Indian Judge, who died just before his pension was sufficient to deal with the problem Victorian parents set themselves by refusing to train their daughters to earn their livings. Few women could have been more highly talented than Ethel, Edie and Mabel Harington. Professor Melville Gwatkin of Cambridge—no mean judge of brains—considered that Edie had the best mind of any woman whom he knew. Ethel, the eldest, had a more clear-cut and trenchant if less deep intelligence than her sister Edie's; Mabel had a sparkling courage. She lived and worked through the Russian revolution as a governess in Moscow. After her hurried flight from Russia she picked up languages and jobs as she went through one European country after another.

149

Edie was exactly like a Botticelli angel, lightly hollowed shell-pink cheeks, great grey eyes and shadowy hair with golden lights in it. When I first saw her she was leaning across the table in a shaft of sunshine, to help cut out some material. She only lacked wings. Edie worked pitilessly hard in a typists' office for twenty-five years; and then became a nursery governess since she could no longer bear the mechanical misery of her imprisoned mind.

Ethel taught all her life in less than first-rate schools, without a teacher's certificate. She was a splendid teacher; but her extraordinary historical and literary knowledge, in spite of her great gift for imparting what she knew, barely earned her keep. "Edie is my special friend," Lislie told me. "Besides, she has heaps of others, and Ethel hasn't—so I want you to make Ethel yours!" I found this allocation momentarily a little hard, for I had preferred Edie, but I was no loser in the end. Ethel couldn't have been a better friend. We were not always in agreement and to disagree with Ethel was a formidable pastime, but we both loved reading; and loved it, I think, in the same way. It was the breath of life to us. Lislie had not the time for much reading. The life she lived required a great deal of up-keep. Yet I never saw her hurried or idle. She helped her mother in everything she did—and she helped her father in everything he didn't do. She wrote all his letters for him as he had—conveniently—writer's cramp. She was the one servant's mainstay. Nothing was done in the house or garden without the greater part of it resting on Lislie's narrow shoulders; but what she did was without drive or tension. She worked as easily as the sun shines. She never needed credit for any of her activities; there was something in the activity itself which suited her gallant spirit sufficiently for all prestige questions to drop. Except for acute periods of lung illness, Lislie's chronic infirmity was neither visible to others, nor allowed to weigh upon her daily life. It was there—things had to be done about it, and she did them; but the difference between people who do not want ill-health and make the best of it; and those who *do* want it and make the worst of it, can hardly be exaggerated. In the great obstacle race of Lislie's life this cruel handicap—the heritage of a neglected childhood-illness—hardly played any perceptible part.

The two people in Lislie's circle whom I came to care for most and who constantly offered me hospitality and friendship to their lives' ends were Lislie's uncle and aunt—Professor and Mrs. Melville Gwatkin of Cambridge.

Uncle Melville, as I was soon allowed to call him, was not only one of the greatest scholars of his day—unique, I believe, in having won five firsts—he was also a man who was very congenial to the young. He did not hamper them with his knowledge, he used it to stimulate and solidify their own.

Lislie spent many of his long vacations with him, and some of these I shared.

We visited Cambridge together often and we loved almost equally Uncle Melville and his wife—"Auntie Lou". Perhaps we were unique in being the friends of both, for they were an extraordinarily "diverse pair". Most people liked one or the other of them; but rarely both.

Uncle Melville was wildly shy, his mind piled high with the knowledge of the ages was not easy to unpack. He held himself back from ordinary social intercourse, partly through ignorance of what people without knowledge were talking about and partly from the natural reticence of one who is too considerate to use in company an unshared advantage. Questions released him, and he loved and needed questions as cows love the hand that milks them, if it knows its job. He said once to a young friend: "You may not know much, but I like to talk to you—you ask such good questions." On another occasion he said to the same friend with great impatience: "Think—you can if you like—think!" But if the questioner was sincere how beautifully—with what pent-up confidence and clarity—came the knowledge that his friend was seeking! His truthfulness was *more* than accuracy—it was the whole content of an intimate and balanced knowledge, channelled into a straight deep stream, by a patient and unflurried mind. Sometimes Uncle Melville would check himself, to enquire earnestly if his questioner understood exactly what he meant, much as a careful surgeon pauses to find out how much pain a wound under his touch is causing his patient. You could not deceive him, because his piercing questions drew out exactly what you understood—neither less nor more. Once he showed me one of his examination papers. It was written in his meticulous minute handwriting on a half sheet of paper. The questions were not more than eight or nine words long. "Anything my students know," he said, "they can find the way to answer in those questions; but of course they must *know* it!"

He was grieved that I knew so much by heart. "That will all stop," he told me earnestly. "It really gets in your way, so don't be alarmed when it stops. I don't know the Creed by heart now— even the Lord's Prayer requires some consideration from me, but I know where each clause comes from and what it means. You will forget as soon as you begin to think."

"No one needs to learn dates," he told me, "if he is interested in his subject. He will not be able to forget the important ones. After all, most people remember their own birthdays without difficulty— a matter of no historical importance whatever!"

Social occasions, when he had to talk—though he was mostly silent—could be catastrophic.

"Now what is your opinion of Tut?" he once demanded from a society lady anxious to impress him at a tea-party, "Tut" being his pet name for *Tertullian* while the lady did not know this great character in early Church history even by his real name.

On another occasion a proud daughter of the Greek Professor of Trinity, Henry Jackson, began a conversation with, "I think you know my father, Professor Gwatkin?" "Of course I know him— disgusting fellow—he stinks miles away!" Uncle Melville replied genially, alluding to his famous colleague's inveterate smoking, but greatly outraging his respectful daughter.

He had nicknames for all his favourites. Auntie Lou was "Pussy —my cat", Lislie was "the animal" with an accent on the last syllable. I was "the slug". I once asked the meaning of this nickname, which seemed inappropriate since I was generally considered rather quick. "Oh yes, no doubt," he replied, "a *racing* slug I admit—but still I think on the whole a slug. You see you're not a scholar—you ought to have been! It's a pity. I should have liked you to attend my lectures, and now they tell me you're too ill— but I don't believe it!"

I went to his lectures on early Church history whenever I stayed at Scrope Terrace. They were amazingly illuminating; it was like watching a skilled antiquarian bringing to the light of day a long-hidden treasure. But I think what I enjoyed and understood best were the hours I spent sitting on a footstool at his knee, in his study, asking him questions.

Once while he spent a vacation with us at Bournemouth he read the New Testament out loud to us from the Greek, translating as he went; explaining why and where his version differed from the Bible version.

I specially remember his translation of one of the beatitudes. "Blessed are the pure in heart for they shall see God." "I do not care for this translation," he told us. "I should rather translate it: 'Blessed are the single-minded for they shall obtain reality.' It is the same thing of course, but I find my version less open to misconception."

While with us, he always gave me his proofs to read for him, and discussed any corrections I thought necessary, as if I were a fellow scholar. Lislie and I spent hours every day painting on glass slides the palates of snails of which he had the largest and most varied collection in the world.

I found as our talks and proof-readings increased that my superficial agnosticism receded. Uncle Melville took my doubts very seriously; and at last I was free to express all that puzzled or outraged me in the problems of this uneasy world. He knew them all; and he knew exactly what I needed to learn, in order to have what he called "a respectable doubt". "You can't *begin* by doubting," he explained to me, "that's silly—you must find out what you are doubting *about* first! An unstudied doubt, not built upon by facts, is a *flimsy* way of thinking!"

He could be crushing; but he never crushed natural ignorance. If he did not think what you said was worth listening to he was usually silent; but if you loved him you knew the difference between his many silences. The silence of disapproval was like that of a person who bites on something he expects to find nice and finds nasty.

At this period of our illnesses Lislie and I were ordered bath-chair drives and Uncle Melville would stroll along beside us. On one occasion Lislie's bath-chair man, a loquacious and boastful person, was obviously straying from the modesty of fact. Uncle Melville stopped dead. We all stopped; then Uncle Melville *very* slowly and wordlessly drew himself up—and away from the bath-chair man, to whom he had been attentively listening—and walked on. The bath-chair man did not finish his story; nor begin another.

Uncle Melville was a Low Churchman though very open-minded except towards Rome or towards those with Roman tendencies. Science and religion were at one with him. He was a strict monogamist, though tolerant of the sins of the flesh in other people, but he had a vindictive dislike of George Eliot—whom he had never allowed Auntie Lou to meet.

"You never judge harshly ordinary bad people, Uncle Melville," I once severely reminded him, "you like them just as much as you like respectable people—sometimes more—so it seems to me very unfair, even if you think George Eliot *was* bad—and most people think she *wasn't*—to judge *her* so unkindly! I don't think you *ought* to have said you wouldn't let Auntie Lou dine with her!"

"You miss the point," Uncle Melville replied. "George Eliot was spiritually base. She ought to have made up her mind what she was going to be—moral or not—and then stuck to it. The moral law is a definite standard—break it if you must; but to pretend you haven't broken it, when you've a perfectly good mind—and must see that you *have*—that's unforgivable! It's just because she fooled most people into thinking that what she did wasn't wrong—

because *she* did it—that I objèct to her so strongly! Arrogance and lying are not my favourite faults." He snorted and glared, one eye ran towards the ceiling, the other pierced me like a gimlet. I held my tongue, but though he had inspired me with awe he had not convinced me. I still thought a mad wife was a very good excuse for living with George Lewes. "Why do you dislike the Church of Rome with such intensity?" I once asked him. "You sometimes speak as if it were worse to be a Roman Catholic than to be an infidel!" He hesitated for a moment, then he said, shaking his head like a dog jumping out of a pool, "Well, it's true—I do dislike Rome! Catholicism may not be as poisonous as infidelity—but it's the shop next door!"

He fought what was left of my Anglo-Catholicism, but he was much kinder about my doubts upon the Virgin Birth. "It doesn't really matter," he explained reassuringly, "whether you believe it or not. It's never necessary to believe an unprovable statement, though it may be desirable. The Resurrection is in a different category. Either it's true—in a spiritual though not a physical sense as Catholics believe it—or Jesus Christ and St. Paul didn't know what they were talking about. Besides there is more historical evidence for the Resurrection than there is for many other generally accepted facts. But as for the Virgin Birth there is no evidence at all. It's just a pious and possible deduction. I myself believe that the laws of birth—and of health generally—*might* be superseded by unknown laws—so I keep an open mind on the subject. The Mother of Jesus was obviously an exceptionally sensible woman; and Joseph believed the angel's acquittal of her in his dream. Still, I had much rather that you accepted natural laws as God's laws, than that you forced yourself to accept a *break* in a natural law—in order to believe a devotional hypothesis." On another occasion he said: "Life is like a drive in a high dog-cart at night. You cannot see its corners before you get to them, so all anxiety is a waste of time! When you do get to them, there is the light you bring with you which is enough to get round the corner. It is well to remember too that fatal accidents only occur once."

When I complained, as a cause for doubt, of the evils life still contained after two thousand years of Christianity, he said: "You are too impatient! You forget how young man is biologically speaking—nothing but a stumbling infant! If you had lived in the third century you would have thought that Christianity was already dead! Besides you should remember, man doesn't descend from the angels—he rises up through beasts; and it's not surprising we have some of their worst instincts still! What *is* surprising is that we are evolving some good ones that they never had."

I once asked him what was the main difference on the world's thought between Roman and Greek influence. "Rome," he answered, "always stood for Law. Greece stood for light; and light penetrates. On the whole I think the Greek influence goes further than the Roman, but we must never underestimate Law—it is the only thing that ensures a people against tyrants."

"Bad temper in an argument," he once said, "is an indication of unbelief."

When he was seventy he began to be concerned that his mental powers might be slowing up, so he set himself to learn the Welsh language of which he knew only a few words. Having completely mastered it in three weeks, he decided that there was no need to test himself further.

The 1914 War was a terrible blow to him. He was an advanced Liberal but he did not doubt that on this occasion war was forced upon us. I remember his saying, with a puzzled frown, after England had declared war "I feel as if I were in need of my dinner when I know that I am *not!*" He was particularly distressed that he was not more personally involved in the sufferings of the war, although later on he was relieved by being asked to write a pamphlet on German, and alleged British, atrocities.

He died from cerebral haemorrhage before the war ended; but after America had, by joining in, made victory for the Allies certain. He suffered from dislocation of speech after his stroke; he would ask for the "Reformation" when he wanted a pocket handkerchief; but he soon slipped into complete unconsciousness, and passed painlessly away.

People said Uncle Melville was plain and strange to look at though I had never agreed with them. His face in his coffin, which Auntie Lou characteristically demanded we should all look at, was strangely beautiful and like the face of one of Michel Angelo's prophets on the ceiling of the Sistine Chapel. I don't know if Uncle Melville was a saint; but I think he was a singularly complete Christian. After his death Lislie and I stayed with Auntie Lou to help her read and sort the flood of letters that came to her from all over the world. The letters came not only from the great scholars of different European nations, or from his former students, but often from ignorant and unlikely people whom a chance word or the shaft of his deep integrity had helped in their private emergencies. He was not only one of the greatest of our scholars. Uncle Melville had as well a deep and child-like heart.

Tragedy had pierced him deeply. He lost an enchanting and promising boy of five years old from diphtheria, and his only other son led a sadly restricted life under a mental cloud. His one daughter was a great pride and joy to him, for Ruth Gwatkin was a fine scholar and became a great educational force as a teacher. In spite of the immense gulf of thought and feeling between himself and Auntie Lou, theirs could be called a happy marriage, for they loved and deeply respected each other to the end. For a short time after they were both over sixty they began to quarrel about their growing infirmities. Auntie Lou was almost incredibly impatient and chafed at Uncle Melville's increasing deafness. Unfairly scolded for what he felt as a sharp physical affliction, Uncle Melville showed resentment and even bursts of anger; but suddenly they both realized that they were breaking up the harmony of their married life, and in a most remarkable way they restored their former tolerance of each other's differences, expanding into a deeper tenderness, until death separated them.

Auntie Lou had a very strong and impressive personality. Their differences of thought and feeling were so great that it was amazing to think of them contentedly under the same roof.

While he was reticent, bone-accurate, extraordinarily sensitive to the feelings of others and minutely observant; Auntie Lou was demonstrative, inaccurate and appallingly outspoken. There seemed no inhibitions in her mind at all, and no sense of privacy. Neither tact nor common sense restrained her. Yet she was intensely warm-hearted and generous to a fault. She always wanted to help, sometimes when it would have been kinder not to see that help was needed; but no effort or personal sacrifice would have been too great for her to make for those she loved. Nor was she a fool, she was an angel who rushed in—sometimes with the effect of folly.

Lislie said truly of her: "If anything happened to Auntie Lou, I should feel as if a fire had gone out." She was beautiful to look at in her old age. I saw her a few weeks before her death from bronchitis, sitting up in bed, brave as a lion and enthusiastic as an eager child. Her white hair and beautiful brown eyes happily contrasted with a scarlet dressing gown. I think she liked the taste of life better than anyone I have ever known.

20

Elena's new home, the Corner Cupboard, was a little slice of a lovely old red-brick house with white portals, sandwiched between two stately mansions; it contained powder closets and had been lived in by Oliver Cromwell. Our garden gate opened upon an emerald velvet lawn opposite the main doorway of Salisbury Cathedral.

I loved it almost as much as Elena loved it; but I must admit that during the many long visits I paid there, the life of the Close never entered deeply into my own.

I think that I came to know, with varying degrees of intimacy, as Elena herself did, all its inhabitants; but when Elena died nothing of Salisbury but the deep imprint of her memory was left to me.

I preferred "the Dog's Dean" as he was generally called to any of its other inhabitants.

He was a very tall, good-looking, elderly man—I think a bachelor —who called on us at stated intervals accompanied by an Aberdeen, who partially, if not totally, controlled his activities.

It was considered that the Dean called oftenest where the dog showed a preference; but I doubt if the Aberdeen cared greatly for any of the Close households. We were, I think, defective in smells; however he knew his duty and had imperturbably good manners. He almost wiped his paws on the mat before entering a house; and even Elena, who hated dogs, welcomed him cordially. He always sat about a yard from the Dean's chair, his ears cocked, his eyes fastened upon his companion's face; and when he thought the Dean had talked enough—he paid no attention to anybody else's conversation—he would advance firmly up to his knee, and place a paw upon it, expressing with absolute lucidity that it was time to be off. The Dean would pay no apparent attention to this hint, but a few minutes later the visit would come to an end. When the Dean died the Aberdeen lay on his grave for five days and nights, then returned to his former home, ate a last meal and incontinently died.

I do not think any Cathedral Close novels, even Trollope's, though deservedly immortal, were in the least like the life which I experienced at the extreme end of the nineteenth century. His generation, earlier than my own, must have been far more robust. The temperature of the Salisbury Close as I found it was tepid; and the life anaemic. Cathedral households, if they contained tyrants at all, contained mild ones. I had the confidence of most of the daughters; and they were not so much crushed as gently dry-cleaned, by example. No one broke, or dreamed of breaking, any of the ten commandments, though I doubt if they were capable of keeping in its entirety the command to love anything or anybody "with all their hearts". A blackmailer would, I am sure, have had a very thin time collecting their past histories; but—except for the Precentor, who burned with a passionate love for music—I was not conscious of any warmth at all.

Nobody really minded the hardships of the poor; no one visited prisons; no one was haunted by the treatment of the insane. They were not glaringly rich, but all were comfortably off and had at least two, more generally four, servants. They went to church very regularly, and had a constant and pleasant social life among people like themselves. They visited any sick they knew all about, one bed-ridden invalid was a special favourite and couldn't have known what to do with the amount of flowers she received daily. As far as they had an aim, it may have been said to be mildly beneficial and to include a careful affection for the Cathedral. Dissenters really ruffled them. Most of them were strongly Conservative in politics; and although Mr. Gladstone had been dead some years they still shuddered at his name, as good Republicans in America to-day still shudder at Roosevelt's.

The Dog's Dean was faintly Liberal in tendency. He had a sense of humour and though extraordinarily shy and needing a lot of thawing, he was eventually very good company.

There was a Theological Training College vaguely attached to the Cathedral and Elena had been asked to entertain a few of the students fortnightly.

She agreed very reluctantly to this male adventure. However, soon after my arrival we prepared a gala tea for the students. I think about twelve of them came. The entertainment was to consist in our showing them an extensive collection of water-colour sketches, chiefly landscapes, painted all over the travelled world by Mrs. Russell Gurney and her niece, Elena. The sketches, though some of them were of interesting places, all looked rather alike, as, shown in large quantities, careful water colours are apt to look.

We gave the students a very good tea, and while showing them the sketches we told them stories of our own late travels and encouraged them to tell us any experiences of their own. The whole occasion became very gay and was punctuated by gales of laughter. On leaving they all assured us that they had never enjoyed any of their afternoon entertainments so much; but the conclusion of the entertainment was much less successful. Elena received a reproving letter from the Head of the Training College. He asserted that in future any entertainment offered must be of a far graver nature. A teacher at the choir school had actually seen a group of theological students coming out of our gate laughing uproariously.

I had never seen Elena so thoroughly annoyed; but to my great relief she was not annoyed with me. She wrote a tart letter to the Head of the Theological College in which she said that she had been present throughout the entire occasion, and that no unseemly mirth of any kind had taken place, what laughter there was had been entirely harmless and that as she had had no idea that her invitations could be open to such impertinent criticism, she must regretfully withdraw them, and would not expect to see his students again. She then sent for the Dean, and showed him both letters. He came out very strongly on our side. "Silly fellow! Silly fellow!" he exclaimed. "If his students don't know how to laugh, theology will be thrown away upon them!" I don't know what he said to the Head of the

Training College, but Elena eventually received a letter of apology. She stuck, however, to her decision not to have the students again. I had enjoyed the occasion, but I had not been specially attracted by any of the young men, so that I acquiesced quite willingly in their perpetual exile.

An incident that I minded much more seriously took place soon after. Elena had arranged for a staid and middle-aged gardener—lent by one of the Minor Canons—to take me out in a pony cart for afternoon drives.

I greatly enjoyed these drives; but unfortunately the gardener and I talked politics. A period of severe unemployment had set in all over England; and the gardener knew why. Hitherto I had supposed that unemployment chiefly depended upon being unemployable.

The gardener opened my eyes once and for all. He told me case after case from among his own extremely respectable acquaintances and relationships. He knew both facts and figures. I was appalled by these family tragedies; convinced; and greatly agitated; and I made the mistake on my return of trying to convince Elena. I failed utterly, and what was worse, she put an instant end to my pony-cart excursions. Had I not been so horror-struck as to frighten her she would even have complained to the Canon of his gardener. This dreadful penalty I managed to evade; but Elena and I remained at variance upon the subject of unemployment ever afterwards.

Sin, in Elena's eyes, was the only cause of social insecurity; and the sin had to be placed upon the shoulders of the insecure. Why, I asked—granting sin to be the only cause—should not the sin rest upon the secure? They had education, opportunity and resources, whereas the insecure had none of these things and could not even like their own sense of insecurity very much.

Elena flushed and became stern. There was always the structure of the Church and State, inextricably interwound, in the background of her mind, while mine possessed no such explanatory architecture.

I also realized that although she must have come into touch with dire poverty while keeping house for Alfred Gurney at St. Barnabas, Pimlico, she had never lived, as I had at Swanscombe, surrounded by nothing else and in perpetual personal contact, often of a highly confidential and friendly nature, with the sufferers themselves. It was true that we did not suffer much from unemployment in Swanscombe, because we had cement works, a large paper factory and the docks; but we had poverty—and sin.

I once greatly admired what we used to call "a corset cover" of Elena's. It was a dainty muslin bodice with a border of lace to be worn over stays. "But, dear," she said, "why don't you get one like it—they are very easy to buy! I will give you the address of the shop where I get mine." "But what does it cost?" I asked her. "Very little," she replied. "This one was only a guinea."

I said no more. My white cotton covers cost one and elevenpence ha'penny.

Elena was infinitely sensitive and tender-hearted. She was besides inured to self-discipline and a spiritual austerity of living that was beyond most people's inclination or capacity; but she was totally ignorant of what kind of life people without regular incomes have to live.

The life of the Close was bogged down by the same sense of unreality; and I think that it had a very curious and restrictive effect upon the human beings who lived it. It was as if they *could* not, rather than *would* not, go beyond a very small and inadequate portion of their own mental and emotional endowment.

They neither felt nor acted with intensity. When they met an emotion they dodged it—if a thought interfered with their pre-arranged beliefs they looked the other way, or broke it up by irrelevance. They did not create. What they knew, and most of them were scholars, or at the least highly educated students, was blocked from percolating through their daily habits by ingrained personal preferences.

The only one of them who could be said to use, with passion, what he had acquired, was the Precentor. I can see him now, rushing bright-eyed, his white hair waving in the breeze, over the velvet lawn of the Close, hugging a piece of music to his breast. He was literally never without one. He knew how to play most musical instruments. He sang like an angel. The choir school palpitated to his resurgent spirit. He was alive, and had an aim. Madrigals were his aim, and all the young, or their seducible

163

elders, of the Cathedral Close sang madrigals in season and out of season.

His colleagues, alas, were bored by his ardour; and even Elena said that she thought the Precentor was exaggeratedly fond of music. The main trouble with the inhabitants of the Cathedral Close, as I saw them, was that they all thought life itself—even religious life— an exaggeration.

21

This last real parting from my home in 1904 cost me more than any other. I think that even then I realized something of my parents' courage and grief in letting me go when they needed me most, but I am amazed at how little in comparison to what they must both have suffered, I suffered for them. It was for Mary and for my boys' club that I felt my heart torn out by the roots. I knew Mary's dilemma was acute and I saw no solution for it. The boys' club still ran on, under my self-sacrificing teacher friends, but they had lost my highway and hedges scallywags. "Bad" boys believed in me and I in them—and now this band of cheerful marauders had withdrawn. I felt this winter was my last chance; I could still win them back; but soon they would be too old to dare to be seen in company with the virtuous. Under the pall of these self-inflated anxieties, I overlooked the long loneliness of my parents; each having gone so far away from the other, and now on the brink of losing permanently the support of both their remaining daughters.

My mother had always had one of us to nurse her, and to react with sympathy and ardour to her needs; but I doubt if my mother felt more lost at this parting than my father, for he had never had to live his church life without at least one child's active and enthusiastic co-operation. We went to all his services, we took his Sunday-school classes, visited and reported on his districts, ran societies and greatly admired his sermons, which were indeed well worth admiring.

Now he had to take the full burden of his work upon his own shoulders; in silence and alone.

I think it must have been the silence which so terrified and discouraged him; and little by little broke down his nerves and sapped his jokes.

He had always prized youth too much—his own backed up by his children's—and now someone spoke of him, though he was only fifty, as "the old gentleman". He told me about it with a wistfulness that showed me he had been stabbed to the heart. "I hadn't thought I was old, Fissy," he said sadly. "Old age seems to come so quickly —and it will stay so long!"

I think that it was about this time that my father rejected his long love for England; and began to wish he had never left the land of his birth.

Yet when he went back on long visits to his mother and brothers, the terrific speed and energy of American life daunted and puzzled him. I think the only time when he was really happy was when he was on journeys between the two countries, when the lost Atlantis of his dreams could shine and beckon him in both directions at once, although he could never reach it by arriving at either of them.

Next to his own journeys he rejoiced in mine.

Both he and Elena came to see me off to St. Moritz; standing side by side on the platform, they were a curious juxtaposition of personalities.

Elena's controlled tender gravity and my father's impetuous wild optimism were left to make terms with each other, after the slender bridge between them was ruthlessly withdrawn; and when I turned to my new companion I felt as if I had inadvertently stumbled over a precipice.

Molly was by far the most human and kindly of a large Punch and Judy Yorkshire family. She was absorbed—and always remained absorbed—in family rows, grudges and competitions; and in the great efforts which she made to satisfy Herbert, who was never satisfied. She was much too fat for her age; and her very good features were spoiled by a bad complexion and a perpetually harried expression. Her health was often far from good, and she would retire to bed mysteriously refusing to see a doctor or to accept food or nursing, threatening dire disaster and breakdown, till I was thoroughly terrified, and even Herbert roused to some form of aggressive reaction. She would then suddenly get up and function as before. Molly was a good housekeeper, economical and hard-working; and her staff worked well with her and for her. The villa was beautifully clean, and totally uninteresting inside and out. This I hardly noticed since the situation was perfect and from my balcony there was nothing between me and the peak the villa was built on but blazing snow. The air was so pure and fine that it was a joy to breathe each separate breath. The sun poured through the house all day long. The sky above was so blue the senses ached with it; and the air tasted of frozen pine and that mysterious cold sweetness of untouched snows. The path from the village only went a hundred yards beyond the villa; and ended in unruffled depths of snow.

There could not have been a healthier place in the world. I had to fight for my promised south room with its single balcony, since Herbert not unnaturally thought the small sum I paid and my slight services would hardly be worth it; but in the end he ungraciously supported his sister's offer and as time went on I think they both found me sufficiently useful, though they never burdened me with duties. I got on rather too well with all the boys. I mended their stockings and helped Molly to nurse them when they were sick and finally Herbert found an even greater usefulness in my handling of parents. Letters to them and visits from them were generally made over to me. Neither Herbert nor Molly could stand parents. Their manners to all strangers were deplorable since their shyness was of an aggressive nature, like the sudden rushes and plunges of distraught animals; and they could not bear, though they knew they must, outside interference or criticism; least of all from people whom they were under an obligation to satisfy.

I often had to tell the parents things which were in themselves annoying; to frustrate their wishes or to upset their plans; but at least I could do all these, often necessary things, without stamping on their corns. I whole-heartedly liked the boys; and the parents soon sensed my feeling for their offspring and believed me when I pointed out the real advantages they acquired by leaving them where they were. No place in St. Moritz was as healthy nor, for young people, so well run. Herbert was quite sensible about rules. He worked hand in glove with Dr. Holland, and when the boys were delicate he took the right precautions without fussing them.

He was bullying and tyrannical with the boys but I think according to his lights he was just. I never let the boys complain to me of him, but their dislike was unmistakable. It would have been easy for Molly to have been liked by them if she had taken the trouble, for she was really kind at heart, but too preoccupied and discouraged to put herself into other peoples' lives. She simply thought the boys were different kinds of trouble, with physical needs which must be met, she never thought of them as enchanting and vulnerable individuals.

Yet if the boys could have judged Molly by the sandwiches she cut for them they would have loved her. I never ceased to like Molly just as much and just as little as I had liked her when we first met, but I had only one moment of real sympathy with Herbert.

It was when Keith Murray, the most delicate of the boys, was very ill with a high temperature. Herbert had to act as goal-keeper in an important match; he was—characteristically—a magnificent goal-keeper. Before he went, he came on to my balcony and stared at me with his fish-like eyes full of misery. "I've got a damned bad headache," he said at last, "and I've got to go off to the rink to play. If Keith's worse you know where to find me."

I suddenly realized that it was a heartache not a headache that he was suffering from; he was in dire fear for Keith, and would have done anything to save him. For that one hour I was genuinely sorry for Herbert, and with him; but Keith recovered and so did my chronic antagonism.

Herbert had six boys that winter, and two young men, patients of Dr. Holland who needed coaching. One arrived soon after the villa opened, but the other was not to come out till just before Christmas. The first one—Mr. Marshall—was a pink shrimp of a fellow with a narrow chest and a tiny fringe of pale yellow moustache. He played no very great part in the winter's life. I think now I might well have been kinder to him than I was. I remember with regret that he once said I had the poison of asps under my lips; and that on another occasion he told me that no man would dare to try to flirt with me—I had too sharp a tongue. I took this latter criticism with philosophy, for there was no one that I cared to flirt with under the villa's roof; but I was sorry about the asps.

The whole atmosphere of the place was one of such inordinate mental savagery that I found myself in self-defence using what weapons I had. Herbert was my chief adversary. He was coarse, foul-mouthed and so relentlessly aggressive that he stirred up a good deal of unnecessary trouble all round him. No one in the house got on with Herbert, the best they could manage was to get away as soon as possible from his onslaughts. I had never heard anyone talk as Herbert talked or behave as mannerlessly as he behaved. At first I was simply appalled and avoided him as much as possible, but as time went on, when I couldn't avoid him I set to work to answer him back. I did not enjoy these conversational controversies which followed; they both irritated and exhausted me physically and mentally, nor did they seem to get either of us any distance from where we started. I supposed that Herbert felt as annoyed and disgusted with me as I did with him; but the reverse was true. He thoroughly enjoyed these verbal fisticuffs, except when they took place in the presence of the boys, and he got the worst of them; then, as was but natural, he became offended. He knew no more of my mind than I did of his; and therefore did not dream that I was chronically offended with him.

Not finding anyone with whom I felt much at home I fell in love with the mountains.

In all sport and pleasure places it is very easy to go beyond the range of hotel guests—half an hour's walking away from the centre of interest does it. I found snow pathways into woods, where nothing moved but an occasional wood-pecker—or a garland of snow dislodging itself from a pine bough.

The silence that surrounds snow mountains is the most attentive silence in the world. There are times when you feel certain that someone has just finished speaking, or if you wait a moment—will begin.

The sea cannot be quite silent, even a lake lisps against its low shore; and the sky is too far away to bring you what it has, but a mountain holds your breath, listening.

Once this winter I woke at dawn and found the whole world had gone blue—the most intense, extravagant blue—a blue deeper than the Capri grotto. Mountains, air and sky were all drenched in this burning, blazing azure. The little town below was the same colour. It was as if I had waked up to find myself in the heart of a jewel.

There was no one in the house who would have cared to share its splendour with me if I had dared to rouse them, so wrapped in a blanket I sat enjoying it alone, until slowly the miracle withdrew and the blue turned into its usual cold grey, the sky separating itself from the earth like a lover parting from his mistress.

In all the five winters I lived in the Swiss mountains I never again saw a blue dawn, though people told me that they too had seen one; nor did I ever find out what caused it. There was no mist, the blue air was quite clear, and everything in it had its perfect form.

There was no sport life at St. Moritz in early November, so on Saturdays we often went on picnics, except Herbert, who wisely avoided occasions of conviviality.

Once we walked all round the lake. Snow covered all the peaks but very little lay on the ground. It was an unforgettable apricot-coloured day. The short larches were still yellow and stood like candles in daylight, against the dark screen of pines. Streams were not wholly frozen, and gurgled and chuckled their way through the creeping ice. The peaks gleamed like polished silver above the darkening valley floor. The walk was far beyond my strength, but I enjoyed every moment of it, till I got too exhausted to move; and then suddenly I experienced the mystery of second wind. I found I could move quite easily again, but in a new way, as if I were lighter and were using less breath. I seemed impelled by a strength which did not belong to me. It was as if Nature held out a crutch to a cripple.

I got home somehow; and was violently scolded by Herbert; nor did I then realize that part of his scolding was anxiety.

On the next occasion, before the heavy winter snows fell, we drove to Silvaplana. There had been several severe frosts, and the lake had frozen hard from shore to shore.

I had just begun to learn to skate, for on their second winter Dr. Holland told his patients that they *should* skate, but not fall, which was rather like telling someone who had never skated before, to walk without breathing. Still, I enjoyed the adventure; and was on this occasion seized by two boys who pulled me rapidly along until I found my feet. The resilient ice above deep water was quite unlike the rink ice. The skates bit into it, giving as well as taking, support

Even one boy—even half a finger of a flying boy—gave me enough courage to float along by myself. Never in my life had I known such joy in movement. A swallow, tossing away the air from the knife-blade of his wings, could not have felt more sure of the sense of flight.

A fiery sunset cut crimson and gold swathes out of the zig-zag pass, the valley spread in an apricot mist before us. The reeds were bright orange fading into spectral gold. The air was still and so cold that breathing seemed another form of strenuous exercise. Ahead of us the Maloja Pass streamed in a golden pathway, towards Italy; behind us was St. Moritz and the approaching dark. I could hardly bear to turn when Herbert shouted harshly to us to come back at once. It was growing late, and the ice beyond us was uncertain in the dark.

There was a little inn near the lake's edge where we all drank hot *Glühwein*; and as we drove back a huge thin-looking moon, enormously round and brighter than the stars, swam in front of a peak, and lit us home.

The new young man arrived just before Christmas; his name was Ernan Forbes Dennis; he had had several chest illnesses and his eldest brother had died of T.B., so although he had not yet developed it himself, it was necessary for him to take careful precautions. His mother and a friend had come up with him to stay in one of the smaller hotels affiliated to the Kulm; and as he was one of Sir Thomas Barlow's patients, Dr. Holland was anxious for everything possible to be done for him. He was a shy young man, Molly told me, unused to strangers since he had been brought up for years on account of his health by an anxious widowed mother, in a lonely Cornish village. We must do our best to make him feel at home, and both Herbert and Molly impressed upon me that they depended on my helping them. Ernan and I were the same age, and they somehow thought that Mr. Marshall was not exactly the sort of young man with whom the new one would make friends.

Molly and I were alone together in our one small sitting room when Ernan was announced. I do not know why I had put on my one full evening dress, of pale yellow satin, because I did not usually wear it for evenings at home.

My husband told me afterwards that he said to himself, "I should like to marry that girl in the yellow dress", but although I can remember everything that happened, and just how he looked on that first occasion, no such idea struck me. I simply thought he *wasn't* only a boy; and that in spite of his shyness, he had very good manners; and I was sorry for him on both these accounts.

Later on in the evening when Molly shouted at him across the table that he was "a damned fool!" for a mistake in his first attempt at bridge, and Herbert shut his eyes and groaned, I felt still sorrier.

Ernan was a tall young man with wavy dark hair, lighter than his thick straight eye-brows, and very dark eyes. He had the high cheek bones of a Scot and one of the finest noses I have ever seen, which had run in his family for centuries, and adorned several ancient portraits. I liked his smile, and that first evening, when he had very little to smile at, I tried my best to let him feel that he was not quite alone in a mad-house being shouted at by unfriendly lunatics.

I cannot think why Herbert and Molly behaved so much worse than usual, when they had carefully prepared me for their behaving better; but I think now that they were embarrassed at being so politely treated by their new guest.

They never did get used to Ernan's manners but Molly became sincerely attached to him; and Herbert, perhaps remembering Sir Thomas Barlow, or perhaps vaguely aware of some dangerous quality in the new young man that might get the better of him if he gave way too much to his natural fits of bullying, behaved slightly better in Ernan's company, and to him personally, than he behaved to the rest of his large family. Ernan had the extremely gentle voice of a Highlander, but he had also the sudden sharp sparkle of the eye common to people whose toes are not wisely trodden on.

It was some weeks before I knew what Ernan thought of Herbert and Molly—but I could guess.

I went to bed much more happily than usual that night, for I thought to myself, "There is someone under the same roof who speaks my language."

22

It was easy to slide into companionship with Ernan.

Molly and Herbert, who looked upon us with a certain indulgence as exotic monsters belonging to the same species, encouraged the beginning of our relationship. Hard-hitting sports, dancing and drinks being beyond either our physical capacities or our tastes, compulsorily isolated us both from St. Moritz life. We were to the rest of the villa's inhabitants not so much outcasts, for we were both sufficiently adjustable to be slightly popular, but players of an unknown game, of which none of them knew the rules. They often liked to talk to us when they had nothing else to do. But I think they privately considered these conversations as "twaddle from the underworld".

We were both ordered afternoon walks—nobody else was— the others played compulsory games; and so without planning for it we began—I think from the third day—to take our walks together; and to play the oldest game in the world.

I don't know how far awareness of his feelings went with Ernan, but my awareness came suddenly and with precision, through a disappointment. A famous orchestra was to come up to St. Moritz for an overnight concert; and Ernan, to whom music was a perpetual holiday as reading was to me, did not ask me to go with him. It was a shock to me since by this time I had supposed he would ask me to share any of his pleasures; but to him it was a still greater shock, for he had taken for granted that we should go together without his asking.

We had been brought up very differently. I expected, and appreciated "les situations nettes" while Ernan had learned as strenuously how to avoid them. To me the *spoken* word was almost as necessary as a compass is to a mariner, while to Ernan thoughts narrowed into words imprisoned, rather than relieved, the processes of his understanding.

He learned by saturation, I by clear and quickly grasped definitions. Our objects were almost universally the same; but our approaches were entirely different.

We went to the concert separately, dismayed and unhappy, Ernan with a friend of his mother's and I with one of mine. I was surprised how much this division mattered to me. It stung my pride like fire, and it did more than sting my pride—it hurt my heart. "If he can hurt me like this," I thought, "I must be falling in love with him!"

We sat just within sight of each other in the packed hall; and the orchestra played Schubert's "Unfinished Symphony".

Our eyes met, and the physical separation ceased to matter. Schubert took us as a great wave seizes on some unwary onlooker, and flung us together—far beyond our depth—into an unplumbed sea. But we were together; and even to me, who liked explanation, no further explanation seemed necessary.

Ernan contrived that we should all take tea together at Hanselmann's after the concert; and in the same skilled manner he succeeded in losing the other two.

The evening was still, and very cold; the sky full of brilliant stars; and the small sickle of a frosty moon glittered like an earring on an invisible head.

Our daily walks went on, and slowly we explained the lives that lay behind us.

There was deep in my blood the unfoliaged plainness of my Quaker ancestors. I moved directly if I moved at all; and trampled pitilessly on the smooth flowers of illusion. In Ernan's blood was high-paced chivalry, deep loyalties and unswerving devotion. He too could be pitiless but in quite a different way. He was moved by angers that were perfectly strange to me, because I had never envisaged the rights which to him were violated; but I often used criticism where he used kindness. We both had a great desire for truth in action, but we had not learned how to apply skill to our actions; nor were we sure of where to look for truth.

The world out of which he had made his life was wholly unlike mine. In both of us our Scottish ancestry had the strongest sway; but the MacDonalds I came from had already been through the sieve of America; his blood was directly Highland. The Forbes clan lived in a glen in the North of Aberdeenshire beyond Strathdon. Ernan's grandfather, Sir John Forbes, had served in India half his lifetime, at a period when great public servants—and he was the finest of cavalry generals—were treated as kings; and when he retired to his glen with the mountain of Lonach behind his home, he felt himself to be—as indeed he was—monarch of all he surveyed.

Sir John Forbes was a passionately devoted servant to Queen Victoria, and was treated by her as a personal friend. He was often summoned to Balmoral; and his whole life was based upon single-hearted loyalty to the Crown.

He was not a rich man, and had married an extravagantly beautiful wife, who took for granted in her gracious and delicate way that there was really nothing they could not afford. She was a Drummond of Megginch, married at thirteen, and left behind, when her husband first took up his service in India, with his sisters, who were more than twice her age and who had expected to train her in the duties of a wife. She asked for the keys of the household on her arrival, and held undisputed sway until her husband's return. Sir John and Lady Forbes had nine living children, and brought them up in a world that was already, had they but known it, no longer theirs. All Ernan's aunts and uncles were interesting personalities, with gifts of effortless courage and good wits, besides very exceptional good looks.

They had their failings, the chief of which was that their sense of reality was dim. They would have died for what they believed, but they believed things for which it is not now considered necessary to die. Gordon Forbes achieved marked distinction and success in South Africa. He was chosen by Rhodes as one of his two executors. "Because," Rhodes wrote of Gordon, "he is one of the only two honest men I have ever met." All Gordon's sisters adored him. He was to have re-made the fortune of his family but Gordon was killed in the regiment which his nephew Fred Dennis commanded, early in the 1914 war.

My husband's mother, Maimie, was the eldest of the five beautiful sisters, Lilla, Emily, Katie and Chattie. Their old family doctor told me that when the sisters came into the ball-room, everyone in the room stood up to look at them. Men leaped on to tables and drank toasts to them out of their dancing slippers. It was a question of great controversial heat which of the five sisters was the most beautiful.

Each had their mother's exquisite features, as if a celestial sculptor had modelled the lines of chin and brow, and if it was difficult to know which was the most beautiful it was also difficult to know which was the proudest. They all had fierce and difficult tempers behind the softest manners in the world.

The two eldest married well enough, but not, the others thought, into the circle they ought to have entered. The other three decided to marry dukes, or to remain unmarried. Aunt Chattie nearly found her duke, but without a dowry the heir's family felt that he must be spirited away across the world, and kept there till Aunt Chattie's pride put up a final barrier against him. In default of dukes the three remained, splendidly refusing everybody else; until their short and lovely day was over.

The aunts had almost nothing to live on when their parents died and Inverernan passed to their eldest brother's keeping; and they made that little less by refusing to live together. Aunt Emily spent many years with her best friend, Lady Louisa D'Arcy Osbourne, a dynamic woman who all but strangled a burglar when she was eighty-four; and Aunt Katie found a devoted friend in Miss Haye, another member of an ancient Scottish family. "How wise dear Katie is," Aunt Lilla commented, "to live with her best friend rather than with one of her sisters! Bosom friends lick your boots—sisters seldom do." All the aunts were witty—and could be the best of company; but Aunt Emily was perhaps the wittiest of them all; and I think when you knew her, the kindest; but she took some knowing.

Maimie, Ernan's mother, married a Cornishman of an extremely old and well-endowed family. At one period of their existence the Dennises, whose name was supposed to come from the Danes, their remote ancestors, had held fourteen estates, in various European countries as well as in their own; but they got rid of what they owned with remarkable celerity, though not of their love for travelling. Mamma and Papa, as their children always called them, had been madly in love. After their marriage they travelled for three years in a long childless ecstasy; and then by some strange whim bought a small estate, six miles from Bude, where it was damp, solitary and not even beautiful, and settled down to found their family.

The Dennises stuck to the Church like glue and when Truro Cathedral wanted a roof the money that should have educated their four sons, and started them in life, went into it.

Through the long, trackless years that followed they became curiously and tragically alienated from each other. Papa was passionately theological and nearly became a clergyman; but lay baptism stuck in his throat, and at the last moment he gave up taking orders, and decided on farming. He felt that the losses that ensued were largely induced by Maimie's taking away his horses for a drive whenever he needed them most. Maimie's health, and that of her children, became her chief preoccupation.

Their passion for the Church dominated both their lives; and they tried with varying success to pass it on to their sons. Both of them were greatly beloved by all their neighbours, and looked up to by the parish of Bridgerule; and they themselves only hated dissenters.

Their sons had to break into life as best they could. Only Ralph, the eldest, was normally educated; he was even sent to Oxford, where he tragically contracted T.B. and died at twenty-one. He was a model eldest child; and his death broke up his home much as Wilmett's did mine. Stanley had the sense to run away to his Uncle Gordon in South Africa, who found him a well-paid but arduous and solitary job in the mines. Stanley was the strongest of the family, and perhaps the one most able to carve his way through the tough hide of the world. After a most successful start he died from pneumonia—unable to survive three days by wagon across the Veldt to the nearest hospital.

Fred was a dare-devil, beloved, inconsequent and unconquerable. Five hundred Boer horsemen rode over him as he lay wounded and left behind by his retreating comrades in the South African War;

and in the World War, as Colonel of the 7/8th K.O.S.B.'s, he won immortal honour. Before he was killed, Fred was wounded in all nine times; he won the D.S.O. with a double bar, and was one of the only two officers to be decorated on the field of battle by Sir Douglas Haig himself. "I think he was without doubt", one of his brother officers told me, "the bravest regimental officer in the British Army."

Ernan fought Fred, who was four years his senior, as soon as he could get out of his cradle. He could not of course master him immediately, but he did him great damage at some expense to himself throughout their nursery existence. Their ferocity was only equalled by their devotion to each other. Ernan gave up his majority and a fair chance of survival, by insisting on leaving the Poona Horse in 1917 when they were ordered to Egypt, so that he could remain in France and serve under Fred.

It is difficult to say why the three younger boys were not educated more normally. I think Mamma imagined that Royal Hands might be out-stretched to place them suitably in their Service. There were always floating about in her mind, three dynamic powers—the Church, the Army and the Diplomatic. And after all, Ralph, who had been normally educated, died. Stan ran away. Fred determined, and somehow succeeded, in getting into the Army. Mamma was sure that Ernan *was* going to die, and in her passionate endeavour to save him she drained nearly all the life out of him. Papa died, soon after Ralph, by taking a solitary walk in winter over the Cairngorm mountains.

Ernan, then thirteen, was removed from St. Edward's School at Oxford, where he was doing brilliantly; and put in charge of their estate. This he managed with some skill, plus a small chicken farm, in utter solitude, and through an endless sense of frustration, till the damp climate and perhaps the loneliness, took its toll of him. He ran away at twenty to London, and demanded Sir Thomas Barlow's advice and help. He could not bear his life in Cornwall any longer, and insisted on being allowed to go to Oxford. Sir Thomas Barlow's advice was a preliminary winter at St. Moritz. Mamma after stormy scenes gave way, but insisted on accompanying Ernan to St. Moritz. Mamma would have accepted any personal sacrifice in order to save any of her children; and Ernan—after Ralph—was her favourite child. Her virtues were "whipped by her faults"; but none the less they were indomitable virtues.

The world of to-day may be more insecure than it was fifty years ago, especially for the more privileged. But what did these privileges, when they were at the peak, deprive us of, as well as provide for us?

No child of to-day could be so mishandled by loving parents and incompetent doctors as both Ernan and I were fifty years ago. In the late nineteenth century all girls—and often exceptionally gifted boys—were at the mercy of parents who were dependent on unrealities and were in a position to let their personal prejudices override common sense.

We might grow up as geniuses; we might force ourselves into jobs we had to learn backwards; we might become clever salesmen or successful crooks; but we were not obliged to learn what could provide us with an "honest" living.

Freedom is a dangerous commodity when we do not know what we are free for; and children cannot well make this decision for themselves unless they are trained in a practical manner to face the open market of the world.

23

The preoccupation of falling in love is so intense that though it is probable a lover never again uses his eyes to so much purpose, he may be accounted blind, since his eyes are wholly absorbed in one particular vision.

This may explain the incredible blindness which hid from me, and I think from Ernan, what our small world thought of our increasing friendship.

I don't know when they began to be seriously concerned about it, but all their thoughts seem to have run on similar lines. We were too young, too delicate, too resourceless, to think of marriage. But we were not thinking of marriage. We were thinking of love and death. Habitations and incomes had as yet occurred to neither of us.

We did not confine our wanderings to woods and remote parts, since we had no idea of concealment. We attended all the big sporting events side by side; and were constantly seen together in the village street. Long afterwards I was told by someone who had shared this winter with us that we were spoken of in St. Moritz as "the handsome twins", although my proletarian nose bore no relationship to Ernan's fine Greek feature. But we were less pleasantly considered by our immediate acquaintance. Mamma, Constance Barnes and their circle; Herbert and Molly, with Dr. Holland in the background, were all united in disapproval and vexation. Yet curiously enough no one attacked us directly.

The first bomb-shell that went off was not only irrelevant but as farcical as the Marx Brothers.

It was my custom always to avoid Herbert's society. My south balcony overlooked the one path up from the village so that I could see his most distant approach; and take steps accordingly. Unless I knew he was tied up with the boys, or could count on Molly's presence, I never went into the rest of the house.

However on one occasion Molly, whom I had expected to find in the sitting room, failed me. Herbert came in, earlier than usual, and with a less belligerent air. After a few preliminary observations, he asked me if I thought a person could or should have more than one friend. I replied that I myself had twelve intimate friends, and hoped to have many more.

We squabbled about this uncertain subject for some time, until to my astonishment Herbert asked point-blank if I considered him one of my twelve. I am afraid I replied only too promptly, "No—certainly not!" Herbert looked aggrieved but persisted, "What am I if I am not your friend—I'm certainly not an enemy!" "You are my host," I replied gingerly, "and of course an acquaintance." Herbert flushed, flung back his head like an angry horse and shouted rather than said: "Well, it doesn't matter to me what you feel about me! I asked Dr. Holland if you were fit to marry and he said you weren't!"

I was so astonished that I lost my breath. I was also exceedingly angry; and when I had recovered it I said, "You had no business to ask Dr. Holland such a question, and he had still less business to answer it!"

Herbert dashed out of the room and banged the door. But not even that bang, which shook the house, did anything to enlighten me as to the nature of Herbert's feelings.

Molly came to my room some hours later, declaring that I had been most cruel to Herbert, and demanding why I wouldn't marry him. I simply stared at her with my mouth open. This slap in the face, then, was a declaration of love! I suppose I should have felt sorry for Herbert, and flattered by his offer.

However I was *not* sorry for Herbert, and I was far from feeling flattered. I had always avoided him, and when I could not help being in his presence, I had always fought him.

I had never shown him by word or look a moment's friendliness, except on that one occasion when I saw his anxiety about Keith.

I thought Herbert a bully, a coarse, conceited and cruel bully; and I knew that I was not alone in my opinion.

Nevertheless, I can see now that I had overlooked one fact that may have misled Herbert as to my feelings.

He knew that I had stood by his interests; and to the extent of my power served them. I had felt free to uphold Herbert and Molly to the general public; and to the boys themselves; so that it may have occurred to Herbert, who never believed in anyone's disinterested actions, that I envisaged my interests as being some day a part of his own.

After several hours of inflammatory talk with Molly, who was not only angry and reproachful but still determined to persuade me to marry Herbert, I finally convinced her that not wild horses—not even the maddened cows set loose upon St. Blandina in the Coliseum —could toss me into such a predicament.

I naturally suggested leaving the house at once, but Molly said this was exactly what Herbert didn't want. If I left, rumours of what had happened would spread all over St. Moritz. The least I could do for Herbert was to stay on, hold my tongue, and stop contradicting him before the boys.

For reasons of my own I wanted to stay on; but as to not contradicting Herbert, I pointed out to Molly that in that case he must leave me alone, and not try to force me to agree with him. This, Molly thought, would be extremely difficult—and so did I—but it was the best I could offer; and finally Molly agreed to it in Herbert's name; and withdrew.

I thought the subject closed. I never opened my mouth; but I expect Molly could not have kept hers shut, for certainly someone blundered. The next attack came from Ernan's side. Miss Murray, Keith's aunt, who looked down on all the world, and was looked down on in her turn by Mamma, insisted upon giving me her unsolicited advice. "A clergyman's daughter," she told me sternly, "with no means and bad health should be only too thankful for such an offer!" How could I possibly expect to do better—or even as well as—Herbert? He had money of his own; and when his father died would have more, and look at the villa—I should certainly never get such a chance again! And I would be well advised not to look elsewhere!

I told her more than once that I never wanted such a chance

again; and hadn't wanted that one. I know now that her persistence was less due to ensuring my welfare than to protecting Ernan's. The Forbes may have looked down upon the Murrays, because their name was not spelt with an 'o', and no bonnie Earl of Moray had come striding through their halls; and the Murrays may have looked down on the Forbes for their own spectacular reasons; but at least both of them together looked down on practically everybody else. Besides Miss Murray's brother had married a cousin of Ernan's. She too could be contaminated by his marrying beneath him. Nothing of this occurred to me at the time. Nor did I grasp why Constance Barnes should have told Mamma that I was an "adventuress", though I enjoyed Mamma's answer, repeated to me by Ernan. "Do you think so, dear? I doubt if adventuresses wear tam-o-shanters."

Mamma herself never attacked me, she much more wisely made friends with me. She said Herbert and Molly took her up so sharply when she explained what ought to be done for Ernan's health; and I am sure she found me sympathetic upon this subject, though I did not wholly share her anxiety when she told me that Ernan, with a temperature of 99°F., caused by a slight chill, might "go down in the night".

I looked after him, as I had helped to look after the other boys when they were sick, but I found him much nicer to look after. Still, if I thought little of these minor disturbances, Herbert's quotation from Dr. Holland had profoundly shocked me. If I wasn't fit to marry anyone, I shouldn't be—if the question arose— fit to marry Ernan. I did not know that the question ever would arise, my nature was profoundly sceptical, and I saw no reason to suppose that even if so young a man had a stronger feeling for me than friendship it would last; or take any more serious form. My feelings, I told myself, were my own affair. If I were going to die soon I saw no reason why, for the next few weeks—the winter was drawing to its golden close—I should not take my joy where I found it.

I felt that Ernan was, for a man, far younger than myself, and if it were true that he had as strong a feeling for me as I had for him, I thought that he would get over it in time. In the spring daffodils quickly give place to roses; and if I wasn't going to have any more than daffodils, I felt that I might be allowed to dance my heart out with them before my spring closed.

We spent more and more time together, and our wanderings seldom brought us back in time for tea. Sometimes we had no money and Ernan would leave his seal ring behind in a village inn till next time. I suppose we must have looked trustworthy, for however far and strange the villages we managed to reach, we always had our tea and were trusted, until we retrieved the ring.

The sharpness of the parting ahead of us was blunted for me by the thought of Elena and Italy; and for Ernan by a curious and unlikely vision of spending our summer together in the Tyrol, with both our mothers.

Again and again I assured him that this prospect *was* wholly illusory. I should go back to England, and even if I must remain in mountains they would have to be Swiss ones; and my mother would never come out and join me, but Ernan blandly but firmly disregarded my absence of faith. He assured me, with unharassed certainty, that we *should* spend the summer together exactly as he had planned it; and exactly as he had planned, we *did* spend it, even to the guardian presences of both our mothers, though not quite so felicitously as we had hoped; since they took an intense dislike to each other.

24

The first two weeks of March melted into a golden mist. The sun and ourselves were of the same mind; but the rest of our grownup world was wrapt in a black cloud of disapproval.

We were uncomfortably conscious of a certain restraint; but I put most of it down to Herbert's understandable rage; and Molly's natural loyalty. Ernan bore a double weight, since he knew his mother's subtle and silent heart; and was forced to hear Constance's warnings and complaints at first hand; but he communicated nothing of what he suffered from them, at this time, to me; and we made no change in our habits. Our hearts were innocent; our propriety inexorable. We felt ourselves to be encased in virtue; although to the rest of the world we were criminal outcasts. Only the boys were our kind and loyal friends. We had always stood up for their rights, and in a silent but adamantine manner, they did the same for us.

I was to drive down the Maloja Pass by Extra Poste, to meet Elena at Chiavenna, and Ernan begged me to arrange my journey on a Sunday, so that he might drive with me as far as Silvaplana; and walk back. This was a capital crime; but as neither Ernan nor Mr. Marshall was under Herbert's orders, short of turning Ernan out of the house there was nothing to be done about it. I heard later that Herbert had considered turning me out instead, but as I was leaving anyway, and such an enforced exodus might have had double-edged consequences, Herbert had wisely refrained; but "sour puss" looks and lofty silences were the order of the day.

We must, I fear, have been most aggravating young people. We felt so good, and were so wildly happy in spite of all the world being against our premature felicity. No one dared to say a direct word to us for fear of precipitating the event they longed to avoid. Were we—or were we not—engaged to be married? No one knew —no more did we.

On Saturday the villa—except for Molly who hated excursions— emptied for a ski tour.

I remained behind to pack; and Ernan remained—ostensibly to study. Instead the sun took us.

It was one of those March days which at high altitudes combine all four seasons. Under the hot brilliance of a summer sun lay the intense still cold of winter; a secret sense of new life stirred the sap of pine trees and sweetened all the air, while beneath frozen boughs the dry pine needles remembered autumn.

We went out early, and I don't know how far we walked, but it seemed senseless to go back for lunch; and Ernan reminded me that I had all the night to pack in. He could, he explained, easily go back to the villa and fetch us something to eat.

They couldn't, he argued, be more annoyed with us than they already were.

We had a rug to sit on; and we felt that we could lean against the pink stems of pines, and look up into the hollow, airy blue of that deep sky for ever.

I stayed sunbound in the enchanting stillness listening to the methodical tapping of a woodpecker and the occasional smart clap of snow plunging from a lifted bough.

Time did not move—it sank—into eternity. A squirrel swung himself into a neighbouring tree, and gazed at me with a companionable fervour. He did not even chatter his disdain. I was so still he might have taken me for a fallen bough, but I think he knew I was as much alive as he was.

Ernan sped back on wings to the villa, where he was met by accumulated asperity; and blank refusal. We ought, we should, we *must* come back to lunch! Molly wouldn't give us anything to eat. I don't know how Ernan surmounted all these obstacles; and it took even him some time to do it; but at length he came away with plentiful sandwiches and a Thermos of hot coffee smuggled out of the kitchen window by the cook, behind Molly's back.

I did not know whether the time was long or short while he was away. I only knew he would come back.

The blue and golden day was all we asked. We did not seem to move much farther forward into it. Yet I suppose we were exploring the possibilities of a life-time.

Our wildest dreams however did not include that we should have to wait thirteen years, five of them linked together but bitterly frustrated; and seven of them sightlessly empty and estranged.

The golden world we shared was free of time, and what we exchanged was a substance as impalpable as the blue air.

The blazing peaks stood round us defensively as if to keep from our young hearts all knowledge of what lay before us in "the wide, dim, lampless, deep, unpeopled world".

We went back in good time for a farewell tea with Mamma at her hotel.

No doubt she looked upon our last day's companionship with ironic tenderness; and unstinted relief. Tomorrow she would have her son wholly her own again, without the startling intrusion of a barbaric girl.

Mamma always treated me with kindness, and with the care with which she would have treated any toy that was dear to her child. I think that at this time she did not take us seriously enough to show —or even feel—disapproval.

Constance Barnes did not hide her feelings. I had spoilt her winter, without even having had the sense to know that I had spoilt it.

She had tried on several occasions to enlighten me; but I had merely thought her unpleasantly shy; and done my best to warm the frozen pool of her aloofness.

Once she had even made a direct attack upon me. She told me that I was bad for Ernan and should leave him alone. I was shaken by her anger, but told myself she thought we had walked too far for Ernan's strength. It is difficult to prove to a clergyman's daughter brought up with the idea of doing good that she is "bad" for anyone with whom she spends her dutifully arranged time. When I repeated her remarks to Ernan, he replied with some firmness that he did not think what Constance said was of the slightest import ance. He was the best judge of how he spent his time; and with whom.

The boys returned late on Saturday night and I bade them a fond farewell. Herbert, they told me, had stopped off at the Kulm. No farewell took place between us; and I do not remember ever having seen Herbert again. Even now—years after his death—if Herbert should rise from the dead to greet me—I doubt if I should feel any differently towards him. He had, however, qualities which I have since learned to regard with greater respect. Molly was in a higher category of human beings altogether, for she had a generous heart. I was glad when she relented just enough to appear in her dressing-gown at dawn to see that hot tea was given us and a magnificent rucksack full of food; but she was stiff with unspoken disapproval. As far as I was concerned I had never felt a moment's antagonism towards her. Our performances had been as good as our promises to each other.

When we made them we had not envisaged the existence of Ernan, nor the unfortunate delusion of Herbert's; so that neither of us was responsible for the repercussions that followed.

Solemnly and in dead silence, Ernan and I slipped out of the sleeping household, into an ice-cold dawn.

The sleigh stood just below the villa, the horses tossed their heads, the bells rang out in that unforgettable gay jingle only given to sleigh bells, conquering the hollowed-out silence of mountain valleys.

Frost flowers covered the lake with a blazing splendour of diamond and sapphire petals. We swept past them into frozen pinewoods that spread—vast and untenanted in those days—between St. Moritz and Silvaplana. We were rapturously free, without restriction or reproach, in the anonymous companionship of nature. No sense of purpose, and no fetter of obligation, troubled those five golden hours.

It is not true that poets exaggerate the beauty of first love. Theirs is the triumph of understatement. When Shakespeare cries: "O spirit of love! how quick and fresh art thou!" he is but remembering, with the sharp sparkle of reality, what he once felt.

Perhaps of all the poets, one of the grimmest and most unhappy has recaptured best the spell of this brief dawn unlinked with the gravity of passion. Thomas Hardy in "The Phantom Horsewoman" and "At Castle Botral" knew what we felt, when he wrote:

> *They say he sees an instant*
> *More clear than today,*
> *A sweet soft scene*
> *That once was in play*
> *By that briny green;*
> *Yes, notes alway*
> *Warm, real and keen*
> *What his years bring back.*

For Thomas Hardy it was a beach in Cornwall, for us it was an ice-blue path surrounded by snow peaks, in their unutterable purity, swimming out, one by one, into the golden warmth of day, while close above them burned the sky's deep, unending blue.

> *What we felt as we climbed, and what we talked of*
> *Matters not much, nor to what it led.*
> *Something that life will not be balked of*
> *Without rude reason till hope is dead*
>   *And feeling fled.*
> *It filled but a minute. But was there ever*
> *A time of such quality, since or before,*
>   *In that hill's story?*

In a timeless flash we reached the long straight line of the Silvaplana lake, black forest on one side of us, and the snow-covered lake upon the other, beyond them both the Pass dipped into depths of sunny mist.

"I shan't stop here," Ernan said firmly, "I shall go on with you, further down the Pass."

I implored him to remember the length of the walk back. Surely he mustn't climb as well as walk? The driver intervened. Why should the gentleman walk back at all? There was the general Poste coming up the Pass as we went down. Inevitably we should meet it much further down; but it would be in St. Moritz by seven o'clock, short of an avalanche, and the frost had been too hard to make avalanches probable.

A lamb had already hung us, why should we boggle at this inviting sheep?

The day expanded, hunger seized us. We ate with fierce enjoyment while we flew on between the changing peaks. If wildness can hold no menace, we were wild with joy.

Birds, in their unfettered flights, may feel as we felt; but not Shelley's skylark nor Swinburne's sea-mew, felt any freer; and after all birds have not so much room for ecstasy as the human heart can hold. If I thought of them at all, and I probably did think of them, for I knew both poems by heart, it was to find that I no longer envied even poets' birds.

We arrived at Vico-Soprano near the foot of the Pass at one o'clock.

The bus was actually there. We saw it standing before the door of the Poste, but alas! the blind sword of parting took too long in cutting us apart—in those few prolonged and perilous seconds we did not look beyond each other's eyes. We neither saw nor heard the noisy passage of the bus, though it must have passed us by inches. I was swept away by my driver, and Ernan found himself at the foot of the Pass.

He did not arrive at St. Moritz till one o'clock in the morning, half frozen and dead with fatigue, after a twelve-hour climb.

The villa was alight with fright and fury. It was supposed that we had eloped. Fortunately they had postponed telling Mamma either the full length of Ernan's absence or of their suspicions of the cause till morning. But the enormity of our proceedings was instantly brought home to Ernan by the enraged volubility of Molly; and the laconic enmity of Herbert.

25

Elena's chief thought in meeting me was for us both to avoid a night at Chiavenna, so that I doubt if she realized that she had a ghost rather than a girl with her, my life having mysteriously disappeared up the Maloja Pass.

We had just three minutes in which to gather ourselves and our belongings together, without snatching the semblance of a meal, before hurling ourselves into the one train in the day for Bergamo.

We arrived in the lower town of Bergamo towards evening and found it commercial and dim, with no hint as to the beauties of one of the loveliest hill towns of Italy. A soft sirocco rain, warm and silvery, blotted out the citadel.

The hotel was worse than the Chiavenna hotel of which we had such bleak memories, a vague varnish of tawdry respectability covered a strong undercurrent of crookedness and dirt; and in our bedrooms there was a piercing and overpowering smell. Elena sternly called the landlord's attention to it. He flung up his hands and his eye-brows, and rolled the balls of his eyes towards Heaven, while he explained to us with an oily smile that what we had noticed was merely the scent of buds from the trees. The windows were all tightly shut; and we could see from them neither buds nor trees. Elena's sternness became decisive. "We shall leave at once," she said; and in five minutes we were back once more in the same horse-drawn victoria in which we had arrived, fringed with luggage, swaying and scuttling over tram lines, through wet darkness.

This time we *didn't* know where we were going, but the driver knew. He was one of those pre-fascist Italians who managed to combine the acutest sense of his own interests with a hardly less lively interest in the affairs of others. No doubt he profited by the hotel he found for us on the citadel, but he saw to our profit as well as his own. No English person, the buxom landlady told us, had stayed with them for two years; the loss was England's. It was the cleanest and friendliest hotel I ever was in—all the floors and passages were of bright red brick washed down daily, most of the restaurant was in the courtyard under a vine trellis. The door to the street was never shut, and all Bergamo seemed to be wandering about in the dusk, and if not playing a musical instrument, listening to one. Gusts of ardent and dramatic dialogue swept in and out of the music.

Opposite our table, with great drops of silvery rain occasionally slipping off vine leaves and falling into his snow-white hair, an enchanting old man played a zither. A little iron table stood next to the one he played on with a carafe of wine and an ample dish from the hotel kitchen; so that whether he was paid in money or not he had one regular meal a day.

It was eight hours since either of us had touched food, and I have seldom enjoyed a dinner more. It was Italian cooking at its best washed down with fiery red wine from the hotel's own vineyard. We ate it in the courtyard, with the old man and the zither, and most of Bergamo looking on.

Dusky shadows from the open doorway gazed at us while we ate, but even Elena did not mind their friendly curiosity, kept sufficiently at bay by protectively hovering waiters.

We were, the chambermaid informed me once our relationship had ripened, the cause of as much interest as we felt. What was the tie between the intensely blond Madonna and myself? If she were not my mother why did she behave as if she were? The blond one obviously had much money—what was she going to do with it? What had we come to Bergamo *for?* Her questions were endless, and as my Italian was strictly limited, her curiosity remained largely unsatisfied. But she managed to find out one thing that Elena didn't. I could not be so anxious about posts—especially posts from beyond the Maloja Pass—unless I had a lover there. The chambermaid became as interested and dismayed as I was myself

hen for five days no letter came; and when at last it arrived her
elief was nearly as great as my own.

The wind changed overnight from a soft sirocco to a withering
ramontana blowing straight off snow peaks, and I developed a
evere cold that settled on my lungs. I had only one morning
oose on the lovely hill-side, to force myself through the main
hurches, clustered in piercing draughts and containing the col-
ected damp of a lifetime, yet I remember with intensity the bright
ints of century-old *intarsia* work in the cathedral; and above all the
ill top itself, with its springing towers merging together under the
rey pall of a bitter sky, while defiantly maintaining its terracotta
nd burnt-sienna tones. After that one morning I retired to bed,
vhile Elena valiantly saw alone, all that we had meant to see
ogether. The tramontana never altered, and Elena decided to
kip Brescia which shared our climate, and travel straight to
'lorence.

I suppose that the extreme vividness with which I remember
Bergamo, considering the blighted little I ever saw of it, must be
lue to the letter which I did at last receive. It was a much shorter
etter than I had anticipated; and it was allegorical in substance, a
orm of writing for which I have never had a predilection, but T. S.
Eliot is probably right when he says that it is the intensity *behind*
vhat is said that counts as literature.

We came into Florence towards sunset; the whole of it—and
Florence is a city specially adapted to sunsets—was concentrated on
he thirteenth-century tower of Sta. Maria di Novella and its
loisters. Black and white marble, and centuries-old, sun-soaked
orick blazed up together. It was a spell-binding first impression; it
s difficult to express what the eye received, since the eye is only a
oart of the receiving faculties, perhaps the millions of brain cells,
vhich biologists tell us far outnumber all the people in the world,
vere concentrated upon my first impression of Florence. We had
olenty of time to take in the dance of towers against the gold and
ourple sky, for we had the mildest and slowest of little horses in
ront of us, and had to drive straight through the city in order to
each the road (for it was a country road then, and not a street)
vhich led to our destination—Fiesole.

The trams had just been laid about the city's core, and we found ourselves, under the balanced lightness of the loveliest of towers, jostled by an intensive yellow tram almost against the bronzed gates of Dante's stern black and white Baptistry.

The Duomo draws the square together, but Brunelleschi's dome only gradually gave out what it was prepared to give. We caught no more than the flash of what appeared to be a leaf pink, tremendous bubble behind Giotto's matchless tower.

We were going to stay for six weeks at Fiesole, in a fourteenth century villa, with a lady who had been a governess to Elena's friends, the Cavendish-Bentincks.

By their help I believe Miss Cook had acquired this ancient villa in a garden just below the Monastery of San Francesco; the walls of the monks' garden touched our own small crowded plot, and our balcony looked straight over Florence, as if we were perched on the rim of a cup. Every morning through a milky mist, the three great buildings rose—tower, dome and octagonal Baptistry—alone at first, and then one by one, single campaniles pricked their way through mist to join the centre group; until all Florence was spread out before us—terracotta, bright burning brown, and sunny gold. Even the Arno was visible, a silver ribbon running through strips of emerald wheat. The almond blossom was out, feathering the whole landscape, while blood-red anemones, with the pointed flame of wild tulips, filled our dishevelled garden. Along our walls mauve and blue iris thrust themselves between the stones; and almost every ancient villa in Fiesole had a sheet of wistaria flung over its walls—or roofing a pergola in its garden.

At night, under a great white moon, our tiny garden shook with the songs of nightingales. "Elena," I cried, gazing over the balcony railings at the almond blossom and the towers, "all we need is Romeo!" "I'm only too thankful," Elena replied grimly, "that there is no such person!" It was on the tip of my tongue, since I was supported by several more yellow envelopes on the table in my room, to cry, "Ah—but there is!"

The words however never passed my lips; and no one was more wholly unaware than Elena during the weeks that followed that such a candidate lurked in the wings.

Miss Cook's Pension was beyond all praise. It was superlatively comfortable. Her cook was a real chef, the house itself furnished with simplicity heightened by ancient treasures.

It was kept like the private house of a fastidious person with unlimited private means. Miss Cook herself was crushed into silence by her own dignity. She had lived under a ducal shadow all her life, and I think dared to love only a small white dog, a toy Pomeranian, which she took, drugged under her cloak, to England every summer; and was never found out. Alas, she let her guests live beyond her means, and she soon had to give up her Pension Paradise.

Our rooms were side by side, mine as small and perfect a one as Carpaccio's St. Ursula's; Elena's more stately salon was large enough for us both to use as a sitting room; each of us had a tall French window looking out over Florence and the garden was open every night to nightingales, bats if they fancied to wander in, and tender mists.

Elena procured, with some difficulty, and as a special favour, a long chair for me to use on the balcony of the general sitting room. I lay there in the lovely sunshine whenever I could, but nothing interfered with our daily descents into Florence.

Elena was a perfect guide. She knew Florence very well indeed and she had made a most careful programme for our daily visits. She never hurried; she never crowded too many things into one morning; and she never forced her own tastes upon mine. What information she gave was always accurate; and about what she did not know she had nothing whatever to say.

Every morning she carried with her in a small basket a flask of boiled milk from our breakfast and a split roll and butter. She would break off from our sight-seeing at a suitable moment, to draw me behind a statue or into some "brilliant window niche" to share this frugal meal.

I think she was a little disappointed that at first I could not be parted from Michelangelo. Pictures meant little to me, I only wanted statues, particularly his statues. Hour after hour I sat in hushed rapture, with the four tremendous figures in the San Lorenzo Chapel—"Day" and "Night"—"Dawn" and "Twilight".

I can't remember what exactly it was that they meant to me, but the emotion they aroused was dynamic—it was like being violently pushed into another world. I loved the bronze boar in the market place—and Verrocchio's boy struggling with his dolphin. What I wanted was more and more human figures, "the beauty of the world, the paragon of animals!"—more robust and lively Donatellos, more Lucca della Robbia cupids, more Verrocchios, with their sly dramatic beauty, more Mina da Fiesoles, delicate as snowdrops in marble of the same fine texture as a flower, although unlike the snowdrop they could never fade!

Perhaps this almost feverish passion for sculpture was a reaction from my illness. Perhaps it was young love enchanted with the chief object of creation. Pictures need mind, they ask a strict attention and some training in values, as well as a natural taste and vigour of appreciation.

Statues accept a more primitive response. They liven your muscles; and warm the cockles of your heart. Elena tried gently to draw me towards the historic Florence. I was quite sympathetic about Savonarola. I had once studied his life and character with some thoroughness in order to write a thesis on him for an examination. I was upset at the idea of his being burned, and climbed all over the Piazza della Signoria not to miss any of the incidents concerning him. I tried hard to concentrate upon his masterful agonies; but my eyes wandered from the imaginary pyre in the centre of the Piazza to rest with a far deeper concern upon Benvenuto Cellini's "Perseus" —which then stood opposite the Palazzo Vecchio under the Loggia dei Lanzi.

I don't know what jolted me out of sculpture into pictures perhaps it was that I loved Elena and so wanted to share her skilled interest; but I can remember the actual birth of my appreciation.

I had gone to the Accademia in search of Michelangelo's "David", and was feeling a little quarrelsome about the size of his head, which I didn't want to think was too large though I saw that it was—when turning away my eyes from "David", I saw through an open doorway Botticelli's "Spring".

"Spring" had a small room entirely to itself; and there were chair in rows before the picture. I sat on one of these chairs; and for th

rst time I *looked* at a picture. I found myself slipping inside the
rame and joining Paris and his apple. The three goddesses danced
n their ethereal splendour on the grass studded with Botticelli's
vind-blown flowers. The winds blew the dancing Flora across the
icture while Spring—central—but much more sedate, mothered
ll her children. It was impossible not to feel a sense of movement. I
ave never felt so conscious of how one art links itself to another as
vhen I watched Botticelli's "Spring". I was caught up in rhythm; and
hought that I heard music. After that episode I took trouble, and
lena read Berenson out loud to me, and told me more and more of
vhat Ruskin had taught her. We spent long hours in the Uffizzi,
nd with her unexampled patience and fastidious respect, Elena
ave me all the knowledge she possessed, without ever forcing my
ttention, or slighting my ignorance.

I did not give up my love for the human form in sculpture, I
nerely added to it a heightened impression of design and its
elease into colour.

If we were very tired and pressed for time we took a little carriage
p our mountain, but oftener we went home by the jostling
nrieking trams, which took the life of the streets into themselves
n a pleasant, desultory, noisy manner.

It was a miraculous time. There was a fresh letter in a yellow
nvelope every day; and all I had seen and thought of during the
norning—all the new names with their eternal gifts, had to be
assed on at white heat to that impatient listener waiting for them
n the mountain snows.

I couldn't have been happier or busier than I was for those six
veeks, though into our paradise a small-sized serpent soon made a
pectacular appearance.

Miss Cook had told us that she was expecting the daughter of a
ishop, well known to Elena, upon her belated honeymoon with
er father's ex-chaplain. Neither of them was young and he was
ery ill.

One lovely day while I was writing on the balcony, a voice like
corncrake's broke over my comfortably cushioned head. "Please
et out of that chair at once," I heard. "I need it for my husband."
faint murmur of protest followed, from a haggard, shambling,

lean and pleasant man. He smiled miserably at me; and I sprang ou
of my chair to face the bishop's daughter.

Her face expressed nothing but autocratic discontent ready t
mount into spectacular fury. "It isn't really mine," I said to th
pathetic chaplain. "Do take it! I don't need it at all!" Elena wa
justly annoyed with me, she had taken some trouble to get me th
chair; and she said I shouldn't have repudiated it so unreservedly
but she hadn't met—as I had—the chaplain's haunted eyes. Th
unpleasantness of the bishop's daughter spread over the whol
Pension. The enchanting and exquisitely mannered servant:
scowled at—scowled back—and became hour by hour less en
chanting. Miss Cook was insulted by being talked to as if she wer
not a lady—more even than a lady—a Cavendish-Bentinc
householder.

The bishop's daughter enraged Elena by saying that she hope
she wouldn't try to talk to her husband who was far too ill fo
conversation. "As if," Elena said to me bitterly, "I were the sort o
person who talked to other people's husbands—sick or well!"
We voluntarily gave up both the public sitting room and it
balcony; but even this was not enough.

The dearest friends Elena possessed in Florence were a well
known and greatly beloved clergyman and his wife. The Jeffreson
had a villa just above our own, with a much more magnificen
terraced garden, called the Villa degli Angeli. We were going to
stay with them for Easter—a fortnight had been mentioned—it wa
to have been the peak of our travels.

But the bishop's daughter put an end to all that. Perhaps becaus
of the chair incident, perhaps because her kindly husband stil
tried to talk to us; she told the Jeffresons (the bishop's greates
friends) that I was a scheming adventuress. This was the third time
before I was twenty-one, that I was called an adventuress, a pleasing
term and perhaps appropriate—except for its connotation.

A wicked, persuasive girl, she declared, destroying alike Elena's
peace of mind and tampering with her property. The Jeffresons
startled and confused, possessing what Henry James so aptly calls
"the imagination of agitated lambs", withdrew their invitation.
They would, they said, gladly entertain Elena; but they begged tha

I should remain at the Pension with Miss Cook. What may have strengthened their conviction of my depravity was the unheralded appearance of one of Molly's and Herbert's sisters. Through the use of my name and wholly without my knowledge, Rose had persuaded Miss Cook, who took in only specially introduced guests, to admit her to our Pension; and Rose innocently filled to the brim the cup of my iniquities. She was incredibly pretty, she was traveling alone; and she saw no reason why she shouldn't speak to the ex-chaplain or sit on the balcony of the general sitting room, beside his chair. She did speak to him, she made him laugh, and when told by the bishop's daughter to stop speaking to him, she gave her the full benefit of the family brusquerie. Rose was far more devastatingly rude to the bishop's daughter than the bishop's daughter had the language, or the presence of mind, to be rude back; and of course Rose was—or appeared to be—my friend.

Hitherto the bishop's daughter had not said she believed me to be immoral; but now the cloak of immorality covered us both alike. We became automatically two "bad" girls.

Elena had been angry at Rose's uninvited and unannounced appearance. All that I had told her of Molly and Herbert had filled her with extreme distaste. Why *should* the sister of this rightly repudiated man turn up to haunt our path? Elena refused point blank to let Rose share any of our expeditions. I was only allowed to speak to her on sufferance.

I myself had rather wondered why Rose had fallen from the blue. Did she wish to know, in order to pass on to Molly, the exact situation between Ernan and myself? Or was she merely interested in taking a look at a girl who had so disastrously shaken her brother Herbert's misogynist nature?

Her curiosity had to remain unsatisfied, and growing bored with her lonely visit to Florence, Rose asked me to lend her a pound, to help her on her journey home. She had run short of money and possessed little more than her tickets and not enough to drive through Paris to the right station. Had I possessed a pound all would have been well. Unfortunately I had spent my last penny on Alinari photographs to take home to my family; and a framed picture of an extremely good-looking St. John the Baptist—Andrea del Sarto's—with which to endow Ernan. Privately I thought it very like him, except the leopard skin. When I asked Elena to lend me a pound for Rose's journey, to my intense astonishment she refused. "No," Elena said firmly, "I don't like the girl. I consider that she had no right to come here, through the use of your name. Considering the circumstances in which you left her brother's villa—and that she herself was actually unknown to you—I am not prepared to help her! Nor do I think she would ever return this borrowed money!"

It was unthinkable to me not to help Rose or to doubt her honesty but I was not without resources. I produced my mother's engagement ring. It was a small diamond but I thought I could raise a pound on it. By chance I had seen a pawn shop in Fiesole with its traditional Medician three balls, which Elena had explained to me, floating in front of it. "Don't bother about it, Elena," I said kindly, "I will go and pawn this instead. The shop is quite near." Elena was cruelly shocked by the suggestion. She tried her best to dissuade me, she found me sympathetic but unshakable. Suddenly she gave in. She produced the pound but she repeated that she was quite certain that we should never see it again. Whether this conversation came through the walls of our room I never knew; but if it did, it may have helped the bishop's daughter to discharge her venom; but it must not be supposed that whatever Elena thought of Rose she took the bishop's daughter lying down.

She went off by herself, white-lipped, with the eyes of a martyred saint, to have the whole matter out with the Jeffresons. She told me about it afterwards; but not, I think, quite all of it. She did not want to put me against the Jeffresons, and feared that if I had known the worst of their reactions I would in my turn have refused the visit.

In the end the Jeffresons came round. They renewed, although they shortened, our invitation. We were to spend three days with them, at the end of our stay.

Elena that night spoke to the bishop's daughter; but she never told me anything that she had said to her. I only know that the ex-chaplain had the courage to apologize to us both before he left. He said he was afraid his wife's neuralgia had upset her nerves, and led her to misconstrue perfectly innocent things; and he added that it had been a great pleasure to him to meet us both. They left soon after and did not go to stay with the Jeffresons as they had intended. I rather imagine that the bishop's daughter had hoped to filch the fortnight that had been meant for us; and that the Jeffresons had seen through her device. The bishop himself turned up at our Pension before they left and spoke most kindly to Elena; and kindly even to me. Rose too left, returning the pound with the utmost promptitude in a polite letter to Elena. I think it says much for the extraordinary justice of Elena that she showed me the letter. "You were right about the girl's honesty," she admitted. "She *has* returned the pound; but I think that *I* was right about her behaviour —she should never have come here!"

26

"The region cloud" that had darkened between Elena and myself dissolved very quickly. Once more we moved together through an April that never for one moment made us want to be in England.

One morning, unexpectedly, for I did not know that Uncle Kennie was in Florence, nor did he know where I was—we ran into him, in one of the endless Uffizi passages.

Elena in the confusion of a surprise introduction did not catch his name. She thought her worst suspicions of Rose justified. Rose had been a designing forerunner to her monstrous brother—and this was Herbert come to try his fate again! Perhaps after all my head had been turned by his atrocious advances, for look with what warmth I was receiving him!

"Elena," I said, "when can he come to tea?" Elena drew herself up with icy dignity, and said these dreadful words: "I am sorry, dear, but I do not find it convenient to receive him!"

Thunderstruck, Uncle Kennie and I gazed at each other; and, trying to hide our grieved surprise, stumblingly exchanged addresses and parted. "Elena," I passionately demanded as soon as his back was turned, "how could you be so unkind to my Uncle Kennie?" Poor Elena, flabbergasted by the discovery that she had banished a person of whom she knew nothing but good, a High Churchman and an Uncle, did not know which way to turn. But all ended well. She wrote Kennie an enchanting note, he came to tea and his mistaken identity was fully explained to him. He, too, it appeared, had never liked Herbert; and our sympathies were complete. We even profited by this incident, because Elena gave him leave to take me out alone for the whole day, an indulgence she would not I fancy have allowed us except for her previous austerity.

Days with Uncle Kennie had a peculiar felicity. Having been himself, and for long years, extremely delicate, we always took things easily. He was an expert traveller and knew exactly where to find what he wanted. He also liked good food in obscure and simple places; and never went too long without it.

He arrived in a small carriage, which was miraculously attached to us for the whole day; and we drove straight to the Etruscan Museum. This we found ostensibly shut, but tips in those nostalgic days opened most forbidden doors, and we had, for an hour, the "Idolino" to ourselves.

This bronze boy, standing in a shaft of sunshine with the centuries thick upon him, is an emanation of eternal youth. In his small, contented, perfect body, "antiquity is young".

We left him dazzled and at peace, and I remember nothing else about the day, except that we wound up by an act of unexampled courage on Uncle Kennie's part. He took me to tea at Fiesole with an old friend of his, a celebrated amateur artist, who lived in a famous villa full of treasures.

His friend was a bachelor like himself, and it seemed to me very glorious and abandoned to be having tea with two such old and distinguished men, who showed me so much kindness and attention. They must have been about forty; and they let me pour out their tea.

Easter broke upon us far too soon, for after it, we were to leave the freedom of our happy Pension, and pay our awe-inspiring visit to the Jeffresons. On Good Friday Elena wanted to take me to the English church in Florence where Father Jeffreson was to hold the Three Hours' Service; and I still more strongly wanted to go. Unfortunately church at all had been forbidden me, and a Three Hours' Service certainly seemed a little beyond the stretch of our scientific consciences. However Elena found a solution which was a proof of her great spiritual courage. She decided that I might go, but only upon one condition, I must eat a beef-steak first, and go to bed directly afterwards. A beef-steak on Good Friday was for Elena so near to being a mortal sin—or perhaps more accurately speaking a mortal slight against the Deity—that I still wonder how she could have brought herself to such a decision. ate the beef-steak and went.

Father Jeffreson was one of the finest and most penetrating preachers I have ever heard. There was never anything extraneous or superfluous in what he said. He cut straight to the bone and never left it.

Like it or not—believe it or not—it *was* religion that he gave you—the religion of a fastidiously honest, and intelligent person.

It was three years since Wilmett had died and I had never faced up to her death, or understood why it so ate into my heart, and coloured my sleeping and waking thoughts. It was not love, for I had not loved her—or thought I had not loved her. I had spent the greater part of my childhood hating her and fighting her. Now during this Three Hours' Service I knew what I had done to her.

There are many kinds of mortal agony and perhaps remorse for what is irretrievable stands highest in the list. Grief wears itself out, acute physical pain can be lulled, but to know that you have caused another human being harm that cannot be undone, strikes at life itself. I think the agony of remorse which rushed through me like a storm on that Good Friday might not have overwhelmed me had I not begun to love.

Love for Ernan still unacknowledged and only half realized refused to take possession of a heart which had been so long tenanted by hate.

Somehow or other I had to get rid of the poison; and broken and scalded with pain I had to realize exactly what part I myself had played in Wilmett's tragedy. I could so easily have loved her if I had understood her; and if I had loved her, she might have let me share with her the physical and mental burdens which had been too much for her single strength.

Even if her death was inevitable, she would have suffered less if I had loved her, and I thought then that had she suffered less she might even have lived. For those three hours I felt I was her murderer.

The next day I went to Confession. Elena had arranged for this to take place, and I had rather reluctantly consented, for my

204

Catholicism—grappling with Herbert Spencer—had already begun to dwindle.

It was in fact the last time that I went to Confession. Yet curiously enough it was the only Confession I ever made which seemed to me real; and in which I felt understood and released by my Confession.

I had tried to tell the truth about my faulty relations with Wilmett to other Confessors, but they had never taken what I said seriously enough. Father Jeffreson went with me into the Hell that I had made, and showed me with ruthless clarity that not to love is always to kill. When he gave me absolution I felt for the first time absolved.

What I had done to Wilmett couldn't be undone, but at least I knew it for what it was; and felt free to love again. I could even take her memory into love.

We took our Easter Communion in the Jeffresons' chapel on the terrace. The chapel was a tiny one with its doors wide open, and Elena had arranged for us to follow the service in the garden.

We knelt between pots of tall white and scarlet carnations, and looked down on Florence, floating up through golden mist, tower, and dome, and palaces.

The Jeffresons invited their whole congregation to breakfast afterwards. Peasants who loved them came down from the hills, in enchanting costumes, with baskets of painted eggs, to wish them a happy Easter.

It was the most happy, and the most real, Easter I had ever known.

27

The Jeffresons had three hundred a year to live on. Upon this sum, and without getting into debt, they kept open house; they employed three enchanting and efficient servants, a gardener, a cook, and a house-parlourmaid. The house-parlourmaid looked after the chickens, and the gardener ironed Mrs. Jeffreson's laced caps.

Their small *poderino* provided them with oil, wine, fruit and vegetables. Every visitor to Florence of any spiritual importance, or anyone in tragic need, came to visit the Jeffresons; and all were made equally welcome.

Mrs. Jeffreson was a most charming old lady, round and rosy as an apple but without tartness. Her eyes shone with perpetual loving-kindness. She could hardly have had time to stop one smile before starting another. Her only moments of gloom were when confronted by the pain of someone else, or occasionally when stabbed by her own sense of inferiority. She was once found weeping at the thought that she could never be worthy of so saintly a husband.

Father Jeffreson was not so easy a companion as his wife. He was very learned; and his sense of right and wrong was irritatingly deep.

The extreme gravity with which he viewed the lapses of anyone in his company from his own high standards of behaviour was perhaps a little too vivid for general comfort. Elena had warned me in advance that it was easy to give him pain, and I must admit, though I deeply revered him, that Atlas symptoms were to be found in the otherwise unbounded generosity of Father Jeffreson's character.

I can never once remember seeing him smile. He took the sorrows of others as his own—but not their joys.

People poured in upon him with their problems all day long, and were placed where they would least interfere with the problems of others. On one occasion I inadvertently interfered with one of these problems. Elena had told me that a distinguished man, who was not expected to talk except to Father Jeffreson, was coming to lunch. Mrs. Jeffreson occasionally made agonizing social blunders— agonizing only to herself—as they were on the smallest possible scale, if indeed they existed outside her own active conscience; and on this occasion she misplaced her guests at table and I was put— where she had meant to put Elena—next to a tall man, with white curly hair, and brilliant blue eyes—curious eyes with an expression like that of a sailor looking for a wind. There were several other guests, and I did not even know that he was the one of whose silence Elena had warned me. I only knew that I had never before met a human being who so instantly cut to the heart of things. To talk to him was a revelation, not only of what he knew, though I think he did know a good deal more than most people, but oddly enough of what he thought wasn't worth knowing. There were strange gaps in his knowledge of topical things. He was English, but he did not know the name of our acting Prime Minister; and once he said of some well-known public event, "I suppose I shouldn't have heard of that."

Was he, I asked myself, an explorer—or perhaps even a long-term political prisoner just released? It was impossible to think of him as anything but good. His bright and burning eyes looked too honest for a criminal's. I was too interested in my companion to notice any other guests, or any conversation but our own. Every-thing he said seemed to come from some deeper layer of being than I had known before. He was not a copious talker. He thought, and spoke, between curious pauses, but with the exquisite felicity of someone to whom a subject has long been part of his deepest experience. At last I became conscious of a curious silence round us and saw that lunch was over—perhaps it had been over for some time.

"We must go on with this," he said to me earnestly as the guests rose, but we never did; and I cannot now remember what we were talking about!

Elena told me to go to my room at once, and rest. She did not scold me, but after tea she said, "That man you talked to at lunch is an ex-Trappist. He left the Monastery only a week ago—and he had not spoken for ten years—that was why I warned you that he might not talk except to Father Jeffreson. Father Jeffreson is trying to bring him back into normal life; and did not wish the fact that he had been a Trappist monk to be mentioned before his visit. Still, you did no harm by talking to him, in fact Father Jeffreson was pleased that he found himself able to talk to you."

The ex-Trappist was gone at tea-time and I never saw him again; but Uncle Kennie told me several years later that he married an English friend of his, and that they lived in Florence under strange conditions. They shared a house together but divided in half; and his wife was never allowed to enter his half without a direct invitation. After a few years the marriage broke down. The ex-Trappist became an Anglican priest and worked, under very austere conditions, until his death, in a London slum.

The Villa degli Angeli was the most beautiful house Elena and I had ever been in together, and we were free to live—between the hours of special meals, or visits they wished us to share—or more often *not* to share—exactly as we chose. I began to feel ashamed of my own silence towards Elena; to part from her without letting her know anything of the subject which was absorbing my whole heart was, I thought, a shabby way of showing the deep confidence I felt in her; and yet I shrank from speaking of what had not yet taken place between Ernan and myself.

One lovely moonlit night, just before going to bed, I summoned courage to say, "Elena, I feel I may be going to face something quite new in my life. I want you to know—although I am not quite certain about it yet—that I expect this change will come soon." Elena stood quite still, with her face turned away from me, and was silent for a long time. I thought perhaps she did not approve of those letters in their yellow envelopes which came every day punctually like the beat of a heart. "Yes, my darling," she said at last, "I *do* know that there may be this great change soon, and I am glad you have told me that you know. I wish I could prepare you for it, but I fear I cannot—I am too deeply involved. Will you, to please me, speak to Father Jeffreson about it before we leave?"

I agreed very reluctantly, for though I had the utmost confidence and admiration for Father Jeffreson, I certainly did not want to talk to him about an uncertain love affair. Of course, he had been married and Elena hadn't—but it was *her* advice and counsel that I had wanted and not *his*.

Elena was moved beyond her normal self-control; she kissed me with the utmost tenderness, and I felt glad that at least we had not parted without my sharing what filled my heart.

The next day Father Jeffreson took me solemnly out into the garden after supper. There were fireflies dancing on the terrace and the scent of wistaria and first roses filled the air. It was not yet quite dark and Florence was there beneath us, thin edged and colourless in the last light.

"I understand," Father Jeffreson said gently, "that a great ordeal lies before you—perhaps greater than any you have ever yet had to face. Will you tell me what your feelings about it are? I hardly feel myself fitted to speak to you on such a subject with authority, but it is true that I have considered it deeply, I have—if I may say so—shared it with many others—and if I could be of any help to you, I should be glad." He sounded so very grave, while I felt so wildly happy—my heart dancing with the fireflies—that I hardly dared to talk about so happy a subject to him as human love; but I said at last, "I don't really know for certain that it's going to happen. I only told Elena, because I love her so much, and I didn't want her to be taken by surprise if it *does* happen! I only know that I shall be very happy if it does!"

There was a long—but I thought kind and understanding silence—before Father Jeffreson spoke again. "If you feel like this," he said earnestly, "really and truly happy, then I don't think you need any further preparation from me. God himself has prepared you! But are you *sure* that what you feel *is* happiness—happiness without fear?" "I have never been so sure of anything else in my life," I told him. "Only of course I don't know if I'm good enough." "That," he said, "is not your business, my dear child. This call—

209

when it comes—is direct from God. You have only to say like Samuel, 'Lord, here am I.' " He told me to kneel down, and knelt down with me, and recited the Twenty-Third Psalm very beautifully. Then he shook hands with me, and murmuring, "I will pray for you always," went off to console another and more anxious heart.

I was glad we didn't have to go into details, but my surprise was great when I met Elena again, after my engagement had taken place, and she reproached me for my lack of confidence in her. "But darling," I explained, "I *did* tell you—don't you remember that evening in Florence—and you told me to talk to Father Jeffreson about it and he would prepare me for it?"

Elena flushed, hesitated, and told me the truth. It was death, and not marriage, which they had thought I rightly anticipated, and for which Father Jeffreson had so kindly and tenderly prepared me.

28

My meeting with my mother was rapturous. She looked better than I had ever seen her look. Once launched upon her adventure, her boats burned, her heart set free, she could not have made a happier fellow traveller.

All she asked was to know well beforehand exactly what we were going to do, and where it would land us, and of course she counted upon Ernan's unfailing escort.

My mother was a real Victorian woman. She might have a horror of sex, and consider men morally very little above the level of the brute; but she was not prepared to take any step without one.

Ernan was to meet us at Basle and to accompany us to Wesen and Tyrol, with or without his mother. My mother could consider no other possibility. Unfortunately Mamma was at a little place called Baden, not very far from Wesen—both being on the main line to Innsbruck—and she preferred to remain at Baden and *not* to come to Wesen with us. Unlike my mother, who was always anxious to arrive immediately at her final goal, Mamma did not like direct action, or haste, attached to any plan. Nor do I think she liked this particular plan. At this juncture of events I fancy she had decided to postpone our meeting as long as it was humanly possible to postpone it, without destroying Ernan's confidence in her self-sacrificing love.

She wished to continue the baths she had begun at Baden, and when her cure was over to take her after-cure in Switzerland. If she went to Tyrol at all, it would do very well in July or August. It was now May.

I had to explain to my mother that Ernan could not escort us from Basle to Wesen; nor leave his mother alone at Baden.

We should pass this little town on our way to Wesen, and stop there for three minutes. Ernan would of course come to the station, and there fix a final date that suited all of us. My excitement was intense but controlled. The little town of Baden was a sea of pink and white fruit blossom under a pale blue sky; but the pretty little station, bathed in sunlight, was empty. Ernan had felt he could not bear only three minutes for this momentous meeting. He stood, had I but known it, on a bridge above the railway station, with his eyes fixed upon our train. The three minutes passed like lead—and we were gone. My mother was greatly disturbed. How could he *not* have come? What did he mean by it? A person who missed trains, in my mother's mind, was next door to a criminal. She feared, she said, that Ernan was unreliable. I found the best possible excuses for him; but though I hoped they sounded convincing to my mother, they did not ring quite true to my own ear. I too wondered why he had not come. I knew he was not unreliable—but could he be a much worse thing—indifferent? Worse was to follow. He could not leave Mamma to join us at Wesen; but he suggested coming over for a day to discuss plans.

A few days later there arrived at lunch time a very handsome young man in an extremely well cut, pale grey, striped flannel suit, whom I almost failed to recognize. This was not the forlorn boy I had parted from at the bottom of the Maloja Pass. In these few months Ernan had become a man. He was no longer forlorn—he was formidable.

He even talked about joining the Japanese Navy. Our new and favourite allies, the Japanese, were being trained by our Navy at the time; and their test for eyesight was less severe than our own. Ernan had always wanted to join the British Navy, and thought his eyes might be strong enough to pass this lighter test. Should he try? I was very much against such a plan, but I could not well press the point.

I could see that my mother liked Ernan; that was all to the good, but I was far from sure that I liked him now myself. It seemed to me that it was I, and not my mother, who was meeting him for the first time.

However, in the course of the afternoon, which we spent in a pine wood by a waterfall, while my mother rested, this doubt was set at rest; nor did I ever hear anything more about Ernan's joining the Japanese Navy.

Our chief remaining difficulty was how we could bend our mothers to an inclusive plan.

Innsbruck was an easy and straightforward journey; and we decided that my mother and I could perfectly well take it unattended in a fortnight's time. By then Mamma's baths would be well over and Ernan, after escorting her to the place she chose for an after-cure, could meet us at Innsbruck, and go on with us to Cortina. When Mamma decided to join us, Ernan could return to Innsbruck to fetch her. My mother was a little restive at this evasion of her settled programme; but I managed to persuade her that it was natural, and not at all in the nature of a slight to either of us, and that Mamma had at least as much right to plans which included the presence of her son as we had. In fact, seeing it from Mamma's point of view, we were highly reprehensible in taking Ernan away from her at all.

"Love takes the meaning in love's conference." We had both begun to understand each other's mothers; and saw that they needed careful handling. It would never do to become estranged from each other because of their differences in outlook.

My mother and I arrived, unattended but intact, at the Tiroler Hof at Innsbruck.

This was a famous hotel, now powdered dust, which my mother had visited in state with her mother and four sisters, a courier and a maid, thirty years earlier.

It still hung in a glorified manner over the railway station, surrounded by a garden full of chestnut trees opening out of the restaurant. There were six different kinds of hot rolls for breakfast; and the coffee and butter were incomparably fine.

This was the end of waiting, for Ernan was to arrive the next evening; and then Nature, at the last moment, determined to disfigure me by a boil—a white hot, unavoidably significant boil—on one side of my undistinguished nose.

I tried everything to decrease its size, including prayer—but it relentlessly unfolded. It was with despair in my heart that I put on a turquoise blue, flounced evening dress, which was much better made than any I could ever have possessed had I not been fortunate enough to pick it up as a misfit for some richer purse.

However, even in this dress—whichever way I looked at myself —I saw nothing else but the boil.

The Tiroler Hof was, in those days, the peak of Innsbruck society. The Hof overflowed into it, as an extra base for amusement; and on the night of our arrival, before Ernan came, my mother and I saw a group of highly distinguished Austrian officers in full dress uniform, covered with orders and medals, enter our lounge. One of them was a tremendous fellow of six foot four. His figure was as splendid as his clothes. We were rather shocked to see that though he was younger than the others, and wore no medals, he sat down before they did, in an arm chair, while the older men stood round him, then he slightly waved his hand and they all took seats in a circle on each side of him. The waiter explained to us that this was the Archduke Eugen; and that he had a right to his manners.

He had been lately banished from Vienna on account of a love affair with a Viennese opera star; and was holding his Court at the golden brown Hof round the corner. The Archduke Eugen belonged to a celibate order, which I could not help thinking was rather a pity, for he was the finest looking male imaginable. He had curly golden brown hair, with a beard to match, black brows; and features that would not have disgraced an Olympian deity.

It was some comfort to learn that though banished in disgrace, the Tyrolese loved him and the Viennese opera star had managed the journey from Vienna to Innsbruck without difficulty. Short of domesticity, Eugen's life till he was fifty possessed every earthly felicity. He was a renowned hunter. Luxury, honour—and the pursuit of happiness—were all his to play with. No one in his life, except occasionally the Emperor, had ever said "No" to him; then like a thunderbolt he fell. His estates were confiscated, his palaces closed, his opera-stars swallowed up in blackness; he himself exiled from Austria. For many years he kept himself alive by teaching English at Basle.

I saw him twenty-five years later for a moment on the platform of a train that was stopped at a halt near Kitzbühel, so that a handful of Tyrolese could still do him homage. Silver-haired and bent, a frail sad slip of an old man, he stood hatless to wave to them, this tremendous Prince I had seen so sure of himself in the prime of his power. Into what world was he now returning? The train took him on, to an empty Vienna, small, starved and trembling on the brink of a new abyss, two years before Hitler finally overturned what was left of Archduke Eugen's empty home. At least he died before the bombing of Vienna; and when he could still drink a cup of coffee at the Tiroler Hof.

The next evening I did not notice if the Archduke Eugen came to drink coffee or not.

29

In 1903 travel in Europe was a rest cure compared to the travel of to-day. There were no crowds of fellow tourists; we needed no passports; officials at frontiers were for the protection and convenience of the public rather than for its restraint. British travellers were treated as distinguished guests, and universally trusted. Their cheques were cashed at sight.

The journey between Innsbruck and Cortina is still beautiful, but when we took it the train went no further than Toblach; and we drove from there through a dustless rock garden, unhurried by any other form of traffic, winding between foothills below tremendous peaks. Amber torrents tossed their way through forests of changing leaves beneath us, while above us waterfalls leaped from the slopes of snow-peaked mountains, in sheets of white foam, catching rainbows of shifting light.

The first part of our journey we took in a sauntering jovial little train which stopped at a dozen small, sweet-scented villages, deep in meadows filled with forget-me-nots, ragged robins, and brilliant vetches, orange, pink, purple and yellow.

Once we stopped for so long that a kindly guard allowed us to descend and explore the nearest meadow, where we sat on a grassy bank and watched our future spread itself before us lost in blossom trees; and drenched with sunny air. We did not speak of love or marriage, yet all suspense between us suddenly dropped.

I knew that whatever was in my heart or mind, by some strange form of alchemy would be transmitted to Ernan's.

We were without health or money and surrounded by a vast, unawakened innocence, yet I doubt if I have ever felt so free from fear before or since. At last the guard whistled for us as he had promised, and we reluctantly left our heartsease and forget-me-nots, to join my mother in the indulgent train.

Everything pleased my mother, the air, the light, even the food; and best of all she had never found anyone so punctiliously reliable as Ernan.

I doubt if she considered seriously either his prospects or his intentions. A French mother would have found this attitude towards her daughter's unavowed lover little short of criminal; but my mother had entire confidence in us both, and as little sense of reality as either of us.

The small wooden Post Hotel at Toblach seemed like paradise to us all three. My mother and I had adjoining rooms, opening on a balcony that faced the Drei Zinnen. These three peaks take the sky into partnership. They tone with the landscape in a group as fascinating to observe as if Michelangelo's constructive intelligence had purposefully designed them.

Ernan joined us for sunset. The peaks, while we watched them, changed from rose colour into amethyst; then darkening slowly in the colourless clear air, they became startling silhouettes of deepest indigo.

One by one, small brilliant points of light pierced the empty dome of sky and mellowed slowly into large golden stars. The air was piercingly sweet and cold, like frozen hay, and perfectly still. The little inn seemed to have been dropped for us overnight, like something in a fairy tale, never to be found again, except in memory.

We slept to the sound of distant waterfalls.

Ernan was out at five o'clock next morning, hunting for places where we could reach easiest the most repaying views.

Yet, when the day's heat brought our escorted ramble to an end, we settled down quite as happily in a small pine wood, devoid of views, close to the back of a summer hotel, still empty, but being rapidly repaired for expected guests. Carpets were being beaten, and sheets hung close to us. What little of the sky we saw was a bright and burning blue, between pine stems, the exact colour of the small star gentians which were spread all round us. My mother went in to write letters; and we began a conversation that possessed a deep flavour of intimacy, without any particular point. In a few minutes, in spite of flapping sheets and blows upon carpets, we discovered that we were engaged.

The strangest part of it was the physiological effect that Ernan's proposal had upon the mosquitoes which had been tormenting us. For at least twenty-four hours afterwards, these rapacious insects forbore their function.

We kept our secret for that day to ourselves; but I felt that my mother must be told before we slept; and Ernan felt with equal emphasis that his mother must not be told for a long time. He had been her whole life for seven years, since the death of her eldest son Ralph, and our engagement was bound to be a severe blow to her.

We must, he explained, break it gradually after she had learned to care for me, a process in which Ernan, at the moment, saw no particular difficulty.

Curiously enough I felt that I would rather have told Elena than my mother; perhaps I needed the encouragement of a more Spartan and less natural sanction.

My mother *did* like our engagement. She had expected it; and was enchanted by Ernan. His health, in spite of a family delicacy, appeared sufficiently robust. She swept aside his immediate lack of prospects. It was obvious that I must get much better before marriage could be considered; so that he had plenty of time to choose a profession. If Ernan was well enough off to go into the Diplomatic Service, which then required private means of four hundred a year, he was well enough off to marry.

If not, why shouldn't he, with his devout Church principles, become a clergyman? A chaplaincy on the Riviera would be just the thing for both of us. But meanwhile it was half-past nine, and we must not forget our long drive tomorrow. We had better stop talking at once and go to bed!

We should both have liked *not* to go to bed quite so soon; but young people in those days seldom rebelled from the *less* drastic suggestions thrust upon them by their elders. Anything more serious than a question of bed-time, I think I might have resisted successfully. But as there were no objections to my marrying Ernan,

I went to bed without a murmur; still I never attempted to go to sleep.

Had I not got my whole life to arrange as well as Ernan's?

Must I not think out this new unknown relationship, and draw into it, one by one, all my old ones?

It was my birthday, the thirty-first of May. The windows of my little room were without curtains and the moonlight shone all night long across the floor. The dawn came before I was ready for it. As soon as it was light enough I started writing long letters to Elena and Lislie; and I think before breakfast time I had added shorter ones to each member of my family. I wished to make my whole future as plain to my immediate circle as I myself saw it.

I believe that I made it admirably plain, yet none of those future arrangements, dove-tailing so logically into each other, ever came to pass.

30

If we had been able to marry within the year of our first engagement, while nature was still prepared to work her faultless miracle with our connivance, our marriage might have been, if not more successful, much simpler in its workings.

We were not only both of us deeply in love, but we were malleable and eager to take our lessons from each other. Our ideals and our habits were strikingly similar, even our childhood frustrations had been the same, whereas when we joined our lives again after long separation, it was as adults who had been forced to learn the chief lessons of life singly; nor could either of us fully understand the steps the other had sometimes been forced to take.

The attraction was the same but the supple material of youth and first love had been wasted. There was, however, only one way in which we could have married immediately, we could have lived with Mamma as she wished us to do, and pooled our slender resources. But before we met, Ernan had decided that he must separate himself from his mother, or else drown in the sea of her protective love.

He had already taken the first plunge out of his mother's clutches. Self-sacrificing, generous and intelligent as Mamma was, it must be confessed that she had clutches; and that she lived not only *for* Ernan but *on* him.

If he married me under those conditions, and I think in his eagerness for our immediate marriage as well as in his deep sympathy with Mamma's loneliness, he would have sacrificed even his new-found freedom, I knew that I could not sacrifice either his freedom or my own. I already knew only too well what living with a devoted, neurotic invalid involved. Mamma was willing to give Ernan everything she possessed—but at the price of possessing him.

Ernan's flight to London and their separation at St. Moritz was her first real defeat, but she had not accepted it as final. Now she was threatened by a greater danger. Ernan had fallen in love with a stray girl—nameless and penniless and half American. The wrong half too, for though when I was young it was not unknown for rich American girls to marry British husbands, nobody expected an English girl to marry a poor American man.

What could Mamma do in the face of such a disaster?

Mamma first ignored the possibility with smiling good humour, when these tactics failed she withdrew herself entirely from the scene of action. Surely Ernan would follow her! Her withdrawal both disturbed and distressed Ernan, much more deeply no doubt than I then realized, but it proved insufficient. He stayed where he was. Finally Mamma, with despair in her heart, decided to re-join us, at Cortina.

She signalled for Ernan's ready escort, and my mother and I prepared light-heartedly to receive her.

The Maioni was little more than a wayside Inn, but we filled her simple little wooden room with flowers, and persuaded the enchanting Maioni sisters to kill a chicken in her honour. She arrived white and speechless and went straight to her room. The next day we sent messages imploring her to join us in our readings and excursions, but she gently refused all our invitations. She was not, she said, strong enough for such undertakings.

We had to meet for the two principal meals of the day, for Maria and Lena were never off their feet; and there was only one table alike for house-guests and chance travellers.

Mamma smilingly ignored my efforts to entertain her; but she did worse than ignore the kindred efforts of my mother.

She fought her with smooth words and fierce eyes whenever they met.

Strangely enough their basic interests were exactly the same; and it hardly seemed possible that High Church Anglicanism—which was their religion—and ill-health, which was their favourite topic, should so lend themselves to lethal purposes.

We had expected that since our mothers had so much in common —including ourselves—they were bound to become good companions; and we could not understand their failure to take advantage of so much common ground.

My mother was the least aggressive of women but when roused by perpetual prodding she could state her opinions with Quaker directness. Both had good manners, and a gift for words; unfortunately these qualities made matters worse.

Mamma retired relentlessly to her room. She went to church at the same time that we went on Sunday; but that was all we succeeded in seeing of her.

I hated to think of how she must have suffered in that hot dusty little room, racked by her fears and tormented by her anger! We took her the loveliest flowers we could find, sweet scented white orchids, and ones that brilliantly simulated bees and flies, but our offerings only made her ill and had to be thrown away. Sometimes she allowed me to come into her room for a few minutes, gently drawn there by Ernan, who still clung to the fallacy that the sight of me might act as a panacea; but it was obvious that Mamma was even more unhealed in my company than out of it. There seemed no question of breaking the news of our engagement to her. If our mere acknowledged friendship reduced her to such misery, what would she not suffer at the thought of our marriage?

In spite of this bitter undercurrent of human misery we remained incredibly happy. We were *in* time but we did not seem to be *of* it; or in the least conscious that it was bearing us away, with all its other less fortunate children. We worked and wandered all day long, Ernan retiring at intervals into a barn where he had hired a seriously afflicted piano, and I into a little green arbour where I wrote an entire book, destined unfortunately to destruction.

I was too happy to write an imaginary story; and too much in love to describe my own happiness, so that I took instead the character of my French teacher friend, and created a plot that seemed to suit it. Unfortunately it turned out to suit her personality only too well, for it was her actual story that I had imagined and which she had never told anyone—including myself. If publicly revealed

222

she would, she explained, have to give up her career in England. So I destroyed the MS.

During this first summer of enchantment Ernan and I never quarrelled, but there were two occasions when we were momentarily shocked apart by two not unfounded criticisms of Mamma's in which I felt, since he retailed them to me, that he participated. She found, she told Ernan, that both my mother and myself were arbitrary in our opinions.

The sting of this remark bit deep, Ernan was astonished at the horror I evinced; and eventually withdrew his part of the criticism, just as I was preparing myself to accept it.

Then it seemed that Mamma found my clothes ill-chosen; in particular she resented a Tyrolean straw hat with a jaunty side feather, which I had bought at Innsbruck, in fond pride, for three and sixpence. She thought it extremely common.

These two dread comments revived in me the nightmare of Uncle Frank's broken engagement. Were they not the preliminary signals of disenchantment? It seemed that they were not. Ernan hastened to assure me that he liked nearly all my clothes, particularly a woollen handkerchief covered with bright pink cherries, which I wore across my shoulders and over my breast in a fichu. Shortly afterwards I gave up wearing the Tyrolean hat.

Perhaps it was just as well that Mamma refused to accompany us on our single driving excursion of two days and a night, shared and presented to us by my mother.

The two fat farm horses Leo and Lena drew up to the door in state, they had bells on their harness and shone like the day itself. The whole household came out to admire them. Leo was a powerful steady horse with rock-like nerves. Lena preferred drama to industry and shied at a dancing leaf. Both were treated as household pets, and we gave them our breakfast sugar whenever we saw them.

All the flowers we had lost when the hay was cut in our valley met us again with a finer, brighter ardour as we climbed Tre Croci.

Ernan and I walked part of the way to spare the horses, and while we rested in the last pine wood, before the trees stopped, a procession of children and dancing kids, led by a little boy playing on a pipe, broke into our delighted vision, like the first page of a fairy tale.

We stopped at Tre Croci to lunch and rest the horses, and then drove along the ridge to Misurina. Misurina, and its little lake, lay in a hollow, held like a cup against the sky. We ate the pink trout we watched caught for supper; and woke at dawn, when the cow-bells first sounded, cold and clear, before the last stars had time to fade behind the nearest peak.

In the extraordinary hush that followed, Ernan and I slipped out of the little inn, drawn by the same compulsion; and rowed out on the shimmering lake. The sun rounded the peak and covered the water with deep gold. It grew curiously hot. Strange puffs of luminous cloud massed themselves together. We paid them no particular attention till we grew aware that the air was darkening all round us and great drops spattered into the boat. Then the whole sky swooped down on us.

The lake rose hissing and pattering, white with fury, clutching at our little boat with fearful ferocity. In a second we were drenched to the skin. The inn family waved and shouted directions to us from the further bank.

Ernan rowed with masterful speed, and I bailed passionately. I don't think either of us had time to feel alarm before we reached the tiny pier, just as the boat sank under us. We ate an enormous breakfast clothed in queer-smelling garments, much too large for us —for we were slender creatures—loaned by the proprietor, while our clothes dried.

On our way down the mountain, however, we had a less innocuous adventure, in which my mother unfortunately was equally involved.

The little stream we had driven through the night before, which had barely wet the horses' hoofs, was now a raging torrent.

Leo and Lena made a valiant attempt to breast the rapids but stuck in the middle. Only the herculean efforts of Ernan and the driver, up to their waists in water, prevented the carriage, with my mother and myself in it, from over-turning. The effect of danger upon Lena's excitable nerves was astonishing. She became perfectly calm, and pulled us into safety as steadily as Leo. My mother prepared for death but was quite quiet about it; although she refused to drive again off the main road. I suppose the driver was in just as much danger as Ernan, but I never gave *his* danger a thought. We arrived in safety on the opposite bank; and by the time we had rested the horses sufficiently to start again, the torrent had once more become a reasonable mountain rill.

The summer ended by my having a mysterious illness. I seemed unable to sleep or eat, and had to sit up at night to breathe with any comfort. The village doctor was called in. It was not, he assured us, a relapse of the lungs, but I had rather seriously, for the moment, over-strained my heart. I must remain absolutely quiet, and he suggested that I give up considering Davos for the winter; and urged that my mother should put off her return to England, till I was well enough to move to a lower altitude. My mother was aghast; but she soon persuaded herself and me that this was after all but the opinion of a village doctor, a man who spoke very little English, and could easily be quite wrong about my heart. Why not instead travel at once to Davos and take Dr. Huggard's advice? Meanwhile my mother decided to go home even sooner than she had intended.

Mamma when told of the doctor's suggestions took a contrary view. She refused to leave Cortina immediately. She always took three weeks to pack, and if it were necessary for me to disobey the doctor's apparently sensible advice, she suggested that my mother might very well take me to Davos herself—if indeed she cared to risk another thousand feet upon a heart already strained—before herself returning to England.

My mother was equally sure that she would do nothing of the kind. The decision about Davos, she left to me; but she intended, with Ernan's escort as far as Innsbruck, to return home immediately.

I understood by now the mingled panic and agony which governed my mother's actions, although I found it hard to make Ernan accept it with the same confidence.

Particularly as he was now obliged, prematurely as we both thought, to break the news of our engagement to his mother before I was left in her charge.

The next day was Sunday; and Ernan decided that Mamma would best stand the shock if it were broken to her during the Celebration. He leaned forward and whispered, "Mamma, I want you to pray, specially for Phyllis". Mamma replied tartly, as far as a whisper can convey tartness, "Why specially for Phyllis? She is far more accustomed than I am to these wretched Low Church observances!"

Ernan temporarily abandoned the struggle, but before nightfall, egged on by my mother's urgency, he succeeded in making Mamma understand what she probably understood only too well already.

She took the blow better than he had dared to expect. Perhaps she still hoped that at twenty her son's choice, though foolish, need not be final.

I was too uncomfortable at the moment to care what anybody thought of anything so problematical as marriage, however I realized that I was to be left alone at five o'clock next morning with a woman who disliked me more than she had ever disliked anyone; and that however fast Ernan travelled, he must be away for at least three days and nights.

My mother was more upset at leaving me than I had ever seen her; and Ernan distractedly begged her to remain, which merely increased her distress. It often seems to an outside observer, that the compulsion to avoid responsibility is greater than the effort needed to accept it.

Leo and Lena bore them both relentlessly away, while a corn-crake ground his persistent note just outside my window.

I had pulled myself together to face these poignant farewells with cheerfulness, but I now relaxed into misery. The one comfort that remained to me in my loneliness was to be as ill as I felt.

A miracle took place. A knock sounded at the door. Surely this was not Mamma who entered? She knew exactly what to do to relieve discomfort. She was exquisitely wise and kind, a perfect nurse, and a delightful companion. All day long she nursed me, as I had never been nursed before. At night she refused to leave me, and had her things moved into my mother's room next door.

When Ernan returned four days later, breathless with anxiety, it was to find that Mamma had accepted a new child; and that I had found a guardian angel.

31

Our journey to Davos was taken three weeks later, at the time and with the leisure that Mamma considered necessary for travelling.

We arrived at Innsbruck on a hot summer night, at a cheap but highly recommended pension, to be told that they had only one single room vacant, the other two were in an annexe, where no food could be obtained, and where it was vaguely hinted there might be a certain absence of service.

Mamma was greatly distressed. Morally speaking, as a chaperon, she felt that she and Ernan should go to the annexe together; but, physically speaking, she knew that she had better remain where she was.

Ernan and I knew very well which we wanted, but we wisely left the decision to her. I had made a very good recovery from my strained heart, and walks to and fro from an annexe by moonlight were greatly to our taste. We had supper with Mamma, who talked herself into letting us take the plunge. We were to be accompanied to the annexe, and most mysteriously more than one porter sprang to our assistance. Upon their heads and in their hands they bore, not only our slender night luggage, but various articles of furniture.

The annexe was *not* next door; it was at the little street's end, and part of a newly built unfurnished house standing alone in a vacant lot. The second story flat, into which we were grandly ushered, had just been painted, and there were two half-furnished rooms, without lights. The September moon conveniently flooded them; the men dumped the furniture they had brought into two bedrooms side by side, which they obviously thought were one too many, and left us with laughing wishes that we felt it better not to understand.

Whether they did it as a joke, or by accident, we never knew, but they locked the flat door on the outside. This however we did not discover, till we woke rather late next morning to find that we were locked into a second story flat with no means of exit. The street was on the outskirts of the city, and for a long time no one came within hailing distance. Finally a man working in an adjoining field reluctantly laid down his hoe, and approached our windows.

He did not understand for a long time what we wanted, and when he did, he did not want to help us. However, when offered sufficient reward he agreed to find someone to take a message to the pension; and late in the morning we were freed by an intermediary with a key.

An atmosphere of intense gloom and terror met us at the Pension. Mamma had been taken extremely ill, in fact she appeared to be dying; a doctor sat by her bedside, holding her wrist in his hand. She was as white as death and incapable of speech. Recriminations were poured upon us by the landlady, and a group of condoling visitors. I think Mamma's anger at our appearing so late had something to do with her speechlessness, but at the time we feared she had had a stroke. Slipping on her shoe, she had trodden on a wasp, and had been very severely stung. It was a long while before everything was cleared up on either side, but at length she realized that we were comparatively innocent. She was for the time being very ill, and completely incapacitated for the next two days.

Greatly relieved by the doctor's verdict, and as soon as Mamma had forgiven us for being locked in, we proceeded to enjoy ourselves.

I doubt if anyone has ever been so happy in Innsbruck before or since.

We radiated rapture and relief, and everyone we met seemed to take part in our felicity.

We ate an omelet of superfine distinction at Igls by moonlight, with the mountains standing round us, still glowing rose red from the lingering sunset. Gazing at the tremendous range of the Nordkette between ourselves and Mittenwald we little dreamed that at the other end of it, on an eye-lid of land two thousand feet above the hidden town of Telfs, we should twenty years later make our favourite home.

In Innsbruck itself we window-shopped for hours planning exotic gifts for each other which we knew we could never buy. We got to know the Armoured Knights in the Hof Kirche as if they were our life-long friends; and were only slightly inconvenienced by the discovery that our clothes were filled by a vast population of excited fleas. I caught twenty-four from one stocking; and Ernan, who was much better at catching fleas than I was, produced forty from one of his socks in half the time.

Mamma never left the Pension, which she detested, until she was fit to travel.

After shuffling about interminably in a puzzled train gasping with heat at Saargans, we climbed in a few hours into deep snow. Dusk turned the foothills into magic; every shining glade and glistening mountain was more lovely than the last. The rising moon touched peak after peak.

> *Each spot an angel, silver shod, had lit upon,*
> *The place shone fresh; and bright, and lately trod*
> *A long track gleamed—where Enoch walked with God.*

Turquoise shadows crossed silvery hollows, and small lilac flames shone out of dark châlet windows as if to match them.

Night "with its stream of stars" deepened the mystery of this new frozen world.

Everything I had ever read of Arctic lands came back to me. Wolves would not have surprised me instead of calm Swiss porters, at the infrequent stations.

We were almost as tired as we were happy; but I think we both wished this moonlight journey might never have an end.

We arrived at Davos with shocking suddenness.

A hard, unlovely light showed up every detail of the spotless hygienic station. A man staggered out from the next carriage carrying his dying wife in his arms. His agonized face and her emaciated form shone clearly in the pitiless electric glare.

It was a shock against the heart to look at them.

Mamma too saw them; but we all pretended that we had not seen them; and drove in stricken silence up the sharply lighted village street.

The Bella Vista Hotel stood at the highest point of Davos Dorf. It was not like a hotel but like a small and well-kept hospital.

Spotless linoleum stretched over every floor; green sound-proof doors stood between us and a faint, persistent sound, which we were not to get out of our consciousness for the next three years, the sound of someone coughing. The bright deceptions of St. Moritz were no more. Davos was run, in those days, like a leper island, a very carefully and well-run leper island. Funerals took place only during the lunch hour; and regular inhabitants never asked invalids how they were or how long they were going to stay. Except for the faint sounds behind the padded green doors, there was complete silence.

We said good-night to each other in whispers and as if there were a chance that we might never meet again.

It was a strange place into which to have brought so much careless happiness.

The next morning the sun poured into my room in superhuman strength and glory.

In spite of the snow, the keen air from the open balcony door was not cold; it had a crisp wine-like quality, fragrant with the smell of frozen pine; and every breath I drew filled me with hope. Summer still lingered in the woods, and when the snow melted from the valley meadows, thin ghost-like crocus, chilled from pink to mauve, sprang up to take its place.

The old stone church had a bell so deep that when the Angelus rang at noon and sunset, the valley filled with music to its brim, blotting out all other sound.

There still lingered a personal memory of Robert Louis Stevenson and his friend John Addington Symonds. The houses they had lived in were pointed out to us with pride, and it was almost as if their eyes still rested on the changeless, incommunicable mountains.

Scientifically Davos was actively alive; X Rays and absonic indexes were talked about. All kinds of new injections were being tried with unpredictable results. One well-known doctor of German extraction was said to have killed his three healthy babies one after the other by an injection which was to prove whether they had tubercle or not; when his eye turned on his fourth and last baby his wife ran away with it in the night; and never returned. Each of the chief doctors had a band of impassioned believers. Dr. Huggard, who was to be the arbiter of our destinies, was a striking exception to British doctors abroad—quite a number of his un-British colleagues respected him—and he had many patients from other countries than his own. He had come to Davos in his youth, a physical wreck; and had first cured himself and then devoted his remarkable powers to curing others. He got up at five a.m. every morning and went to bed at midnight. A great deal of this extra time he spent in study. He was a determined psychologist and practised what he knew upon his patients' minds as well as upon their bodies. He was too clinically minded to arouse affection in his patients but we all admired him even when we trembled before him. He had a scathing tongue, and used it remorselessly upon the careless or unwary. Patients either obeyed Dr. Huggard or were driven from his door. He refused to use a telephone; and had a scale of charges which varied according to whether he considered his patients ill enough to send for him or not. If they sent for him for little or nothing, he charged exorbitantly, but if they really needed him they found his charges reasonable, and I believe there were even cases to which he gave a great amount of attention for nothing at all.

All three of us were to be in his charge, without the presence of any other counsellor or guide for the next three years; and he was particularly benevolent towards us. "Your united ages," he said on one occasion, "do not amount to mine. I therefore feel myself specially called upon—if you act intelligently—to be of use to you." And of use to us he certainly was.

Ernan and I put off going to see him for nearly a week, unable to face the possible end to our happiness. At last we summoned the necessary courage and called upon him together by appointment, while Mamma decided to remain at the Bella Vista to pray for us.

Ernan saw Dr. Huggard first, while I sat in a cold little waiting

231

room. Time came to a stop, till at last the door opened, and I saw Dr. Huggard's immense bald head shining just behind Ernan's shoulders.

As soon as we were alone in his consulting room, Dr. Huggard said to me kindly, "Your fiancé is going to get quite well—completely well—in a year's time or even less!" Then he turned his attention to me. I had never been asked so many questions in my life; most of them seemed to me irrelevant; and some of them unanswerable. "And now be quiet," he said with smiling abruptness before proceeding to examine me a great deal more thoroughly than I had ever been examined before. When he had finished he said, "I think you will get well too, but not quite so soon as your fiancé; and you must go into a sanatorium while you are up here because you are a sanatorium case."

This was a terrible threat. Tremblingly I begged to be allowed to escape my doom. I could not afford it; and I knew that apart from the loneliness and separation it involved, I should never be able to do uninterrupted work. Dr. Huggard listened, not unsympathetically. Perhaps my awed docility saved me, perhaps he too disliked the routine of hospitals; at length he said, "If you really want to work I will give you a single chance to remain free. If you follow my written instructions faithfully for a fortnight, cure in the open air nine hours a day, and never dance, smoke, or attempt any sports, you can improve as well where you are as in a sanatorium; but if you break any of my rules—and I shall know by your symptoms if you do, and *not* take your word for it—you will have to go into a sanatorium for the rest of this winter." Fervently I agreed to an implicit obedience; then I ventured to ask him if Dr. Maioni had not been wrong about my heart.

"No," Dr. Huggard said, "he told you the truth. You have a dilated heart, high altitudes are not good for you, and you may easily have over-strained it by climbing; but I should think the condition it is in now is of long standing and in time you will no doubt acquire compensatory muscles. This altitude, though higher than is quite suitable, is necessary for your lung condition and I think with due care you can adjust to it. But I must tell you that you cannot marry yet—not for another four or five years. I

232

things go well with you, you might be able to bear a child then, though I cannot promise this. No doubt you will both consider waiting a great hardship, but you are extremely young; and you can remain engaged. Happiness is very good for both of you!"

I left him, feeling full of confidence and freedom. The weight of the long years before our marriage could take place was not yet on my shoulders, and I felt convinced that I should be able to bear a child. I had expected a life sentence; and Dr. Huggard's verdict seemed to me in the nature of a reprieve rather than a penalty.

It was not until, with every cheerful aspect uppermost, I had told Ernan, that I realized the pain I was inflicting; and must share; for Ernan envisaged, as I had not, all the frustration and distractions of the years ahead.

Mamma took our sentences with unspoken relief, and deep kindness. We soon felt renewed hope. After all we loved each other, we were together; and life closed round us again with the spacious elasticity of time, which is youth's great prerogative. In the course of the next few days Mamma went to see Dr. Huggard for herself, and this proved the hardest of our immediate prospects. Dr. Huggard was quite pitiless. Mamma could not remain in Davos after November. She was too arthritic and too sensitive to drops in temperature. Arrangements must be made for her to go to the Riviera and wait for Ernan to join her in the spring.

Meanwhile the three of us had Davos almost to ourselves for the next two months; and in spite of our shadowy futures, it was—for Ernan and myself at least—a magic period. We were out all day curing together on our balconies; rowing upon the lake or wandering in pine woods. We talked as if time were never long enough for all we had to say to each other.

We felt just as happy with Ernan's mother as we had been with mine, perhaps even happier, for Mamma had no sense of time, and never seemed to care how early we started out on our wanderings, or how late we returned. We ran her errands, and if we wanted her companionship she was always there eager to give it to us. She even read Henry James out loud to us while we rested—in a most skilful manner—as if she were long accustomed to those intricate delusive sentences instead of just having been introduced to them

—overnight as it were—at the height of his middle period. We were reading at the time *What Maisie Knew* and *The Awkward Age*, books of which I never tired.

Lislie was to join us early in November before Mamma left. How would she and Ernan like each other? Blinded by the singleness of my preoccupation I came within an ace of destroying the felicity I had so ardently anticipated.

The Bella Vista, where Lislie had already spent a happy winter and consolidated pleasant relationships with returning guests, was in many ways less suitable for us than for her.

Ernan, for the sake of soaking himself in the German language, had decided on a German Pension, remote and cheap, with no English tongue under its roof. Mamma, who had to leave us in the course of the next few weeks, wanted to be close to him till the last minute, and had taken the only vacant room in a much warmer hotel near his Pension; while Ernan discovered, just before Lislie's arrival, a hotel close to Mamma and to him, with two south rooms and private balconies for Lislie and myself at the same price for which we had north ones at the Bella Vista. Davos was rapidly filling, and we had to give an immediate reply. There was no time to consult Lislie, and I felt assured of her consent, but it was a fatal precipitancy. Lislie did not care in the least about a south room or a private balcony; still less did it matter to her being near Mamma and Ernan.

She knew no foreign languages and the Kaiserhof, where we were to stay, was exclusively inhabited by Poles and Germans.

She wanted her pleasant English acquaintances, nor did she consider that I would have taken the Bella Vista hill at all seriously if I hadn't wished to be near Ernan. Besides, she feared—rightly as it turned out—that if we went off at tangents to three different hotels we should arouse a considerable amount of unkind talk. Her whole prospect of social entertainment for the winter was left in the lurch.

I might have understood better what I was asking Lislie to sacrifice had I ever had a social life, but that was an advantage of which I was entirely ignorant. We passed through terrible hours; but our friendship held firm; and Lislie never once threw up at me,

234

though all that she foresaw happened, the advantages she had had to forgo. To my intense relief, however, she found that she *did* like Ernan; and he had from the first moment generously accepted her. Both of them made adjustments so handsome and so entire that I doubt if I ever knew what it had cost either of them.

"I have been waiting," Dr. Huggard once said to me, "for you to quarrel, either with your friend or with your lover, for much longer than I had anticipated. Pray when do you propose to begin?" It was a question that many people asked themselves through the long years that followed.

Perhaps we could afford to combine so much harmony with so much intimacy, because our separate pursuits never came into competition. Ernan and I worked steadily apart, from four to six hours daily, while Lislie joined her Bella Vista friends on the skating rink, which was fortunately no further away from us at the Kaiserhof than it was from the Bella Vista. The social ban upon her soon lifted, in spite of the sinister effect of our living under three separate roofs, though I believe I was still considered by some of her Bella Vista friends as beyond a pale, which I never attempted to pass.

32

The winter of 1904–1905, in spite of tragic incidents, was one of the happiest of our lives. We worked, played and lived to suit ourselves. Nobody interfered with us, and our delight and confidence in each other increased with the time we spent together. We had intimacy without responsibility, and, moving in the same direction, our minds fixed on the same aim, neither of us realized that we did not know how to make a practical or sustained effort towards reaching an independent married life. We had set forth upon the ocean of life, like unwary mariners without training or discipline; and having never learned the simplest laws of navigation.

Ernan set to work under terrific tension to make good the gaps in his education. It is not easy at twenty-one to acquire, in six months' time, from worse than mediocre teachers, sufficient knowledge to pass a university entrance examination, learn two European languages sufficiently well for a diplomatic career; and to become an expert skier. Dr. Huggard had insisted on at least three hours' snow sports a day, exclusive of tobogganing, as part of Ernan's cure; and added to these pursuits Ernan had a natural desire to spend part of his time with a fiancée who was unable to join in either his work or play.

Pavloff's dogs were in a better situation than we were, for at least they had a master who knew to what purpose he was dedicating their conflicting efforts. The morality we practised as a matter of course undermined our nervous systems, while our constant anxiety as to each other's health acted as a spur to our passionate affection. There was no chance of our getting tired of each other, when there might be so little time in which to get tired.

With the sanatorium hanging over my head, I was the most Spartan curer of the three. I seldom missed, whatever the temperature or the temptation, my full nine hours a day in the open air.

Soon after eight o'clock every morning, established in a magnificent sheepskin-lined sack lent by my Grandmother Fowler, plus a hot water bottle on my knees, on which to unfreeze fountain pen and fingers, a wooden writing board designed by Dr. Huggard stretched across my chair, I took at a long, steady gulp, the first five hours of the day. No one else cured at so early an hour, so that I had perfect solitude and silence in which to think out my work before the temperature rose sufficiently for me to use my wool-clad fingers in the act of writing.

I loved the company of the cold, blue-white peaks, my eyes learned every visible curve and hollow, so that when I revisited Davos forty years later, I felt as if I had been suddenly put back into a nursery in which I had played as a child.

Far down the valley to the south the twin ranges opened, and through the narrow gap shone the first apricot light. Sometimes the stars were still visible, their gold sharpening into diamond against a background of pale blue. Slowly the light increased, drinking up the valley mist, until with a bound the sun shot over a distant peak pouring a flood of golden warmth over the waiting valley.

There were mornings when the mountains had a rigid, wizened look; and a colourless light came up the valley. The sky lost its cold purity; and filled rapidly with ragged clouds churning down huge snowflakes, each like a separate flower petal carved in crystal. The flakes fell gently with unhurried persistence, turning back upon themselves in the still air, as if uncertain whether to come or go. The mind grew dizzy watching them, and yet there was something inexplicably soothing in their purposeless, unhurried flight.

Our private balconies, side by side, with their due south exposure, were a great gain to Lislie and me, physically and mentally, for both sun and time streamed round us uninterruptedly. They were our sitting-rooms, and though they cut us off from our fellow guests except at meal times, the language barrier was already a sufficient, and perhaps not unfortunate, obstacle to social intercourse. We were told by Ernan's French teacher, who had several friends among them, that we were described as "good girls without pride", and we were also told, though too late to do anything about it, that the hotel we were in was considered markedly disreputable. However we never suffered the slightest inconvenience from the habits of our neighbours; perhaps the daily appearance of Ernan, who was tall and of a robust appearance, may have acted as a safeguard. I was not without fears of our open balcony doors at night, but Ernan reassured me by showing what an admirable missile a glass water bottle would make in case of need; and having placed mine within reach of my bedside every night, my fears subsided.

Lislie had no fears. She always took for granted that when dangers turned up it would be time enough to deal with them.

Late one night there was a loud crash, followed by screams, pictures fell from walls, vases from tables; accompanied by a strange, intermittent shaking. Lislie called from her adjoining room: "Oh Phil, what is it?" to which I replied soothingly, for my mind had leapt for one terrified moment to a slightly intemperate Pole next door, "Don't be frightened darling, it's only an earthquake!" "If that isn't like you Phil," Lislie replied with scorn, "no man is anything *like* as dangerous as an earthquake!"

The earthquake, which for Davos was a great event, had much smaller proportions in my mind than an incident which had taken place the day before we left the Bella Vista. This incident, caused by a clergyman, rankled for weeks afterwards.

Mr. Pentecost, the name was his real one, had a belligerent nature, and was not generally liked by any of his fellow guests. He had, I think, a wish to be jocular; and it is very hard to be jocular without a friendly audience. Unconsciously we had, by the natural exuberance of our youth and freedom, snatched away his rôle. Mamma had left us for a warmer hotel as soon as Lislie had joined me. It was only a matter of days till we followed into her neighbourhood; and perhaps though her absence did not add to our good spirits, it may have made them more openly buoyant. There were four of us, in our early twenties, who sat at one table, and our jokes were highly congenial to each other.

One day after lunch Mr. Pentecost followed us into a small

sitting room off the hall. The hotel gossip had wound herself across the heater, the hall was full of replete guests well within earshot, when he proceeded to attack us.

Were we not aware, he shouted, of the extreme gravity of the place we were in, its constant heartbreaks and terrible physical suffering? Our atrocious laughter at meals, our lightheartedness generally were a constant source of annoyance, and our presence disturbed and displeased everyone in the hotel. When he first began his attack in a high, excited voice, I thought he meant to be funny, and to show my appreciation of his jocular intent I fatally laughed again; this naturally increased his rage. Our feeble efforts at self-defence he dashed away, with increasing violence. The hotel gossip, all eyes and ears, listened, enchanted by the scene. One of us said at last, with sufficient firmness to be listened to, "Mr. Pentecost, we leave tomorrow, do you not think you have said enough?" With a furious gesture he cried out: "I don't care where you go, or what you do!" and tore out of the room.

The hotel gossip unwound herself from the heater, and very kindly told us not to take Mr. Pentecost's words too much to heart. She had heard no complaints from the other guests, and rather thought she would have heard had there been any. For her part, she liked a little laughter in so sad a place as Davos; and she hurried away to spread Mr. Pentecost's remarks to any of our fellow guests unfortunate enough not to have overheard them.

Perhaps we *had* laughed too much, perhaps our laughter when unshared might be unpleasant to others. Perhaps, worst sting of all, our laughter itself was but a form of cowardice? But these reflections came long after the event. The immediate reaction to Mr. Pentecost's remarks was rage shared by all three of us. Had *we* no sorrows? Was it not true that the worst cases in the Bella Vista were our best friends? It was true we laughed, but we did not laugh *at* people, we laughed *with* them!

Ernan took the situation with extreme gravity. He must, he said, take some form of challenge to Mr. Pentecost. Lislie and I had been insulted; and as our protector he could not let the matter rest.

Ernan was twenty-one and Mr. Pentecost perhaps twenty years older. He couldn't be knocked down since that might produce a haemorrhage. He should, however, Ernan thought, be horse-whipped. None of us unfortunately had such a thing as a horse-whip about us. Well—then he must be driven to apologize, and we all three set to work on how Ernan should drive him, with all the felicity of "l'esprit d'escalier".

The scene took place under our balcony window at dusk, and Lislie and I listened with avidity.

Mr. Pentecost was asked, in no uncertain terms, to apologize. He made matters worse by explaining in a fatherly manner, that his remarks were really meant more for Lislie than for myself; he realized that Ernan's fiancée was a much more serious person than Miss Brock and rather misled than intentionally wild. Ernan then remarked that this made matters very much worse, as I should resent the insult much more seriously for Lislie than for myself, and that it was a pity he could no longer challenge Mr. Pentecost to a duel. Mr. Pentecost tried to laugh this off, but in the end he lost his temper and retired in a passion. He had got the worst of it, but we were all three doubtful as to whether he had listened to the worst. People in a passion are seldom able to take in what is said to them, about what has caused it.

We held a further council of war, and I suggested a letter, one which could be calculated to produce the most unpleasant results in the fewest possible words; and since this form of expression was my métier, I soon produced such a letter, reading it aloud, to the admiration of my two companions. Ernan felt that the letter was exactly what was needed. We would all three sign it; and Ernan would push it under Mr. Pentecost's bedroom door. In it he was told that he was neither a Christian nor a gentleman. It was a good night-cap.

But Lislie said, "It's a lovely letter Phil! And it's done us a lot of good already—now let's tear it up! After all Mr. Pentecost's very ill!" So we tore it up; and Mr. Pentecost went unpunished, except that when we infrequently met him in the village street we all three solemnly cut him; and he—rather regretfully, I sometimes thought—whistled as he passed us.

In our new hotel we were no longer exposed to such temptations. Lislie and I had a table to ourselves in a corner. The Poles and

Germans sat at one long table down the middle of the room; and all the noise was made by them. Prussians barked, and from the Poles and Russians a Slav hurricane of conversation drowned out all other sound.

Our defence—if defence it were—of laughter was rapidly put to a severe test. In the course of one week we were summoned to attend three death beds.

Lislie was wholly unfamiliar with death, and Ernan and I were if anything more vulnerable from our recent family losses.

The first of our friends to die was Winnie Thomas, the sister of our special friend Muriel. She died the hard way, without compunction or complaint, as Emily Brontë was said to die. She sent for us, she explained, because we had often amused her, and she wanted to ask us to stick to Muriel. She would see no one else, not even the Davos Chaplain. She could pray by herself if she wanted to, she explained, and it wouldn't make her cough so much.

Winnie had been a famous hockey player, and it was when she realized that she could play no more hockey that she had given up the already hopeless struggle for life. "I don't mind dying now," she told us. "I'm very uncomfortable, as you can see for yourselves, but I shan't die till I've seen my father and mother and can leave Muriel with them. I only hope I shan't keep them hanging about here afterwards." I don't know how she managed to keep alive another twenty-four hours, for she was choking to death when we saw her; but she did just manage it. Her parents arrived at midday. She insisted on their resting and having a meal before they saw her, and died in their presence three hours later. She *was* successful in not keeping them hanging about afterwards.

We were appalled by this interview, but much more heart-rent by the one that followed two days later. Gwen Smeaton was a young married woman with a baby of four months old. She was a great friend of Lislie's and both of us had hoped against hope that she would recover. She had everything to live for, an adored and adoring husband, and after nine years' waiting this one child crowning their lives with joy.

She had brought the baby and its nurse to Davos with her; but she only saw it out of doors on her balcony, handling it with exquisite care and precaution against infection, while she had strength to hold it.

She had had six months' savage, hopeless illness; and she died completely undemoralized and serene. She sent for us, she explained, partly because we were her special friends, but chiefly because she knew we were ill, and she wanted us to realize—if we *did* get worse —that death came as a friend. She had been so intensely happy in her earthly life as to make her feel sure the Creator of the life she knew must be the source of happiness in the unknown life she was about to enter. There was nothing terrible in saying good-bye to Gwen. Nevertheless the fact remained that she was leaving her husband and child; and a few hours later she had left them.

Cold disgust without fear had been what we had faced with Winnie; for Gwen we had to face nothing but the sense of our own inadequacy. Yet it was as if Davos itself—with its myriad, variegated dooms—had settled down on us. When we came home to be comforted by Mamma it was to find a letter which added to our distress. It was from a young St. Moritz boy, whom I had only met once or twice at the Invalids' Home the previous winter. Dr. Holland had declared that his was a mere precautionary case after an attack of pneumonia; and that he would be well in three months. I had caught sight of him a few weeks earlier in Davos, and had been shocked by the change in him. The note was to ask me if I could possibly call on him, as he was unable to go out, and there was something he wanted specially to ask me. I had thought him on first sight a conceited, uppish boy; and nothing had changed my opinion. Now I was frightened. I knew that I must go to see him, and find out what he needed. Neither Ernan nor Lislie wanted me to go. Ernan offered to go instead, but I felt I had snubbed the boy unfairly and owed him what reparation was within my power. Ernan, who accompanied me to a poor little châlet which we had never noticed before, on the outskirts of the Dorf, waited for me outside the gate.

The landlady was busy scrubbing a kitchen floor which needed it. There was no sitting room.

She told me to go to the top of the house, and that I would find her lodger's room opposite the stairs. She added that had she known he was so ill she would never have taken him in. She had never anticipated having to carry up his meals.

I found him in an ice-cold attic in which there seemed to be nothing else but his paper-thin, white figure, poured out like milk, on his small camp bed.

His shallow breathing shook what was left of him every time it came and went. It was insufficient for more than a word or two at a time. He would pause, quite calmly, till the next breath came, like a clever mechanic using a run down machine. "You must think it very funny," he began, "my asking to see you. I know you don't like me. But I'm dying now, so I thought you wouldn't mind."

There was the same light of battle in his eyes that I had thought before was aggressive vanity; I knew now that it was courage.

I quickly said that of course I didn't dislike him—I had only not known him, that I would do anything he liked, and would come often to see him. He didn't listen to me. He simply waited, until he had collected enough strength to go on. "I am sure you can write the sort of letter I want sent to my mother when I am dead," he explained. "Tell her how comfortable I was—and people kind. Say that I had everything I could possibly want. Will you?" I said I would. I knew that his mother was a widow and that he was her only child. Very cautiously he spelled out his mother's address. "Say that I didn't mind dying," he went on, "except leaving her of course—and that it was—easy!" I said that I would say that it was easy. "That's all," he whispered. It had taken him a long while to collect his last strength, but I could not leave him quite like that. "Can't I do anything?" I said. "Haven't you any friends—wouldn't you like to see the Chaplain?"

"Oh yes!" he said. "I forgot! She'd like that. Tell her I saw the Parson—often!" "Wouldn't you like me to get him now?" I pleaded. "No," he said, "please don't! Once—was enough!" His eyes meeting mine smiled. I saw that he could do no more with what was left to him, so I went. Ernan was still waiting for me when I came out. "I'll never let you go and see sick people again!" he said firmly. "You're too upset!" There was however no need for me to go again, because when we went together next day with flowers, it was to find him dead. We all three attended his funeral. We were

243

his only mourners. Three deaths in a week were too much for us; so we decided to spend all the money we had in one wild orgy, and get away into some healthy place in the mountains full of cows and peasants.

We took a sleigh with two horses, skis and food, and tried to drive beyond what we had had to share.

It was a perfect day. The sky a burning cloudless blue, the pines intoxicated us with their scent. We drove deeper and deeper into the mountain silence—far away from that low persistent sound of coughing that we had learned to dread.

The peace, the sun-warmed air, the heavenly light plunged us into ecstasy. Nothing moved in the motionless trees; no living thing stirred in the silent woods. The earth lay lifeless under the sparkling snow. There seemed nothing to be afraid of any more. The old catholic prayer beat through the beauty of the day its endless reassurance, "May their souls rest in peace and may light perpetual shine upon them!" We climbed higher and higher, until at last we reached an opening in the woods, where below the glittering peaks a little village lay curled like a sleeping dormouse. I have forgotten its name, but there was a Posting Inn where we could put up the horses. We ate our lunch in a courtyard with a magnificent view and laughed so much over it that it was a good thing Mr. Pentecost was nowhere near to hear us. Suddenly a girl appeared, leading a long string of very beautiful cows behind her. The cows were an alluring beige in colour with huge eyelashes and clean as household pets. She took them to a trough with a pump and they drank with great good manners, as if eternity were before them, returning in the same order to their dark stalls. Ernan and Lislie found a treeless slope to practise ski-ing on; while I sat and watched a huge sapphire-coloured icicle melting in the sun. I had nothing to do but think, and I found it better, now that I was alone, to let the experiences of the past week filter through me, and no longer to try to dodge their deep significance.

I was prepared to face death for myself, or thought that I was, but not to face the loss of my two companions. I felt that I might physically survive them, but the loss of my lover would have killed all that I meant by joy; and Lislie was at once my conscience and my sister. I felt sure that there was no one in the world to be compared with either of them; and I had so fastened my identity into their personalities, that I could see nothing at all over the rim of their lives. It was into the pit of this nothingness that I now forced myself to look.

Dr. Huggard had scolded me severely on my last visit to him, and once more threatened me with the sanatorium. "You seem to me to lack discrimination," he said. "You should remember while you are in such a place as this that no one—including yourself—should have more to contend with than his own symptoms. Each patient has his own consolations which you know nothing about, and is very often unconscious of his doom. When he isn't—he is probably far too uncomfortable to resent dying. If you have to think about another ill person—pray do not add to his suffering all the others you have heard about in Davos. It is quite unnecessary. No one up here has more to bear than his own illness; and death is not repeated twice. Besides I can assure you that there are many worse forms of death than tuberculosis." Now I repeated his words to myself with a deeper significance.

It was impossible to fear anything alone with this beneficent stillness. The sunlight, and the unsullied snow peaks rose above me, soothing every nerve. I found that I could accept the thought of death as easily as the thought of life.

I even began to believe that I might *not* lose either Ernan or Lislie; and when they returned from their ski-ing, bringing our lost gaiety with them, I was able to share it.

33

Our first winter in Davos together, under the sarcastic but stimulating probes of Dr. Huggard, proved a triumphant success. Ernan's tubercular trouble was checked for life; Lislie's general health improved greatly; and I put on nearly two stone in weight; and felt that I could take on the world.

We were, however, kept up in the high mountains longer than most of our friends. The three of us, left to ourselves, explored by rail or Post the nearest villages, where we made friends with startled sleepy Swiss in mountain inns, ate austere lunches out of paper bags, and returned full of light and air, enriched by some new peak in our mind's eye. The days began with long celestial dawns, and closed late, with flaming sunsets. The bright and living air was *Herrlich wie am ersten Tag.*

Dr. Huggard agreed to Thusis, which he said was no damper than anywhere else, for the month of April, before we were allowed to go home. The day before we left Lislie developed a poisoned thumb. She cajoled the young surgeon, to whom she had been sent to get it lanced, to allow her to postpone the operation till we reached Thusis; and did not tell him that we were crossing the Passes between Davos and Thusis by Post. The shaking and bounding of these medieval vehicles over half thawed roads released the poison into her system. By the time we reached Thusis I was horrified to see how ill Lislie looked; finding on arrival that her temperature was 103° and that she had a swelling under her arm, we summoned the nearest doctor.

Dr. Schreiber was one of our best medical finds. He had the tough resiliency of a cricket ball, a wild and wonderful command of the

English language, and the cheerful courage of a bull terrier. He lived at full tilt, working twelve hours a day, ski-ing, riding or climbing over his mountain district, in all weathers, on one enormous meal a day, which he ate when his day's work was over.

He operated that evening on Lislie and ordered her to be given a wine-glass full of brandy neat every hour, straight round the clock. Lislie became brilliantly conversational by morning, but remained cold-sober and coherent, to the treatment's end. There is very little doubt it saved her life. On his second visit Dr. Schreiber saw Ernan and myself, alone, and without Lislie's knowledge. He told us kindly but frankly that though Lislie might pull through her present illness, she must die of T.B. in the course of the next few months. He begged us to telegraph immediately for her parents and meanwhile to authorize him to send her by ambulance to the nearest sanatorium. "You are young," he urged. "You have your whole lives before you, and you are exposing yourselves to great risks, and for a person who, however dear she is to you, is beyond saving!"

It was a dreadful dilemma, for we knew that the Brocks could not afford to come out together for an indefinite period, nor to pay heavy sanatorium expenses. I felt that I was trying my young lover very hard, but Ernan did not fail me. He agreed without hesitation that we should nurse Lislie by ourselves. Dr. Schreiber respected our decision, and said, "Very well then—we will do the next best thing—care for her as well as possible, until she is able to travel home." For three weeks we nursed her night and day. Lislie's recovery was like watching a tide inch backwards in the teeth of a gale. At first it was doubtful if she moved at all—and, even when we saw she was not losing ground, her recovery was very slow.

A clergyman cousin of Ernan's stopped for a night with us, on his way down from St. Moritz, and finding how ill Lislie was, begged us to let him administer what might well be the last Sacrament.

Lislie had no idea of the gravity of her own condition, but it was Easter, so that she agreed readily to taking the Sacrament with us. When I had prepared the room, and was about to call the two young men to her bedside, she stopped me. "Phil," she said, "you've forgotten my rouge and powder. I must make up before these two men come in here!" I was both astonished and horrified. "But Lislie," I exclaimed, "you forget, Harold is a *Priest*, he will never notice what your face looks like while he is administering the Sacrament!" "Nonsense!" Lislie said firmly. "Priests are men, and aren't blind! Do as I tell you!" And to my astonishment, when the Service was over, Harold told Ernan over the breakfast table, "You know I think Miss Brock must be going to recover, she has such a lovely complexion!"

Lislie was always inspiriting to nurse. Nothing shook her fortitude, nor clouded her alert curiosity; nor did any physical symptoms, however dire, demoralize her gaiety of heart. Whatever she could do for herself she enjoyed doing, and what she couldn't, she left without protest to her nurse. At first we went out singly, so as not to leave her alone, but as soon as she was safe to leave, we took our walks together, between patches of late snow, in the pine woods and up the mountain sides.

The woods were full of hepaticas, wind anemones, and violets of every colour; and day by day the spring drove fear further from our hearts.

In five weeks Lislie was able to travel to Basle, where we spent the night, parting next day from Ernan, who was joining Mamma at Zürich. It was a hard parting. For eighteen months Ernan and I had been continuously together. I doubt if married people of many years' standing knew each other as well, or depended upon each other's company nearly so much.

We had no money for sleepers, but Ernan had managed to find us a free side, so that Lislie could lie down all night. Whenever, for brief intervals, I slept, I heard Ernan's voice, with terrible urgency, calling to me; and when the slow pale morning dawned, I felt as if half of me had fallen over a precipice; and the half that hadn't fallen, envied the other half.

After leaving us at Basle, Ernan rejoined Mamma at Zürich and they travelled to Geneva, where Ernan was sharply ill for several weeks. They were to summer on the lake together, and as soon as Ernan had recovered from his illness he went to live in a French Professor's family.

There he found what he most needed, a life with healthy young

contemporaries, and out-door amusements. He combined swimming, mountain climbing and fencing with hard work; but it was
congenial work against a background of mountains and music.
Here he found Robert Pollak, a violinist of wonderful promise,
who became his life-long friend. His fortunes belonged to us, as
ours to him.

Robert Pollack was one of the world's great violinists, though
his reputation as a soloist was broken—in that of a teacher he is
to this day unrivalled—by the impact of two world wars.

The first war came as he was rising to fame, and for seven
years he was interned in Russia. The shadow of the second war
drove him to accept a ten year appointment at the Imperial Con-
servatoire at Tokyo. Before leaving Europe in the late twenties,
that fine critic, Robin Legge, wrote of him in the *Daily Telegraph*:
"Robert Pollack gave one of the most beautiful performances
of Brahms' D minor Sonata I have ever heard in a concert
room."

Every evening set itself to music. Ernan's health and his ambitions were alike freed. He wrote to me constantly of his expanding world; and I lived on and for his letters.

Hitherto I had seemed the older and the more experienced in
life. Now our positions imperceptibly changed; Ernan's was the
mind that shot forward, his companionships were more varied, his
physical life freer than any I had ever known. My eager imagination
filled itself with his new growth. It never occurred to me that his
recovered health and his maturer mind could act as hindrances to
our relationship. I had always lived more in my imagination than in
actual fact; and now I found Ernan's imagination to live in as well as
my own. My letters took fire from his, and, as often happens to
those whose profession is writing, I gave him the unfettered
sympathy and full stimulus of my answering mind, which I might
have been incapable of giving him had we been together, and our
pursuits been different.

The changes these six months brought me were the reverse of
free-ing. I had to submit to a too long delayed operation, which
suddenly became urgent, and though I made a quick and good
recovery, there were long painful weeks before and after the clumsy

249

surgery of our old friend and family doctor, which greatly restricted my activities.

My family's troubles, too, were thick upon me. Mary had grown worse, and the relationship between her and my mother was extremely painful. My father could not but feel that the greater part of this trouble was of my mother's making, and this added to my mother's constant resentment against him. Adoration was what my mother lived on—without it she became obsessed by fears and ill health. I still adored her, but I could not give her the support she felt that she needed, in her attitude to Mary, or even in her inexhaustible complaints against my father.

We had taken, for the summer, a pilot's cottage, sparkling with brass, full of models of old ships and treasured oddments from the sea. It was on the village green of Southwold, under immense Suffolk skies. The weather was unusually fine, the hedges thick with honeysuckle, the scent of bean fields filled the air. Bird life and old churches were my outward satisfactions.

Suddenly the MacCords, from our far away American life, reappeared. Mary, George and I were enchanted to have them. We chose lodgings close to our cottage and spent all our time with them. But this new felicity did nothing to dislodge the grudging unease of our parents. Stronger than the honeysuckle, a sense of doom was in the air. Betty and Maida were accompanied by an old aunt, who was fast losing what little mind she had once possessed. Her depression and her illusions played their part in our gloomy domestic atmosphere.

Betty, now twenty-five, looked like a handsome young widow who has had experience without joy. This visit to Europe was her bid for freedom. Since we parted, she had lived through ten years of almost incredible shocks and strain—the divorce of her parents, the sudden death of her mother, her father's remarriage and the nursing of an extremely unpleasant grandparent. Now she had reached a calm determination no longer to be used as a domestic slave and prop to irresponsible and selfish relations, but to go to Paris, where she could study painting and music and live her own life, seeing that Maida had an equal freedom. They had only two hundred pounds a year to be free on, with the added expense of a enniless and distracted aunt. Maida, whom we had last seen as a poilt and sallow child, had changed into a slenderer edition of the Medicean Venus. She had big grey eyes, well cut features, and her hair was the colour of buttercups. I never looked at Maida without remembering the cry of the Prince in the fairy tale, "Rapunzel! Rapunzel—let down your golden hair!" Rapunzel was imprisoned in a tower, and she had to let down her hair for the Prince to climb up by, as a preliminary to her rescue. Maida, whose disposition had markedly improved since childhood, would, I think, have shown the same self-sacrificing courage for the right Prince; and for several enchanted summer weeks it looked as if George might be the prince.

How far Maida fell in love with George, or George with Maida, I never fully grasped, but I was prepared to do my utmost to support them. What more satisfactory daughter-in-law could my parents find? Maida was the daughter of their greatest friend. She had the sweetest disposition in the world and even a hundred pounds a year. George was just going up to Cambridge at nineteen and Maida was very little older; but I had been allowed Ernan at approximately the same age, and with even greater handicaps. Why should George, generally given everything he wanted at once, not be permitted his own choice of a wife? But family disapproval seethed around us; my divided parents were firmly united against such a prospect. Secretly for five hours George and Maida became engaged; then something even more efficacious than the opposition of parents tore them asunder.

Christabel our first cousin, half sister and half friend, perhaps even more than half sister and half friend to George, who spent the main part of his holidays at her country home, intervened.

George asked Christabel, on a visit to Cambridge, to post a letter to Maida, confirming their engagement. Christabel wanted to know who Maida was. George told her. The letter somehow or other never got posted.

The engagement to Maida, like a wisp of cloud caught in a sunbeam, lost its transfiguring light. Fortunately Maida's heart became more seriously re-engaged shortly afterwards in Venice.

What happened to George's heart was for the next few years George's own affair.

I quarrelled with Christabel permanently for the part she played in George's young life, but like most quarrels it was useless. I lost Christabel and became less rather than more useful to George. There would indeed have been far more reason for quarrelling with her had Christabel ever intended to marry George, since she was older than I was and required the sort of life George could never have provided for her. Seeing there was nothing I could do to lift George's clouds, I returned to the problem of Mary.

Dr. Schacht had warned me that Mary must not continue to live with my mother, but he was by no means pleased with the alternative I promptly offered him. Mary could come to Davos for the winter with me.

In the presence of Ernan her problem—like all others—would, I felt sure, be happily solved. No-one, except Mary, agreed with me. Nevertheless I had my insistent way; breathless with hope and joy, I travelled to Zürich, where Ernan, equally expectant, rushed to meet the princess of his dreams. I do not to this day know which of us was the less provided to give what the other wanted.

34

If the modern young underestimate their emotions, forty years ago we ran the danger of over-estimating ours.

There was no cold storage element in our romantic existence. We had endless time to concentrate upon the affections and few amusements to break up our concentration.

When Ernan and I had to face a separation of six months, after a year and a half's continuous intimacy, absence not only made the heart grow fonder, it imperceptibly expanded our images to far beyond life size.

Mary and I arrived at Zürich, a little dishevelled after sitting up all night in a second class carriage. I saw the sun god I had expected to find upon the station; but I did not realize—blind with joy for several hours—that I had failed to provide him with a sun goddess. I was indeed a liability rather than an enchantment, and an unsuitable partner for Ernan's new kingdom of health and freedom. When at length I bit upon this unpalatable truth, I immediately demanded an end to our engagement. Ernan insisted that we must take time for re-adjustment, and refused to hear of an instantaneous parting. Neither of us understood what had happened. There was no one else. We had written to each other with increasing devotion day by day, our confidence in, and respect for, each other were intact.

We were completely bewildered, and sure that our suffering was unique. At length we decided to say nothing to anybody, and to carry out our plans as if nothing had happened. A miracle had taken away our joy: another miracle might return it. It was difficult to say whether we found it more painful to be apart or together. We tortured each other when together, and tortured ourselves when apart; it was worst of all, perhaps, to be in the presence of those who sympathetically wished to share what they supposed to be our joy.

It might have been easier if my feelings had changed as Ernan's had; but for me nothing had changed about my lover, except his joy in me.

Lislie, who had made one of her dauntless recoveries, joined us after Christmas, and from her it was impossible to hide anything. She had been too much a part of our lost kingdom.

Her presence lightened my load; but it made Ernan's heavier. For the first time an element of contrast entered our unchallenged relationship. No matter how careful Lislie and I were to hide our serenity, the fact that no "region cloud" had blotted out our sunshine added to his darkness. Neither he nor I knew that long engagements physically affect men differently from women. Nor could I realize into what prison of his childhood I was driving him back.

Free at last from his own ill health as I was not yet free from mine, denied the natural relationship of love, while in constant nearness to its object; trying to carry the burdens I had thrust upon him as well as his own, Ernan felt himself once more chained to an adored and adoring invalid as he had been all his long childhood to his mother. His ambitions devoured him, and through his choice of me the future closed down on them, rather than opened a way for them to be realized.

Ernan was pessimistic by nature and did not share my confidence that, for me as well as for him, recovery lurked round the corner. I was certain that my recovery would be complete; Ernan was equally certain that the future would but prolong the present. Mary's needs were, for part of the time, predominant for all three of us, but as we were without the slightest knowledge of how to help her, we mysteriously failed. We had been told that she should apply herself to some form of winter sport, and we urged her to avail herself of these opportunities; but Mary disliked all sports, and Davos had neither duties nor attractions for her; so she devoted herself to running errands for invalids instead, and got worse.

When spring came in sight, Ernan and I at last decided to take Elena—and Mamma—partially into our confidence. If they could

254

ot throw any light on what had happened to us, then we both knew
nat our next parting must be "the poor last".

I was without hope, for I felt sure that Elena, who had always
isapproved of our engagement, would now demand its close.
Mamma too, I thought, could not fail to wish Ernan freed from so
much misery; but instead Elena suggested our consulting Dr.
Huggard before taking any further steps, and Mamma wrote to me
ehemently, and with tenderness, refusing to hear of a break in our
ngagement. Ernan, she said, was certainly ill. He had never got
ver our separation forced on him by Dr. Huggard. She was sure
nat his affection for me had not really changed and never would,
nd she was now satisfied that we were permanently suited to each
ther. She begged that we both join her immediately. This we knew
o be impossible. Elena's advice—though we shrank from it—was
t least within our power to carry out, so we decided to visit Dr.
Huggard separately.

Dr. Huggard's talk with me was both caustic and illuminating,
nd I came away equally startled and relieved. He actually thought
nat Ernan's feelings *would* change. He counselled a short pre-
minary parting. Ernan might join his mother at Lugano, while
islie and I remained where we were for the next few weeks. If
rnan sent for me, as Dr. Huggard suggested he probably would, I
nould join him. It would be time enough to start talking of break-
ng our engagement if Ernan did *not* send for me. Mary he des-
atched immediately to England, having given her very wise advice
nd even some comfort.

Before we could carry out our immediate plans, a cable arrived
om South Africa saying that Stanley, Mamma's second and
trongest son, with the best prospects of re-making the family
ortunes, was dying of pneumonia. Ernan went straight down from
ne mountains to Mamma; while Lislie and I lived through a
rilliant, hollow thaw.

I do not remember for how many weeks we were chained to our
Davos balconies above the flooded valley, watching the splendid
ageant of the March sun burning the snow off the white peaks one
y one, till they became mere green and sodden hillocks sinking
ut of the sky to merge themselves in the wet earth.

There were no letters. I finished my third novel—a poor top-of the-mind book, that curiously enough went through three editions and caused old H. B. Pinker, the best and kindest of agents, to say "This child is going to be a novelist!"

I made up my mind that I could never write again, and decided to become a hospital nurse. "Thought is," without doubt, "the slave of life"—and mine at the moment was both motionless and incredibly tasteless.

One hot and empty noon a telegraph boy climbed through the stream of our path to the door below our balcony. He brought—this messenger of the gods—a telegram from Ernan saying he had got rooms for us in Mamma's hotel at Lugano. In the April that followed by the green lake side, slowly and tentatively at first, and then with a rush like the Italian spring, our lost joy returned to us.

Ernan implored an instant marriage—however financially insecure, unwise, or wild; a further separation—though this time we contemplated only two months—was, he felt, beyond our capacities.

Mamma was full of sympathy and understanding, but Stanley's death had brought fresh financial and physical strains upon her. How could we short-circuit our way to paradise at her expense?

We *almost* ran away and left Lislie and Mamma to their own devices; but we had been brought up to the idea that sacrifice of desire was in itself meritorious, and family affection was very strong in both of us; so that once more we gave way to the tyranny of time and space.

35

It was decided in my family circle that at last my father must meet Ernan; and as a half way meeting place where French was spoken, we chose Ste. Adresse, a small suburb on the cliffs above Havre, where there was both a *plage* and a golf links.

The presentation of Ernan to my family took place in a small hotel sitting-room, very French, and overcrowded with spiky furniture, gilt mirrors and dusty plush. It was a terrifying hour. My mind was absorbed in apprehension about my family's reception of its new member. Would they, whose opinions so greatly swayed my own, be content with my superlative choice? Would Ernan like his new family, which was as near to me as a vine is to one of its branches?

Ernan came into the room a little late, but looking like the prince out of a fairy tale. All my fears died down at the sight of him. He was five foot eleven and a half in height, broad shouldered and slender waisted. There is a self-portrait of Andrea del Sarto's which might have been taken of Ernan at twenty-three. He seemed to bring the sunshine out of the garden into the room with him; and all the stiffness melted out of the furniture. Instinctively I knew that my family *had* accepted him, and felt a pride in its new member. Our American blood contradicted his traditions—time in us went to a different beat. With great physical strength, Ernan united extreme gentleness of manner. The core of his being was *noblesse oblige*. A fellow officer in the 1914 war well described him, "as the sort of fellow who would give you his last shilling if you were hard up— and then apologize for its not being more." He had a keen, quick Highland temper and fierce pride; but it was the rights of others that Ernan fought for more willingly than his own.

The golden weeks in Normandy that followed, under a harvest moon, were among the happiest of our lives. The days flew by, each one more full of beauty than the last. Scarlet geraniums grew like vines over my ground floor window and scented all the air. Honfleur and Harfleur were within our immediate neighbourhood; pink and white carnations hung from the balconies of their old steep pitched houses above their small gay harbours.

One day we went by ourselves, still further afield to visit St. Jouin and Bruneval. In 1907 they were unspoilt villages set deep in gorse and pines, close to the sea. At St. Jouin we ate prawns of an enormous size and succulence with home-made brown bread and butter, following them up by wild strawberries and cream, with which we drank long draughts of golden cider. When we demanded coffee and cream to follow, "La Belle Anastase", the huge moustached landlady, beloved of visiting artists, said firmly, "No, my children—do not tempt me to sell it to you—my conscience prevents me—you have already tried your stomachs to the uttermost—be advised by me—ask no more of them!" The day passed so quickly through our reluctant fingers that we missed our train and there were no others. Strongly against the advice of La Belle Anastase, who showed us the loveliest of bedrooms, and urged us to spend the night, we drove across country to a distant junction and flung ourselves into the last possible train—arriving at our disturbed hotel just before midnight. No amount of reproaches could efface from memory the round pink moon, spreading waves of rose and golden light over the bare stripped fields.

On another occasion we got lost, this time *with* my mother, in a forest near Le Touquet.

Deep in the centre of the woods we came on an open glade. A rose brick château sprang out of an ancient bricked courtyard. There was a stone wall in its centre, and softly stepping, cloud-white fantail pigeons cooed and bowed on its roofs and walls. There was no other sound, no dog barked; and we were told when we found our way out of the forest that there was no such château, or at least there had not been for several hundred years.

As our parting drew near, Ernan tried to make me see that Mamma would be very seriously annoyed if I did not return with him to Zürich, to stay with her for the few weeks which separated us from our winter in Davos. My instinct and my whole heart pulled me towards this plan, but alas! I perhaps too fully realized that to do what we both wanted—and what was due to Mamma— would be to shock and dismay my whole family. Where, they would have asked, would be my winter clothes, and what was to become of a non-returnable ticket! They had gone far to meet this most elusive of sons-in-law. My father and George had spent our only common holiday in a foreign land, playing golf on strange links and swimming in alien water.

I broached the subject, but how could I expect them to let me throw over a month's visit to Elena—long planned and costing nothing—added to the only three weeks in the year that I was allowed at home!

I saw at once that I should greatly displease my parents if I insisted on going with Ernan to Mamma. They would probably have given in, but all their pleased acceptance of Ernan would have vanished, that blessed sense that he was exactly what they wanted him to be—and what I knew he in reality *was*—would have been set aside. Had I dreamed that Mamma was to die in two months' time, and Ernan be left to face this mortal blow alone, how differently I would have acted! But fate gives no hints to prepare us for its immeasurable disasters. Nor did I then know that unilateral decisions are as fatal in love affairs as they are in the affairs of nations. Against his will I let Ernan go alone to Mamma, and to an extremely hurt and reproachful Mamma. A few weeks later he left her for Davos, only to be summoned a fortnight later to her death-bed. Nothing that followed would have been the same had I been with him then.

Fred arrived from England too late to see his mother alive, and returned to England before Ernan, who brought back her body to Bournemouth, to be buried by her wish in her son Ralph's grave. I went from Cambridge, where Lislie and I were staying with the Gwatkins, to Bournemouth to meet him.

I found him ill, surrounded by hostile aunts, and under the shadow of the imminent arrival of Frank Lascelles. It was not supposed that I would insist on seeing Ernan alone in his room; but

I insisted. We groped about in a blind pain, out of which we never seemed quite to emerge until two years later our engagement ended.

Ernan was not only ill; he was overwhelmed with grief and that remorse which is half anger against life, and half a savage oblation of ourselves upon the living altar of what is left precious to us.

Elena wrote that she would come immediately to Bournemouth and invited me to join her at her hotel, but I refused as I should have been further away from Ernan; and took once more a wrong decision, staying on with my kind but inappropriate hosts the Jacksons.

I half knew that I was refusing my salvation, for Elena's presence would have fortified me, relieved Ernan, and impressed the aunts. But I also feared that Elena would discover that I had a return of lung symptoms which I was trying to conceal.

Elena was displeased with my ungracious decision; and neither of us guessed in those grim hours we spent together in a cold hotel drawing-room that we were seeing each other for the last time.

Ernan's greatest friend, Frank Lascelles, arrived to console him, much as Elena had arrived to support me.

Frank had been for many years the Dennis's family hero, sustaining Mamma through all her tragic losses, and discovering in Ernan, who was eleven years younger than himself, many of the traits he had loved in Ernan's eldest brother Ralph, his Oxford contemporary.

Mamma had however, with time, changed her devoted affection for Frank. Her absorption in Ernan could not brook a rival, and I think too that she had cause to feel that Frank's friendship would always be narrowed to his own interests.

"Frank," she warned me, "is selfish and I don't trust him. He was bad for Ralph and he is worse for Ernan. Be very careful that you do not let him spoil your lives."

I had naturally accepted Ernan's own glowing accounts of his famous friend rather than Mamma's warnings. Besides, I had a curious and intriguing first hand memory of my own.

At fifteen I had jumped a large flower bed and landed at Frank's feet. It was as far as I had got, for the senior curate of St. Peter's, Bournemouth—with whom Frank was talking at the garden gate— though a great friend of mine, had refused to introduce us.

Still I had looked at Frank, admired and been forbidden him, when he was in the splendid bloom of his youth, flushed with triumph at being the finest Romeo the O.U.D.'s had ever produced.

Frank had large, brilliant blue eyes, chestnut curls and the carriage of an emperor. Nor was he merely good-looking. He was, in romantic parts, a fine actor. He had indeed queered his own pitch by the splendour of his presentation of Nero in a chariot race—as Beerbohm Tree's understudy. No actor manager could afford so superb a substitute.

Frank, I now think, was a man born out of due time. Twenty years earlier he might have rivalled Irving, twenty years later he could have trained himself to wear the austere laurels of Bernard Shaw's coldly intellectual heroes; but he could not survive the drastic scepticism of the twentieth century, and as an actor he fell—with romance—a pre-war casualty.

However, the stage was far from being the only background for Frank's resilient personality. He had all the flair and magnetic drive of a great producer. His pageants at Quebec, at Bath and the London Festival of Empire at the Crystal Palace proved him the finest pageant-master of his day.

Our second meeting, if less dramatic, had a two-fold significance. I did not admire Frank less, but—in spite of eager expectations—I found myself unable to like him.

I had hoped that Ernan and I would find him with us on our long, up-hill climb, but instead I found him a more ruthless opponent of our marriage even than Ernan's family. Fred—in spite of his deep anxiety for Ernan—was always chivalrous and kind to me. The two brothers looked alike and had many of their finest qualities in common; both had personal courage, unflinching integrity and deep tenderness of heart. Fred was intellectually lighter and gayer than Ernan, and he was physically the most active person I ever met. His relationship to his mother had been one of continuous, if affectionate, opposition, and he suffered far more lightly than Ernan at her death. I did not see much of Fred over the funeral period, as he had an intense dislike for Frank, who was managing everything for the family with effortless zeal and ability. Fred became invisible whenever Frank entered the room.

I had no right to feel surprise that Ernan's family should object to our marriage. What hurt me was that while Ernan was confined to his room they should have treated me with insolent unkindness.

I had my share of grief. Mamma had loved me as a daughter, and I felt her death as if she had been my mother. Frank, I thought, would surely support me in the presence of these fierce aunts, and lift the burden of my failure from me. On the contrary, Frank—who had never been a favourite of the Forbes family before—now became a highly prized confederate and completed my ostracism. Frank's was a double-faced attitude, for he came to see me at the Jacksons' in the light of a friend; and when Ernan was with me he treated us as one.

The aunts, when far later in life I made their true acquaintance, I found charming, and in many ways kindly, women. One of them I numbered among my best and kindest friends for the rest of her life. They dearly loved Ernan; all that they did was for his benefit; and two of them when they died left him the little they possessed. But at the time of Mamma's death they hung over our happiness like a menacing wave about to drag us down.

Ernan insisted on seeing me daily, but during these brief intervals I realized how little comfort it was in my power to give him. The grief of a son at the loss of a mother, who has too long and too devotedly consumed him, has no remedy beyond the slow healing of the spirit of life.

I was concealing trouble of my own, my one terror being lest I should be held back from my journey to Davos—for there I knew Ernan would be free to take what comfort I at last could freely give him. But by the time I arrived in London concealment was no longer possible. Dr. Schacht saw me, and was inflexible. I must go to bed and stay there for at least a week. I must be nursed; and I must not speak.

My mother was horrified at the expense of either a hotel or a nursing home; and wished to return to Swanscombe immediately. Ernan, shocked and frantic with fresh anxiety, persuaded—perhaps over-persuaded—a kind cousin of his with a London house to take me in for a week. My condition was insufficiently explained to her, nor did Ernan dream that she was part of the family determination to prevent our marriage.

The days spent under her roof were unmitigated torture. I found a whisper a most inconvenient form of expression for one who does not wish to be convinced of doom and has quite sound reasons against it.

Ernan was not, except under bitter protest, allowed in my room, while the doctor refused to allow me out of it.

The cousin, ably seconded by Frank, managed to convince Ernan—to whom the idea of impropriety was as foreign and as inconvenient as it was to myself—that he was endangering my reputation; and that he would completely shatter it if he travelled out to Davos with me alone.

These were Ernan's relations—Frank was his dearest friend. I had to accept their verdict; and, what was harder still, to reconcile my father to it.

Ernan and my father saw me off together. In a few days, we thought, we should be together, and the worst edge of our first great grief be assuaged by each other's unhampered company. In time we were not three months away from our golden days at Ste. Adresse—but in everything else, although we neither of us knew it, an unplumbed sea stretched between us.

36

It had seemed to me in London that the only important thing was to get out of that Edwardian strait jacket into which I had found myself inadvertently compressed, and to be free to receive my lover in our old surroundings, where no one could intervene against us; and where at last his pent up sorrow might find its natural relief.

But people who have active natures are apt to blind themselves to all but one aspect of their problem. What interferes with their activity seems to be their main enemy, although there may be other far more sinister influences at work.

The journey to Davos was easy enough but no one, however determined, can manipulate the effect of an icy mountain wind on a damaged lung. This wind caught me at Basle; and by the time I had reached my familiar little room in the Hotel Buol—warm, spotless, empty and kind—I found I had an enemy within me whom I could not control.

I struggled for forty-eight hours alone with increasing illness before I could acknowledge that I was beaten, and dared to send for Dr. Huggard.

The Dr. Huggard, who sat in my tiny room surrounded by my unpacked things, was no one I had ever seen before. He was no longer cold and gay; but extraordinarily kind and grave. Did I not know, he told me, that he was my friend? Then why did I not send for him at once? Had we not worked together to produce a cure for over two years? Why should I make things difficult for both of us? If I was thinking of money, that was absurd; he charged for frivolous calls what they deserved, but for this illness I would find there would be no extra charge at all. He would come and see me as often as he liked and he would send his nurse for the next few days. When was Miss Brock coming out? Not before the middle of January? That was nonsense! She must come immediately. Was this also a question of expense? How much money had we got?

I had earned sixty pounds which had been put aside for Lislie's winter from mid-January to the end of April—this, we had thought, would be the best use she could make of it.

We must spend it now, Dr. Huggard told me authoritatively; even a fortnight of Davos would do Miss Brock good, and when the sixty pounds were finished, more would inevitably follow. Relations of such girls as Miss Brock, Dr. Huggard drily informed me, always paid up in the end; and he himself would see to it that they did. He was now going to send a telegram to Miss Brock, and would return with something to help me as soon as the porter could procure it.

Four days later Lislie stood by my bedside. I had not seen her since we parted at Cambridge before Mamma's funeral. The spirit of life came into the room with her.

Nevertheless this time I did not get well quickly. I had hidden the gravity of my illness from Ernan and inadvertently played into the hands of his relations. That he did not rejoin me immediately was partly due to their importunities, but also to the clearing up of his own and Fred's affairs. When he arrived at Davos I found him completely masked by grief, partly for Mamma, but also from despair as to our future. For these weeks he had had to stand alone the full battery of opposition to our marriage, both from his relations and from Frank. Finally the family oracle, Sir Thomas Barlow, was called in to proclaim that our engagement must end, that marriage would be madness for both of us. Had Ernan not lost a brother and I a sister from T.B.? What hope would lie in such a disastrous marriage? The fact that Sir Thomas Barlow had never seen me, nor taken the trouble to consult Dr. Huggard, who had treated our lung trouble from practical observation over a space of years, did nothing in those days to qualify the harshness of his verdict.

Ernan, however shaken, did not yield to it. He insisted on coming to Davos to see me again, and, finding me not yet recovered from my illness, could not bring himself to tell me what had occurred in London.

I was therefore without a key to what followed, and could not understand why Ernan's gloom never lifted. At Ste. Adresse we had discussed many possibilities for our future, among them a plan we had neither of us relished, but which had eventually taken form.

Herbert found the Villa Adriana impossible to run successfully without a modern language teacher, but a fully qualified one was more than he could afford. It was therefore suggested that Ernan should return to St. Moritz to teach what he knew, and to learn from Herbert what he needed for Oxford. Herbert wished eventually to leave St. Moritz. He might in a year or two agree to sell us the villa, and leave us to carry on his job.

We had decided—Ernan, Lislie and I—to stay at Davos for Christmas and then transfer ourselves to St. Moritz. Ernan went at once to St. Moritz, but I was held back by the condition of my heart from following him, for several weeks. St. Moritz was 1,000 feet higher than Davos, and Dr. Huggard gave me only a reluctant leave to try it. The trial failed. My heart refused to adjust itself to the extra height, and Lislie and I were ordered down at a moment's notice to the Lake of Como, where I was severely ill.

We stayed at a little empty hotel at Tremezzo on the Lake of Como, where Elena and I had been together; and it was here that I received the news of her death. Helen wrote that Elena had asked if she were going to die, and been told the truth. It was early spring and the new-born leaves of a poplar were visible from her bedroom windows. She held her hands out to the leaves, dancing in the sunshine, and laughed with joy.

A few days later I had a telegram from Ernan. Frank had made him a sudden offer to which he must make an instantaneous reply: would Ernan go with him to Canada and help to prepare the Quebec Tercentenary Pageant under Government auspices? Should he accept or refuse? He would abide wholeheartedly by my decision. I wired immediately "Accept". Nor did I ever regret this decision. Frank was still Ernan's hero, though I knew now he could never be mine. Still, he was the nearest either of us had ever known to a genius. Perhaps this Quebec Pageant, planned by the Government of

Canada, might be the stepping stone to greater and more permanent prospects, and certainly it would be an experience so adventurous and releasing as to break down the walls of Ernan's grief.

He had no real prospects where he was, besides being miserably unhappy. He and Herbert were bitterly antagonistic, and it was extremely dubious whether what Herbert was fit to teach was worth Ernan's learning.

If I did not get better, this distance and absorption would be in themselves an anodyne. Before I had left Davos for the last time, I had asked Dr. Huggard if it would not be fairer to Ernan to break our engagement. Previously he had laughed when I had made this suggestion, but I noticed this time he looked grave, and delayed answering me. Finally he had said, "You have cared for each other for a long time. Do not decide anything till you are stronger. Then think it over very carefully and make your decision together."

I had the greatest confidence in Ernan's powers, and I knew that what he would not do for himself he would always do for others—especially for Frank. At last he had something to hope about, and I hoped with him, and for him. Even if I had foreseen that in the long run Frank would swallow all that we had of hope and joy, stripping Ernan bare of his heritage, and forcing on him liabilities which Frank himself had no conception how to meet, and under which Ernan staggered manfully for years, I doubt if I could or should have acted differently.

Certainly as far as the Quebec Pageant was concerned we were both fully satisfied with the result. It was a magnificent success, and it was a direct service to our country, one of the many bricks that England has set in the wall of time, to strengthen the race of man. Nor can I doubt, as Lord Grey wrote to Ernan in 1914, that without him it could never have been achieved.

The dramatic vision was Frank's, and even the power to put his vision into the minds of others, but the wise interpretation, the untiring attention to detail, and above all the considerate dealings with fellow workers, were Ernan's. Frank had driving power, but no understanding of the human beings he set himself to drive. Without such an intermediary as Ernan he lost touch with reality.

It was Ernan's integrity that business men trusted; and his

sympathy which, with his knowledge of the French language, drew together the sharply divided French and British Canadians into one sustained effort. Young, untrained and unprepared as Ernan was, he was able—by the use of every ounce of moral and intellectual capacity he possessed—to save Frank's dreams from wreckage. In the process—sometimes a very gruelling process—Ernan learned how to handle men. Supported by the extraordinary kindness and common sense of the Canadians themselves, and backed by the private friendship of Lord Grey's Military Secretary, General Sir John Hanbury-Williams, and that of Monseigneur Matthieu of the Seminary at Quebec, he had the personal triumph of overcoming what looked like the insuperable deadlock between Catholic French and Protestant English. Mysteriously and overnight the tense and silent opposition which had brought all their preparations to a stand-still, died down.

History turned upon its pivot. Montcalm and Wolfe no longer antagonised each other from their heroic graves; but met together beneficently, moving towards a peaceful goal, upon the bloodstained Plains of Abraham.

37

The next eighteen months were the longest and most unpalatable of my life. I saw Ernan only for snatched and inconclusive meetings between ominous decisions. The greater part of the time he was absorbed in the desperate struggle to launch Frank's grandiose plans in London and Canada.

I less and less believed in the viability of these plans, or in Frank's sense of responsibility towards Ernan and his future. I knew that the capital left Ernan by Mamma, on which our hopes for the future were based, was fast melting away to cover their initial expenses. What else would Ernan have to fall back upon when this was finished?

I did not realize that Ernan was already too deeply involved to withdraw from what he still passionately hoped might be turned into success; and my lack of faith turned his difficulties into nightmares.

Whenever he saw me I appeared to be worse rather than better. Dr. Schacht took a very grave view of my condition, and no hopes were held out to either of us. I frequently suggested ending our engagement; but Ernan as frequently refused the suggestion.

It was some slight relief to me that my parents were now very much better off, since the death of my Grandmother Fowler, so that my failure to provide for myself, and frequently for Lislie, was no longer an anxious drain on the family exchequer. Still, these eighteen months, when I earned nothing, sapped my sense of freedom, and decreased my hopes.

During this time I lived with my parents in the summer, and spent the following winter of 1909 with Lislie in lodgings at Bournemouth. Here we had a two months' delightful visit from Professor Gwatkin.

Lislie only partly shared my passion for acquiring knowledge; still she worked for hours with me, painting the palates of snails on glass slides, while Uncle Melville translated Greek for us. "The *animal*," as Uncle Melville used to call Lislie, "is a gregarious animal! We must not keep her head too long in books." So Lislie led our social life for us, while Uncle Melville drilled me in Church history, or whatever he had in hand. He never ceased to regret that neither "the unfortunate young man"—his name for Ernan—nor "the Slug"—myself—had had a University education; and he tried hard to make up for my deprivation by constant tuition.

Professor Gwatkin was not only a born scholar, but a born teacher, with a glorious mind, furnished from end to end with deeply digested knowledge, which he could impart in the most original and sparkling manner to any attentive ear, however ignorant the mind behind it. "To love him was a liberal education."

Indeed, it had to be, for he was fiercely discontented if my attention wandered, however severe the task he set me. Stupidity I think he would have forgiven, but carelessness or evasion, under the guise of facility, he pounced upon like a hawk upon its prey. I *had* to understand, or work till understanding came. Yet, curiously enough, however absorbed he seemed to be in our subject, no-one was quicker to spot physical fatigue in his pupil, although he had his own peculiar way of dealing with it. "Now stop!" he would say, one eye fixed upon me, while the other swivelled up to a corner of the ceiling. "You are tired! Another subject is what we need! We will begin on something else immediately!" Nor did I ever find this measure of re-application fatiguing; indeed, I enjoyed it as much as he did. Science and religion were the two poles between which his mind moved. They included anything—and indeed everything—except art.

During this visit, Uncle Melville painstakingly extracted from me the last vestiges of my High Church training—there was very little left to extract, except my love for Newman's prose. "An untruthful mind *has* no beauties"! Uncle Melville snorted when I pleaded for the clear beauty of Newman's style. "If you like lucid prose, read Swift—it is much better for you—since you cannot read Greek—which would be best of all!"

Perhaps Uncle Melville did not notice that, while I willingly gave up what poor remnants were left of my Anglo-Catholicism, I had nothing to put in their place. Uncle Melville's attitude to knowledge deeply impressed me, and I hope improved my mind; but his attitude to faith, though it won my respect, did not quiet the rebellion in my heart. There is little I can look back on during this time with satisfaction. My heart, my spirit and my body were all three in insurrection against life. I could not have my way and all other ways seemed barren to me.

I had, however, one visitor during the summer that followed whom I deeply prized. My Uncle George had been sent from his slum parish in New York, on the collected pennies of his Polish peasant congregation, to try insulin as a last chance. The only place for this treatment for diabetes then known was a sanatorium near Vienna. Uncle George took the cure there, and it prolonged his life for ten years. But when he came to see me, in a cottage near Hindhead, there seemed very little hope for either of us.

In my early childhood I had decided that Uncle George was the only person on whom I could rely for absolute honesty upon religious—or indeed any other—questions. He was a sceptic by instinct; and a believer by practice. My father would have given me a beautiful answer to any hard question—Uncle George never any but a true one. Had he not been able to give me a true one, he would have said he had no answer.

Now here we were, both of us in the same dilemma. Passionate in our love of activity, we had been flung from the highway of life into a backwater—there, at best to die—at worst to remain unused.

I knew that I was in danger of losing my love as well as my life; but I did not know then that Uncle George had long ago lost his. "Uncle George," I demanded, "do you not think it very unfair of God—if there is a God—to let people who want work stand all day idle in the market place; and still more unfair, when they are at last allowed to work, to pay them the same as those who have worked all day? I don't think what is happening to either of us *is* fair, do you?" Uncle George was tall, and so thin that he seemed more like

271

a shadow than a human being. He bent towards me, with his great tragic eyes fixed on mine for a long time before he answered me.

"Those men," he said at last, "did not want to be idle or they would not have stood all day long in the market place where they could be hired; and when at last their chance came--and to such men I believe that it always comes—no man knew how hard they worked for the eleventh hour, except the man who had hired them! A thing is worth what we put into it, Phyllis. I do not know if there is any other fairness."

38

Psychologically speaking there are three good reasons—or excuses—for ending a love relationship: (1) if one of the partners feels at too great a disadvantage to the other; (2) if outside factors are overwhelmingly against the partnership; (3) if third parties mislead or undermine the confidence of one partner in the other. In our case all three of these played a part.

We had both been brought up on love and fear, instead of upon love and courage. The best way to decrease fear is to increase love; but this was not the way chosen by our mothers in our upbringing; their fears corroded their love. I think we owe them a life-long debt for the love they poured out on us, but we were weakened, and let ourselves be weakened, by the invasion of their fears and their lack of common sense.

I spent the winter of 1910 at Sta. Margherita on the Italian Riviera, devotedly nursed by my kind and generous friend "the aristocratic Dragon," Julia Farrer.

Ernan's involvement in the preparation of the Festival of Empire grew deeper and deeper. Julia's nursing was less than successful; and the future at last looked hopeless. Our engagement came to an end—a destined end as it seemed at the time. We made a clean job of it, and neither knew where the other was for the next few years.

As soon as I stopped my frantic efforts to get well, I began to get better. There was nothing to struggle about any more, and, though the future was unthinkable without Ernan, there seemed to me no particular reason why I *should* think of it.

I released my mind, and no doubt my body released itself with it, by trying to put into practice a sentence from Foggazzaro's "Il

Santo": "To be like a leaf in the wind, is the will of God"; but what I was really like was a leaf when the storm of self-will has ceased to blow, and it is left at last, unchivied, on the bough.

As soon as I was less acutely ill, Lislie and Uncle Kennie, replacing Julia who returned home, decided to move me by easy stages to the Lake of Garda.

Uncle Kennie never accompanied us upon our travels; he always—whether from motives of propriety or pure terror, we quite never knew which—preceded or followed us. We had to travel very gingerly on this occasion, since I could not walk, and was not allowed more than two hours' travel at a time.

Uncle Kennie awaited us at Spezia, where he had chosen an old-fashioned hotel, in which I had a room so enormous that I felt as if I were lost in a field. Knowing that I loved nothing better than Shelley, Uncle Kennie had arranged a visit by carriage to Lerici, as soon as I recovered from my journey. Meanwhile he showed even greater courage—at my passionate instigation—and gave Lislie a day's real sight-seeing at Pisa. Uncle Kennie had a horror of being seen with any unattached woman unchaperoned, and Lislie and I considered this a mutual triumph of the highest order. To be alone with me was nothing—this he could dare with impunity, for I was a niece—if only a step-one—but to be alone, and for a whole day, with anyone so dangerously captivating as Lislie—was indeed an act of heroism.

We were not far off Lerici; and it was April.

There was a soft haze of sunshine over the tulip-shaped hills. High, slender poplars, topped with plumes of green and golden leaves, wandered over the countryside. Silvery olives climbed the slopes of little hill cities, while cypresses struck their erect black notes at every turn of the landscape, like companies of pilgrims knowing exactly where they intend to go—and where to pause upon their journey.

The Gulf of Spezia stretched before us, a dancing blue.

We lunched at Lerici, overlooking the dock where Shelley's ill-fated boat was built, and then drove from its rose and yellow walls along the very road where the two frantic wives of Shelley and his friend, Williams, sought their young husbands after the storm, not yet knowing that they were already widows. Somewhere along this road they met Trelawney, riding fast, to put an end alike to both their hopes and fears.

Through the mist of olives on the hill-side rose the raspberry-coloured walls of Byron's villa, where Mary and Shelley walked every evening to enjoy those conversations, in which Byron tells us Shelley "talked like an angel".

The Villa Magni, a much less pretentious affair than Byron's, stood by the roadside, almost in the waves. The lower floor, as in Shelley's day, was filled with nets and the trappings of fisher boats, while above it were the four small rooms—and the terrace balcony —which had housed such splendid company.

The present householders, full of excitement and sympathy, urged us to enter. They were deeply interested in our excursion, and alive with memories, as if Shelley had been drowned yesterday.

The very walls of the little white villa seemed to whisper with their bygone speech. We stood in the room which Shelley had walked through, dripping and as God made him, while poor Mary was trying to give a respectable dinner party.

The blue gulf that had held so often Shelley's live body, and stilled forever his wild and gentle heart, broke in harmless ripples at our feet. There was nothing that we looked at which Shelley had not seen with his enchanted eyes.

This day's pilgrimage had a strangely healing effect upon my spirit. What was immortal in what Ernan and I had once possessed beckoned me towards courage:

> *For Love and Beauty and Delight,*
> *There is no death nor change.*

A few days later, Kennie left us for Florence, and Lislie and I continued our journey to Salò, where we found ourselves most comfortably installed, in a hotel with a lake garden looking across to Catullus' "olive-silvery Sirmio".

Here Fate prepared to smile upon us once more in the shape of three generations of large German countesses, grandmother, mother and daughter.

They were exceedingly "hochwohlgeboren" ladies from Meck-lenburg-Streslau, sent by the infuriated papa of the daughter, Marie-Louise, for her to get over the wicked notion of marrying beneath her—a mere, though an attractive and intelligent, pastor. Both grandmother and mother were upon Marie-Louise's side, and she never did get over it. Their united docility, backed by rivers of tears, melted the father's heart, and a year later Marie-Louise married the pastor. Forty years have washed away their ancient name, but Marie-Louise's eyes—blue as cornflowers—and hair like golden straw—haunt me yet.

They were all three affectionate, warm-hearted women, who spent most of the time sitting on each other's knees singing Lutheran hymns. Two years earlier, Marie-Louise's mother had been at death's door with a dilated heart, and miraculously cured by a German genius at Nauheim. I too must, they declared, go to Nauheim for the cure, and be saved by Dr. Schott.

Encouraged by the enthusiastic consent of my generous parents, we slowly crawled on to Nauheim.

The cold green Neckar, swollen with melted snow, raced through floating clouds of apple blossom, down the valley and under the castle walls of Heidelberg. I always like to remember Germany as we then saw it in 1910, so clean and mild, so like a fairy-tale with a happy ending!

Yet, even then, there was a flaw in the fairy-tale. Under the pink castle walls, and among the apple blossoms, we were conscious there was something a little grim in the slashed faces of healthy boys on bicycles, with pill-box hats glued to their round hard heads; and still more grim in the university attached so oddly to a prison, where we read Bismarck's unwavering scrawled name on the walls of his frequented cell.

I was sceptical about this visit to Nauheim so curiously made easy to me. I was sick of trying to get well, only to find myself slipping back into pits out of which I had crawled. I had tried so hard to get well; and failed so often. Now, without even a goal, what reason had I to succeed? I disliked the genius charlatan, who roundly scolded me for coming to Nauheim at all with a half-cured lung. At first I had to be carried to and fro from the baths and bandied about between stodgy bath-women; but in a month I could walk. I had a rest, a further six weeks' cure. I was unbelievably better but how oddly fate had worked upon my rebellious heart!

When I had wanted to recover with an overwhelming desire, I had gone full tilt towards death; and now here I was wanting to die, for the better I got the more I disliked my widowed state, yet finding myself bursting with rude health!

Lislie had soon to leave me, alone, except for the ineffectual ministrations of a clergyman lover of hers, whom I did nothing to assist in his forlorn mission to entertain me.

I was sorry for this poor young man, for I considered Lislie had treated him rather harshly; she had thrown a wet sponge at him, when he was taking evensong for us, on my balcony, and when he had asked her if she did not think a priest should put his Church before his love said: "Certainly not!" The poor fellow was not a suitable husband for Lislie, nor did she for one moment contemplate him in that light. But that he remembered her with a certain halo of fascination all his life I had reason to know, for he sought me out with some difficulty thirty years later after a long, successful Church career, to ask what had become of her.

Although I could not contemplate my future without distaste, I found myself taking great pleasure in my increasing physical powers. To walk again was an enchantment to me; and I never remember feeling, before or since, so bound up with the processes of nature. Every leaf and bud of spring was a beloved companion to me.

39

I looked forward with a strange mixture of hope and fear to a long holiday visit from my parents. My hope was that their love might soften this stone that was in the place of my heart; my fear was that I should find I could not regraft myself—after five years' separate growth—on to the family tree.

The doctors had told me I must, for the next few years at any rate, winter abroad, so that I should have six months out of the year alone, free from family life; but I had not yet learned how to live alone.

Lislie, if she could leave England, must winter in Davos. How could I even afford to keep her there? I should have to earn the money by writing, but I did not feel sure that I could ever write again.

There were plenty of subjects crowding all about me, but they seemed as uncertain of me as I was of them. Healthy writers attract subjects; they do not have to scurry round looking for them. Solitary, self-made professions depend more on courage than professions with colleagues, who, even if antipathetic, act as lively counter-irritants.

Courage was what I lacked. How was I to acquire it? I had given up religion when Elena died, or rather, when Elena died I ceased to be supported by *her* religion. I knew that when my parents arrived they would expect to find a cheerful and entertaining daughter. Could I bring off this facade of living on the strength of my own personality? Meanwhile they had left all the details of their trip to me to prepare for them, and I took a good deal of trouble over it. My mother was to stay with me longer than my father; and Dr.

Schacht had recommended Vevey as an after cure, on my way to the Italian Riviera for the winter. I had made up my mind to go back to Sta. Margherita. I did not want to go there but I couldn't make up my mind to go anywhere else. The people who ran the little hotel had been very kind to me; and it was cheap.

The Swiss tour proved successful. We went first to Berne, and then to Thun, which is perhaps the loveliest town in Switzerland. The Mönch, the Eiger and the Jungfrau preside over the lake. Brahms wisely spent his summers there, and weaved their beauty into his music.

My father was always a restless traveller. He was afraid of missing anything, and wanted, like the hero of Leacock's skit on the Russian novel, "to mount his horse at the door and ride away in every direction".

My mother preferred to stay fixed; and only to see what was in her immediate vicinity. I took turns in doing what each of them wanted, for I had no preferences of my own; everything tasted like dishwater to me, and felt as hollow as a drum.

As soon as my father went home, my mother and I settled above Vevey on the slopes of Mont Pélerin.

Every evening the Dent du Midi wrapped itself in flame; and every morning I woke at dawn to see the thin peaks of the two Aiguilles, ice-white, against the coldest, lightest, rose-coloured sky.

The Lake of Geneva has a separate charm from that of the Italian lakes: its waters look cooler and less sensitive to romance, but it has an unearthly evanescent beauty of its own. Its pale waters gleam the colour of a pigeon's breast. There are days when there are no mountains, but only a moonstone floor with walls of mist; and others when the lake is like a polished shield, holding with startling vividness snow peaks carved in silver.

I have seen the lake black with fury, its "wild white fingers snatching at the sky". But on these summer days it had an airy blue and silvery splendour, unsubstantial as a dream.

My mother and I were alone, more alone than we need have been, for the hotel was large and full of visitors, who made not the slightest impression upon either of us.

I could not tell if I had succeeded in convincing my parents that I was a devoted and happy daughter, but when at last I had left my mother in the train, and climbed the long hill-side which led to the hotel garden, I knew well enough that I hadn't convinced myself.

I now had to find how much I liked my own harsh and indifferent company.

During this bleak interval I received a short letter from Ernan, and wrote one to him. This was the first and only communication that passed between us for the next few years. Ernan's letter told me that he was finding help in Christian Science; and he begged me to study it. I immediately bought Mary Baker Eddy's book, from which however I drew no sustenance whatever; but I also read, as Ernan had suggested I should, the four Gospels on end, extracting and collecting in a list as I went all the miracles that concerned healing. I was, as anyone must be who reads the gospels in this manner, enormously struck by their amount, and by the emphasis Jesus put on making people well. He did not take illness as a matter of course. He often spoke as if it came from a mistaken way of living; and as if it were not enough to get better, but necessary to change the way of living as part of the cure.

It was not quite clear exactly what connection there was, because the Evangelists being simple men who liked the taste of miracles, put their emphasis on the miracle of recovery rather than on what had caused the sickness. They were not looking for first principles; and Jesus seldom gave them more than they could take.

I wrote to Professor Gwatkin on the subject and asked for his opinion. He replied immediately that he had been convinced by his own study of the Gospels that there was a direct connection between health and holiness. He was, however, unable to tell me how this connection came about, though he supposed that it must be due to a moral approach towards "wholeness". A whole man, he suggested, Christ endowed, *must* have a healthy mind in a healthy body.

The Greeks had always taken this for granted without Christianity and there was no reason to suppose that anything in Christianity contradicted the Greek theory, rather the contrary, Christianity supported it. Christ said: "I have come that ye might have life—and that ye might have it more abundantly."

It was not, however, till twenty years later, when I began to study Alfred Adler's "Individual Psychology" that I found science could provide a method for achieving the aim of "wholeness".

There is a law that man shall love his neighbour as himself, and it is by obedience to this law that man becomes "whole"—and perhaps may find this wholeness of the personality includes health.

I made no such discovery at the moment; but I think it was about this time that I vaguely began to notice a particularly cheerful and congenial group of Americans in the hotel. Half of them were young, sunburnt mountaineers of both sexes; the other group included a charming old lady, curiously like Whistler's Portrait of his Mother, who was generally accompanied by a devoted, middle-aged son.

I discovered that these were students from Columbia College travelling with two Professors, both sons of the old lady, who chaperoned the party.

The younger son—in whom I took no interest—was good-looking and climbed; the elder, who had the appearance of an india-rubber doll, bottle-neck shoulders and a slightly harried expression rather like that of the rabbit in Alice in Wonderland, attracted my favourable attention. He did not climb and was seldom seen without a book. One day the elder Professor asked if I would join a picnic he was getting up. Unable to think of a good excuse to cover a refusal on the spur of the moment, I accepted.

I dreaded this social experiment extremely; but there I found myself, on the higher slopes of Mont Pélerin, overlooking one of the most lovely scenes of lake and mountains that exist; surrounded by a rather sensible party who looked at it as speechlessly as I myself.

I had taken no part in the conversation on the way up; and I now took very little part in the handsome feast provided for us by the Professor; but I enjoyed the view.

The Professor, who was a most charming and considerate host, said at last,

"Only poetry is suitable in a place of such beauty! Let's have some!"

281

He began to recite, but hindered both by a stammer and a lack of memory, he got tied up; and as no one else seemed able to extricate him, and he obviously could not extricate himself, I suddenly found my own voice giving him the words he wanted. He appeared surprised, but pleased. "Look here," he said, "you obviously know the whole of this poem better than I do. Please go ahead with it."

It seemed silly and churlish to refuse.

He had chosen Browning's "Guardian Angel", and I went on with it to the end.

"Now," he said when I had finished, "what about 'Fears and Scruples'?" I gave him "Fears and Scruples". With the excitement of a fellow expert, he went on picking and choosing what he wanted—it was all one to me. I followed where he led. We skipped to Tennyson and back again to Browning. By the time the picnic was over we found that we were friends. The students then discovered that I had spent six years in America and were thrilled at the opportunity this gave them for international discussion. We must have one, they said, nightly, till they left for Greece.

When I went back that evening I wanted to retreat. There should, I told myself, be no such evenings; but by the time I was introduced, after supper, to Whistler's Mother, I knew that retreat was impossible.

For the first time for six months I had made a slight contribution towards social interest and the very cockles of my heart were warmed by it. Before the kind and intelligent party said goodbye to me, they begged me to contrive to cheer up a compatriot they had to leave behind them.

Elinor Proctor's story was a sad one. She had come on a visit to Europe—it was the first time she had ever left her husband and her native town in Maine—she was to join an artist brother who lived in Paris, and who had promised to take her to Italy. This faithless creature left with a party of friends to paint in Norway a few days before his sister arrived. Kind compatriots had brought her with them as far as Vevey. Italy was only a few miles from her, but she would never see it, for they must go on their more expensive way; and as soon as the false-hearted relation returned to Paris, Elinor must meet him there and catch the next ship home. Time and money would by then have expired; and she would have seen nothing of Europe beyond the unpretentious town of Vevey.

I liked the look of Elinor Proctor. She was an active, quiet woman in her early thirties. Suddenly I saw the solution of her problem. "But why not come to Italy with me?" I cried. "Sooner or later I shall set off for the Italian Riviera—you can take a train direct from Sta. Margherita to Paris—and there are heaps of Italian towns we can see on the way!" I seized a map and showed her. Stresa—Pisa—Siena—Florence! They could all be worked in without the slightest difficulty.

Elinor was enchanted, but how could we manage the expense? We each had about the same amount of money—I knew hotels in all of these places far cheaper than the one we were now in—we could manage perfectly! We had time to stay "en pension" in every one, there would only be tips extra; so into Italy we incontinently plunged.

Nowadays it would not seem much of a plunge; but Elinor's mind swam in alien seas of dread conjecture. She had never travelled anywhere at all till now. She knew no word of any foreign language. She did not, for that matter, really know me. It was a great act of faith on Elinor's part; and like most great acts of faith, it came off.

We had a wonderful three weeks together. The experience to me was an even deeper experiment, for the plunge I was taking was back into life itself.

Tickets, money, arrangements, programmes—all these hung on my unaided wits—and how I enjoyed using them! In a rush everything came back to me, all that Elena had built up in me, every wandering, well-taught hour, sang in my empty mind again.

I still possess a copy of the notes Elinor asked me to send her as a remembrance. Never had anyone a better or more passionately receptive fellow traveller than Elinor! Nothing escaped her. She wanted to see everything there was to be seen, and to know all about everything there was to know.

She never tired, she never grumbled or was irritated, sick, or sorry. She had a natural taste for beauty. As a traveller she was pleasant, punctual and calm.

It was September weather, bland, windless days, full of sunshine; and purple evenings lit by enormous stars.

At Stresa, where the sun was too hot and the hotel too cheap, we got poisoned by bad food, but managed, on a starvation diet, to visit and enjoy each of the Islands, leaving no inch unexplored.

Three days at Pisa cured and sustained us, while Siena and Florence fulfilled our wildest dreams.

We had no trouble, except Elinor's looks. Curiously enough I had not noticed that Elinor *was* beautiful, until we were inconvenienced by it. It was the kind of beauty that sets off amorous Italians like fireworks; and we had to take daily measures to stave off their importunity.

Poor Elinor was greatly flustered by having her hand seized in trams; and at the kind of overtures so astonishingly made to her in corridors of trains. I think now that it was not surprising, for she had a delicate sea-shell colour, thick strands of shining chestnut hair wound round her well-shaped head, and big hazel eyes like a Botticelli Madonna's.

Elinor was aghast at the effect of these hitherto unembarrassing features. Her husband, of course, had liked her appearance, but there had, she piteously assured me, been no one else who had endeavoured—and in such unwelcome ways—to attract her attention.

We overshot our arrival at Siena—and finding ourselves on a small empty station, with only one rather amorous caretaker, and four hours to wait for the next train, I implored Elinor to take advantage of a boy with a donkey cart, who offered to drive us across country the few intervening miles into Siena itself. It was sunset. Vineyards stretched, heavy with purple grapes, over the deep red earth; clear-cut silver leaves of olives shaded the burning colour beneath them. The sky was colourless with small curled clouds, gold and rose colour, floating in it like the sails of toy boats. The grapes hung knee high between the olives in every shade of red and purple—fantastically beautiful. I had implicit trust in the donkey boy—Elinor none at all.

I knew from the pride and fire of his generous dark eyes that we should be perfectly safe with him; but I failed to convince Elinor. "Wait! Wait!" I said to the donkey boy and he waited. At length the smouldering advances of the station-master proved too much for Elinor and she yielded to the lesser evil. I have often thought that the approach to Siena at twilight—towers and palaces and the orange glow which swept over them—was the most beautiful sight of my life. The light seemed part of the earth itself—it lingered long after the sky had done with its pageantry. "At last!" I said to Elinor, "at last I know what 'burnt siena' in paint boxes really means!" The glow covered the neatly tripping donkey, and the boy beside him. All our luggage had fitted in somehow. We sat above it while the boy walked encouragingly by our side. He and the donkey understood each other perfectly. Just to show off at first he belaboured and goaded the donkey into unnatural swiftness; but when I told him that there was no hurry and begged him to desist, he used instead his persuasive voice. The "Arrh!" with which he besought the donkey to go just a shade of a beat faster touched the animal's heart; but not for long. There *was* no hurry. The sun had gone, the towers moved deceptively towards us—and away from us. It was nearly dusk when we reached the small, renowned and extremely cheap pension where we were to lodge. What the boy asked was incredibly little; and Elinor in her relief at not being robbed and murdered by him, agreed to double it. I only hope the look of dramatically intensified astonishment and gratification with which he received his tip spread to the donkey.

In the garden of our pension there was a pomegranate tree covered with fruit and flowers; indeed as I remember it, when we woke on that first sunny morning, the garden was simply composed of the pomegranate tree, the rest of the hillside crumbling sharply away beneath it, into towers.

The interior of the pension was full of inexpensive but imposing antiquities, a little brittle and ramshackle, but dark wood and shining brass can go quite a long way towards romance, when the rest of the Middle Ages are their background.

Elinor was deeply interested in the lean, learned, hushed English ladies simmering with pious activities under our roof. Perhaps the ladies, all much older than we were, were not quite so learned as they sounded, but we made the most of them, while sitting together at meals round one long refectory table, exchanging our day's adventures.

The only slip in our whole harmonious tour as far as I was concerned happened in Siena.

We had arrived—and I expect the donkey boy had told us about it on the way but I had not taken it in—on the last night of the *Palio* races; and when Elinor gathered what the *Palio* was like she shrank from going out to see it. Races—at night by torchlight—crowds from every surrounding hamlet—noise that already sounded like a bombardment blended with a massacre of the Innocents—without the escort of a man—she couldn't. She really couldn't—her husband wouldn't like it. "Very well then," I said with quiet determination, "I will go alone!" But here the landlord intervened. "No," he said firmly. "Signorina—that I couldn't allow! Not from this Casa!" Together—two English ladies especially—he could answer for their safety—but one alone! No—I was too young—and, so he kindly told me, too handsome! It would never do—such exposure asked for male companionship and it would certainly be thrust upon me. His own family would have loved to take me, but they were already visiting their quarter's horse—and he, alas, must remain to guard the Casa—besides he had seen many Palios. He regretted it deeply—it was the sight of a lifetime—but I could not go alone!

I looked imploringly at Elinor, but she had already stood much. She had endured the terrifying splendour of the bare hill-side with an unknown male escort; her New England conscience closed down on us both. I can only hope that the donkey boy enjoyed the *Palio* as much as—or more—than I should have enjoyed it. It must have been a grand one, for the next day every second young man we saw was heavily bandaged.

The night was pierced with shrieks, the gutters still ran with wine next morning—Elinor tried hard to convince me—perhaps blood.

In Florence we were regally housed in an old Palace on a narrow street, dedicated to Dante. Florence was my greatest effort and it was there I met with my greatest reward.

We could only afford eight days; and into those eight days we crammed churches, museums, palaces, picture galleries, gardens, whole hill-sides.

I began to feel, as I showed Elinor those accumulated felicities of the Renaissance, as if after all, in losing one young man, however dear, I had not lost everything. "Beauty, beyond all feathers that have flown, is free." We are not—even during periods of intense unhappiness—jailed against it.

Perhaps Venice is more beautiful as a sheer spectacle than Florence—Rome was eventually to be the city I loved above all other cities—but Florence in spring or early autumn moves to music.

It is in Florence that observing eyes are "teased out of thought" by the marvels they behold; and that the heart knows for certain that however heavy the burden it bears:

> *Beauty is truth, truth beauty; that is all*
> *Ye know on earth, and all ye need to know.*

40

The most startling part of my return to Sta. Margherita was that
neither Sta. Margherita nor I was recognizable one to the other. The
garden had shrunk from an illimitable wilderness to a terrace the
size of a pocket handkerchief, the distant luminous hills were just
across the road, and the town itself—once inaccessibly far away—
was now a stone's throw. It was like the morning after the Resurrection.

Enrico—the illegitimate and preferred son of the proprietor who
actually managed our hotel—and the Signora his sister-in-law who
nominally managed it—received me incredulously, but with open
arms. The German doctor, who had attended me for weeks daily,
six months previously, declared stubbornly that I had never been
his patient. That young lady of the same name was going to die; he
had said so—and so it must have happened. A pity, Enrico sympathetically observed, that I paid my bills so punctually, otherwise
since I was an imaginary patient I might well have sent the doctor
an imaginary cheque!

We celebrated my return from the dead with the best wine the
family could produce and drank it together in the garden. The vintage was on, and the hills were a soft purple like the bloom on the
grapes themselves. While we were drinking our wine and exchanging our news, Enrico observed that I might be rather surprised to
hear that he had joined the Church of England. I was exceedingly
surprised, since he had once told me, "I see so many strange things
in this hotel that I feel I cannot afford to believe in anything I do *not*
see! It would be too surprising!"

"It came about in this way," Enrico explained. "You remember the good Miss Thompsons—how they were religious? I used to think to myself they could have afforded a more expensive hotel than ours had they gone less often to that uncomfortable church at Rapallo. Every day the Miss Thompsons gave me something to read about God—though I had so little time for reading—and the next day they would ask me questions about it. 'What shall I do?' I asked myself. 'I cannot be constantly answering questions about God!' Besides as you may remember they had been extremely good to me, while that disagreeable little episode took place in Tripoli! Constantly they sent me food parcels and even cigarettes. Since I was never a Catholic, why not—to please them—call myself a Protestant? So now I am a member of the Church of England!—and often we go to Rapallo in a carriage together, for which they pay, of course!"

"But Enrico," I said, rather shocked in spite of my agnosticism, "surely you do not take the Sacrament with them?" "But why not?" Enrico replied complacently, "a little bread—a little wine—I take such things every day! Whether I sit *at* a table, or kneel in front of one—what difference can it make?"

The Signora shook her head sadly so as to be on the safe side. Her position was a delicate one. She was extremely pretty and as good as gold, but her husband—one of the legitimate sons who owned our hotel, though he was seldom seen in it—neglected her shamefully, and indeed for many years actively ill-treated her because she bore him no child. Every year on the right Saint's day in August the Signora climbed up Monte Allegro, a stiffish mountain above Rapallo, on pilgrimage to a little church on its summit opened once a year for the express purpose of increasing fertility, and prayed hard for a child. For thirteen years she prayed in vain—and then the Saint relented. She had a boy baby; and her husband promptly bought her a pink silk blouse and took her out to a party. Enrico was very kind to her even before this happened. "You will enjoy the winter now you are well," he told me. "There is a young Signorina here who is very beautiful and paints. She will make a nice companion for you."

I found the Signorina bathing in a pool among the rocks at the bottom of the garden. We soon discovered that our outlooks on life, though dissimilar, were not antagonistic.

Sylvia was acting as companion to an elderly lady from the West Indies, who was extremely indolent and a little ill.

Sylvia could hardly have been said to "companionate" Mrs. Brown, who paid her handsomely for the purpose; but she ate her meals at the same table, and from time to time she allowed Mrs. Brown to accompany her upon excursions for which Mrs. Brown paid.

Sylvia was a shameless flirt. She went very fast, but perhaps not very far; and all Sta. Margherita's male inhabitants were in love with her. This was what took up most of her time, although it included a little painting.

As there was no one else in the hotel so early in the autumn, Sylvia and I spent many hours together upon the halcyon, purple and azure sea.

Sylvia had completely captivated a boatman called "Luigi" who had just come out of prison for manslaughter. Luigi had not meant to kill his brother-in-law, but they were having an argument on a stone jetty, and when his brother-in-law fell over backwards, his skull, which was thinner than skulls have any natural right to be opened like an egg-shell. Unfortunately his brother-in-law's family refused to take the judge's lenient view of the accident, and threatened the moment Luigi reappeared, to shoot him at sight.

He was not, he explained to us, afraid of these relations in the daytime; but when it became dusk he never moved without his revolver. Sylvia and I took it in turns to sit with the loaded revolver on our laps, while Luigi rowed us over the darkening sea.

Sylvia was a good woman of business and made a bargain with Luigi, that since we were obviously a great protection to him—for no Italian would be likely to shoot him with an English lady on each side of him—he must charge us considerably less for these evening excursions.

There was an evening when the sky changed from ice green to lilac, darkening slowly into purple, while the San Lorenzo cypresses closed in against the side of the mountain. Suddenly we were swallowed up in velvet blackness without the light of even a star. There was no sound but the soft grinding of oars against their rowlocks, when out of the darkness came a cry, and a sail gleamed

290

over us, so close we could have touched it. Our startled boatman shouted: "Dove andara Lei?" Deep as music, out of the blackness, came the long vowel sounds of the answer, "Anderemo—Spezia!" A month later a barque, on its way home to Spezia—perhaps this very one—caught off its course in a night squall—was dashed to pieces on the rocks beneath my window. Unknown to me, all three of its crew were drowned in the shrieking darkness. I lay awake most of that stormy night and heard no cry; but a sound of incredible and exquisite music filled my little room till dawn.

The hauntingly beautiful, and empty, month of October was barely over when the Miss Millers arrived.

They were the last surviving daughters of an old military family; their father had been a cruel martinet and they had been brought up in an atmosphere of overpowering respectability.

The elder Miss Miller had modelled herself upon this repressive parent. She was a rigidly correct woman of fifty with the British Empire running through her veins like fire. The younger sister must have been very pretty as a girl, with blue Irish eyes and black hair; but after forty she ran to nose, a high Wellingtonian feature, which needed the constant assistance of powder. Her eyelashes had failed her, and her eye-lids were too strong a pink. Her resemblance to a harassed and over-controlled rabbit was painfully clear.

She had never been allowed to be young and could not give up trying. Towards the last season's end Julia had reported to me, with crisp contempt, that the younger Miss Miller was behaving in a foolish manner with one of the Italian waiters. Conrado was an ex-prize fighter, and I do not think Enrico would have employed him except in a rush season.

Insolence lurked behind his flattering manner and coarseness behind his superficial good looks. Both sisters had, as the season slackened, become involved in the dubious pastime of learning Italian from him.

They appeared to look upon Conrado as something rather less intelligent and more harmless than a pet dog. They took his impertinence as jokes; but the elder Miss Miller soon had the sense to withdraw her attention from him. She dropped the lessons and froze away from his insinuating bursts of flattery with cold disdain;

and she also froze away from her sister. It was a relief to be told by the Signora that Conrado had been dismissed by Enrico and gone to Naples; and that the sisters were again upon the best of terms.

One afternoon a knock came at my door, and the younger Miss Miller followed it. Her face was white as a painted clown's and she shook all over; it was some minutes before she could speak at all, then she gasped: "Conrado!" and collapsed shuddering upon the nearest chair. When she had recovered sufficiently to speak coherently she told me the whole piteous story. Before she left for England the previous spring she had met Conrado secretly in Milan, under the pretext of visiting a dentist. She had planned an elopement and had expected marriage.

Unfortunately Conrado had not expected marriage; he was indeed already married; and when the younger Miss Miller realized what he *had* expected her fear and fury knew no bounds. She was terrified of ever seeing him again; and had succeeded in keeping her address in England from him.

When she knew that he had gone to Naples, she had agreed, though very reluctantly, to return to Sta. Margherita. What explanation could she give to her sister for *not* coming? Yet she had been always secretly terrified that he might turn up—and now he had. Conrado had letters of hers which he threatened to show her sister if she did not pay him well—and regularly—for his silence. If her sister were ever to see these letters, the younger Miss Miller said she would kill herself. She had instantly given Conrado all the money she had in her purse, and had promised more. She simply dared not see Conrado again. Nor had she any more money. They were not well off, and her sister controlled their finances. Could I help her? Would I see Conrado for her and threaten him away? I said that I thought we must consult Enrico. He was the soul of discretion, and in a sense he was partly responsible for her trouble by having employed a criminal. I had no power over Conrado— but it was quite possible Enrico might have some authority unknown to us. At first Miss Miller refused with tears. No! No one else must be told! She couldn't bear it. No one must ever know about Conrado! If anyone spoke to her about him she would simply die of shame.

Her whole soul rose up against her ever having thought of him as anything but a waiter. She not only repudiated Conrado as a lover, she repudiated him as a human being. He existed only as an act of God—or rather as an act of the Devil—a sword of Damocles hanging loosely in the air above her own, and her devoted sister's, head, for she now wholly loved and identified herself with her austerer sister. They had been so strictly brought up, she explained, they knew no evil. They were naturally and immaculately chaste, and invulnerable to social disaster—and yet there was Conrado lurking behind every bush in the garden, ready to pounce out upon them and destroy their sacred edifice of security—as if it were a soap bubble.

It took me hours to gain her consent, but at last sheer desperation wrung it out of her. Enrico *must* be told—but by *me*. She could not speak again of Conrado; and under no circumstances must anything be done which involved the knowledge of her elder sister! I was sorrier for her than I had ever been for anyone. Enrico too was sorry for her, but he was even more shocked than sorry. "Could you suppose," he asked me gravely, "that a woman of that age could *possibly* know so little of life? Why, Signorina, if you will forgive my saying so, an Italian girl baby of a year old would have known enough to keep clear of Conrado!"

However, Enrico thought of a plan, which involved his starting immediately for Milano, from where Conrado had originally sprung. "He must have a record!" Enrico explained, "and when I get that—I get everything! Fortunately I know a Police Officer at Milano—I shall tell him nothing of this matter because it is always well to keep the Police innocent—but by making a little exchange of one kind or another—for there is always some little detail of local knowledge which they would be glad to pick up—I will hope to gain the information I need. Then—I myself will blackmail Conrado! Something shall hang over *his* head in exchange for those letters! You must pray, Signorina, that his past is even worse than his present. While I am away the Signorina Miller should be ill in her room. You and the Signora will, I know, take her meals in and look after her. No one else but the sister must have access to her day or night. The old one must be told enough to keep her quiet. She can be trusted to hold her tongue; and she too must not leave the hotel grounds till I return. The Signora will see that Conrado stays outside *our* premises, but I cannot be answerable for either of these poor ladies except *inside* them! Conrado is *mal educato*—should he be unable to obtain money out of these sisters he might even attempt to kill one!"

The Signora and I had a long and nerve-racking week-end. Twice we caught sight of Conrado lurking on the rocks beneath the garden. The elder Miss Miller, when the younger managed at the dagger's point to give her a mitigated version of her dismal plight, refused to see or speak to her again until Enrico returned. She might never, she asserted, speak to her again, if Enrico's mission failed.

Nothing, neither tears nor prayers, nor her sister's complete physical collapse, moved her. She agreed to inform the other hotel guests that her sister was ill; but there her compliance ended. Still, she faced the hotel with heroic composure, and insisted on going out for her usual walks. Oddly enough, Conrado did not molest her; he probably thought it might pay him better to await the re-appearance of the less courageous sister who had more to lose. At the end of forty-eight hours Enrico returned, grinning all over like a Cheshire cat. "Have I evidence, Signorina?" he exclaimed gleefully, as soon as the Signora and I were safely closeted with him. "I have evidence enough to destroy a dozen Conrados! And evidence too that will not require Police intervention! I myself will meet Conrado in the café of a friend of mine—and the glass of wine I shall treat him to will—I flatter myself—be the last 'that one' ever drinks in Sta. Margherita!"

Exactly what took place at that café between Enrico and Conrado I never learned; but Conrado realized that the game was up. He handed over all Miss Miller's poor little letters, and was thankful to escape to Naples, his ticket paid for by money he had already received from her.

Released from disaster, the younger Miss Miller showed an incredible resiliency. The Church and State once more swallowed her completely, and the only change observable in her was an even more pronounced moral strictness than that of her elder sister. The elder sister immediately unbent and no one in the hotel ever learned anything about the incident. Both sisters seemed graciously to overlook the part played by Enrico and myself, and regarded us for the rest of the winter with a forgiving but slightly disapproving air. The Signora they had never noticed, so they simply continued not to notice her.

Deprived of the two greatest intimacies of my life, I felt unable to take more than a superficial interest in those around me; but with increasing health, I managed to keep at bay the icy sense of inner loneliness from which I had not recovered.

41

On the last of sixteen rainy days in November when all nerves were rasped, hopes dimmed and daily habits burdensome, I became suddenly conscious of a faintly pleasurable stir in the little hotel dining room. Glancing up from my solitary corner table I saw a young man walking through the row of dreary little tables, as if footlights were before him.

Paul was not handsome but there was about him the agreeable air of consciously bestowing and receiving pleasure from human contacts, especially from contacts with the female sex; and almost all of us at the Hôtel Métropole were women.

I knew at once that Paul could not be English, in spite of the Savile Row cut of his impeccable suit. He carried a tempting primrose covered volume in his hand; his tie, his socks, the edge of a silk handkerchief just showing above his breast pocket, had a complete relationship.

All men were but stubble from my cheated harvest; but however superfluous I found Paul, or however gingerly my burnt imagination handled him, I had noticed him and he was the first man, unless he got in my way, that I had noticed since my broken engagement. After that one glance, however, I resigned him with relief to Sylvia. He was exactly, I said to myself firmly, her cup of tea.

But he was not the kind of young man that even Sylvia was likely to retain for long at the Hôtel Métropole. The Ritz was his native shore.

I managed to avoid meeting him with some skill for the next few days. Rumours however reached me that Sylvia and the smart young Frenchman were as glued together as postage stamps.

However successfully I avoided Paul, I could not keep the same game up with Sylvia. Impatiently she knocked at my door, pouring out the charms of her new friend, and imploring me to consent to a meeting.

He was French, but he talked perfect English, he had constantly enquired after me. Everyone else in the hotel was delighted with him. Why was I so tiresome? I was busy—I did not want to meet him. But I *must*! He had written half an article on Shelley and wanted my help before he went any further. Surely I would not refuse to assist a fellow writer? I wavered. The French rarely appreciate English poets. Shakespeare they accept as an international misfortune; and Byron for political reasons and because he was rude about his fellow countrymen; but never yet had I heard of a Frenchman appreciating Shelley. "We think the gas he had in his stomach mounted to his brain!" my French friend, Mellie Darius, had disrespectfully informed me. "Besides his private life lacked common sense. He seemed to think one should have wives instead of mistresses, instead of a mistress as well as a wife! A far more economical arrangement!"

I capitulated to Shelley; and met Paul.

I thought it an extremely intelligent article; and we exchanged ideas on Shelley and verified quotations since he had not brought his Shelley with him.

They were the first ideas I had exchanged with anyone for months.

On the second occasion we talked together I realized that Paul had a haunting resemblance to Ernan. He was not like him in feature, for Ernan was undeniably handsome. It was like looking at a shimmering and slightly distorted reflection in lake water.

The weather cleared up, the last of the vintage was gathered; and on the first fine night there was a Festa.

All the villages round about collected in the town Piazza. Bonfires blazed on the mountains, and music and dancing seized the air. Paul and Sylvia went off into the gold and purple evening together, after I had rather reluctantly refused to go with them.

They remained out all night; and were heard, by practically every old lady in the hotel, breaking their way into the house at five o'clock in the morning, in fits of ungovernable laughter. Ours was not the sort of hotel in which such an escapade could get off lightly.

Enrico came to me in despair. What was he to do about it? Her own Signora Brown repudiated the *bambina*! As for all the other ladies, led by the Miss Millers—whose faulty memories overlooked Conrado—they threatened to leave the hotel in a body unless Enrico turned out Sylvia. Would I use my undoubted gift for advocacy and see each outraged matron or old maid in turn—beginning with the Signora Brown? But first I must see the *bambina* and implore her to remain incarcerated in her room till I had deflected the lightning.

I found Sylvia unrepentant and furious. The old women were hell-cats. She had as much right to be out as they had to be in. She and Paul weren't even drunk. Nothing had happened. And if I had seen the face of the night porter when they broke in on him, through a window, I should have laughed too! She meant to defy them all, and go off, singing her way down into the village, as usual. However it might be a good thing if I talked with Mrs. Brown—Sylvia wouldn't apologize to her in person—but I might apologize for her. After all they had been later than they had intended. It was not until she saw Enrico's face in the hall that Sylvia, realizing the full gravity of the situation, retreated to her room; and begged me to do the best I could for her.

At first Mrs. Brown was adamant, nothing I could say would move her. Sylvia had ruthlessly applied the last straw—the camel's back was broken. She must go. There was far less of a mother's heart to Mrs. Brown than I had expected, however there was a lower motive I might try. Mrs. Brown loved a title and Sylvia's uncle had one. With shame I worked upon this leading trait in our national character. I reminded her that at Easter Sylvia's uncle would pick her up to take her on to Rome. If Sylvia were dismissed, there could be no pleasant and gratifying meeting with this august personage in the Spring, no thanks for a family responsibility taken so inexpensively off his aristocratic shoulders! At last Mrs. Brown grudgingly succumbed. After all, Sylvia *had* sent me to apologize and *had* promised to behave better in the future. The rest of the hotel, except the Miss Millers who were stubbornly vituperative were an easier affair. There was nothing in Sta. Margherita that matched the Hôtel Métropole for comfort and cheapness. Since Mrs. Brown agreed to overlook Sylvia's scandalous conduct it might be unnecessary for them to do more than register their very strong disapproval. But it must be understood that there could be no more unseemly laughter at dawn, nor unchaperoned excursions that lasted all night.

Paul, who had refused to appear until the front line of resistance was carried, did the rest. He was a glorious advocate. His mixture of dignity and apology, grieved consideration and deep respect, melted everyone entirely towards himself, and partially towards his fellow criminal; only the Miss Millers insisted, if they did not actually leave the hotel, in acting as if Sylvia had left it. They cut her dead for a week. After that week, armed neutrality took the place of belligerence, for by then it was plain for all to see that Paul and Sylvia were barely on speaking terms.

The day after the Festa Paul came to thank me for my efforts, and to explain his part in their mutual indiscretion. He was, he told me, in a distracted condition. He had not told anyone else, but he had come straight from his father's funeral, and his father had died—indeed had killed himself—in a *maison de santé*. Paul was in error of inheriting the same tendency.

By profession he was a pianist; but he could not—for a few months at least—return to so arduous and emotional a profession.

He must have a quiet life—with some form of occupation which would take his mind off his father's tragedy. Did I think he could write—and would I help him if he tried?

There would be no more outbreaks like last night. That had been a *bêtise*.

I replied with caution that I should think, from his article on Shelley, that he might very well be a writer; but that I thought writing was an individual profession and that I gravely doubted if one writer could be of much use to another. Paul thought differently, he begged that I would at least try to help him. Plots were his trouble, perhaps he could write something if only a good plot were put before him which stimulated his fancy, so that he could make a start.

I had several stories afloat in my mind, as well as the one already shaped upon which I was working, so at length I offered to think one out overnight, and tell him the result in the morning.

I went to sleep however before I had visualized any particular plot, and woke up at five o'clock in the morning with my brain alight, and what I thought a remarkably fine story on the tip of my mind. I was almost sorry I had promised the plot to Paul as I thought it rather better and clearer than the one I was at work upon, but there was nothing to be done but hand it over to him when he joined me in the garden.

I retailed it with satisfaction, for clothed in words it sounded better than ever, but to my great surprise Paul stared at me with angry eyes, and said with that icy politeness only the French can attain, "Mademoiselle, will you be so kind as to tell me from where you have learned these facts about my private life, since they are not among those that I have repeated to anyone?"

It was some time before Paul would believe that I had never heard of him or talked with anyone who knew him before he arrived at Sta. Margherita. When he did he was wholly, and I was partially, bewildered.

It was true I had invented my friend Mellie Darius' unknown former life—but that was far less astonishing since I after all knew her intimately, and she might very well have dropped sufficient hints, unconsciously, for an observant imagination to hatch into actual happenings. But about Paul I knew nothing whatever, except what he had told me about his father—which had not come into my plot—and I had only talked to him twice. I suppose that I must simply have paid a visit to his nocturnal mind. Paul asked me rather sharply if I had told him *all* that I had picked up from his experience. I said yes—this was the whole book as it had unravelled itself before me in a series of pictures. Streets, cities, characters, all had been as plain and verifiable as daylight—but they seemed to have gone no further than his breaking a rather odd, Protestant and Catholic, engagement with a Swiss girl at Lausanne when he was twenty-five. He was now thirty-four.

"There is a good deal more that I may one day tell you," he said finally, "but for to-day we have had enough. You must see for

300

yourself I cannot write my own life story!" I agreed and offered instead to furnish him with one of my unfixed plots, which I had been considering before I met him. He agreed to think this new plot over, and we parted, each of us rather shaken by our shared experience.

When he joined me again in the garden a few days later, he asked if he might tell me some other facts about his life, which I had *not* imagined but which he now felt I ought to know. He began his story in rather a startling way. "Mademoiselle," he said, "I must tell you at once—before we go any further together—that I am corrupt. I have been corrupt from a child. I cannot make love to you, though I might very well want to—but you must not let me! You must remember that I have no right. If you do not stop me—you will regret it—and so shall I! Your friendship would be invaluable to me—if after hearing my story you could permit such a thing."

In those days I did not know what a corrupt person implied; I knew what it meant, but I thought of it as an accidental moral illness. Paul had been corrupted as a child by a Priest—well, the Priest had gone—why should not the corruption also vanish? I had not realized that we are not easily divisible from our functions or our experiences.

I was ignorant and in consequence arrogant; it was easy for me to believe that I might be of very great use to Paul. I told him, what I believed to be the truth, that falling in love with anyone was as impossible for me as for him. My heart was broken. I loved the people I had once loved, but I was incapable of fresh emotion.

"But you have affection," Paul said quickly. "You have shown affection for Mademoiselle Sylvia!" I shook my head. "I act automatically," I explained, "in the direction I am accustomed to act. I have no particular affection for Sylvia; but I also think as I have been brought up to think. If you and I were to be friends, I should feel that I might be supplanting Sylvia with you—and I could not agree to supplant her." Paul explained then that he and Sylvia had fallen out for good. It was true that he had been madly excited about her for a few days, and she with him.

It was a violent flirtation and had had a violent ending. If I didn't believe him, I could ask her. She had made it perfectly plain to him that she wanted no more of it than he did.

Such things happen in just such a way. Sylvia was extraordinarily pretty. Each had set out to conquer the other, each had resented the other's power to charm. Neither had succeeded in proving whose charms were the strongest. There had been nothing more to it than that.

To my surprise Sylvia endorsed Paul's verdict. As a flirtation it had been, she explained, immense fun while it lasted, but it had petered out. Paul was too vain and too selfish. Everything had to be the way he wanted. "If a man begins this way, Phyllis—*before* he is a lover—just think what he would be afterwards!" Sylvia told me impressively. But on the other hand, she and I were friends, and she would be extremely hurt if I deserted her for Paul. Let him write a book if he liked—and I could help him with it if I must—though she thought it great nonsense his writing if he was a pianist, but anyhow let us stick together as before. I gave her my word that our relationship should remain unchanged.

The next morning our more difficult bargain was also struck. Paul and I were to be friends. We were to write a book together; and neither of us was to fall in love with the other.

42

A day or two later Paul told me that he found the act of writing irritating to his nerves, and could not interest himself in the plot that I had given him. He suggested instead that we should collaborate over some of his Paris experiences, which he thought I should find dramatic enough to turn into a novel. I could make my own plot, and he would provide me with scenes and characters, which I could fit into it, at will.

For two and a half years Paul had acted as chief accompanist and private secretary to one of the world's most famous retired singers; and the most famous of its singing teachers.

The *atelier* was run as a business racket by the wife of the ex-singer, a beautiful and aristocratic woman devoted to the career rather than to the person of her husband. It is doubtful if Monsieur X. himself knew what a racket she ran.

Madame X. had discovered that private secretaries acting as lovers served her husband's interests better than if they were merely secretaries. Paul had been both her dupe and her lover. Even when he found out, as he very soon did, that the *atelier* was run upon semi-criminal lines, featuring rich young women with poor voices, and finding them the jobs already promised to poor young women with good voices, he had believed Madame innocent of the persistent bribery, blackmail and general dupery that went on. It was only when he found that the arch-criminal was also her lover that, enraged and aghast, he had thrown up what was from a financial point of view a very good situation. To play second fiddle to a criminal was more than Paul's *amour propre*, let alone his innate decency, could swallow.

"Broken Music" was the title we eventually chose for our experiment; and, although he did not accept it, it was the first of my novels to attract the eye of an American publisher.

I hesitated considerably before falling in with Paul's suggestion. It meant giving up a novel in which I was already deeply involved, and undertaking a mise-en-scène with which I was totally unfamiliar.

However, it was obvious that Paul in his nervous condition was incapable of continuous interest in any other subject than himself.

If I wanted to help him this was the only way in which he was likely to be helped. By taking up his immediate past and weaving it into a novel in which everything was to be seen at his own valuation —with all the impetus and clarity of inflamed and defeated vanity— I could relieve his mind from grief, and give his nerves time to settle down.

It was many years before I learned that you cannot do for others what they are either untrained or unwilling to do for themselves.

Paul passionately wished to re-instate himself in his own eyes, and to go back with fresh courage to his music; but he intended— though no doubt unconsciously—to remain at the same time the person who had caused his long series of defeats.

I was both flattered and excited by the prospect of reforming Paul, but I warned him that I was an unknown and so far unsuccessful author. I could only offer him half profits on our adventure; and half profits on what I had hitherto earned would not amount to much. Six months would cover the first draft and would need his constant attention since I was writing with an unknown background and dealing with purely French characters. However, once I had successfully mastered the first draft, the last six months I could manage alone. Nothing, Paul assured me, could be easier or more delightful. He needed six months to restore his nerves. Although he had very little money he would have enough for a quiet life, and he was a person who knew how to make his economies. His risks would be no greater than my own. For both of us it was worth trying; even if the novel's immediate profits were as small as I had feared.

For me at least the experiment was an unqualified success. I lived in Paris through Paul's eyes. I thought, I even dreamed in French. A sense of form which had hitherto escaped me now gave precision to my thoughts and their expression. Day by day, week by week, the English clergyman's daughter slipped away from me, and I became a mind avid for reality.

There were many painful lessons for us both. Paul was a cruel task master, impatient of faults and insistent on the preeminence of materials and facts.

There are no hiding places for intellectual untruthfulness in a good French mind. Paul's lucid and outspoken candour was untinged with mercy. He never let a thought escape him till he had scraped it bare to the bone. "Broken Music" only failed to become as good as it should have been for two reasons. One that my natural narrative power was constantly held up by favourite scenes of Paul's which he wished interpolated; and more seriously still by a sort of dual control, caused by the diversity of our two minds. Paul saw the story as one of a heroic young man pursued by harpies; and finally overwhelmed by ill-deserved bad fortune. Inspissated gloom, through which his sympathetic and chivalrous spirit unwaveringly shone, was what he wanted to present to the world, through my imagination; but unfortunately the blasted heath motif was not my natural element. I agreed to a certain amount of gloom, and to heroism, but not to undiluted heroism, on the part of the young man; and I enjoyed doing the harpies, of whom Madame X. was the chief. I am bound to say that from the point of view of interest she completely knocked out the one nice young girl—over whom we both wasted a good deal of time and attention. Paul wished to save this hunted innocent from suicide and/or starvation; but not to have to marry her afterwards. I wished the girl to save him. I did not mind what happened to her afterwards—nor incidentally to the tragic hero. Let him be a tragic but a spirited hero. I envisaged them both getting their musical noses on to successful grindstones in the end, even though their hearts could well remain permanently broken. Paul wished the grindstones to be failures as well. Finally—after much amicable discussion—I got the grindstones; and Paul got the gloom. I invented for my own amusement a French man about town—uncle to the hero—who became a channel for my cheerfulness and was one of the best characters I ever drew. Paul too enjoyed him and greatly helped me to gallicize his wit. We used both our languages, English when Paul was not excited, and French when he was.

Sylvia disapproved of the whole affair. "Why do you give Paul half profits for talking about himself?" she scornfully objected. "He would do it for nothing—and in your place I should insist upon being paid for listening to him!" But I felt myself repaid a hundred times over. Nor have I ever lost the magic sense of a door opening into other lands, and other languages, than my own.

However I soon found out that I had over-estimated Paul's interest in poets. He refused to talk any more about Shelley and when I tried to turn our conversations towards literature—French or English—he told me succinctly that he took no interest in the subject whatever and never had. He hated what he used to call my "cold, intellectual gaiety", and would shake his head sadly, murmuring, "Quel dommage, Phyllis, que vous n'êtes pas assez physical!"

Paul had agreed to share Sylvia's company with me because I had insisted upon it, but they bickered continuously, neither being able to endure the radiant self-presentation of the other; and each objecting strongly to sharing their audience.

We had made a good start on "Broken Music" when Paul developed a tooth abscess; as he refused to visit a dentist he soon became very ill indeed, with sky high temperatures, until the abscess broke.

The Signora and I nursed him alternately by day, and Enrico, who seldom went to bed before three o'clock, kept an eye on Paul at night.

Paul was not a good patient. He refused treatments, objected to doctor's orders, and threatened suicide. He often turned the Signora out of his room in tears. I was made of sterner stuff. I did what had to be done for him, and paid no attention to what he said. When at length Paul recovered he told me that he would have died except for my nursing and my *fermeté*, but he added, to my dismay, that what I had done for him as a nurse had totally disenchanted him in me as a woman.

We often gave each other these salutary shocks.

To celebrate Paul's recovery we decided to take our lunch to Portofino. Through the silver tracery of olives the sky was burning blue. The sea was satin smooth. Impecunious fishermen tempted us, and we all three decided upon a visit to San Fruttuoso, where in former centuries the Doges' corpses were carried by night from Venice, to hide them from their enemies, and buried in exquisitely carved marble tombs. Later on in history the bodies had been carried back to Venice again, or perhaps their enemies *had* discovered their hiding-place after all, for now the arched embroidered tombs were empty, but the tiny inlet, with its half dozen stone houses hidden under olives, and tucked against the mountain, was still a lovely port of call.

In our day only birds and fishermen visited San Fruttuoso. The path that led over the mountain back to Portofino was steep; and the sea—as we might have known had we stopped to consider it— was during the winter months a dubious method of travel for an open boat. We were just about to drink what passed for tea on the stone balcony of an ice-cold Trattoria, when the boatmen returned in a great state of excitement to warn us to come at once. The wind was rising, the sea was even at this moment "*Molto-molto pericoloso!*" and might shortly become worse. Why did we not return by foot over the mountain? They must take their boats back, but they could return quicker without us. There was a hurried conflict of ideas. Paul suggested staying where we were for the night, and letting the boatmen return for us when the sea was calm. Sylvia declared she must return at once or send a message through Paul across the mountain to Mrs. Brown. I could not climb the mountain. Why could not Paul go back on foot alone, while we stayed where we were? Paul said he neither could nor would scramble down a mountain side in the dark. So the path of least resistance seemed the sea. We ran down to the inlet with our excited boatmen, and launched ourselves with peril, from the rocks into the madly dancing boat. The sea was clearly alarmingly rough, but the highly skilled fishermen got us safely out of the rocky inlet on to the open sea. By keeping close to the precipitous shore, in the trough of the waves, we were getting along nicely, though I remember thinking that it would have been wiser to have posted a long letter to Lislie still in my handbag, on the shore, when with a sound like the splitting of yards of stiff calico, a squall broke out of the yellow sky. In a minute the sea churned itself into white and snatching foam. The waves, breaking on the rocks a few feet from us, dashed back over us; the wind, and the boatmen, shrieked together. I don't know how long we struggled in that dancing surf, but it seemed a lifetime. Sylvia sat at the bow. Her blue eyes sparkled, the wind tore at her golden hair plaited round her head. She looked like a little *Cinque Cento* angel about to take wing from a Bellini picture.

Her voice rose above the mingled prayers and curses of the fishermen. She sang song after song, while the storm rose higher and higher, with unfaltering courage. There was a moment when it seemed the end had come. The boatmen flung down their oars shrieking; the boat spun round in a cauldron of white foam—but still Sylvia sang. Her eyes, her voice, her spectacular serenity re-inspired the terrified men. She put their hearts back into their bodies. They started to row again, flinging their last strength against the sea; and suddenly we rounded the point; and were in the little harbour of Portofino. The boiling surf was gone. The smooth green backs of the swell were easy to surmount. We were safe.

When we landed, the fishermen caught Sylvia's hands and kissed them. They said she was an angel, they had seen the golden halo round her head as she sang. We had returned from the dead. She had worked a miracle! From henceforward they would pray to her as if she were the Virgin herself! We gave them all the money we had on us, and they insisted on treating us to a glass of wine, before they went to their church to return thanks—and to find a cheaper *Vino* on which to spend the remainder of their tips.

As soon as we were alone, waiting for our carriage in the pouring rain, I told Sylvia with great warmth that she had certainly saved all our lives by her courage, and presence of mind. To my delight, Paul followed by a set speech only possible to a Frenchman—of exquisitely turned compliment.

It looked to me as if the occasion was to be nicely rounded off, and that we might drive home for once in peace. But alas, nothing of the kind occurred!

Sylvia, pleased with her due round of applause, now wanted more, and began a long, highly coloured version of past heroisms, so varied and so spectacular that I found myself doubting again if they could all have happened to any one person in so short a life-time. Unfortunately Paul went further than doubt; with merciless clarity and persistence he stripped these little tales to pieces, till they became under the lash of his cruel tongue more and more ragged and insecure. Finally Sylvia lost her temper. She said she would have nothing more to do with Paul, and that I must choose between them for companionship. She would never speak to him again. We lapsed into frozen silence. The rain came down in torrents. It was dark before we reached Sta. Margherita. Sylvia had forgotten to leave a message with Mrs. Brown, before starting out on our excursion; and Uncle or no Uncle, Mrs. Brown could bear no more neglect and anxiety. She dismissed Sylvia at sight. I took Sylvia to my room. She had used up all her salary; she would of course be given her return fare, but to what would she return? Her uncle had closed his house, and started on a round of visits before setting out for Rome. He would be furious, he would probably disinherit Sylvia (not for the first time, but perhaps for the irrevocable last), there was no one who wanted her and nowhere she could stay. It was a pity that we had not all three been drowned.

It was very hard for Sylvia to have to descend from being the Virgin Mary's substitute, to being a dismissed companion, and we spent what was left of the night discussing her problem.

The next morning things looked a little brighter. Mrs. Brown, having now heard the full account of Sylvia's heroism, said Sylvia might stay at least until she had time to make other arrangements; Paul apologized. He finally confessed to me that he had been upset at not having been the hero of the occasion; by some oversight on the part of Providence, he had not been taught either to row or to sing.

I consoled Paul with the thought that we were mutually deficient; and we had after all shown no cowardice. It was hardly our fault that we were not blondes with thrilling voices and a large repertoire of Italian peasant songs. Paul was however inconsolable. Passive courage was a very good rôle for a woman, he explained, but as a man he should have put on more of an act. After such a débâcle, he must leave Sta. Margherita at once. He would go to Rome; and of course I would go with him. How otherwise could we write "Broken Music" together?

I was stunned with horror. How could I go to Rome? Why should I leave Sta. Margherita where I was almost part of the Signora and Enrico's family? Rome would be too expensive, too unhealthy and above all, to go with him alone unchaperoned was impossible. On the contrary, Paul said firmly, it was going to be perfectly *comme il faut*. He had thought it all out in the night. We need not travel together, he would go ahead, and get me a room in a French Convent—very cheaply indeed. The Mother Superior was a friend of his, and who could make a better chaperone than a Mother Superior? The climate of Rome was dryer and calmer than that of the Gulf of Genoa—look at yesterday! Such an affair could never take place in Rome.

I had never seen Rome, and it was a crime to be so near the Eternal City and to avoid seeing it!

Besides did I not think I ought to take Sylvia? Was not the Uncle coming to Rome at Easter? And such an uncle must be good for twenty pounds; this would keep Sylvia—for whom by now Paul was genuinely sorry—until he came. Sylvia was enchanted with the plan. She forgave Paul; and the Uncle *was* good for twenty pounds. My parents put up no resistance. They thought a Convent under the care of a Mother Superior a perfect setting, and my father having been to Rome was enthusiastic as to my sharing his experiences. He would see Rome again through my eyes.

Sylvia and I bought a Central Italian Baedeker between us; and used it till it dropped apart.

Paul hated sight-seeing so we explored Rome in peace; and when we weren't sight-seeing as Paul pointed out, Sylvia must paint. The French convent was on a hill exactly opposite the Colosseum. It was a workmen's quarter and not markedly salubrious.

The Mother Superior was not anxious to take us but on hearing that I was writing a book with Paul, which would convert me to Catholicism, so Paul had surprisingly informed her, she gave a qualified consent. We must both be in at nine o'clock every evening. Paul could only be admitted at certain hours for stated intervals, in the visitors' room—or later as a concession on the terrace where I worked daily. Also I must see a doctor since I had been a lung patient, and abide by his decision. The doctor was re-assuring and saw no reason why I shouldn't be accepted as a guest, though he said firmly I must go to bed at five o'clock during the winter months since otherwise my lungs might not stand stone floors and sudden drops of temperature. I stood everything and turned my life upside down to meet Rome. From early morning till five o'clock I lived on, and in, the city. Sometimes with Sylvia, often quite alone, I strolled in and out of galleries and churches; and up and down the seven hills. At five o'clock I went to bed and wrote till I was sleepy. I saw very little of Paul and could have dispensed with what I saw. The Paul of Rome was a different and not nearly so pleasant a person as the Paul of Sta. Margherita. He had become passionately worldly and was swallowed up by the friends he had told me previously had been his moral and financial ruin. Complete quiet and careful economy seemed no longer necessary for his health.

Sylvia reluctantly shared a studio in the Via Margutta with an old acquaintance, an elderly Miss Williams, whom she didn't like. Sylvia was furious with Paul for not introducing us to his friends; refusing to share my relief that he didn't; and she was barely consoled by long days spent in the Campagna sketching, while I read aloud to her.

I was by now deep in the stream of "Broken Music". All that I wanted of Paul was an occasional attentive ear, and a little caustic criticism; and it was all I got.

Paul said it made him nervous to sit in the visiting room of a convent; and even on the terrace he became very irritable and restless. Suddenly he was taken ill. I must go at once to the hospital of the Blue Nuns to see him. I did not find him very ill; but very cross. He thought he had appendicitis; but the doctors found he hadn't. He couldn't possibly stay in Rome. He couldn't see enough of me to do his share of the book. I was losing my French touch. I must come at once with him to Capri. That was the proper climate for both of us, Rome was impossible in February—see how ill it had already made him! Besides his friends did him nothing but harm as I might have known they would! I thought of all the things Rome had been six weeks before, and to me still was; I thought of Sylvia brought there to be deserted; I thought of my parents, and I said a firm "No!" But fate conspired against me. The Mother Superior and I had always taken to each other; I had been brought up in a convent; but she did *not* like Sylvia. Sylvia's virtues were not those which suit convents; and her venial infelicities soon became crimes. It was forbidden to make a sound in corridors, yet Sylvia constantly sang, at the top of her voice, Italian love songs of the most ardent nature; and the nuns, though French, knew Italian. Finally she sang one of the most startling of these songs straight into a procession of nuns on their way to chapel. The Mother Superior sent for me and said that Sylvia must go. She would be enchanted to keep me, but alas, my friend was not a young person suitable for convents. Her room was always untidy, there were cosmetics on her dressing table—and now these songs! What was to be done about it? At a pinch Sylvia could have a bed in the Via Margutta studio. We were not likely to find anything else cheap enough for both of us. Yet I longed to stay in Rome—it suited me as no place I had ever been in suited me. My whole imagination was saturated with it—I felt as if Rome had suited me for a thousand years. Besides I had no wish to see more of Paul than I was already seeing; nor could I believe that even my indulgent parents would much care for their daughter going off to Capri with an unknown Frenchman.

But how could I, if I refused Paul's plan, keep what I needed for "Broken Music"? It might well be true that I was losing the French touch; and it was certainly true that I couldn't afford to lose it.

I had started the book in order to save Paul; but I now wanted to save the book, and I fear the salvation of Paul—besides being a very dubious affair—had now become subsidiary.

However this new plan might still save him—and he was strongly under the impression that if I consented to go to Capri with him he *would* be saved. At last I agreed to write and ask my parents for their consent, privately hoping that they would refuse it.

Sylvia was, with some justice, exceedingly annoyed about the whole project; but in the end she acted with great generosity and consented to stay in the Via Margutta if it should prove necessary.

My parents—to my dismay—wrote expressing complete confidence in me, and leaving the decision to go or stay in my hands. No social laws pressed upon me. I had no acquaintance to be scandalized. I was to be from henceforward my own law-giver.

I think I had begun, though not very seriously, to realize that Paul wished to be my lover; but I also realized that this did not prevent him from being the lover of other people. I need not therefore feel that too much was at stake for him if I kept to our original bargain.

I now think that it was unfair to go to Capri with Paul on this basis; but at the time it seemed to me that we were mutually advantageous to each other.

I was not as Paul once explained to me "une femme initiée" or else perhaps I would have been a little kinder to him—or far less kind.

43

The first stage of my journey to Capri was not auspicious. Sylvia came to see me off, and unfortunately, while waiting, formed one of her violent if fleeting flirtations with an unpleasant man who was to be my fellow traveller. Naturally enough he supposed that I would be prepared to carry on the flirtation where it had left off; and it took a considerable amount of time before my freezing tactics succeeded in getting rid of him.

I was shaken by this experience, and inclined to panic. What if Paul failed to turn up in Naples and I was left alone in that particularly evil city with an awkward customer hovering at my heels? What if Paul *did* turn up but also proved to be an awkward customer? What did ᴛ know of Paul—except from his own self-histories? His behaviour in Rome had been both irresponsible and unsympathetic, though it had suddenly changed to dangerously lover-like docility when I had at length consented to go to Capri.

We were not to *be* lovers—that had been well understood—but with all these sudden changes of place and behaviour might not also this estimable bargain find itself subject to spontaneous lapses? The train was an express but it stopped once at Velletri. Should I get out there and return to the complete, if austere, security of Mother Françoise?

This would be false and cowardly on my part and might give Paul, if he did turn up at Naples before my telegram could reach him, both trouble and anxiety.

We stopped at Velletri—a small and uninviting town. It was pouring with rain, and my mind was still not made up when the train moved on. Paul *was* on the platform at Naples, in his most

314

kind and reassuring mood. It was still pouring with rain, but neither of us cared, as we flung ourselves into a *carozza* to dash for the last boat to Capri.

We caught it by the skin of our teeth, an archaic and dingy piece of boat-building, which rolled in a most terrifying manner on the calmest crossing. With half a gale blowing from the north the little steamer showed every intention of seeking the bottom. I had avoided the dining car for fear of my fellow traveller, and this did not seem the moment to think of tea. Paul and I sat facing each other across a small table in a crowded cabin punctuated with excruciating sounds. Paul was in the highest spirits while he explained to me that he could not find two hotels for the sake of *des convenances* as we had planned, since in Ana-Capri there was only one; however it had an annexe across a garden and he could sleep there if I wished. I would see for myself that Ana-Capri was the most perfect spot on the island.

I think it was while I was looking at his face across the table that I first realized Paul's likeness to Donatello's Marble Faun. One side of his face—which reminded me of Ernan's—was gentle and humane; but the other profile was—like the Faun's—inhuman, malicious and irresponsible. Taken both together, when Paul laughed, they formed an engaging contrast.

By the time we reached Capri the wind had blown the rain out of the sky. The island rose from a black sea, a deep indigo blue; in shape rather like an arm stretched out in welcome. The small harbour of the Marina was full of row boats manned by sturdy matrons, who seized upon our luggage and ourselves, eventually disposing us, with much conversation and laughter, in a small carriage drawn by a pair of ponies; the driver being no doubt the nearest male relative of the strongest matron. It seemed to be the Capri rule forty years ago that women met the steamer in row boats and carried the heavy luggage, while men were the drivers of carriages and lifted wraps and baskets.

The Capri ponies had the hearts of lions, and the legs of chamois, and no sooner were we settled in the small open vehicle—something between a victoria and a dog-cart—when they tore up the mountain at full gallop.

315

The sky was clear and high above us, and one by one the full-blown stars rushed out. "In one stride came the dark". What lay ahead of me was wholly unpredictable, but the immediate moment was pure rapture. I wanted those lively ponies, rushing at full tilt up a mountain, never to arrive; indeed I think I would have welcomed accompanying them over a precipice, so fragrant and heady was that wind, tearing the sweetness from sea and mountain, and tossing it back in our faces, beneath those splendid stars. "It is perfectly safe," Paul told me, "in Capri horses know nothing else but hills—a horse that would not gallop could not exist!"

Nicolino and Rosina, the brother and sister who managed the hotel, did not expect us. People very seldom caught the last boat to Capri from Naples; and even more seldom tried to catch it.

The question of the annexe had to be left till morning, since it was unheated, with its rooms unprepared. But we could have dinner: cheese, a salad of superfine excellence, followed by fruit. Wine came of course from their own *podere*. The gods may have eaten such meals but I doubt if even the gods had a better appetite than I had. I slept the clock round, not minding in the least what questions were to be left unsettled till morning.

Paul had left all financial arrangements to me to make for both of us. He thought women capable of bargaining better than men, but he told me he could not pay more than seven lire a day. I could make my own price. He would remain in the room to assist my struggles. He was of no help whatever. On the contrary he rushed to the aid of the indignant and grasping Nicolino. We must, Nicolino declared, pay ten each, though it was out of season and Paul had previously told me that none but the Grand Hotel in the town of Capri ever charged more than eight in February. In the end, after a fierce and exhausting battle we compromised. Paul was to pay seven lire, and I was to pay nine. This was the very least Nicolino would take us for, and even this, he said, was a dead loss to him, since they had no other visitors so early in the year, and keeping open at all was a mere concession to chance wanderers.

I willingly chose the unheated annexe room for myself, and left to Paul the steam-heated one in the hotel itself. An outside staircase led from the garden to a large room, that opened on a balcony, and had easy access to a pillow-shaped roof, white as a snow flake. Pigeons bowed themselves into my room every morning with my breakfast from a small and fragrant garden full of lemon and orange trees. From my balcony I could see pink almond blossom, like tethered clouds, floating above pale green vineyards that dipped sharply down towards an incredible blue and purple sea. Standing like a tall tulip on its bed, Ischia rose out of the sea. I was unaware that this island was full of ex-convicts, mainly murderers; subject as well to hideous calamities on the part of nature, in which a small but vicious volcano played an active part.

Almost anything of a disagreeable nature could and did happen on Ischia, while on Capri nothing happened but the succession of the four seasons, soaked in light.

Nevertheless, in spite of its evil reputation nothing prevented Ischia, seen from a distance, from looking lovely as a dream.

The sun does not shine at Capri, it shines through it. Everything hangs in light, and is penetrated by it. There is very little sound, since all birds are shot at sight: sometimes far off the murmur of the sea, and occasionally the rather hard note of a church bell jangling from under the sulphur coloured dome of the Ana-Capri church, which was on the opposite side to my balcony. It was fortunate I had one window overlooking so respectable and considerate a neighbour.

Forty years ago Ana-Capri was a tiny and remote village, miles away from any habitation except what remained of Tiberio's villa; and an equally ancient tower with a few rooms attached to it, belonging to Axel Munthe.

Beautiful and simple girls wandered over the hill-side, frequently accompanied by goats and carrying magnificently shaped water jai on their unbending heads.

These daughters of the gods, Greek featured, with the enormous velvety eyes of cows, were as the years passed and distances narrowed, mysteriously transported to Naples, to live lives of quite a different kind. Beauty, and that simple upright kindness that dignified peasant life, slowly withdrew from Capri. Even in my youth, too many sinners, anxious to survive their past, or to start a future of the same kind unobserved, came to Capri, where they could live as they liked uncriticized. Artists and writers with perhaps more commendable motives came for a week-end and often stayed for twenty years; but these visitants—savoury or unsavoury—lived in or near the little city of Capri in the centre of the island, or in the Marina above the tiny harbour; they seldom penetrated to the wilds of Ana-Capri.

The first thing Paul did, after he had finished reproaching me with the bluntness of my bargaining, was to bring me his loaded revolver. "This," he said, "you shall take care of now for me— while we are together. Lock it up in one of the drawers in your room—and hide the key. Some men put their lives in women's hands. Mine is perhaps the higher compliment—for I shall put my death in yours. One thing I promise you, Phyllis—whatever is the outcome of our friendship—I shall not kill myself while we are together."

We arranged our lives on a fixed plan, arranged by Paul. If we ever altered our relations, he explained, we could alter the plan. Meanwhile I never saw Paul till we met at lunch. From early morning to mid-day I wrote on my pillow-shaped roof shared with the washing. After lunch Paul strolled over to the annexe to hear and criticize my first draft, chapter by chapter. Sometimes, when it was read, we wandered together over the mountain side till dusk, sometimes we separated early and met again for dinner. Punctually after dinner Paul vanished; and I returned to the annexe, either to the roof and the stars, or to my room and a book.

Paul gave me marvellous descriptions of all the people he met and their strange histories, but he never allowed me to meet them. He explained that I had entrusted myself to him. He must be careful about my acquaintance.

I don't think I felt particularly lonely. I was deep in the stream of "Broken Music". Paul looked well and happy, and seemed to enjoy working on the book as much as I did. The conditions were perfect for writing, so that the iron curtain that Paul drew between myself and his amazing acquaintances did not distress me. It did not occur to me till much later in life that iron curtains are the precautions taken by those who have something to hide, or who fear to share.

I doubt if Paul's disreputable friends were any more disreputable than Paul himself, and since I was able to take care of myself with him, it is probable that my morals could have survived even this further challenge. However, closer at hand, the iron curtain was lifted by chance.

Almost opposite our gates there was an artist's studio, run by a German painter, perhaps the best in Capri, and his immensely fat and rather horrible Viennese friend—who in his youth had been as beautiful as Antinous.

"*Il Porco*", the name by which the Germanic friend went in Capri, was a remittance man from an aristocratic Austrian family; two young men worked at the studio as well, Francesco, a young Italian student, and a youth who might have walked out of Eton College, so Anglo-Saxon and distinguished was his type. Vincenzo's father had indeed been an English earl. His mother was a Capri peasant girl who now took in washing and—when I knew her—though more than middle aged and partly toothless—danced the tarantella better than any person in Capri.

I made the acquaintance of the studio through an Airedale. This sagacious and well behaved animal entered the dining-room daily at his master's heels, and became instantly invisible under the table until Otto—the painter—departed.

Unfortunately on one occasion the waiter handed his master a dish on the wrong side, and it appeared to the Airedale an offensive gesture. Instantly his teeth met in the waiter's leg. Screams rang through the room. The waiter seized a knife; Otto flung himself upon the waiter; Paul leapt up to separate them, calling out to me to secure the dog, who was about to execute further damage upon the waiter.

There was no trouble about the Airedale when once I had gained his attention. He had done what seemed to him right and with an easy conscience now devoted himself to making friends with me. I was well accustomed to dogs, having brought up from infancy two bull dogs, a mastiff, a red setter, and several smaller fry. But it was supposed by my Italian audience, and even by the returning Otto, that I had achieved a miracle.

I was thanked, congratulated and applauded, and the whole *atelier* was thrown open to me at any time. Paul must bring me round this very evening—the moment the light had gone. Paul somewhat reluctantly agreed; and our acquaintance flourished.

I particularly liked Otto and the Airedale. I did not care for the two young men; and I loathed Il Porco, though I must admit that he sang Schubert's songs extraordinarily well.

The waiter did not go mad as Nicolino and Rosina had prophesied. On the contrary, he merely grasped from that day forward the right way of presenting dishes at table.

Paul wisely collected a handsome sum from Otto and his friends, including ourselves, with which to present the damaged waiter. "You see, Phyllis," he told me, "we must all make a little sacrifice otherwise the dog will be dead from poison within twenty-four hours."

The sum collected must have been sufficient, for the dog survived.

44

I took one whole day's holiday during the two and a half months we spent on Capri. Not that I felt the need even of one, for every day's writing on our growing book was to me more of a release than an effort. Paul however grew restive. It was, he said, a mortal crime to be so near Pompeii and not to visit it. Since I refused to go to Naples with him for a night or two at least I must consent to take a day's trip to Pompeii.

Unfortunately there were no connections between Capri and Pompeii. At last we discovered that sometimes a schooner sailed at dawn with oil and wine from Capri to Castellamare; and from Castellamare the Naples steamer could pick us up, and drop us at a port beneath Vesuvius well within reach of Pompeii.

As for coming back, some connection could no doubt be devised by which we could get to Castellamare from Pompeii and catch the evening steamer to Capri. We should then be home soon after dark.

When we started at daybreak, the stars still pierced the colourless clear sky. The whole island was asleep, not a dog barked.

It was April and every breath we drew was sweet with the scent of wild herbs and young vines.

We could barely see our way along the precipitous path, old as the island itself, that dropped straight down the mountain side from Ana-Capri to the sea.

We reached the Marina in time to be rowed across with the last load of barrels.

The *Stellamaris* hung above us, all sails set, a lovely, lively

321

creature, swinging at her anchor like an impatient horse pawing for its freedom.

The sailors dragged us up a rope ladder under the ship's figurehead, a gigantic mermaid lashing her tail at us as we climbed.

The sailors were full of jokes and laughter at their unusual cargo; they put me on a coil of ropes covered by sacking, where I could lean against the mast. Their great ringing cries as they lifted the anchor were music from a remote past, and seemed to wake the day. The ship, her white wings fully spread, sailed out across the bay into the dawn mist, over a patch of beaten gold. A deep pink glow spread behind Naples. Ulysses, Greece, the long adventure of mankind, were part of that early dawn.

The ship moved along its golden track, effortlessly and without a sound:

> *Like those Nicean barks of yore*
> *That gently o'er the perfumed sea*
> *The weary, way-worn wanderer bore*
> *To his own native shore.*

We could hardly bear to part from the schooner and her friendly sailors; but Castellamare soon closed down upon us, a bleak, surly port, without distinction or comfort. We waited shivering on the jetty, scanning the empty sea, shaken by the doubts of the inhabitants, for the Naples steamer, they explained, was a perfunctory visitor; and certainly at eight o'clock in the morning we could not get a vehicle or expect a breakfast at a place like their own. At last a little plume of smoke against the pearly sky put our anxiety to rest. This was no cloud—for the clouds were white or rose coloured—but our dingy friend, the Naples steamer. The port below Vesuvius was also breakfastless and grim, the sun beat hot upon us, and we had a long climb before we reached the gates of Pompeii. "That one," the Padrona of the one small restaurant told us, referring to the absent custodian, "is always uncertain. No one cares to walk about alone in the city even by day, and yesterday there were only two visitors—who gave small tips—so to-day he may feel too discouraged to appear. Perhaps if you took a meal here first——!"
We said we certainly would, and after the Padrona had retired to d

her hair, which had not been done for some time, she reappeared, with a bottle of Monte Vesuvio wine—a rich and pleasant beverage. The custodian, she suggested, might well agree to let us into the city if he were invited for a drink first. Mysteriously the custodian appeared, I fancy he was her husband, and we all sat round a small iron table, and had a glass together.

The winter, the Padrona explained, at Pompeii was sad, but in another month—what a pity it was we could not have waited and come later—we could not have heard ourselves speak! Such crowds from Naples—and when they were Americans, what tips! Truly you could say that not lava but gold covered the sides of Vesuvio!

The sun clamped down on the mountain side, but the gates of the city were opened to us and for long happy hours we wandered through the city, Paul and the custodian explaining its roofless memories in alternate French and Italian. New discoveries and restorations had just begun, but for the most part Pompeii was still as Shelley saw it, and even as Monte Vesuvio had stormed, shaken, and left it, nine hundred years ago. All that had happened in the interval was that the sun had sunk deeper into the biscuit-thin Roman bricks—while the frail wind-flowers, and the tall grasses, had grown higher over them.

The marks of the chariot wheels were still plain on the stony highway.

Pompeii might have been a glass slipper left behind by an enchanted Cinderella fleeing to escape her cruel sisters into the mountain side. The walled highway wandered along under its umbrella pines and then stopped suddenly, against Vesuvius. The mountain looked consciously mild and reassuring as it rose over us into the cloudless April sky; only a tiny flag of smoke stained the translucent blue.

For an hour, while Paul gleefully vanished with the custodian to see indecent frescoes from which I was, by my sex, happily debarred, I sat alone in the garden of the Faun's House.

His statue in bronze, horned and goat-hooved, spun alone, above a little fountain, under its roofless walls.

I lost all sense of time, perhaps I fell asleep, for although it was bright noon I felt darkness surround me and heard a rustling sound, as if thousands of dry leaves rushed past me, "like ghosts from an enchanter fleeing."

I woke shivering into the blinding light; and when Paul returned I had no need to see mummies, or that petrified dog searching for fleas when the lava caught him, to recapture the burning darkness that fell upon Pompeii and all its citizens.

When he had taken us out on to the hill-side above the circus the custodian left us to get his dinner. The air was full of small golden bees, and the scent of thyme. Between the green arches of the young vines far below us danced the "innumerable laughter" of the waves. To my bereft and vulnerable heart such beauty was unbearable and my eyes filled suddenly with tears. Paul seized my hand and kissed it. "You are the most sympathetic woman in the world!" he exclaimed. "You feel for me, more even than I feel for myself! I see that you are re-living my parting with the Golden Rose! You were right, it was here—on this very spot—that we spent our last day together two years ago!"

I had forgotten about the Golden Rose. She was, I knew, the last but one of Paul's serious mistresses. I dried my eyes, and listened to the saddest of his stories. The Golden Rose had been for many years a well-known and much admired woman, the mistress of a famous English writer. He had been faithless to her, and she had found consolation in Paul's new young love. She was ten years older than Paul, and had been to him both mother and mistress. They had lived together a year in apparent happiness. The Golden Rose had plenty of money, and took a house at Posillipo, where Paul was her free and happy guest.

Suddenly her old lover re-appeared. He had lived too long with her not to miss being without her. He came in order to reclaim her. She confessed to the astonished and heartbroken Paul that fond as she was of him her heart had always belonged to her older lover. "Never before," Paul finished sadly, "nor since, Phyllis, has a woman left me of her own free will! This had a most serious effect upon me! I find that you forget the woman you have left—but the one who has left you—her—you never forget!"

In spite of Paul's grief—and my own—we ate a hearty lunch, and drank together to the slow healing of time.

Pompeii too had taken a long while to heal; but now the miracle was accomplished. On this brilliant April day even her scars were beautiful.

It was growing late. The custodian and Paul tried *not* to find a driver to take us to Castellamare, but I persisted; and one at length was found.

It took half an hour for him to climb down, and for us to climb up, to a less fantastic price, and while Paul wandered away to have his last joke with the custodian I took the opportunity to promise the driver an extra ten lire (when lire were worth ten times or more than they are worth now) if he caught the steamer; otherwise I am quite sure we might have reached Castellamare but not Capri, for the night.

It was an unforgettable drive. The road was divided between rocks and holes—the horse was a skeleton tied to his shafts by a curious cob-web made of pieces of string. We were tossed continuously between earth and sky. Spurred by the driver's enthusiastic whip and deep reproachful cries, the poor ghost of a horse fled like the wind—and the vehicle behind ricochetted after it. We caught the last steamer to Capri in the purple dusk. The stars came out like a troop of buttercups, but their brilliance was soon eclipsed by a fantastic golden moon. There was no dark. Never have I seen such light poured out from the hollow lady of the skies as swept those wine dark seas! Even the Naples steamer was irradiated and I think Paul forgave me, that we got home on time.

45

The quiet stream of our collaboration was broken by two enlivening incidents. The first was of a festal nature. Once a year Ana-Capri gave a fancy dress ball shared alike by Capriots and artists.

Paul came to me in great excitement. "This is an affair," he told me, "in which I propose that we should take the leading rôles. You shall be my 'Manon'—and I shall of course be 'Amelio'! Bring me your entire wardrobe! You do not know what can be done with good make up, but you shall find out! Mascara—under and over your eyes—and then perhaps you will learn what use to make of them! My costume will be that of the Boule' Miche in the 1880's."

After considering my wardrobe with mounting gloom, Paul threw my ineffectual dresses on the floor in despair.

"All this is more suitable for a funeral!" he told me, "but we will buy five yards of Japanese silk, and I will myself draw a sketch for a costume. I used to take my holidays in Spain with a designer from Paquin, and once I gave him, from watching a leaf in the wind, a design that was the success of the season. It will not cost you more than fifty lire, and since you cannot sew Rosina and Margherita shall make it up for you, under my directions!"

Rosina and Margherita were two of Paul's devoted flames, and I felt that they would deeply resent this use of their spare time; but Paul, flying on the wind of his brief enthusiasms, was irresistible; and we all three reluctantly obeyed him.

The dress turned out a masterpiece, though it seemed to me that I need not have been so continuously pricked with pins as I was during the fittings. Bell-shaped trousers of a brilliant pattern, an open shirt, a flowing tie, a *beret* on one side of his head, a marvellously concocted moustache and small goatee, transformed Paul from a man about town to an artist of the Boule' Miche in its finest hour. However, the pains he took about his own costume were nothing to the pains he took about mine; and it was not until some days later that I discovered Paul had promised that as well as payment I would finally consign it to Rosina. Paul himself trimmed my broad-brimmed hat and tied it under my chin with cherry-coloured ribbons, presenting me with a basket of flowers to carry in my hand. Whirled into the ballroom on Paul's arm at the psychological moment to create the greatest sensation, we led the procession, and both received first prizes.

Later on I disgraced myself, by leaping up to extricate a baby, who had wandered under the dancers' feet. My prize scent bottle fell to the ground and was shattered. Paul was furious with me. "Never have I seen such a clumsy and unnecessary action!" he declared. "So discourteous too, and the worst possible omen for our relationship!" and he took no further notice of me for the rest of the evening.

It was my first ball, and the baby fell asleep on my lap, and remained there till one o'clock in the morning. Its pretty peasant mother took full advantage of my inactivity, and I was thankful for the excuse not to accept the dance offers, ceremoniously made to me through Paul, by enterprising Capriots, since I had never learned to dance.

I heard afterwards, through my friend Otto the painter, that the Ana-Capriots forgave me, both for breaking the scent bottle and refusing their offers. "*Poverinà!*" they said. "She had an attack of the nerves on account of the furious jealousy of the Frenchman! She even had to hire the baby for the occasion, since had she danced with us the Frenchman would have killed her!"

The more rowdy artists, from Capri proper, turned up at midnight led by 'Il Porco' insufficiently clad as a lady in evening dress.

Paul, still sulky about my clumsiness over the scent bottle, took me home soon afterwards, returning to lead the revels till dawn.

I woke at five to the unaccustomed sounds of shouts and songs, and saw from my window the whole cavalcade of dancers, devils with horns, and mermaids with tails hung over their arms, streaming into the church for Mass.

I dressed quickly and joined them. Paul slid into the seat beside me, and murmured as we knelt together, "You did very well to come to Mass, Phyllis, it was a good gesture, and will please all Capri!" I was thankful to realize that the scent bottle disaster was forgotten.

The second incident was more tragic in its nature. I was just going out to my lonely roof after dinner, when Paul beckoned me to join him in the hall. "Please spend your evening in the salon," Paul told me urgently. "*Il s'agit d'une vie!* The poet, who lives in the cave behind the Madonna, is about to commit suicide. He is in the salon with his revolver on the table, writing his will—and a farewell letter to his mother. You must sit there with him while I go for the *Guardia*! I will sign to you from the doorway when I have succeeded in bringing them, and you may then retire. The poet will certainly *not* shoot himself in the presence of an English lady!"

I was not wholly reassured by this optimistic surmise, but I accepted the task; and entered the gloomy little salon, decorated by stiff and dusty palms in tubs, and very little else. The revolver lay on the table. The poet, pen in hand, was gazing into space, thinking out his last and most cutting words, to his rather heartless mother, a German Baroness, who was gambling away the last of their fortune at Monte Carlo.

The poet looked very white and miserable, and to divert his mind I asked him if he would like to share some coffee with me, if I ordered it. He agreed quite eagerly and added to the coffee a suggestion that I might also order toast and butter. He had not eaten since breakfast, Nicolino having refused to supply him with anything for which he did not pay. I ordered two portions of ham-bread, both of which the poet ate, sitting on the opposite side of a very small fire I had lit for the occasion. Anything but the simplest speech was denied us, since neither of us knew the other's language. Still, we did what we could with the smattering of Italian we shared—neither of us looking at, or mentioning, the revolver.

It was a great relief to me, however, when Paul reappeared in the doorway, and I could hand the situation over to him.

The suicide, they decided between themselves, was now to take place over the precipice of Monte Solaro. The revolver was given up out of consideration for my feelings, since I should probably hear the shot even in the annexe, and guess its purpose; besides there was no hurry. They would take a walk together first. This they did, singing songs, and exchanging last words, while the *Guardia* lurked under cover behind them. The *Guardia* had arranged with Paul not to arrest the poet, whom they already knew intimately, until he showed unmistakable signs of really carrying out his suicidal intention. However as they neared the precipice, the *Guardia* thought it best to spring from behind their rock cover—and they then gently escorted the poet back to a cell, which was considerably more comfortable than the cave he lived in.

Paul went with them providing a bottle of Capri wine, which they all drank together in a most cheerful spirit. In the morning a telegram was sent to the Baroness to inform her that her son would remain in prison until she came to remove him from Capri. "The cave nobody minded," Paul explained to me. "The peasants often fed the poet and he sometimes sold a poem on which he lived for weeks. His mother, too, occasionally sent him a part of her winnings—but suicide, the *Guardia* say, is bad for tourist traffic. Besides all the hotel keepers have got tired of paying for his last meals."

Towards the end of March Paul heard of the imminent arrival of two young Englishmen, one a former acquaintance of his. I was distressed to think of how they would consider our unchaperoned relationship, but Paul reassured me. "Do not," he urged, "have one moment's uneasiness about the matter! I will explain everything—besides their own connection is not even dubious—I know all about it! They will accept whatever I say about ours. Indeed they would think none the worse of us if it were—what it would be only natural to suppose it to be!"

I had my doubts as to what Paul really wished them to think; however, as soon as I got to know them I took my own precautions, and I know that at least one of them firmly believed in the innocence of our connection, though he was extremely worried about my lack of chaperonage.

Both had been unknown to me, but by a queer freak of destiny the one *not* Paul's friend turned out to be a distant connection, through marriage, of my mother's. I liked this one the best. He was an ex-soldier who wanted—quite vainly—to be a painter. For many years I carried about with me a sulphur coloured lump, which he had thought resembled the dome of the village church under a Capri sky. In 1914 he once more joined the profession he had always detested and was killed in 1915. I never knew a man who more longed to be what he wasn't—and who died more bravely being what he was.

Neither of those two young men entered at all deeply into my life, but by a curious coincidence they had a definite effect upon it. For two summers later they met Ernan, and by chance showed him their Capri photographs, among which were several of Paul and myself. They had no idea what they were effecting by this unnecessary introduction, nor did Ernan inform them that he had ever known the girl in the photographs. They had simply been surprised as I was at the haunting physical likeness between Ernan and Paul, and wanted to compare the photograph of one, with the original of the other. But I think that the sight of those photographs, and what the two men said of me, may have wakened in Ernan the desire which grew slowly into the intention of meeting me again.

One night, when Ernan heard from those two friends that Paul was actually in London staying at the Langham, he waited in the foyer till nearly midnight, in order to catch sight of Paul; but Paul did not return till after Ernan's patience had become exhausted; and left for Paris next morning.

46

While I was in Rome and Capri, Lislie was at Davos. The bond between us had never weakened. All that happened to either of us was revealed, by weekly letters, to the other. When we had parted at Nauheim the previous summer, Lislie was already planning a new life at home, with light work, rather than a return, shorn of her two companions, to Davos.

I had fought this project with all my might, but when Lislie and I very rarely differed, I always found myself at a disadvantage; for in the back of my mind I knew that she was far more often in the right than I was. Dr. Huggard had plainly told her that while Davos was of great value to her general health and as a preventative of T.B. it could be of no use to the permanent lung abscess. She therefore felt that as a cure was denied her she might just as well enjoy her home life, which she really made enjoyable both for her parents and herself by helping to lift their financial difficulties.

In the end she overcame everybody's resistance and found herself a job as part-time secretary to a Distressed Gentlewomen's Society, patronized by Royalty. The Royalty in question unfortunately liked Lislie. The Distressed Gentlewomen proved to be even more distressing than distressed; and not in the real sense of the word gentlewomen. They were highly jealous of their Patron's slightest favour, and as soon as the Royal back was turned they found the means to discredit Lislie in a humiliating and most painful manner.

After three months' work in an ill-ventilated London room, this galling failure seriously upset Lislie both physically and mentally, and greatly to my relief means were forthcoming from her two generous and devoted aunts to send her to Davos early in January. It was a great relief to think of Lislie safely in Davos and instantly responding to climate and fresh companionships. I doubt if I should have gone on to Rome with Paul had I not been certain of her immediate welfare.

I do not think Lislie wholly approved of Paul but she accepted him for the sake of "Broken Music" and also because she thought that the society of young men in general was good for young women —heartbroken or not.

It was March before I noticed that Lislie's description of one of her new companions was different from her descriptions of her other admirers.

Wyn was a soldier, twenty years older than Lislie. His sudden lung breakdown came from an attack of blackwater fever which he had barely survived, and he was by no means the usual type of lung patient. He played polo, killed tigers, was rather fierce and laconic to most human beings but very kind to Lislie. They skated together and took their lunch out afterwards on the Schatz Alp. Fierceness in men was no challenge to Lislie as it was to me; and her own conversational powers were ample for two. I soon realized that Lislie was in love with Wyn, and I had no doubt whatever that Wyn must be in love with Lislie.

Marriage was Lislie's best opportunity for happiness; it was an added blessing to me that Wyn should be older than she was, a responsible successful man, who had done well in his profession, faced danger and trouble and already knew how to meet with those two "dread imposters". Wyn, I felt, was exactly the man I would have chosen for Lislie.

The thunderbolt followed a week later. Wyn loved Lislie passionately and had told her so; but he had also told her, simultaneously, that he had a wife and three children.

This knowledge came too late for Lislie; what could she do with a situation that destroyed every hope that either of them possessed? At first I could not despair of their future. Wyn did not like his wife. Theirs was an uncomfortable, superficial union. His wife had flirted dangerously with other men. Therefore Lislie was robbing her of nothing she had not already forfeited. Why could they not divorce? Divorce in our day was a very serious act, but both Lislie and I had thought it out and come to the conclusion that there were cases which exonerated the breaking of a marriage. Here, I thought, was one of them. I wrote at this time daily to Lislie, letters full to the brim of sympathy, anxiety and all the hope I could pull down out of her relentless sky.

I told her to read John Stuart Mill on divorce. He was stiff reading, but convincing; and he burned through and through with respectability and release. The pain of others must be the only limit to freedom in marriage. Since Wyn's wife could suffer no such pain, why should she be allowed to be a permanent obstacle? Lislie received none of these reassuring epistles. Our Capri porter steamed off all foreign stamps and sold them. By the time I had discovered this breach of trust and telegraphed to Lislie, fresh and more serious news reached me.

Lislie couldn't explain all the difficulties but they were worse than I had thought—much more difficult—much more hopeless. She would come to Capri with Wyn for the last ten days of his leave—money must be raised somehow—and Mrs. Melville Gwatkin, "Aunt Lou", would join us there after Wyn's departure and share Easter with us in Rome. We must dispose of Paul; Wyn must never be mentioned. Fortunately his boat sailed from Naples before Auntie Lou was due to arrive. I would see for myself what Wyn was like and how hopeless—since he was like it—their future happiness.

Paul was highly sympathetic and gave me the full benefit of his almost unlimited experience. He saw no reason to take a gloomy view of so simple an affair. Naturally homes shouldn't be broken up but the lovers could live together, they were probably—whatever I might think to the contrary—already living together. It was of course terrible that Wyn should have to go to India without Lislie and that they must part so soon; but there would be other leaves. I must arrange to take a villa—possibly in Capri—where the lovers could spend Wyn's leaves under my roof.

I could let the villa for the rest of the time if I wanted to go elsewhere. Nobody would be upset by this arrangement. Did I not grasp how simple a plan this would be for all of us? Paul too could come sometimes as a guest, it would be most convenient, and everybody could share expenses all round! I said I must see Lislie first. I must know exactly how she thought and felt. I should know directly I saw her what to do—if anything; and I should then know Wyn. I could not make plans in the air that might suit none of us.

The great thing was, Paul told me, to give up my clumsy Anglo-Saxon prejudices and become a civilized European. I had not the excuse of being *dévote* and surely I could see that morals without religion were a *bêtise*! These I must really—and in advance—be prepared to waive! I said my morals depended upon seeing Lislie. Paul needn't be afraid I shouldn't support whatever she was prepared to do. As for our own future relationship, it must wait too—everything must wait until I had seen Lislie. Paul asked me sternly if I did not see where this brought us out? I was putting Lislie before him—did I care for her then more than I cared for him? I was astounded at the question. But of course I did, I explained, I had thought this was always understood between us. If this were really so, Paul told me (not, as I now see, without justification) then I would never have any adventures beyond those of the imagination! Did I not see that, granted as he was prepared to grant, the innocence of my relationship with Lislie, such confidence between women acted as a *"cabal"* to any man's allowing himself to be attracted by either of them? I agreed that I was very fond of Paul but I tried to explain that my friendship for Lislie was of a long-tried fundamental nature. I could not say what was the truth—that I had been—and would be again—attracted by men, more than Paul had attracted me. I simply appealed to his sympathy, for I was frantic with anxiety, and Paul relented. Never had I liked him so much as during the terrible week of suspense that followed.

All letters ceased, the journey from Davos to Capri—in those days a long one—had begun.

I knew on what day and by what boat to expect them: nothing more. My heart pushed senselessly against the reluctant hours. If only I could see how Lislie was! If only I could know she need not have to endure this long, hopeless pain, that I foresaw for her—pang by pang—because I had experienced it myself!

Paul drove with me to the boat. "Phyllis," he explained to me kindly on the way down, "remember that you go to meet—not your friend Lislie—but two lovers! I go with you to support you—*C'est entendu*! But this is their first opportunity for freedom—and I foresee that they will not be on this boat at all! They will spend at least one night—probably two or three—at Naples. It is what I should do in their place. Prepare yourself then for disappointment!" "You don't know Lislie," I said. "If she had meant to spend the night at Naples, she would have told me so. If she had missed the boat—she would have telegraphed."

The boat arrived on time; and there was no Lislie on it. I felt as if the solid earth had slipped from under my feet. At that moment there was nothing but Paul's kindness—a slightly triumphant kindness—to which to cling; and I clung to it.

That evening at dinner Paul said, "To-night we will break our rule, and I will stay and talk with you, Phyllis." I felt glad that I was not to be alone with those cold stars. How did I know that Lislie had not been taken ill on the journey? She could be taken desperately ill, with appalling suddenness. What was Wyn really like? Where were they? Was Lislie safe with this stranger? A man who had not told her he was married until he had won her love? A man who was not prepared to divorce—for her sake—a woman he did *not* love? These were the questions I wanted to talk over with Paul; but Paul, this suddenly discreet, very gentle and tender-hearted Paul, chose to be taken off, under my very nose, the moment dinner was over by a rather horrible little girl of fourteen, who had turned up without any reason—but to take him off. She was the child of an unspeakable American woman, who spent her time and her daughter's on any quantity of little affairs, with relays, according to Paul, of Neapolitan army officers; while her heartbroken husband drank himself to death.

These visitors had even managed to shock Capri; and now Paul proposed to escort this trampish child home at eight o'clock in the evening. "It is dark, Phyllis," he explained, "one little quarter of an hour is all that it will take! She says she is frightened of the dark! Wait here—till I return."

I waited half an hour, and with increasing resentment another

335

half hour, then I crossed the garden to my annexe, locked my door, and went to bed. I was more amused than angry with Paul, still I *was* angry with him—and I found it salutary to be angry.

Next morning Paul appeared, heartbroken and full of apologies; and also of fresh consolation. I needed consolation and made light of the apologies, for there was still no telegram.

Paul came with me again to meet the morning boat—he had got up on purpose at, for him, a most unusual hour. I don't know what I thought was going to happen when the boat arrived; but I was without hope, until I saw Lislie waving from the deck.

I had never seen her look so radiant or so well. I needed no explanation. She was wildly, completely and contentedly in love with Wyn. They had spent the night exactly as I had supposed they would; not at all as Paul had supposed it.

The Roman train was two hours late, the last boat to Capri had been unexpectedly punctual; Lislie had telegraphed immediately. The cable from Naples to Capri—always a vivacious piece of mechanism—had gone out of order for twenty-four hours; and I received Lislie's telegram on our return to the hotel.

Perhaps the summons of the little American girl had not been an unfortunate one.

As for Wyn, he had a broken nose, remarkably broad shoulders, and bright brown eyes with a glint in them, like the glint in the eyes of an Irish terrier. I liked him at once, and for always. I saw with relief how deeply he was in love with Lislie, not as a boy loves, with fruitless idealism and unpredictable reactions, but plainly with ardour and integrity. He loved Lislie as a man loves when he is over forty and knows that he is in love for the last time. The best of Wyn's whole nature went into this final passion. He lived only four more years and I am sure that he did not survive his love for Lislie. Wyn had an Englishman's old-fashioned code respecting women. They were "bad" or "good" and to be treated accordingly. However much he might feel towards Lislie like a lover, since he could not marry her, she would have been no safer with her father.

Everything would now have to be thought out at a different level. Even Paul, though at first incredulous, and then disgusted, agreed as to the cruel innocence of their connection.

"Well then," he concluded, his shoulders raised to their extreme limit, "I believe that they are lunatics! Still I admit this is a grand passion; and we must accommodate ourselves to it accordingly."

I doubt if Lislie and Wyn, absorbed merely in being together, had any idea how beautifully Paul stage-managed their affair.

We gave them all the privacy and sympathy they needed; while Paul drilled the staff into the watchful tact which he felt their situation required. Even Otto, the Airedale and *Il Porco* were hushed into insignificance.

Slowly the rest of their tragedy passed from Lislie's mind into mine. Money was the chief obstacle to their union. Wyn had no private means. He must support his family. He loved his children. Their mother was a bad parent and he was needed by his three boys. A divorce would ruin his military career.

None of these obstacles meant anything to Wyn, at the moment; but they meant what they actually were, to Lislie.

If she gave herself to Wyn she made it harder for them to part and she risked his remorse. For according to Wyn's code he mustn't "do anything to spoil her chances." If he did, he would respect neither himself nor—eventually—Lislie. They must just take all that was within his code to permit; and then part for ever. I doubt if we said as much as this at the time to each other. I simply realized that this *was* what Lislie felt, and would act upon.

I offered her Paul's plan. I was earning money, I should earn more. What he had suggested was from my point of view feasible, but Lislie did not think it could be carried out. Her parents loved her, she was completely at home with them. She could not go on telling lies all her life, and it was doubtful if Wyn knew even how to begin. Devastating candour was his chief attribute.

The day before he left, Wyn asked to talk with me alone. At first he was fiercely hostile and intractable; but when I assured him that I would always do, at any time, whatever Lislie wanted for them both—she had only to choose and whatever she chose I should support; he broke down completely, kneeling beside me and sobbing with his head in my lap. I thought his body would break before his heart did.

Lislie went alone to the boat to see him off. She was completely worn out physically and mentally and I kept her in bed for four days afterwards. Then she got up and started to live again with her old serene, open-hearted detachment.

Paul was disgusted with the whole affair. "How you mismanage these things, you arrogant Anglo-Saxons!" he expostulated bitterly. "Nature arranges one thing—and you arrange another—and then you are surprised that it hurts!"

47

The imminence of Auntie Lou did not upset Paul as much as I had feared it might. He too had a plan to break to me. A rich young American of rather an inferior type, whom he had once introduced to me in a café, and then bluntly dismissed, had invited him to Venice for three weeks. Paul was to start immediately after Auntie Lou's arrival.

He was particularly anxious to meet Auntie Lou, since he felt that Lislie and I would miss his expert hand in concealing from her the unchaperoned history of Capri. Paul intended to come to Rome for Easter so that we should all meet again.

The day before Auntie Lou's appearance I received an incoherent letter from Otto, the painter. Would my charming English friend and I come over for the afternoon to help him sell his pictures to some rich Americans who couldn't speak any language but their own? Paul brought the note and added further explanations. "This matter is important for Otto," he explained. "I found these Americans for him, but I think they must be rare, this type! They are suddenly, immensely rich, having discovered oil on their land, but simple and religious—people of a respectability *incroyable*. It would be a serious mistake for them to find Otto, surrounded by all his young men—and above all, in the presence of *Il Porco*, whom no one, the most innocent, could mistake for anything but what he is! *Il Porco* of course insists upon being present to arrange prices, since he too lives on what Otto earns. I have told Otto that what he needs is the appearance of English women—of high respectability. Faustina, our chambermaid, will have made it plain to all Capri that in spite of appearances you and Lislie are patterns of virtue. Otto's reputation might also reach these Americans. As I have frequently pointed out to you, though you *would* make a friend of Otto, he has the worst reputation in the island! But we must always do a friend a service—so you will come?" I said of course I would, but that naturally Lislie could not be asked yet to make such an effort. However to my astonishment Lislie called through the open balcony door that she would like to go very much indeed.

Paul seized my best hat, tore the trimming out of it, and rapidly proceeded to make a far smarter new one, by turning the trimming upside-down and cutting the hat in half.

Lislie brought out all our best clothes on to the balcony, and after a long and heated discussion with Paul as to which of us should wear what, we retired; and transformed ourselves into looking as "mondaine" as possible. Paul gave us careful and impartial finishing touches, and then we all hurried across to the studio. Paul looking, I think, far the best dressed of the three, for he had the gift of appearing as if he had been born in the right clothes, for the right occasion.

The whole studio was in an uproar. It was being cleaned for the first time for years, and Vincenzo and Francesco were quarrelling bitterly over the cleaning, while *Il Porco* egged them on.

I always liked Otto's appearance myself, but I must confess that it was of a trampish nature; and half a dozen of his friends had just looked in to offer him slightly tidier garments of their own. Otto looked very worried and unhappy over the choice so generously afforded him, but Paul swept him away into his bedroom, with all the contributions over his arm, and soon turned him out a model of staid propriety.

While they were gone Lislie and I succeeded in calming down the young men. Francesco told us that Lislie looked like Venus, while I resembled the Madonna—this was a dangerously mixed compliment, for Lislie resented being kept out of holiness, while I was still more irritated by being denied fascination. "And have you not been told," *Il Porco* sympathetically explained, "that here on the Island—it was long ago discovered—these two ladies were but one?" After this satisfactory solution I insisted on having several unsuitable pictures moved to an out-house where I persuaded the

Airedale to stay and look after them, since I was unsure how he would react to strange visitors.

We sent Vincenzo off to the village for cakes and Paul cut exquisitely designed ham sandwiches, while Lislie and I made tea and coffee. It was explained to *Il Porco*, who simply could not believe it, that wine was out of the question. Paul had ascertained that his Americans were teetotallers—teetotallers with an extravagance! *"Unmöglich! Unmöglich!"* *Il Porco* sorrowfully chanted; and then they were upon us; about six of them drove up from Capri in relays of small carriages. They were a kind, pleasant, rather solemn group of Middle Westerners, who realized that the sudden wealth thrust upon them required careful, and even religious handling. In spite of Paul's having told them, at a chance meeting in their hotel, that Otto's pictures were the last thing in culture and the best art on the island, they were not convinced that it would be right for them to go so far as to buy any, not at least without most careful consideration. Paul had indeed made an impression on them; but not quite so reassuring a one as he had imagined.

I do not know how far, if at all, the introduction of Lislie and myself soothed their anxious morality. Paul's idea had been to make us look as smart as possible. Lislie had pink and blue veils floating about her head, and looked ravishingly like the Bacchante portrait of Emma Hamilton. What Paul had done to my best hat, though it may have been becoming, was not sobering in effect. The pictures, which were full of unbelievable Capri light, glowed and shone on the walls. I had rigorously kept the show to landscapes, since Otto's figures, which he loved to paint in sunlight, never had anything on, except sunlight.

Only Paul and ourselves were understandable conversationally, although *Il Porco* talked a great deal during tea and Paul and I made free translations, frequently inventions, of what he was saying to the visitors. Otto looked unhappy, listening to the far away barks of his banished pet, and said very little. He told me afterwards that he couldn't speak because his collar, lent by a friend, that Paul had made him wear, was too tight. However the Americans, oddly without humour for Americans, gradually thawed. We explained what a pity it was they should have missed Lislie's aunt, by twenty-four hours; and we told them all about Uncle Melville and that my own father was a clergyman. We got a good deal in that was reassuring one way or another; and all our statements were factually correct; but they did not sound very likely. *Il Porco* got more and more boisterous, the Americans quieter and quieter. Still we cannot have made too bad an impression on them since we were gratified to hear after our rather subdued return to the hotel that they had finally decided to buy two of Otto's pictures.

I often wonder where those vivid Capri landscapes hang, and what became of Otto, who vanished from Capri in the first world war, leaving the inconsolable Airedale behind him.

The next day Auntie Lou was upon us, voluble, excited and intensely curious. She seized upon Capri and rushed through grottoes, asking innumerable questions. She was shocked at Lislie's lassitude which, however, she put down to ill-health, and she was determined to make some kind of romance for one or the other of us, out of Paul.

Paul enjoyed her so much that he nearly refused to go on to Venice, which would have upset all our plans. Auntie Lou's greatest friend was a French Marquise, with whom she stayed yearly; and she was, though in general very easily shocked, prepared to make great concessions to French habits and expressions. Paul played up to her for all he was worth, and gave her a hairraising, possibly veracious, history of Capri Society. Of course, he explained, he had never introduced me to a single one of these doubtful characters! His own connections with them had been of the lightest, he simply knew who—and what—they were.

Two daughters of an American bishop had been my chief companions. It was a pity Auntie Lou had just missed them. This statement was what Henry James once described as "a mitigation of rigour." It was true that my Uncle George's devoted friends, the two Miss Potters, daughters of Bishop Potter, had spent one day on the island, and lunched with me alone, Paul inspecting them from a distance; but Paul now managed to make their stay extend into something limitless. They would not, of course, he explained, have left for New York so soon had they not realized their place was so happily to be taken by Auntie Lou! As for Wyn, a week ago consuming all our thoughts and powers, he was sunk without a trace—only Lislie's sad eyes bore evidence of his passing.

"Perhaps," Auntie Lou suggested, having wrung me dry as to the possibility of a romance between Paul and myself, "perhaps Lislie may have a sick fancy for him! She doesn't look at all herself, and Paul is a most attractive young man! I gather he hasn't a penny and doesn't believe in marriage! Such a pity when he is so charming —but perhaps he may get over that in time—even Frenchmen do!"

I agreed that Paul might settle down in time, but not, I somehow thought, with Lislie; and Auntie Lou had reluctantly to let Paul go, without attaching him to either of us.

Paul's parting with me was an anticlimax compared to the one we had just witnessed, yet it was not without emotional significance. We had done what we set out to do. "Broken Music" was finished. I gave Paul back his loaded revolver. "And now," he said to me, "I have never asked it of you, but *now*, I want to see a photograph of that ghost who has stood between us—all these months. Please show me this Ernan, to whom you were—for an eternity —engaged!"

I had destroyed my photographs of Ernan, even those Mamma had given me; all but one which I could not bring myself to destroy, and this I now produced from the bottom of my trunk, where I had kept it hidden so that no one should think I had not fully recovered from my broken heart.

Paul studied it for a long time in silence.

"Yes," he said at last, "but yes—it is true we are alike—this man and I—but we should have acted differently!"

I knew how differently, for Paul had often explained to me his views on successful love affairs. What he looked for was three months' undiluted ecstasy—and then a slammed door. No relationship could, he believed, last at white heat longer, nor was a love relationship bearable once it had cooled down. "And why not this variety of choice?" he had demanded. "Here you are with me in a garden full of flowers—is it confined exclusively to violets? No! it contains as well three kinds of anemone, tulips and lemon blossoms. Why should human love be more stingy than nature's? A man wishes all these beauties to be made part of himself."

I could not accept this analogy, for I knew there was—as in most analogies—a lie in it. Women are not flowers; they are fellow human beings, and they require what I had once had, a man's true and lasting affection. Ernan's love had been real and so had mine to him. We had had to live without this companionship, but at least I did not have to give to feelings which were unreal and impermanent what I had not given to a deeper and truer affection. Paul attracted me, he tempted me—for I was starved of accustomed tenderness—but he never went near the depth of my heart.

I have little doubt that unreal love can readily be accepted by the inexperienced man or woman, for the charm of sex attraction glitters like gold; but I do not think any woman who has known a true and strong devotion will mistake a lighter one for it. I knew Paul too well to expect from him anything but conflict and caprice. I therefore parted from him with real affection, but no great regret. We had carried out our bargain. Paul had completely recovered from his breakdown, and looked and felt better than he had ever done in his life. He had had an incentive; he had been greatly amused by Capri and had benefited by its climate. As for me—I had finished "Broken Music".

It was a bridge book. I did not arrive at fame by it, but I crossed some barrier in myself between fear and courage. The books I wrote after it, and alone, were no longer written without organic perception.

I went to Capri still an amateur: I left it a professional. I do not say that I owed all of this change to Paul. I think indeed that I owed some of it to having mastered my loneliness.

I tried to thank Paul for all he had done for me. I knew it was a great deal, though I did not then know how much. Had he not broken down the barriers of my mind, and carried me out of an island on to the mainland of Europe, from which I have never wholly returned?

"I have kept my honour to you," Paul said at last, "and you have given me an affection, which I neither want—nor can return! As a Frenchman you have insulted me—I know you do not realize how deeply. I could have loved you very much—this you have refused me—and now we part. If you ever want to see me again I will come

344

to you, but only on the condition that you accept me in advance as your lover. I do not mind meeting you in Rome, en passant, at Easter—but this is our real parting—and I think it is a final one. *Alors—c'est fini—Phyllis!*"

It was symbolical of our relationship that I gave Paul for a parting present, at his request, an edition of "Cranford", and that Paul gave me, on his own initiative, the "Tales of Boccaccio", in which he wrote that I was the best "Compagnon de voyage" he had ever had and the least exacting woman he had ever met. Perhaps I had not been exacting enough, but it was at least as great a shock to me to lose Paul's friendship as it was to him to lose my love —perhaps it was a greater, for Paul had many lovers, while I had never again quite so ruthless, or so gaily unpredictable, a friend.

48

The high wind of Auntie Lou's affectionate curiosity blew through Lislie's broken heart without doing it the harm I feared.

In the Naples Museum Lislie laughed, for the first time since Wyn left her.

Auntie Lou's exploration of museums was enthusiastic but not profound. She passed rapidly from statue to statue, pausing where her heart held her, and for Lislie or myself to read aloud from Baedeker the facts attributed to her favourite, before saying in a loud carrying voice, "Please find me a picture postcard of that, dear, and put it down to my account!" "Ah!" she exclaimed on this occasion, "what a lovely little boy, sleeping under a tree I should think—do come and look at it dears! What does Baedeker say about it?" "He says," I replied, "that it's a drunken Faun!" Auntie Lou—teetotal to the core—was horror-struck. "What a dreadful thing!" she exclaimed. "Don't either of you go near it! Quite hideous too! And tell Lislie *not* to get a picture postcard of it!"

Our two weeks in Rome is a compound memory of wistaria and golden roses, soaked in sunshine and constant reunions, rather like transformation scenes in pantomimes. Sylvia, for instance, was now beautifully dressed and bored, installed with her two Uncles in the Hotel Eden, concealing all the things she had done, and most of the people she had known in the Via Margutta, under a network of lies, hissing under her breath at me, on the rare occasions when we met, the things she was most anxious to conceal from her new companions.

Paul reappeared and, on the terrace of San Onofrio, looking down the Borgo Santo Spirito made me a curious proposition. He had, he explained, in Venice entirely got over any attraction I had ever held for him, but he had also discovered that he missed my companionship more than he expected. What he now suggested was that I should marry him for the sake of my own freedom, his name, and a home, for which he mentioned I could probably afford to pay the greater share, he paying only his expenses for short intervals. This would leave him absolute freedom to travel for any length of time he liked, with any companion of either sex whom he might choose. I did not think of saying that marriage without love was as one-sided a proposition as love without marriage—his previous proposition—indeed with a personality such as Paul's an infinitely more dangerous adventure.

A moment of temptation seized me; a lump rose in my throat. I gazed down some fifty feet below, to where Lislie was sitting on a rose-drenched wall, and ran down to her, crying over my shoulder, "No! No! it couldn't *be* like that!" leaving Paul permanently behind me.

To my surprise Lislie told me she was expecting Paul to propose to me, and had dreaded the result. "He would have made you terribly unhappy," she told me. "Paul is like a bad dog—he bites the hand that feeds him. I have never liked him from the first moment I saw him—nor would you have liked him if he hadn't looked like a caricature of Ernan done by a poor artist. I daren't tell you this before because I was afraid you would give way to him. Thank God you had the sense to say 'No'—and now let's forget all about him!"

The curious part of it was that I found Paul very easy to forget. My heart and its memories had never really strayed from Ernan. Paul had but ruffled my senses and given me a nostalgic longing, like the sight of an old photograph of a dearly loved scene which you can never revisit. I found that I felt a great deal saner and happier without this feeling.

In spite of her heart-break Lislie shared my deep Roman enchantment, and we determined to spend our next winter in Rome together. Davos had become unbearable to Lislie. Auntie Lou had introductions to learned excavators and authorities on art and sculpture, so that we saw long-buried temples and had access to

347

unexpected ancient treasures that we should never otherwise have seen, yet I think we both prized most the hour we took off alone together in the cloisters of San Giovanni Laterano.

Attached to the great church, on the outskirts of Rome as it then was before the city overtook it, with the wind and light of the Campagna brooding over its great square, there was perhaps no place where an onlooker felt more the sense of timelessless which gives such ease to life in Rome. Lost in so much history, what can matter to the Individual?

The exquisite carved cloisters, no two columns alike, were empty except for sunshine. The square lawn they surrounded was still an early green. Above them rose mysterious stone houses, roofed with terracotta tiles, their window-sills full of climbing flowers. Vague songs drifted through the afternoon light, and charming Italian heads gazed down on us from open windows. I did not speak to her of it but the sense of Lislie's grief was like a weight on my shoulders. "Phil," Lislie said to me, in a quiet, determined voice, "I want you to understand that this loss of Wyn is not the deepest thing in my life—and I'm going to get over it. After all, I've only known him for six weeks and not been in love with him for more than three. I'm not going to let it haunt or blight me. I dare say I shall fall in love again. I'm going to try and you must help me to try, by not thinking I'm too unhappy. I may be unhappy *now*, but I promise you that I'm not going to be unhappy *long*!"

I knew that Lislie said this chiefly to lift the weight of her sorrow from my heart, but I also think that she had set herself to accomplish what she said. The attitude of never minimizing, but always disposing of her difficulties, was part of her bottomless courage. Lislie's was the least aggressive and the most equable and steady courage I have ever known.

She was never an optimist in the accepted sense of the word. Where tragedy was inevitable, she both foresaw it and acknowledged it. Nor did she minimize, as I was apt to do, the cost of what must be paid by the individual for what he values most. She paid ungrudgingly, and without resentment, to the uttermost farthing. For a few weeks after this parting Wyn's love, like the aftermath of a splendid sunset, coloured her whole sky. She had been so deeply and thoroughly in love for the first time, and each had had such trust and delight in the other, that she could not feel life had betrayed her, or that a single one of her dreams of love were falsified. By the time the long sense of loss caught up with her, she had already gained her second wind. What perhaps helped her most over the next few years was a wholly unexpected joy caused by a new friendship which included both of us, and came to us through the generosity of Uncle Kennie. He was always terrified of introducing one of his friends to another. Something catastrophic he felt sure would immediately happen, in which he would find himself guiltily involved. Yet he had the courage to overcome this terror for our sakes, and to ask his most prized friends, Lilian Beit and her sister Marguerite Carter, to call on us. They were to be at Nauheim this spring, where I was to take my final cure; and they invited Lislie and myself to tea. We were a little loath to go, for we knew they were immensely rich, and somehow thought of them as two old ladies who—probably accompanied by a pug dog—might take us for a dull and awe-inspiring drive. But for Kennie's sake we dressed ourselves up as smartly as possible, and walked into the grandest hotel in Nauheim as if we were used to splendour.

There we found, sitting upon a sofa, shoulder to shoulder, two of the loveliest young women of our time. The Carters had originally come from Virginia, but after the disaster of the Civil War, their suddenly impoverished family had broken up, and one branch of it had moved to New Orleans. The deep south was in them, with its sense of privilege, its high acceptances of obligation and its exquisite courtesy. Their grand-parents had ruled a dark world, and even their parents could remember old cruelties and luxuries taken as a matter of course. Their own youth had been hard but somehow or other enough money had been raised to send these two well-connected young beauties to stay with relatives in Rome. It was considered a terrible *mésalliance*, when Lilian married Otto Beit for love, before the immense fortune of his elder brother Alfred was left to him, forcing them to become—out of the domesticity Lilian loved—part of the great world of their day. Marguerite lived with Lilian to help her bear this new burden of responsibility.

349

It was difficult to say which of the two sisters was the more beautiful, Lilian with her cream and roses complexion, big azure eyes and golden hair, or the darkly lovely younger Marguerite, with her beautifully moulded features and great velvety dark eyes. Both were equally kind and generous, but Marguerite had the more active and dramatic nature. She burned with ardour and initiative, while Lilian, possessed of a curious innocence, simply opened her heart like a flower to the sun, giving out all its fragrance. Both had dignity, but Marguerite's had a touch of something withheld and formidable about it, while Lilian's was the unconscious dignity of a child. No one more innocent and willing to accept whatever life offered—without exacting tribute or suspecting evil—could be imagined. I always thought Lincoln's first love must have been just such a girl as Lilian—to inspire his greatest speech with those immortal words, "With malice towards none."

The four of us became at Nauheim cordial acquaintances, soon friends, and then for the rest of our lives deeply intimate friends.

We knew, and they knew, that their society life must remain a thing unshared by us. We had no social value, and no money, with which to enhance our youth; besides both of us were workers. What they gave us was a friendship of the heart, but this friendship implied constant meetings in their homes, both in London and at Tewin Water, where we found a beauty of living we had never known. Otto and Alfred valued works of art, and possessed some of the greatest pictures in the world. Lilian and Marguerite shared with us operas, theatres, concerts and many of the great spectacles and high values of London at perhaps its richest, and most illuminating hour.

They shared our home problems as well; and we shared theirs.

They came into our lives at a time when economic pressures, ill-health and sorrow had long been our companions, and they took the weight and narrowness of these hard visitants away from us.

I have loved few friends as much—and none more—than I loved Lilian and Marguerite. They managed to transform and sustain our lives without ever making the mistakes of the rich, when dealing with friends who are poor. Nothing they ever gave us cost us anything, either materially or spiritually. Their sunshine was our sunshine; and when grief struck them we entered into it as if it had been our own.

I often think if we had never met Lilian and Marguerite at Nauheim we might have become dulled down and broken by the persistent weight of the older lives we could not help and yet had to support. Unmarried daughters in homes ruled by hidden pressures or neurotic character—burdens, which cannot be lifted, inevitably become the backs that have to bear them. One of the most releasing of our social changes has been that so few unmarried daughters now are obliged to live at home; if they do, they are given the rights of wage earners; and need not become domestic slaves. They can take their share, but not more than their share, of home obligations. Lislie and I took all there were.

49

When Lislie came home, she found everything at Alstone Lawn gradually disintegrating. Chinks had widened into gaps; less money came in; and just as much went out. It is not easy for old people to restrict their comforts, and Lislie's parents belonged to an age when certain standards of personal habits were accepted as rights.

Lislie saw that the gay life of her youth was over. For her parents' sake and her own she must again find work. I made many protests against this risky adventure. I thought work of any regular kind impossible in Lislie's precarious condition, but fortunately for Lislie it was her own judgment that she relied on, not mine. She had never been trained for any kind of work, but she had both charm and courage, and very soon found suitable work for herself with an intelligent American lady, who was losing her sight, and wanted a bright and trustworthy companion to write her letters, read to her, and run her errands. It was a well paid, half day job, compatible with living at home. The Roman winter, which we had planned together, had to be postponed; I went instead alone to Valescure in the Esterel mountains.

In 1911 Valescure consisted of a few hidden and majestic villas surrounded by cork forests, three miles from St. Raphael and the coast.

The Hôtel des Anglais was filled with English guests of a witheringly respectable kind, and somebody in their circle decided that I was the much discussed and morally repudiated writer, "Victoria Cross". In consequence of this discovery, an icy spiritual boycott exiled me into a world of speechless silence. I suffered considerably under it, but it never entered my mind that there was any particular reason for this cold shouldering; I simply thought that nobody wanted to know me, and tried to make the best of it by attaching myself to the cork woods, and taking long walks up the easier slopes of the Esterel.

The Century Publisher who had been so much interested in "Broken Music" offered to publish it if I would either change its ending, or write a sequel which should prove as good as "Broken Music". With appalling speed and concentration I wrote "The Common Chord" in three weeks, and rewrote it during the months that followed.

The first six chapters contained some of the gay aftermath of my Capri winter, but soon my spirits began to flag; surrounded by people who would neither look at, nor speak to, me, the thrill of existence died down. I wrote more than ever, and at fiercer speed, and a very bad and superficial piece of work I turned out. If anyone was ever an escape artist I was one that winter; but the trouble with most escape artists soon tracked me down—for what I escaped from was not myself, but art.

However, after a time my loneliness was slightly mitigated by a fierce but fascinating old lady, who had entertained for a bachelor Viceroy of India and little she cared if I were Victoria Cross or the devil himself if I were competent to make a fourth for her at bridge. Lady C. was an inveterate gambler, forcibly removed at last from Monte Carlo by her family, because of the ruin she had brought on herself and indirectly on them. She was now placed at Valescure on a remittance and played excellent, if avaricious, bridge. A kind but inarticulate chaplain, I think purposely, introduced us. He had hitherto acted as her fourth, but he would not play for money and disliked being carried by his partner. I was to take his place. The other two members of our nightly game were an Irishman, Mr. B., who had taken to drink in order to keep up spirits reduced by a coldly contemptuous wife, without any marked success; and an enchanting Colonel who had won a V.C. when he was over sixty. Both men were terrified of Lady C. and looked on me at first with anxious pity as a lamb thrown to a tiger. But to me Lady C. simply wasn't a tiger; she took a grim, protective fancy to me; she chuckled,

353

and unbent, till our bridge became less a slaughter upon a battle-field and more of a game of skill. On the occasions when Mr. B. was the worse for drink, Lady C. would give him a piercing but not hostile glance and say, "Mr. B., I perceive that you are not up to playing bridge this evening. Will you have the kindness to ask the Chaplain to take your place?"

One day Lady C. proposed taking me to tea with friends of hers, who lived in a stately villa set in a marvellous garden. I knew their name. My heart sank for I realized that I must refuse her invitation. Lady C. stared at me with icy severity. "I don't know whether you are aware of it or not," she said, "but you are guilty of very bad manners. It is not everyone that I invite to take tea with my friends. I shall be seriously annoyed if you do not reconsider your refusal." There was nothing for it, but for me to tell her the truth. The people she wanted me to visit—Colonel Call and his wife—were near relatives of Ernan's. Colonel Call had married Laetitia, the daughter of Shelley's friend, Edward Trelawney, and Lady C. had thought I should prize the literary connection. I was certain they would remember our broken engagement and know my name.

I must say no one could have made handsomer amends than Lady C. "My dear," she said, after a moment's pause, "I am not in the habit of apologizing, but I apologize to you profoundly. I should have guessed you had a good reason for such a refusal and not have pressed for it. The bad manners are my own." We never referred to the subject again; but Lady C. was markedly kinder to me, and I felt a little less lonely after this incident.

When we parted she asked if I could arrange to spend the following winter in the hotel in which she proposed staying. "I shall not take up much of your time," she graciously told me, "but I like someone to nudge." The flavour of this slightly familiar word from her formidable presence was inexpressibly entertaining. I cannot imagine even a V.C. daring to return the nudge.

Lady C. had accepted the new cult of Asiatic origin called "New Thought". "My husband," she once told me, "was practically faultless, but there must have been a hidden flaw in his otherwise perfect character, for—quite unnecessarily—he died. I find it hard to forgive him." She had taken up "New Thought" after her husband's death. "It is better than any other religion I know," she explained to me, "because it is the only one that explains why I am so irritable to my maid. I used to suffer remorse for some of the unkind things I said to this poor creature—I frequently reduce her to tears—but I now realize I am only carrying out the pattern of a former life, when it is quite probable that I had slaves; and killed them. Under these circumstances it can hardly matter if I make her cry occasionally or not."

Uncle Kennie turned up for my last weeks at Valescure, and soon found out, and rectified, the undue fame under the shadow of which I had led so solitary an existence. But I no longer needed the open arms which now awaited me. My book was finished and Uncle Kennie and I took daily excursions together. We started off on exquisite April mornings, full of the sweet scents the sun struck out of sage and thyme. Anemones and grape hyacinths poured over rocks, and every variety of cystus—yellow, pink and purple—opened to the sun. Kennie, having previously brooded over a map, would take me to some little-visited bay, or to a crumbling old tower crowning a pink hill-side. We caught slow and pleasant trains full of friendly peasants, and often drank their wine and shared our sandwiches with them.

When we reached our destination, which, however small, would boast some little restaurant or point of vantage, I would be left, propped by a knapsack, to my own devices, while Kennie took the climb he had planned, within his powers but beyond mine, returning flushed with triumph to a late tea, and a hurried race afterwards to catch a sympathetically belated train.

We were the best of companions. I had only to remember that the Church, Politics and Society were sacred subjects to Kennie; and in general to avoid depth or unnecessary emotion. Sex, for instance, was utterly taboo this winter, while the winter before sex, with all its ramifications, had been the chief subject of discussion. The difference between Paul and Uncle Kennie, however, was so vast, that there was no danger of giving to one what was the main diet of the other.

Towards the end of March Lilian presented Lislie with enough money to give us a month together in Venice. It was like being offered Paradise, with Beatrice thrown in.

We arrived in the rain, but our first sight of Venice—the Grand Canal, a deep silvery grey, flowing beneath its multi-coloured palaces—was one of the greatest moments of our lives. Venice is probably the only place in the world which never disappoints the seeing eye. I have visited it nine times, under snow and drenched in summer glory, and have never failed to recapture the incredulous wonder of that first glance from the station steps, down the Grand Canal.

Two incidents happened on this first memorable visit, which had in themselves nothing to do with Venice, but which, perhaps partly because of the vividness and splendour of their background, became landmarks in our lives.

Wyn returned to Europe with a second lung break-down, and wrote asking Lislie to meet him wherever she chose.

I shall never cease to regret that I opposed this meeting. It required a courage that Lislie possessed, and I think she would have been happier for the rest of her life if she had accepted the challenge. She had never changed her mind, nor regretted her decision, and I thought then that to meet again would but throw her back into a whirlpool of useless conflict; but it is always a mistake to act from fear rather than from courage. Lislie went out alone, to make her final decision, walking up and down the Zattere in the rain, while I watched from my window her slight erect figure against the grey background. When she came in she said, "I have decided to refuse Wyn—but I think I'm wrong." Two years later she read of his death in *The Times*.

Our second shock was an impersonal one. We were sitting at a table in the window of the little Calcina dining room watching the Campanile of San Giorgio shaking in golden ripples on the water, when some one came in and said, astonishingly in English, aloud to a room full of strangers: "The *Titanic* has struck an ice-berg and gone down and more than half her passengers are lost." A woman at the table next us cried out, "I don't believe it!" and burst into hysterics. It was as if security itself went down with that one ship.

Now with our indurated imagination, after two world wars, with the shelving of our moral values caused by legalized inhumanity, we should take such an accident with objective calm; but then we shared it. All of us in that little sun-warmed room faced those icy waters, wondering, had we been the few lucky ones, should we have rowed away from the sinking ship in half-empty life boats, rather than risk being dragged under by the tossing arms of the drowning?

One year's road-toll to-day is more than three times as great as the loss of those long dead passengers in the *Titanic*; and we are no longer even surprised at such multiple and unnecessary slaughter.

Humanity is not surprised enough to prevent war, though it may wipe out what is left of civilization. But then, we *were* surprised; I doubt if any of us slept that night.

50

We had planned, earned and saved for our Roman winter with ardour for eighteen months, and now in 1912 it was ours at last. A month of it Lislie and I spent pursuing our two quarries, history and art, with equal zest, when fate—Lislie always asserted—through the eyes of Velasquez's Pope in the Doria Gallery laid her low.

After a long morning, riveted by that greatest of all portraits Pope Innocent the Xth, in which the whole genius of Velasquez glows with incredible force, through the haunting eyes of the most docile of the Popes, Lislie became suddenly and dangerously ill. We never knew exactly what her illness was, but I was told by the handsome and fashionable doctor, who controlled British invalids in Rome, that Lislie was fatally and infectiously ill, and must be packed off immediately to the Blue Nuns. On discovering that Lislie was a doctor's daughter and that he could expect no fees, this hollow potentate retired, and never called again.

Lislie couldn't stand the idea of the Blue Nuns, and urged that we should sweat it out by ourselves. I knew she was too ill for this attempt, but I found a thoroughly competent Italian doctor through Uncle Melville's friends, the Balzanis, and though he thought gravely of Lislie's condition, he agreed to my nursing her where she was. Dr. Galenga thought she had Roman fever with lung complications, and advised us to spend the rest of the winter at Frascati, as soon as Lislie was fit to be moved.

There was only one hotel at Frascati, which called itself the Grand, but as it was usually empty in winter except for a stray guest or two, it proved most accommodating as to price. Uncle

Kennie joined us for a month, and for the only time in our long, serene relationship I found myself violently angry with him for daring to say that this time he did not think Lislie could recover.

As soon as I could leave Lislie for an hour in the day-time, I made friends with the gardener custodians of the vast empty villas of Frascati, within easy distance of the hotel, so that when Lislie came out into the world again we had the freedom and grandeur of those great landscape gardens, stretching up the hill-side towards Tusculum, in which to wander at will.

The Aldobrandini was our nearest neighbour, and I remember one winter hour, in an ilex grove of pale sunshine and dense black shadows, that was like an incident in a fairy tale. We were sitting on the rim of an empty fountain, a splendidly entwined, moss-grown group of figures rising behind us, when I became suddenly aware that we were being stared at by living and hostile eyes. "Look at the toads!" Lislie exclaimed, and there, advancing from all directions out of the ilex hedges, were large, stone-green, unpleasant monsters in regimental order; and it was upon us that they were advancing. I was terrified, but Lislie said: "Nonsense, Phil. I'm not going to let a little thing like a toad upset me! Let's just stay where we are, and see what they will do. We can easily kick our way out of them if they try to attack us." I had not the courage to await the on-coming horde at so low a level, so I sprang to my feet and jumped across the fountain basin; but Lislie sat on unmoved, a slim and vivid figure in the wintry sunshine, with a scarlet scarf across her shoulders, while the toads advanced slowly but inexorably towards her. They stared at her, and she stared back at them. Their mottled throats moved in a horrible manner. "They will spit venom at you!" I cried in terror. "I don't believe what they spit *is* venom!" Lislie coolly replied. "Anyhow they haven't started spitting yet, they're only thinking it over!"

The toads hopped ponderously, in unbroken formation, to about a yard in front of Lislie, and then stopped dead. They did not attack. It was probably *their* fountain; and when they saw that Lislie's was not a destructive force they merely concentrated on a massed watchfulness, till, tiring even of that, they broke line and hopped off singly into the dense shadows of the ilex hedges.

Among all the villa gardens so courteously placed at our disposal by friendly gardeners, the one in which we lingered oftenest was a garden of the Falconieri family. Planned in 1550 by Cardinal Ruffini, the grey fortress walls, seen through a stately avenue of trees, looked undefeatably strong.

But it was not its strength; it was a hidden beauty in the garden that took us there day after day. Behind a screen of tall black cypresses lay a small rectangular lake. It was completely surrounded on all four sides by these trees. In the unrippled water each single cypress duplicated itself in the shining mirror of the lake beneath; while through the arrowy tips of the trees the sky dropped its bright azure. There among violets and wind anemones time had stopped. Our voices were the only sounds we ever heard. We thought the beauty of this hidden lake was as immortal as the light that fell upon the dark stems of the cypresses. Yet in 1914 William II used the Villa and its garden for his Headquarters. This was a mere invitation to destruction, for Villa and garden survived the first visit from Mars. It was thirty years later that Hitler's hordes reduced the Villa to rubble, uprooted the immemorial cypresses and dispersed the shining waters of the little lake.

I wonder if on that hill-side now even the stones remain; but the violets may still grow thick along the grass, purple as the robes of vanished kings; and sweet as the memory of those unforgotten hours.

By the Falconieri lake we used to recite Alice Meynell's poems aloud to each other.

Once, straying further down the road into a villa garden yet unvisited, we tried to drive Prince Muti away from his own flower beds. "You must not pick those hyacinths!" I told him sternly in my best Italian. "Please come away at once! Do you not realize that you will get the gardener into trouble for admitting you—and that we shall never be allowed into the garden again?" "But I *am* Muti," he explained in perfect English, "and the garden, and the gardener, are my own!"

It was a pleasing incident and led to our being presented with a handsome bouquet; and even greater freedom of access than we had enjoyed before.

As Lislie's strength returned, we took longer excursions into the Campagna itself. An ardent and enchanting boy, with eyelashes half a yard long, for inconsiderable sums produced a donkey, on which Lislie rode astride, with a complacency I envied. We climbed to Tusculum, by the ancient Roman way, passing Cicero's villa half lost in brambles, to the wooded summit, where the ruins of the loveliest of amphitheatres looks down across long waves of the Campagna, to a silver line of sea.

Wherever the eye rested, Rome mastered it. Michelangelo's gorgeous bubble of a dome, sometimes white as a snowdrop, or glittering gold when the sun caught it, shone with determined significance. The pink Roman arches wandering across the plain led towards St. Peter's. Soracte pointed its solitary peak at the city like a warning finger. The whole landscape bowed towards that romantic symbol. We had had to leave Rome, but Rome throughout that long but enchanting winter never for a moment left us.

One warm March day, as we were having tea on the hotel terrace, two unknown ladies decided to follow our example. It was an hour before sunset and the Campagna was a dim sea of periwinkle blue, in which the willows shone, crimson and bright orange, in the distance.

We could not see the faces of the two women, for their table had been placed behind our own, but we could hear their voices. One of them made a cheap and easy sneer against the English suffragettes and their—as she thought—foolish and unnecessary sufferings. The other began to answer her. Noiselessly, Lislie and I put down our cups, and left our tea unfinished. Never had I heard so beautiful a voice, so rich in quality, so varied in cadence; merely listening to the sound of it would have been pleasure enough, but it was the words that caught us—unpredictable and jewelled words, sentences in which verbs had an active quality that stung the mind like a whiplash.

I suppose it was what is called Shakespeare's English. The poor, astonished woman, to whom the voice spoke, was swept out of her world of cheap catchwords, into a sea of spontaneously perfect prose. The voice spoke quietly, marshalling her arguments for the freedom of women with an objectivity dipped deep in ardour. It was as if her whole being impregnated each word she uttered.

The subject was one that Lislie and I had been discussing all winter long, without having come to any positive decision. "If there's one thing," Lislie used to say, "that I hate more than a suffragist, it's an anti-suffragist!" Deprived of half our years in England, and limited by ill-health, I suppose we should not have been able to play an active part in the struggle even if we had understood it. We knew no one who fought on either side, and as the newspapers were in the hands of men—sometimes highly skilled and intelligent men—we saw only one side of the question. Both of us were strong feminists, well supported by Uncle Melville; but what we believed in was the higher education of women, and the opening to them of all careers for which they proved themselves fitted; and we feared the suffragettes' political aim might impair our objective. We knew nothing about politics, and had not grasped that the vote was a key to all fundamental freedoms. Now as we listened to this melodious voice putting forth well-balanced arguments in lucid prose, we looked at each other like stout Cortez "with a wild surmise, silent, upon a peak in Darien." Who was this oracle, who had so deeply and permanently convinced us?

A sudden stretch of silence succeeded the convincing voice, the poor overwhelmed lady bleated a little into it, and then both ladies rose and walked away.

We related the incident to a kindly middle-aged woman, to whom I had lent my fountain pen for an hour some days before, and who had continued to talk to us whenever we met, in a friendly manner, without disclosing her name. "We think she must have been someone rather special," Lislie explained, "because it was such a miracle to listen to her!"

The lady laughed. "I haven't told you my name yet," she said. "I'm Lady Butler—and I can easily tell you whom you heard talking in the garden this afternoon, because it was my sister Alice—Alice Meynell, the poet—and I agree with you she *is* rather special! If you want so much to meet her, it is not at all impossible. To-morrow she leaves Rome, but I am visiting her in London this June, and I am sure I may invite you to come to her house."

We were so awed that we could scarcely speak, but at length we explained to her that Alice Meynell was our chosen poet. Neither of of us could imagine our lives without her. The pattern of her words expressed the deepest feelings of our hearts.

Lislie was the more complete and devoted of her worshippers, though I think she had never read, and re-read, all that Alice Meynell had written with the same desperate thoroughness that I had. I resented bitterly however the poem most usual in current anthologies, "The Shepherdess of Sheep." I resented it with such vigour that I felt, even where it did not exist in her other poems, the sense of being tied down and self-restricted. Besides, however willingly I accepted intellectually the taste of doom which was Alice Meynell's deepest flavour, I was fundamentally joyous. I wanted to be able to bear grief if I had to bear it; but my whole nature rose against being *made* to bear it. I wanted the world open: the Catholic Church wanted it shut; and I felt that the Church's rigidity had crept into Alice Meynell's writing, at the expense of her art.

Nevertheless her writing, both in poetry and prose, made an immense appeal both to my heart and to my intellect, so that I tried hard to make myself docile to her deep channelled resignations. Now, I had heard her voice; and I knew that she was deeper than her denials.

Lady Butler did exactly what she had promised: she invited us to meet Alice Meynell in June. We had two openings to the Meynell household—one through Lady Butler's kindness, and one through cousins of Lilian's and Margurite's who knew both ladies well.

We made use of both channels; but we never penetrated to the inner circle of the Meynell household, nor counted ourselves as among her special friends. Nevertheless Alice Meynell was extraordinarily kind to me, and until her death, and after, she was one of the great literary influences of my life.

She told me I might come to see her on Sunday afternoons, and that I did not go often was by my own choice, for she said to me once, with her direct and truthful generosity, "I wish you would come oftener—very often indeed."

I felt that since Lislie could hardly ever spend a Sunday in London I should be taking an unfair advantage of our great privilege, if I enjoyed it more frequently than we could share it together; but I had also another reason. Each time I saw Alice Meynell I felt that I was watching a magnificent, wild creature—a tethered angel—suited for enormous distances and stately freedoms, closed into a narrow space behind the iron bars of a cage. The sense of this disciplined self-control was so severe, and yet so impassioned, that it hurt me. I wanted to break down the bars and I knew that I never could. I knew that Alice Meynell meant never to have the bars broken down. She was going to die behind them as she had lived; but then she meant to be free! She had not written that sonnet called "Renunciation" for nothing.

There was sympathy between us, more even than her generous and gracious kindness would naturally have granted to any young woman who loved poetry, and was trying to learn to write.

Once or twice, when I was in an agony for her, because of something said or done, against her spiritual taste, her eyes had met mine and I knew that she not only knew what I was feeling, but was glad that I shared the distaste with her.

Very often she sat remote in a deep pool of silence, while her husband kept up a pleasant, kindly chatter with her guests. A chance word might recall her: and then she would spread her wings like some great bird of Paradise, and speak for a few moments as I had heard her speak in the garden at Frascati. The room would glow and pulse with her thoughts, and then, as suddenly as if a hand had pulled her back, she became dumb; and the great light would fade.

The impression she made upon me each time I saw her was of entire wholeness. As if her words, her thoughts, and her heart were single as a drop of blood; but it was not blood that flowed easily.

Alice Meynell was extraordinarily wise about literature; I do not know how wise she was about life. I think, like all women of her age and up-bringing, the danger of ugliness had been too much impressed upon her. The greatest danger of all is probably the danger of taking too many precautions; and Alice Meynell had not escaped this peril.

Once she said to me of Jane Austen, for whose work she had a strong, almost personal dislike, "She is too little heavenly." Perhaps Alice herself wanted heavenliness too much. I had the feeling that she distrusted life, rather than realized that all that we know of spirit must come from the use we make of everything else on earth.

Alice Meynell was a sound, scholarly critic, with sharp prejudices and occasional blind antagonisms. She said once of Henry James, whose writing she shrank from, as a retreat from lucidity—but whom she knew I passionately admired—"Yes—perhaps he has the key to the imagination, but he fumbles so long in turning it!" and on another occasion, "I think every writer has the right to make his readers think; but he has no right to make his readers think, because he has not thought sufficiently himself."

I loved to talk to her about words, and her special use of them. Besides her strong love of active verbs, she used often, and with special skill, past participles. She liked the prefix "un" because, she said, "It is short and to the point, and does not clutter up a sentence."

Her heart was locked, a piece of it separately, in each of her many children; but there were, for her physical strength, far too many of them, and with her curious gift for seeing only one thing at a time with the whole of her being, there must have often been tragic family situations and misunderstandings.

I remember H. B. Pinker, my agent and hers, telling me how shocked he was as a father when two of her little girls came in unaccompanied out of pouring rain, and stood drenched to the skin in the doorway. Alice Meynell gave them a remote and speculative gaze, then, murmuring "Darlings—how wet!" returned with concentrated zest to the literary topic they had just been discussing.

I liked—but with the same sense of baffling strangeness—all of the Meynell children whom I met, especially Viola, with whom I had for a time a period of direct intimacy, cloaked by her Catholic restrictions, and never wholly—on either side—attaining complete understanding. Perhaps we could never have understood each other even if we had wanted a completer friendship, but I have still retained the admiration and perplexed affection that I felt for her, when we were girls together.

I thought her mother was right in believing that Viola was more naturally a poet than a novelist; yet her novels had beautiful qualities. They were static in action, but deeply original in thought. Some people who read them proclaimed them dull, yet Viola's single thoughts were never dull. Whatever she saw or said had a peculiar sincerity, enriched with ardour, that was like her mother's, and yet definitely her own, for Viola had a modern mind; but I had a feeling that although her emotions and imagination roved in fields unvisited by her mother, she had been caught in the same spiritual strait-jacket, and could not move at will.

As a girl, Viola was an introvert and did not easily project her thoughts through the medium of other people's minds. This was against her as a novelist, and although the sense of drama was deep in her, she could not make it run into her stories. She lacked narrative power. It was as if she saw too much, through too many avenues of approach, yet every thought she had was natural to her and deeply rooted in her being.

That the truth about this strange and deeply moving, yet inharmonious family has never been told seems to me a public loss. We need to understand what has made—or marred in the making —gifted persons who have given a contribution to the world. Perhaps we need these lessons in living, far more than we need to understand the lives of criminals and delinquents, so liberally presented to us by artists at the present time.

The Meynells were rare beings, whose spirits—shackled by difficulties—had a meaning for mankind. I still hope that the one who knew and understood the Meynell family best may one day give her version of it to the world.

A direct-speaking, ill-mannered young man, who nevertheless possessed intelligent perceptions, once said to Alice Meynell in my presence, after Wilfred Meynell had read aloud to us, without her permission, an extremely intimate letter from George Meredith, "Do you *like* having your private letters read out loud to strangers?" Alice Meynell did not answer him in words; but she shuddered and gave a long sigh as if it came from the bottom of her heart—it was nearly a groan.

Arthur Koestler has a theory that human beings live on two

conflicting levels, the tragic and the trivial. Conflict existed between "this diverse pair," because Wilfred Meynell lived wholly on the trivial and Alice wholly upon the tragic level. I do not know when or how they met; or if they had not, when I knew them, at the deepest level, already parted; but there could be very little doubt that, though the nine points of the law were meticulously observed on Alice's part both in public and in private, the spirit had escaped.

51

After the winters in Capri and Rome, I found adjusting to my old position in my family extraordinarily easier. This may have been partly caused by the fact that my health was better and that Paul's affection for me—singular though in many ways it was—had helped to restore my courage. I no longer felt completely robbed of all feminine attractions; and if you have courage you can use it on anything that comes along. I now used it on my family relationships, and found my family a good deal easier to get on with than Paul had been. They loved me, they were sorry for me; and, once I grasped that I could give them pleasure and take it from them again, they found a way of making life at home comparatively rose strewn.

My only real concern was about my father's health. While I had been away he had had a serious attack of bronchitis, and seemed to have only partially recovered from it. My mother attached no significance to his chronic cough, except that she found it disturbing at night; but two of his best friends took occasion to warn me very gravely about his health. Both wanted him to leave Swanscombe; and, for different reasons, my mother too wanted it. I could, now, live at home eight months out of the year in any ordinarily healthy place in England, and whatever place would be suitable for my father would be equally so for me. I felt that they both needed me, more than they had ever needed me before, and would increasingly need me.

My sympathy and love for my father had grown stronger, while my fixed adoration and self-identification with my mother had gradually loosened, ever since I went abroad, so that I could now act between them rather as a bridge than as a weapon.

I still loved my mother with tenderness, and the strong force of habit; while my father's generosity prevented him from taking advantage of the fact that my understanding of life had widened in *his* direction, and no longer supported hers.

I was to be the only child in their home, even while they grasped the fact—and found a certain comfort in it—that I was no longer a child, but a mature woman with a world of my own.

George was still under their roof at intervals, but he had fallen seriously in love, and all his thoughts and efforts were moving towards a home of his own. My mother wanted George to have whatever he really wanted, and supported the engagement; but my father was definitely, even passionately, against it, as he had been against George's possible engagement to Maida. I don't know quite what he wanted for George—something, I suspect, in the nature of a royal marriage—but it was in this instance not what George wanted for himself. I strenuously threw in my lot with George and Margery, and did everything that was possible to help their love affair towards a happy ending. I felt as if their success in love would be my own.

About the Swanscombe problem I was much less sure. I felt certain it would break my father's heart to resign, and yet I feared for his life if he tried to struggle on. Finally I went privately to see the local doctor who had attended him for bronchitis. It was my old enemy, the alarmist, but when he told me that my father's bronchial tubes were permanently blocked, and that he was unlikely to survive many more winters in the smoke of the cement works, I felt that he spoke little more than the truth.

I hated to go against my father in the family discussions that took place, and I sometimes wondered whether life without Swanscombe would be much better for him than death under the pall of smoke in which we lived; but there was a further reason for leaving Swanscombe which turned the balance against our remaining.

My father loved me dearly, and I tried to companionate him in every way I could, but my companionship had come too late. The avenues to his heart and mind were blocked by loneliness. All the support and sympathy he had for so long needed from one of his own family he now received from our district nurse. Their relationship was perfectly innocent but extremely annoying to all of us; and a desperate trouble and unnecessary anxiety to my mother.

This was the strongest of her reasons for leaving Swanscombe; and equally strongly it pulled my father in the opposite direction. What other life had he now than the little circle of devoted church people he had built up round him for fourteen years? And of this circle, who could be more of a support and help to him than our faithful, good little district nurse? It was she who had brought him to the sick and dying, a ministry which he never neglected, and in which all his best gifts were released. She never missed one of his sermons, and admired them all alike. From her, he had no criticism, only the warmth of admiration.

The death of Wilmett had shaken my father to the core; the further separation from Mary and myself left him completely without the support he needed. He probably cared more for George than for any of us; but George was the most opposite to him in temperament of all his children, and understood him least.

Looking back at my father's history, with eyes now older than his were when he died, I think it one of the saddest human stories that I have ever known. He was a man of brilliant parts, great dramatic and intellectual powers, and ceaseless energy and generosity of heart. Yet he allowed himself to be sucked down into a back-slum in the country for fourteen years; and even there retreated from the task he had set himself. For the first few years, while Mary and I were acting as his devoted curates, he worked with *élan* and great success, adding astonishingly to the meagre life of the church; but then this power too dwindled, he ceased to visit his parishioners, and spent most of his life in a sort of intellectual wilderness, relying for human companionship on chance contacts made on golf links. His brilliant conversation became a hesitating monologue. His sermons floated, back-boneless, on the wings of his beautiful voice.

My mother was no doubt responsible for having made these retreats easy for him by taking no interest whatever in his work, and by refusing to entertain any of his friends; but she could not be held responsible for all of it.

My father made—like all of us—his own choice. He gave up all serious reading. The life of his mind retreated with the life of his heart. Hitherto his summers and his open air life on golf links had saved him physically; but now something in him snapped. Through the long, unending, rainy summer of 1912 his mind began to move towards resigning Swanscombe. Finally he agreed, when the autumn came, to go and see the Bishop of Rochester and talk over the future with him.

He came back from his visit to Bishop Talbot with the dark clouds of renunciation transformed into cheerfulness.

The Bishop, who must have had great wisdom and understanding of men, had begged my father to become his visiting chaplain, and created this new position for him. My father was to take week-ends in turn preaching for the tired and over-worked clergy of the diocese. Retiring from Swanscombe need not be the end of his work for the souls of men. Perhaps my enthusiasm for his future was more ardent than his own. I promised to go with him, wherever he went, and pointed out the tremendous power he might exert preaching to ever wider and wider circles. I saw him as a travelling apostolic light, and I remember, while I poured out my hopes and eager anticipations, that my father looked at me with tired eyes in which a twinkle lingered. "It's too late, Fissy," he told me with a sigh, "to be quite so much of a light as you make out!"

While I was at Valescure, a house at Bromley had been decided upon and bought. It was like the houses Jane Austen's heroines usually ended in, on rising ground, with gravel soil; and the garden contained the oldest oak tree in Kent. "Just the tree for hanging myself on," my father wrote to one of his brothers.

I cannot truthfully say that I ever liked Bromley or the house, but there it was on my return; and my parents had generously allotted me a large sunny room to work in—the first work-room, other than a corner of my bedroom, that I had ever possessed.

It was spring, and I loved the garden. There was a pink may tree in full flower and a tall anchusa as blue as the sky; and there—to our family consternation—two streets away, was little nurse! She had resigned as well. She was a Queen's Nurse with a first rate record; and there was no reason whatever why she should not find a job in Bromley, upon which she could successfully live.

371

My poor mother was horror-struck, and she made all the mistakes jealous people can make. All her children's sympathy was with her; but I could never manage a personal dislike to little nurse. She was small, round and rosy, competent and kind. She adored my father, and had never in all her forty years of innocent life had anything, or anyone else, to adore.

The final break with Swanscombe had not yet taken place for my father when I arrived at our new home. He still had a month of Sundays. I went with him for one week end, and saw for myself how exhausted he was at the day's end—and how much he was loved.

A week before the final leave-taking a cable arrived saying that Uncle George was dead. There had been no warning.

My father loved all his three brothers passionately; each of them suited him in different ways, but the one he needed most—and, since his mother's death, his spiritual support and counsellor—*was* my Uncle George. This blow, coming as it did on the eve of his leaving Swanscombe, was a terrible shock for my father. A week later he went alone to say his farewells to his last parish.

I begged and implored him to take me with him. I reminded him how much I too had loved Swanscombe and worked for it while I could, but he refused. He did not want any of his family with him. At last, seeing how distressed and even alarmed I was at his decision, he said gently, "Don't you see. I should break down if I had you with me, Fissy!" and I was forced to let him go alone.

He came back in an extraordinary mood of exhilaration as if a great load had fallen off him, and talked brilliantly and continuously for hours. He had not come straight back from the anguish of his parting. He had spent Sunday night with friends, and taken Monday on the golf links. It had been a cool windy day, and it was late evening when he came home. All the scents of the spring garden were in our new and pleasant room. In spite of his gaiety and evident relief, I felt more uneasy about him than I had before.

The next day my mother said he had taken cold by travelling with the windows open. He would come down later than usual, but didn't want his breakfast sent up to him; and she did not think that she need put off the day she had planned to spend in town.

I waited to go to my room till I had seen him, and was then

certain that he was really ill. I persuaded him to lie down on the sofa in the sunshine, while I brought him a cup of coffee and his letters. He was pleased to find one from his best friend in America, Harry Thompson, the brilliant sub-editor of the *Saturday Evening Post*. "Read it aloud to me, will you, Fissy?" my father asked me. Harry's letters were always good reading, and this one was specially interesting to us both, with several good jokes in it. He had enclosed some beautifully pressed pansies from his garden that gave my father great pleasure.

I wanted to take his temperature and send for the doctor, but he refused. "Only sit with me," he said, "if you don't want to write." Soon after he fell asleep, and I was able to creep away to telephone little nurse. She came at once, took his temperature which was 102°, and persuaded him to go to bed, while I telephoned for the doctor.

The doctor, when he came, did not take nearly so serious a view of my father as we did; he said my father only had tonsillitis, and must stay in bed for a few days.

My mother, when she returned home, was very much annoyed with me for having sent for nurse; and not at all alarmed. The next day the doctor admitted that my father had pneumonia.

George was just about to go to London for a three days' Chartered Accountancy examination. He wanted to give this up, though it meant postponing his career and his chances for an early marriage. My father was determined George should go, and used his last strength to make him promise to stay in London and sit for the full three days' examination, not coming back till it was finished.

There was a moment of complete understanding between them when they said good-bye. George made an effort he had never made before, and perhaps never known how to make, to show his father his love for him; and father, looking at George in the full height and beauty of his young manhood, felt his last hope satisfied.

Nurse looked after my father by day and the doctor sent in his own night nurse. I sat up in his dressing room to help her, for acute pneumonia is a terrifying illness to nurse and she was young, and sometimes frightened.

It worried my father to see me up at night, but he never guessed that I was a few yards from him in his dressing room, sharing those long fighting hours. He was only sixty-one, and, except for his bronchial trouble, an exceptionally strong and active man. Little nurse was angry that the doctor kept him alive on oxygen. She said if he had been a poor person he would have had no struggle, but become unconscious almost at once.

The last night George slept at home, I had to ask him to go to the nearest hospital for a fresh cylinder, as our spare one leaked. He came back at dawn with two cylinders on his shoulders, between the red may trees, with all the birds singing. He had to leave at nine o'clock and never saw my father alive again.

I had sent for Mary; and Dr. Schacht came down for a consultation from London. His examination merely irritated and exhausted my father, but I think it was a great relief to my mother to have his advice, and lessened the load on all our shoulders.

The night before my father died, I was seized with anger and rebellion. All night long I felt as if some merciless hand was dragging at my father, to pull him through a gap in a stone wall. As fast as we tried to fill the gap, this unseen Power widened it. I could feel the weight of the stones against my hands. Suddenly, towards dawn, I knew with relief and astonishment that it was *we* who were merciless: my father *wanted* to get through the wall. The hand that dragged the stones apart to let him through was helping him to escape. I had heard him tell little nurse that he wanted to live ten years longer; but now I think this wish had left him. Soon after he became delirious, and all day long his beautiful deep voice rang through the house saying the doxology over and over again.

Towards the afternoon his lungs became water-logged, and it was difficult to understand what he said, though he was fully conscious. He said in a bewildered way, though his room was radiant with light, "My eyes are growing dim." Soon afterwards they became fixed, on a photograph of George; and he sank deep into unconsciousness.

Mother had sat with him all through the afternoon, but she went to bed as usual at nine o'clock, and little nurse stayed on with me. The night nurse was worn out, and did not come again. At ten o'clock, my father came round again. "Where's Daisy?" he asked anxiously, "I want Daisy!" This was his tenderest name for my

374

mother. I had not heard him use it for a long time. I ran upstairs and waked her. At first she was terrified, and refused to come down; so that I had to tell her he was dying.

When she had pulled herself together, she behaved with wonderful composure and tenderness. It was still quite light, and the birds had only just stopped singing. My mother sat close to the bed, her hand on his, with her eyes full of smiling love. Peace came to my father like a miracle. Half an hour later, he started up in bed, his eyes brilliant with light, his voice cleared, and he cried with exultation: "I am off on the great adventure!"

I think he saw quite plainly the faces of his beloved dead, for he called their names over one by one in a ringing voice, with an ecstasy of relief and delight, then, in a flash, he fell back, dead.

I took my mother into my room for the night. She cried a little but astonishingly said to me: "Now all my anxieties are at an end!" When I had settled her off, I went back to little nurse; and we did together all that there was to be done.

I sat on the floor at her feet with my head in her lap, and cried at last. I felt like an up-rooted tree—and she comforted me for a sorrow that was far less deep than her own.

Afterwards I went into the garden. I have never seen such colours, or heard such music as on that bright May dawn.

My father died on the 26th of May 1913, so that he missed the shadow of war, and died in the unshaken world to which he belonged.

George struggled magnificently through his nightmare days. I telephoned to him night and morning, and he somehow succeeded in passing this stiff examination before coming down the day before the funeral. Mary arrived the morning after my father's death.

The worst thing I had to do by myself was to cable to Harry, my father's last surviving brother. Harry was going through the crisis of his life. He was parting with a wife he had deeply loved, but whom he had not understood, and who I think had loved, but not understood him.

All through my father's illness, Harry's unhappiness had been uppermost in his mind; in his delirium he had constantly asked me,

"Are Harry and Mary in the next room, or only in my heart?" Now I had to tell Harry that the last of his family was dead.

While I was struggling to write the cable out at the Post Office, I fell fast asleep across the counter. I had been awake for five nights; but I think it was the pain of telling Harry rather than the fatigue that made me fall asleep. I had to force my whole will against itself to send him that cruel message, in his grief. I had already warned him by cable, but for such shocks there is no warning.

I could not do for my father what I wished still to do. I knew well that he would have wanted to be buried at Swanscombe, with all the people who had loved him at his funeral; but nothing would move my mother. My father must be buried immediately, in this new raw place that he had never loved. I only gave way when George said to me: "We must think of the living now, and not make things harder for mother." However, I insisted that at least we should invite all his nearest friends to the funeral and entertain them in the home which had been his. My mother refused to see any of them except her trustee and solicitor, and remained in her room.

About twenty of his friends came, and saw his home, his garden and his books, for the last time. E. H. Coleridge came with an original MS. of Byron's tied round his neck with a string, for fear he might absent-mindedly lay it down and forget what he had done with it. Some of my father's fellow clergy and Mr. Elliot, his beloved friend, our Swanscombe school master, were there, and older friends still from a wider life—among them two of the Wroughton girls, and Bob Arnold from Rochester. The house was alive, strangely alive for the first time, with love and memory, and even laughter. "How he would have enjoyed his own funeral!" one of his friends said to me, "and how he would have made *us* enjoy it!"

52

I did not at first grasp how widely the gulf of my years abroad had separated my mother and myself until we were actually left alone together.

Had I been told, up to the age of nineteen, that I was to be my mother's sole support and companion for her declining years, I should have accepted the prospect with rapture, for until that age I considered my mother to be the most saintly, the most beautiful and the most enchanting personality known to God or man. I asked nothing better than to devote my life to serving her. But when she told me nine years later that I was to be her guardian angel for the rest of her life, I felt my heart slide down into my boots; and there—as regards this prospect—it remained.

Directly after my father's death all my energies were bent upon making this critical change in my mother's life bearable to her, and in hastening on George's wedding so that he might the more quickly and naturally recover from the fearful shock and strain he had just been through.

Four months later, George was permanently and happily married to the prettiest bride I have ever seen. My mother could not face the emotional strain of the ceremony, but Mary, just back from a Paris visit to the MacCords, and dressed by them in grey and violet, in spite of her advancing thirties was quite the smartest person in the church, looking nearly as pretty as the bride. I forget what I wore, but I well remember what, to my intense and private astonishment, was pinned on my dress. It was a spray of white heather and lilies of the valley, sent to me by Ernan.

For many years we had lost sight of each other when, in 1913, just after my father's death, I received a letter of sympathy from Ernan, through my publishers. He suggested that, since our broken engagement was so long a thing of the past, we might well meet again as friends. I had no reason to refuse, for there had never been a quarrel or as much as a discussion over the breaking of our engagement. Yet I accepted his suggestion with as much fear as joy. To me the past had been devastating and irrevocable. I never thought that I should see or hear from Ernan again; and here I was, four years later, wearing his flowers at my brother's wedding!

The time that followed between this letter and our marriage was not the easiest part of my emotional life. I told no one but Lislie of Ernan's partial return.

I did not know what was in Ernan's mind or heart; but it was inevitable that after the intense intimacy of the past the old tenderness, the old words even, might—like a dangerous Fifth Column—infiltrate into the composure of our platonic life. The past still meant everything to me, but I thought that it might mean nothing to him. Although we had not been in personal touch for four years, in 1911 I had seen his name with that of Frank Lascelles all over London.

The Festival of Empire, with its spectacular appeal and its thousands of performers, was perhaps the last great public symbol of our "far flung" Empire. In the transformed grounds of the Crystal Palace, every Parliament building of each of our Dominions was duplicated. It was the most grandiose and comprehensive of all Frank's creations as well as the most successful. The part Ernan played in it was that of counsellor, exponent, partner, and interpreter, not only of the Festival, but of Frank himself. Royalty opened, and supported it. On his birthday, King George V invited as his guests two hundred thousand London school children. King George V, Queen Mary, Queen Alexandra and her sister, the Dowager Empress of Russia, visited the Pageant in turn.

I greatly wanted to see it, but fear held me back. I was afraid of two things: I might see Ernan again, and he might think that I intentionally wanted to see him; and if I did see him I was still more afraid that my new adjustments might break down, and memory throw me back into a conquered pain. Lislie, with her greater generosity and wisdom, urged me to go. "It's the greatest thing of his life, Phil," she told me, "you ought to see it and enjoy it! Nothing could please him better and surprise him *less*, than that you *should* go! What does it matter if you *do* see him—though you're not likely to, in all those thousands, but if you do—he is the same Ernan! He won't think anything, except that you wanted to share his Pageant with him—and he wouldn't be human if he didn't want you to share it!"

I couldn't explain to Lislie, though I knew she was right, that I was *too* human! I couldn't face the re-opening of what had once been closed. Yet I always regretted my lack of courage, for had I seen the Festival Ernan and I would have possessed, in all the years that followed, the great bond of having shared the greatest of his efforts, and the most shiningly successful of his experiences. Instead I asked Lislie to go and see it for me, and to let me look at it through her eyes. So the Festival ended, and the next two years slipped by without even the sound of Ernan's name.

It had not been difficult, though more difficult than I had expected, to persuade my mother to sell the Bromley house and live in London. She had always preferred London to any other place, and had nothing but painful memories of Bromley, but I was increasingly to find that any change, or any activity, unless I undertook the whole of it for her, was now beyond her powers. She had retreated from the time of Wilmett's death; after my father's, she became incapable of any advance. She reluctantly agreed to go abroad with me the following winter if I made all the arrangements, but she was without choice as to destination. Rome, if it had sunshine, would do as well as anywhere else. I asked her if there was anything I could do, to make this first winter more bearable for her. Her eyes lit up. "Yes," she said promptly, "there is one thing you can do to please me. Promise me to make no friends at all on our travels!" I promised with a sinking heart, for to me the chief joys of travel were its human contacts, nor could I ever separate them from the scenes of which they were so substantial a part.

I fear I did not keep strictly to the letter of this promise, but I cut away any developing of opportunity as faithfully as I could.

It was a gloomy winter in spite of Rome. My mother must have found me an exhausting and provoking companion. I wanted her to share my delight in pictures, statues, palaces and churches. I gave all this up very slowly and reluctantly. Surely—surely—however unhappy she was, she must want to see the Boy with the Thorn? The Dying Gladiator? The Marble Faun? I reproached myself for not sufficiently considering her grief; but I found that it was not only grief that held her back from the pursuit of beauty. She *could* find pleasure in the Borghese Gardens, where stout Roman nurses, with brilliant coloured ribbons floating down their backs, balanced rather grim little olive skinned babies on white laced cushions in their substantial arms. She enjoyed the Roman shop windows, the English tea-shop, and the Library where she changed her books. She would not set foot in the Campagna; though I once had a happy experience with her, in the Villa Adriano. Here among the roofless pink walls, where the Emperor Hadrian stabbed his best friend to death for making too pointed a witticism, the purple violets grew so thick it was impossible not to step on them, and their scent sweetened all the air. My mother was shocked at my buying a whole bottle of the famous Adriano wine to drink with our meagre hotel lunch, but when she had once tasted it, to my delight she drank more than half the bottle. She was in theory a stern teetotaller, but on this occasion she threw theory to the winds, and really enjoyed herself.

It was during this interminable and sunless winter that I had finally to admit to myself, my discovery growing in painfulness with my understanding, that my mother refused, and would go on refusing, the two things on which my heart was set—human fellowship and the pursuit of the imagination.

My social activity horrified her; my work-life she brushed aside, as she had my father's. What she wanted, and what she failed to get, was a nurse-companion sufficiently delicate to share all her exclusions. What she got instead was a creature active as dynamite, who wanted to exclude nothing that adventure prompted.

We both suffered ferociously, and without intermission, till my marriage four years later; but my poor mother was the least to blame and the worse sufferer of the two—she was also the more lonely.

I know now that I could have improved our situation if I had realized that all my mother's exclusions were the result of fear, fear which had been unassimilated throughout her childhood, and haunted all her life. Had I shown greater tenderness, and a non-conducting firmness—where her weaknesses assailed my own contribution to life—I might have done much to free my own activities and to diminish her fears. As it was, I gave in without much show of tenderness on occasions when I should have quietly gone my own way; and refused to give in where it would not have hurt me, and would have benefited her.

Nor was my domestic attitude greatly assisted by the forceful impact of a new friend—Ezra Pound. Parents in Ezra's eyes were the natural enemies of children, and a child who did not try to get rid of his parents was a superfluous nonentity. Surely, he asked me, I did not want to go down to posterity as an example of filial piety?

It was at one of May Sinclair's literary parties that I first met Ezra.

I had been looking forward to this rare party with longing, for here at last I expected to meet the fine flower of intellectual London. It was a great occasion, being the first public appearance of Mrs. J. M. Barrie, who had recently left her husband for another and younger man. It seemed to me an insufficient fact to account for their being treated like royalty, and I thought a little wistfully of Capri, since, if it was a question of immorality being successful, I thought that Capri could do considerably better than London; and without awe.

I could not help thinking it a pity that everyone in the room except this young man, who was my own age and whom I found markedly distasteful, should look over forty and dye their hair—especially the men. This particular group, of which May Sinclair was the centre, called themselves Graeco-Romans, and managed to be both earnest and apathetic at the same time.

Suddenly the door opened, and a tall slim young man projected himself into the room with the force of a bullet. He had red hair, a gold-red goatee, and wore an open shirt. If an electric eel had been flung into a tank of half conscious fish, its effect must have been the same. A strange, aggressive, bark-like cough heralded his utterances, and he had incredibly bright blue eyes. Ezra, I delighted to envisage, had no awe. I had risen abruptly to leave Barries' successor, whom I found insufferable, when May Sinclair introduced me to Ezra, telling him that I was half American. It might have been the worst of introductions, since Ezra had lately shaken off vituperatively, and by intention for ever, the dust of his native land; but instantly we found that we could both laugh. We could say anything we liked to each other and laugh at anything either of us said. We laughed at England, we laughed at America, we laughed at each other. We had a wonderful time together. The rest of the room drew away its skirts from us, and stared in offended silence. We were enjoying ourselves. We were not respecting the dazzling portent of living in sin, presented to us in the person of Mrs. Barrie and her new partner. It was life that we respected.

Ezra was at this time prepared to hurl incendiary bombs of wit and scorn at every roof in London. He was a born debunker; and London was his immediate target. To shock and to shock again was all Ezra ever asked of life.

His mind was like a rapier, and it struck, with keenness and force, from an impeccable core of integrity. Religion—sex—money; all were to go down before him, in the light of concrete fact. Ezra's thoughts may all have been heresies—and indeed most of them were at this period when they first occurred to him—but they were the kind of heresies that stakes were made for. You could not have got rid of Ezra except by fire. Perhaps you could not have got rid of him even then, for some of his thoughts are still, nearly forty years later, the leading lights of the newest generation of poets.

When I got up to go—and nobody wanted us to remain, least of all the now thoroughly offended Mrs. Barrie and her companion —Ezra came with me.

There was never anything either romantic or even intimate— —unless to be intellectually direct *is* intimate—about our subsequent relationship; but to me it was a priceless and permanent possession.

At one time Ezra thought of bringing Yeats—whose poetry he was stripping bare to the bone—to live near us at Bromley, and asked me to find a place for them to live in. I found a broken down mill on a common covered with gorse, which looked precisely the place for them and could be picked up for a song, but it came to nothing. Nevertheless Ezra came to spend a week end with Lislie and myself at Bromley, in my mother's intentional absence, and it was then that Ezra started to teach me how to read and write. Unfortunately Lislie took a deep and lasting dislike to him. "If I could only make up my mind," Ezra said to me on this occasion, "if you were a romantic or a realist, I should know what to do with you!" "But why can't I be both?" I persuasively suggested. That was the point at issue. I couldn't according to Ezra's creed *be* both; and according to mine I could not give up either. I was as willing to learn as Ezra was to teach; but I wished to make up my own mind as to the value of what I learned. In fact I was a fellow rebel. I was never the stuff out of which satisfactory disciples are made. Nevertheless I have profited all my working life by this impact with Ezra's disruptive, iconoclastic mind. "I don't know whether you can write or not," Ezra eventually told me, "but I do know that you're damned easy to read." If I was, he made me more so. Half a dozen at least of his dictums stuck in my mind like barbs.

Almost immediately after meeting him I wrote one of my best short stories, "The Liqueur Glass," and I finished "The Captive," the first of my novels which really became mine.

If Paul opened my mind, it was Ezra who showed me what to put in it; and also what to throw out of it.

At a time when he was—as usual—nearly penniless, he gave me the best meal I had ever tasted, and drove into me a respect for food and drink which greatly contributed to the satisfactions of life. He helped to place my stories in "The Smart Set" when he was acting as its sub-editor.

If I had done what he wanted me to do, left my mother, and lived on and for my work, I think he would have done still more for me; for I should then have had the advantage of living among the youngest and keenest minds of my day and sharing their adventurous outlook. Ezra and I were the same age, and our contemporaries were the brains of the rising twentieth century. There were, however, far greater advantages that I should have had to resign, had I become one of the band of intellectual Plymouth Brothers led by Ezra Pound.

I should have lost the larger life I was to live in Europe; and the deepest of my human relationships.

I might have had to give up Lislie as well, for she had neither the time nor the inclination for intellectuals; and it is probable that I might never again have met Ernan.

The art of writing, though a skilled profession, is greatly dependent on the art of living; and I am thankful to remember that at this juncture of my life I made the right choice—effortlessly—and without even realizing that the choice was made.

The mere name of Ezra was anathema to my mother. I think they did once meet at Brunswick Gardens in the hall; but never again. In 1912, when Lislie and I went to Rome for the winter, Ezra gave me an introduction to his great friend and disciple, H.D., and I later met Richard Aldington through Hilda.

I made a great many mistakes over these two. I laugh now when I think of their nature: but I found them highly stimulating as companions, though I agreed with Lislie, who was violently shocked at their unkind treatment of H.D.'s simple and kindly parents. We were also struck with H.D.'s ignorance of nature. "She cannot be a real poet, Phil," Lislie told me indignantly, "or she would know a lamb's bleat and not ask what kind of a bird it was!"

H.D. was a mysterious girl, an introvert with a curious Victorian streak of docile femininity which had to battle with her twentieth century revolts. I thought—and still think—her poems as lovely as salted shells washed up out of reach of the tide. I made the mistake of admiring these poems of H.D.'s as much, or more than I admired Ezra's, and I thought Richard Aldington's inferior to either. No one was more annoyed by these heretical opinions than Hilda. Richard Aldington in his turn considered me 'Meredithian'—a term of abuse in those days—but he was a kindly and generous hearted person, and grateful to me for introducing him to Tusculum, which he and Hilda had hitherto overlooked, and subsequently giving them both introductions to my artist friend in Capri.

Richard would, I think, have liked to give me a helping hand when H.D.—not altogether surprisingly—repudiated me forever.

The morals of this literary circle differed fundamentally from Lislie's and mine. If the occasion had arisen, we would not have been averse to considering the world well lost for the sake of a serious, lifelong passion; but we still considered the world to be well worth keeping. The set to which H.D. and Ezra belonged were not only prepared to lose the world, they wanted to kick it away from them on the slightest provocation, or even on no provocation at all; indeed it was a pleasure to them simply to kick it.

Perhaps it was not their world; but it was Ernan's, Lislie's and mine.

Looking back on what I knew of Ezra, linked with a much later renewal of contact, I think it a sorry business to have thrust this honest and kindly person, with his strange far-reaching gifts, into the exclusive society of homicidal lunatics for no better reason than fascist utterances over a microphone during war-time. Especially it seems to me odd, considering that Ezra's political ideas as then expressed are passionately supported to-day by a large proportion of the Republican party of the United States—who are still allowed at large—that the only American poet to share these ideas is held behind bars for the rest of his natural life.

53

At one of the Crystal Palace auditions in 1911 Ernan had met a musically gifted mother and son. The boy, though only seventeen, had already composed several songs, and his mother was a well-known singing teacher. Ernan's chief interest had always been music, and he set himself to encourage and release the boy's exquisite voice and troubadour talent. It was in this way that Madame Clara Novello and her son, Ivor Novello, became a part of Ernan's life.

Ivor, in spite of his natural beauty and unlimited musical aptitude, was at this period a brilliant but spoilt child, living in the grip of his mother's strong and possessive personality. His family background, though passionately affectionate, was stormy.

In the early autumn of 1912, in a sudden fit of fury, Ivor's Welsh parents parted dramatically. On this occasion Ivor chose to join his father in Cardiff rather than remain with his mother in her London flat. His father agreed to take him, on the condition that he promised never again to communicate with his mother. Ivor promised; however he soon began to miss his mother intolerably, and, having passed through many parental rows, he did not feel that this sudden choice between his parents need be considered irrevocable. He made a pretext to go to London and visited his mother clandestinely, but since he still took his father's side, the quarrel with his mother broke out afresh; and Ivor decided to return to Cardiff. The cause of this quarrel was an ill-mannered pupil of Madame Novello's to whom Ivor and his father took a strong and jealous dislike.

By ill-fortune a friend of his father's had seen Ivor enter his mother's flat. This busybody hastened to report to Mr. Davis, before Ivor's arrival. A trap was prepared for the unsuspecting Ivor. The friend waited in an adjoining room. Mr. Davis asked his son if he had visited his mother's flat. Ivor denied it. He was instantly confronted with the friend, and turned from his father's house.

For the second time that day Ivor travelled the distance between Cardiff to London, exhausted and practically penniless, to discover that his mother was still implacable, and her roof denied him. He dared not return to Cardiff, and did not know where to stay in London without enlarging the scope of the quarrel. Ernan's address was not known to him, but he managed to abstract it from a club porter; and with tear-stained cheeks turned up at midnight on Ernan's doorstep.

Ernan was staying in the home of his mother's oldest friends, two *grandes dames* of Norman descent and rigid Victorian conventions.

The Miss Malets were not the kind of old ladies who entertain angels unawares; they would have expected credentials even from the heavenly host. But there was no denying this young and importunate angel—and Ivor was given sanctuary.

The next day Ernan started to reconcile the Davis parents.

This was a long embattled process, but eventually the parents became fully reconciled to Ivor (who now had his two homes again open to him) and partially reconciled to each other.

The question of Ivor's future, however, still remained a bone of contention. Which should be his home? Mr. Davis wanted Ivor in Cardiff. Madame Novello did not want him in Cardiff. Both parents wanted him out of London to avoid further quarrels with the still unbanished pupil.

Ivor was not anxious for either of these parental shelters. Why could he not, he demanded, go to Canada with Ernan? Someone must co-ordinate the music of the Pageant which was to be prepared in Toronto. Why not Ivor?

Ernan had both the projected Toronto Pageant and the Empire scheme on his hands, and he was now asked to add to these responsibilities the immediate future of this unique and unpredictable boy. The parents were delighted to shelve their problem, and Ivor enchanted with the adventure.

All Ernan's Canadian friendships opened whole-heartedly to entertain the two young men. Ivor was not only thrilled and released by the society of these new friends: he learned habits of disciplined will and social manners, which were to be of permanent value to him.

Ivor's whole nature blossomed out under this strenuous combination of education plus congenial society.

It was in Canada that he wrote his first operetta called "Fickle Jade" and, although it was never published, "Fickle Jade" proved a quarry out of which Ivor drew many of his most successful later songs.

During the winter of 1912, Ernan took Ivor with him on a business trip to New York, where he settled him in rooms opposite the select Home Club. Ivor enjoyed the cooking of the famous French chef and was introduced to the best musical and dramatic society of New York. When Ernan was obliged to return to Canada, Ricardo Martin, the Metropolitan Opera tenor, and his wife, who lived at the Club, took Ivor under their wing.

The spoilt child was gone. No longer forced to be an unwilling battle ground between the strong and uncontrolled natures of his parents, Ivor rapidly developed into the spontaneous and enchanting young man who took and held London, not by storm, but by a faculty which never deserted him of evoking sunshine in others from an unlimited supply of his own.

The Toronto Pageant received considerable Canadian backing, but after promising and prolonged negotiations, local jealousy as to the choice of a site, and other complications, led to its being indefinitely postponed. Ernan returned to London with concrete proposals for the Theatre Scheme, but no immediate and—as he and Frank had hoped—money-producing Pageant. Ivor, with "Fickle Jade" in hand, and full of poise and confidence to face London, returned with him. His prospects of a musical and theatrical career in London with Ernan and his mother's backing were as dazzling as their fulfilment.

Ernan's candle was now burning at both ends and even in the middle. There was the British support to be won for the Theatre Scheme in order to meet the Canadian proposals; there was Ivor to be launched; there was even for himself time to be squeezed into studying drama with Rosina Philippi, and to appear successfully in several parts at the Old Vic. Rosina believed in Ernan's capacity to make a career on the stage, but it was plain that the efforts he was making to become an actor while still desperately struggling to keep the Theatre Scheme going were dangerously taxing his physical powers. I felt convinced that he ought not to jettison his career to save the Scheme or to launch Ivor. I knew what his powers were and I longed to see them used on his own future.

No doubt my anxiety was heightened by jealousy. Besides the preoccupation of Ivor's career, Ernan was emotionally involved in the sentimental attachment of two devoted women. The elder was wildly in love with Frank, the younger with Ernan. Naturally I was like prussic acid to both these women, as well as to Frank, to whom my return must have been intolerable; nor was I much more palatable to Ivor, though in the course of time, through Ernan's patience and understanding, Ivor and I became lifelong friends.

Meanwhile this intimate circle tried their best to destroy an influence which they could not assimilate; while I reacted with great unwisdom, and often invited the wounds which I received.

Perhaps if these two women had not looked on me as a powerful vampire, and I had not thought of them as triumphant rivals, we might have accepted each other with kindness as fellow human beings, and lessened the emotional distraction of Ernan's life.

Our return to our old intimacy ran a hectic and obstructed course, though during the year and a half after my father's death we met increasingly often, and when my mother and I came back from our winter abroad in the spring of 1914, and took No. 15 Brunswick Gardens, Ernan and I saw each other constantly.

Yet it took some time for Ernan's life to filter back into mine, or for me to grasp the strength of the obligations that he felt still bound him to Frank, and even more strongly to the ideal that had inspired them in common, from the days of the Quebec Tercentenary in 1908. They had both believed they could support and strengthen the ties of the Commonwealth by the cultural bond of the Dominion Theatre Scheme; but Ernan now fully realized that Frank's creative power had come to an end. His power of showmanship remained, but he no longer desired to show anything except himself.

The Festival achieved all that it had set out to do, on a scale of the utmost magnificence, although its guarantors had to be called on to the full. Two unforeseen financial burdens were forced upon its producers. One was the great transport strike, which involved the cancellation of heavy provincial bookings; and the other was the death of Edward VII in 1910, just before he was to open the Festival. This not only caused fresh expense, but a year's postponement.

Lord Plymouth, who was a most loyal and indefatigable chairman, bore the full brunt of these misfortunes; but that the Festival survived in all its glory into 1911, was also due to Ernan's determined foresight in insuring against the death of the King.

Never had England seen such a Festival; it included an historic Pageant which ran in three-day cycles during the whole summer and was carried out by ten thousand voluntary performers, each borough of London contributing a scene.

In the Crystal Palace grounds were exact replicas of the Overseas Dominions Parliament Buildings, each standing complete in its own grounds, and containing exhibitions of its chief produce.

The splendour of this Festival of Empire, supported by great names and fortunes, and visited by Royalty, went to Frank's head. He was now determined to ignore all danger signals of a practical kind for the Theatre Scheme. Everything must bend to his will—men, money, time and opportunity. He could not adjust to the business world as it was, the business world must adjust to him. Ernan, warnings and advice overlooked, must somehow carry out the practical side of his dreams.

For two more years Ernan continued the long up-hill battle. Canada was behind him, but wanted the parent company to be floated in England, with England contributing half the capital. Ernan managed to interest many influential people with whom he had come into contact during the Festival. But it was an uneasy moment for uncertain financial ventures. The men he approached wanted Canada to make the first commitments.

After endless negotiations, arrangements were finally completed;

but Lord Strathcona's death in 1914—before his promised agreement to underwrite the share capital for £200,000 was signed—darkened the hopes of the Empire Theatre project; the war finally extinguished them.

The spring of 1914 was the most beautiful and brilliant spring London was ever to know—the last miraculous moment before a great rose drops.

The window boxes in the West End were as individual as their inmates in glory.

The sun shone with exaggerated benevolence. Dutch tulips invaded London parks in great streams of colour; never had the bluebells in the woods of Kew flamed in more burning azure. The endless shops were filled to the brim as if a giant hand had poured from an invisible cornucopia all the riches of the world.

At the peak of her incredible loveliness, Pavlova danced with Mordkin. She was like a woman in shape, a bird in flight, and her motion was as unpredictable as a leaping wave's. She could float and soar; she could leap and run; she had discovered both a new medium and an unknown physical power. She danced like "an unbodied joy whose race has just begun."

Chaliapin, singing for the first time in London, may have been said to bring on the war: in "Khovantschina" by Moussorgsky his effortless great voice carried us through the music until—at the end of that last tragic act—it was we, as well as the persecuted Brotherhood, who passed under his leadership into the flames.

Nor was this life of magic beyond those of small means. For half a crown we could see a new Bernard Shaw play; and for five shillings, after standing for hours in a queue, we could dash up the crowded stairs, clasping a brass token, to the gallery of Drury Lane, and watch Nijinski in "L'après-midi d'un Faune" reach the mad peak of his tremendous skill. "How can you stay in the air so long?" an admirer asked him. "The real question is: why should I ever come down?" replied Nijinski.

Even more thrilling than the pinnacle of art was the life of that tremendous spring. Slums and war clouds were forgotten. Park Lane pulsed its brilliant way crowded with resplendent diners out. Never had there been so many dinners—weddings—dances.

Footmen on doorsteps whistled for taxis all night long. We even had a new poet—Rupert Brooke—to read aloud to each other on our home-coming.

There was only one uneasy moment when an Austrian Arch-Duke was murdered in a far away and inconspicuous place called Sarajevo; but our startled wits soon returned to our fools' paradise.

Three days before war was declared our private lives came to a stop. I found myself unable to read a word except headlines in newspapers.

We talked breathlessly of total war; but none of us knew what it meant.

On the evening after war was declared we rode on the top of a bus to Westminster. The whole, vast city swam in light and laughter.

Street sellers offered crêpe rosettes for the Kaiser on trays, or handed out black-edged cards with "In Memoriam, poor old Bill," printed on them.

No one guessed that war—like peace—is indivisible.

The crowds filling the streets cheered and sang as light-heartedly as children promised a treat.

54

The first world war was more human and I think more individually agonizing than the second.

The casualty list was far longer; and a daily diet. The life of a second lieutenant in France was reckoned at fifteen days.

From our coasts we heard the sound of the guns upon the battlefield. The men's leaves were more frequent, yet the gulf between the imagination of men and women was much wider. The women of the first world war could not know, since few of their men could tell them, what they suffered. Rats, mud, dirt and noisy death cannot be readily transferred from experience into imagination. In the second world war the boys and girls of 1939 joined in one service and spoke the same language.

Ernan and I wrote several times a week to each other, and shared at least half of his short leaves, but there was still no defined relationship between us.

The moment war was declared, rather than wait for the slow process of enlistment and training Ernan bombarded the War Office to be sent to the Front immediately, on the strength of his languages. He had done the Government a service in 1911, and the War Office agreed to give him a French and German test, which he passed A.1. No doubt the excellent references from General Sir John Hanbury Williams, Lord Grey, "Lulu Harcourt", and Colonel Drummond Hay, who at that time was commanding the Coldstream Guards, expedited Ernan's hopes.

In September 1914 he was ordered to Marseilles, where he joined the 34th Poona Horse as interpreter. The Poona Horse had just arrived from India. Two of its Squadrons came from the old Third

Bombay Cavalry once commanded by Ernan's grandfather, Sir John Forbes, and with whom his name was a household word; so that Ernan found himself accepted as one of themselves. Few working relationships could have been happier or deeper in the years that followed, both among officers and men. This "band of brothers"—a very exclusive and fastidious band—gave Ernan a fellowship he never forgot or ceased to prize.

Before he left England, Ernan had passed his last few days at Brunswick Gardens, and left me his Next of Kin, before he vanished into a sunny silence.

We still thought the war—and that a victorious one—would be over by Christmas.

My mother, who had always found Ernan's society most congenial, made no difficulty whatever about his re-entry into our lives.

Mary had just gone to Egypt with her great friend, Sister Margaret Clare, a distinguished social worker; and they were trapped in Cairo together, for the next five years. George was now married, an expectant father with a home of his own.

The long September days were empty, but not unendurable until the hammer blows of the war began to strike down on us.

One Sunday morning, on the way to an early service at St. Mary Abbot's, I saw people standing like stones reading their newspapers. They were not only reading them, but glancing over them at each other in deep concern—some of them actually spoke of their concern—to perfect strangers. It was the retreat from Mons.

Betty and Maida, who had been on a visit to us that spring, suddenly reappeared as refugees on our doorstep. I had telegraphed them to come, and they had had a terrible week escaping from Paris in a crowd of fleeing tourists. After an unimaginable journey in an overcrowded boat, they arrived at Brunswick Gardens, immaculately clad with clean white kid gloves on. No more welcome guests ever came to share mutual misfortunes.

The German blunder on the Marne gave us a momentary respite; but for the next three years I never left the house without expecting to find the telegram I dreaded on my return.

By Christmas the Poona Horse were in the trenches at Festubert.

As the war dragged mercilessly on, Lislie and I felt unable to bear our lack of participation. We were not strong enough for nursing or land work. Lislie was now acting as morning secretary to a West End doctor, and she decided as well to book-keep the finances of the Fund for Belgian Refugees, of which Dr. Des Voeux was treasurer; this involved always two, and often four hours' extra work a day.

I joined my friend, Florence Bonus, at the Hammersmith Town Hall, to help look after three thousand Belgian refugees posted to the Hammersmith and Shepherd's Bush district.

Florence worked all day at the Town Hall, managing the accounts and making all decisions in our many emergencies. My part of the job was to find—and keep—the Belgians suitable lodgings, to translate for them in their difficulties, and to take them to hospital when they required medical attention. I had to deal with any incidents that turned up on my visits—shocked or irate landladies were the form these incidents usually took—and it was upon the information that I raked in for her that Florence based her decisions. For eighteen months we worked in the utmost harmony together for eight or ten hours a day; then Florence fell ill and had to be away for over a month.

I managed to find two inexperienced but efficient girls, who could do my outside work, while I took over Florence's job.

I had no knowledge of book-keeping, nor did I know much about the Law, though here I had the kindly help of the Town Clerk as well as the police to fall back upon. Some of our problems came from dubious passports, some from secret funds while claiming grants; and among our very fine average of industrious and decent workers there was a handful of remarkably black sheep.

I had several memorable interviews with the police about these tough propositions. Some I felt were more sinned against than sinning, and I tried to get them off. Once a policeman said to me with stern kindness, "What you want to remember, Miss, with these 'ere Belgians is that we have to act on what you say. So if you don't want us to act, you'd best say as little as possible." I took this wise advice deeply to heart.

Uncle Melville too helped to preserve my sanity. "Since you have more to do than usual," he wrote, "I should advise taking your first half-hour off completely. Refuse all interruptions, and spend this time planning how and when to do what lies before you. By doing this you will save both time and confusion." This was not only true, but I also found that this period, in which I did nothing but plan, greatly relieved me from nervous tension.

I do not know how I managed to do the accounts, but at the end of the month I was only sixpence out, and that to the good. However, I am bound to admit that the Chartered Accountant, who looked through the books on Florence's return, told me that in all his long and varied experience he had never come upon a more curious, and to him difficult, method of accountancy. "I should have hardly thought it possible," he said benevolently, "for accounts to be done in this manner; never mind, since it has all come out quite successfully, but I must confess I was glad that I had had some training in cypher reading, before I was asked to audit your accounts!"

While Florence was away the Government demanded an exact report on the means of each refugee, upon which they intended to base a more stringent arrangement of grants.

There was a mother and child in whom both Florence and I were equally interested. The child was dangerously ill with heart disease, and Florence had allowed them a considerable amount of the marginal fund, which was no longer at our disposal. It seemed to me that I had no option but to state the actual facts, while pressing the difficulties of Mme Best's situation strongly upon the authorities.

Mme Best was immediately docked of all her extra grants, and Florence upon her return was furious. Florence, I found, once annoyed stayed annoyed; and I too was resentful at having my friendly relations with mother and child ruthlessly broken. I knew that I had done quite as much for them as Florence had. I had nursed the child two afternoons a week, to free Mme Best, and was deeply attached to them both. Now Mme Best not unnaturally regarded me as a fiend.

I had worked hard and not unsuccessfully at my double task; and I felt that with all the Belgians more or less settled in, and catered for, I could now withdraw; so I persuaded my two half-timers to stay on with Florence, and resigned.

I had been asked to join the Ministry of Information under the writer, John Buchan, later Lord Tweedsmuir; and after a short holiday at Tintagel, I started to work for him. There was probably no one in Europe easier or better to work for than John Buchan, if you wanted to work. The jobs he gave me were more suitable, both for my health and for my working capacity, than the Hammersmith work had been.

In 1915, almost overnight, and as it were by accident, "The Dark Tower" became the book of the hour in the U.S.A.—just as, twenty-five years later in 1940, "The Mortal Storm" took the same place, in the same country, during the second world war.

It had been a great surprise and reassurance six months earlier to have "The Dark Tower" accepted as a serial in "The Century Magazine"; but when on publication it soared into the full American limelight, I was placed on a different footing both as an author and—although I did not grasp it—as a human being.

Under its English title, "Secretly Armed", "The Dark Tower" had dropped quietly like a stone into the silence of my small British public. It was hardly noticed by reviewers, and I was no better known after its appearance than I had been before it.

Perhaps I should have taken my American future more seriously had I been on the other side of the Atlantic, or less overclouded by the war shadows and my bitter personal anxieties. As it was I accepted the fact of my new prosperity with gratitude because it meant that I could free Lislie from her financial anxieties, and exercise more freedom about my own future; but the impression it made on me was extraordinarily slight. My work for John Buchan continued, and did not prevent my writing; that was all, during those war years, that I could carry.

Ernan was now in possession of a second star and had been asked by the G.O.C. Fifth Cavalry Division to become his A.D.C. This meant for a while comparative safety, and, when the Division was moved to the St. Quentin area, entailed vital liaison work with the French.

Ernan resigned this personal appointment as A.D.C. when the

Indian army was transferred to Egypt, in order to join his brother Fred's hard-fighting regiment, the 7/8 K.O.S.B. east of Arras.

This "act of insubordination", as the G.O.C. called it, cost Ernan a Légion d'Honneur that the French wanted him to have as a token of their warm appreciation of his special services; but this was now firmly side-tracked by his truculent General.

Rage and affection combined in General MacAndrew's treatment of the man he used to call "the best A.D.C. in France"; but the General's fury at his decision did not prevent Ernan's being mentioned in Despatches.

If I had not been working for the Ministry I might not have been given a travel permit to Paris in 1915, which enabled me to spend a long leave—as long as a week—with Ernan in the Boulevard Arago.

On my way to the boat, I fell into conversation with a very young girl, quietly crying behind a copy of *Punch*. I discovered that she had missed her uncle at Charing Cross, who was to have provided her with funds for the journey. She had only her ticket to Paris, and nowhere to go when she arrived. She said she had heard there was a Travellers' Aid Society, and hoped they would put her up till her uncle could wire funds.

I doubted if the Travellers' Aid Society functioned in war-time, and rather gingerly offered myself as a substitute. I feared Edith might think me an agent for the White Slave Traffic, then very much a subject of dread to young girls travelling alone. However, Edith must have had an unsuspicious nature, for she eagerly accepted my offer, and we arrived on the boat together in a dense fog, feeling far more cheerful for each other's company.

It was a still night and we slept well, only to find on waking that we had never left the dock; and that the fog was quite as thick.

All day the fog never lifted, but towards evening the Captain was galvanized, by some very important persons in a temper, to put out to sea. It was rough as well as foggy, which, while it reduced the danger from submarines, increased that of collisions. During the night five different boats hooted madly within a few yards of us.

The night was further enlivened for us by a lady in a black crêpe de chine nightgown who had constant fits of hysterics, which were not subdued by her resorting constantly to a bottle of brandy. She passionately refused to put on her lifebelt, when the order reached us; and I went to beg the stewardess to help persuade her into this slight measure of security. "I'll help you with the young lady, with pleasure," the stewardess told me, "if things get any worse; but that sort had *better* drown!"

Drowning, however, was not to befall any of us. We reached Paris late at night in safety. There was no Travellers' Aid on the station, and after a night together at an hotel, I was greatly surprised to find, when we arrived at the Boulevard Arago next morning, that Betty took a dim view of Edith. When told that the friends with whom Edith was going to stay in Switzerland—they were called Masaryk—were going to set up a republic in Czecho-Slovakia after the war, with the help of the U.S.A., Betty's suspicions deepened. "Phyllis," she said, "now I know that girl is an impostor! Whoever heard of such nonsense!"

However, everything was eventually stretched into security, and Edith sent off with sufficient funds, which she promptly returned, to Switzerland.

Nearly thirty years later I asked Jan Masaryk if he remembered Edith. "Of course I do," he said, laughing, "she lived with my people for two years—and I very nearly married her!"

This leave of Ernan's was both transient and agonizing.

On my way home I ran into the victims of the first gas attacks.

All civilian travellers were hustled out of their train on to a side platform, to enable the Red Cross train to unload more quickly from the main platform.

We stood for two and a half hours watching the men being lifted out on stretchers. They were not really men any more, these tortured boys, but green and grey spectres, asphyxiated and gasping.

A young doctor with a loaded syringe in his hand sprinted down the long platform to fall on his knees by the side of the first stretcher. "There—there, my boy!" he cried with the tenderness of a mother, "there—there!" The whole of pity was in his voice and in the stern dedicated face of the nurse who waited on him.

When I found myself on the boat I only wanted one thing, and that was for the boat to go down immediately. My wish was very nearly gratified. While I was still wondering if it would not be possible for me to slide over the railings unobserved, a sailor on the look-out sprang down on deck gesticulating towards what looked like a harmless black buoy. The engines reversed in time to escape a mine; and being congratulated by two staff officers on the calm with which I shared a danger I had not understood, I reluctantly postponed my personal exit.

The ship drove on over a calm azure sea, into the grimmest April man ever gave to his fellow-man.

During the next two years I continued my work for the Ministry and wrote "Second Fiddle" and "A Servant of Reality". I shared Ernan's leaves, and spent summer holidays with Lislie and her mother, on the Yorkshire moors, and in Cornwall at St. Ives.

In 1917, in mid-July, I went to stay with friends in Amberley. Lislie and her mother were there, and it was there, surrounded by kindly Americans on a green lawn, that I found a letter from Ernan awaiting me. It was a short decisive letter. Would I marry him on his next leave but one?—If I consented he would join me wherever I was next day, from Folkestone.

I had by now given up all thought of marriage, and this letter came as a shock of overwhelming joy. I telegraphed immediate consent; but that evening fear took the place of joy.

I was now thirty-three. I knew nothing of marriage. Was I not too old to learn? A deeper fear than this stirred my heart. Was I sure—in spite of all the good and wise reasons for breaking our former engagement—that there was not some inner failure of my own to meet my lover's need, stronger than any of them? The pain of the past rose up like a wall between us. It was Lislie who demolished the wall. "It's such nonsense," she said severely, "to talk as if there was anything particular about marriage! It is Ernan's being Ernan that matters! All you've got to do is to be happy! You've never been happy without him, and if you can't be happy with him, then all I can say is that you must have taken a dislike to happiness!"

When Ernan arrived next day I knew that I had not taken this dislike.

At last we wholly understood each other, and our happiness was complete.

Ernan was now able to explain why he felt that the old obstacles to our marriage could be ignored, and why he was confident of the future. War had greatly simplified his outlook. The open air life suited him physically, and the companionated discipline freed his over-sensitive conscience. While he was in France, a lion-hearted, hard-headed Scottish solicitor, William Fairchild Greig, had freed him from his business difficulties, clearing up the last complications caused by the Theatre Scheme, so that his house was now in order.

With no greater responsibility ahead of him than death, Ernan felt that he could afford love.

55

It was during the first serious air raid London experienced that I bought my wedding dress.

I stood in the open doorway of Marshall and Snelgrove's where I was choosing the material, and watched twenty-five planes, striped yellow and black like hornets, sailing in undisturbed formation over the defenceless city.

The alarm had emptied Oxford Street and sent all the buyers and shop assistants into the basement. Having a greater fear of frightened people than of distant planes, I remained in solitude.

The riches of Eldorado spread about me: counter after counter was filled with silks and satins equally desirable and unguarded. It was almost a pity I felt, in spite of the proverb, that it takes more than opportunity to make a thief.

A belated horse and cart, that had no chance to vanish suddenly like motor vehicles, clopped peacefully down the wide and empty thoroughfare towards Holborn. It must have been the first time in his working life that this horse found himself unimpeded by motor traffic in Oxford Street, at mid-day. London was soundless except for the noise of his hoofs.

I felt as if I had inadvertently dropped out of time into an empty world.

Then the All Clear sounded, and with a roar, traffic returned, and I once more set to work to buy the material for my wedding dress.

I was to wear a terracotta costume with a long coat, a velvet picture hat of a darker shade, and an apricot chiffon blouse with hand-painted butterflies on it; and it was going to be made by the best dressmaker in London.

My mother had said that it would be sheer wickedness to buy a trousseau in war time, but I could not forget that Ernan's mother had told me no one could be legally married in any dress that cost less than thirty-six pounds—then the equivalent of sixty. I compromised between the maternal visions. Lislie had backed the more generous estimate.

After our honeymoon I was to return and share my mother's home at 15 Brunswick Gardens till the war ended.

The only great change that faced me was the parting from Lislie. I had to leave her behind to live her own life, instead of the one she had long weaved into mine.

Fortunately Lislie had made this parting easier for both of us than it would otherwise have been by insisting on separating her work life from mine. Although she had consented, for the sake of her parents and their necessities, to share the over-plus I received from my American successes, she had always firmly refused to be my full-time secretary. She chose instead to earn her living apart from her main preoccupation. Twice a week she spent the night under our roof, and gave me the full benefit of her criticism and advice on my writing as well as typing business letters for me; but her main work remained her half-time job as D.V.'s secretary. This had always been against my wishes, for I had for so long, and so often, guarded her menaced life that I knew I could spare her, in her work life, in ways nobody else could. But on the whole I am sure that her decision was good for us both, and made our parting easier.

For two years after my marriage there was no perceptible difference in our relationship. To love Ernan more was not to love Lislie less. Our affection never changed, but when I left England to live in Vienna our activities were severed. After the war Ernan was offered the post of Passport Control Officer for Austria, Hungary and Yugoslavia with headquarters in Vienna, and then the pattern which Lislie's life and mine had weaved together inevitably fell apart.

How much we had enriched, perhaps how much we had impoverished each other, I shall never know. I only know that without Lislie's serene, untrammelled friendship my life, for many years, would have been denied its sunshine; and that when I lost her, I lost an influence which made me behave—and wish to behave—with considerably more courage and consideration than I found myself behaving after her death.

Lislie had her imperfections, but she never seemed to realize that basic integrity and flawless courage are not a matter of course. She took these great hurdles effortlessly, nor did I ever know her fail to surmount one. She had charm without falsity and courage without aggressiveness. I was not alone in my estimate of her. All her friends, men and women, had the same admiration and confidence in her. Her only brother Basil said to me after her death, "I have been trying to remember if Lislie had any faults but I can't find any."

When I left England in October to await Ernan's marriage leave in 1917, England was half-starved and Paris frozen.

At the Boulevard Arago Betty and Maida were able to procure only a few green sticks for a fire, and the gas we cooked on at the lowest of pressures was only turned on for three half hours a day.

As the bitter winter progressed we went to bed at five o'clock to keep from freezing.

A shell dropped from Big Bertha every quarter of an hour, preceded thirty seconds earlier by shrieks from two clipped sea-gulls, who shared our garden.

We had this punctual warning without fail, but there was no defence except the battlefield. Whatever unusual noise was made we knew must be either a shell or a bomb.

Our wedding had to be postponed for Cambrai. At last the cavalry were to ride into the blue, the way opened for them by the newly invented, preciously secret tanks. But alas! this splendid prospect faded. Our cavalry, after five tense days of hope, were thwarted of their break-through. Paris turned from a frenzy of admiration and joy into sullen reproach. What kind of an ally were we?

The dark December days dragged on—slow, cold and empty.

A blizzard struck the city the day before our wedding. Maida and I walked through it across Paris on pavements like rivers of ice. One of us fell down every few moments. I do not know what Maida felt; but my sensations were those of complete invulnerability;

it was as if I walked on air, and fell, when I had to fall, on a substance softer than a cloud.

Ernan's General had promised us a Queen Anne tea-set and a lavish three weeks' honeymoon; but we were not going to waste a moment of it. Everything that we could prepare before he came, tickets, sleepers, hotel accommodation in the south, were to be arranged before he arrived.

He came that night, powdered with snow, but polished and shining as only cavalry officers knew how to be; and carrying with him a tall white lilac bough the size of a small tree.

We had wanted no audience next day, but to Betty and Maida a wedding without a reception was unimaginable. They stayed up till the small hours transforming the studio and preparing with Maturine, their French cook and my fellow-bride, the full festivities allowed in war time.

Seventy people came to the reception, most of whom neither Ernan nor I had ever met.

Lislie had been refused a passport; but we felt as if she were with us.

Maida's courage and generosity were unforgettable. Her own long engagement to Amerigo had been recently broken, and her heart with it; but she acted as if our happiness were hers.

Betty kept all our heads as well as her own. She had to leave us at the last moment, on our way to the Consulate, to search for a wedding ring. My confidence in her was so deep that I never turned my head to see if she had got it, when, half way through the ceremony, she reappeared with the last gold ring in Paris—just in time to thrust it into Ernan's hand.

We began to get married very early in the day at the Mairie in the Apache Quarter, swept there by friendly Americans in a big car. This was followed by a second civil ceremony at the British Consulate on the right side of the river, and we finally wound up with a celebration at the Embassy Church, still lavishly decorated in red and white flowers for Christmas. It was New Year's Eve, and though all day long it poured with icy rain, I felt as if it were a day in June.

It was a pity, we thought, that we could not go on being married in order to prolong the sensation.

At the wedding reception Ernan nearly came to blows with an Australian soldier friend of Viola Meynell's. He had spoken disrespectfully of the cavalry action at Cambrai.

Ernan announced with fierce gravity that they must go into another room to discuss the matter in private. I was horrified to discover the limitations of a bride's influence, for I could not stop the threatening storm; I was not even allowed to share it.

However, eventually Ernan's exposition of the event, in which his Division had taken part, convinced Viola's friend that the cavalry had not disgraced itself. The real reason for the tragic setback was that the tank penetration had not been deep enough to pierce the German defensive network on a broad enough scale to enable the cavalry to exploit the first surprise advance. The wedding guests sighed with relief, and the reception continued without bloodshed.

When the last guest had gone, Lendall Pitts, Betty's chief admirer, reappeared carrying with respectful solicitude, in a long basket, a bottle of Château Yquem 1870.

At midnight, we boarded the Riviera Express, which ran into a snowdrift at Valence, holding us up for twelve hours longer.

However, Betty had provided even for this contingency by a picnic basket; and nobody could possibly have met a snowdrift on better terms. In the basket there were pâté de foie gras sandwiches, white bread and chocolate, and a bottle of good red wine.

Next day at sunset we found ourselves under a sky of sapphire and apricot, and heard the chattering of palm leaves.

Night dropped on us as we drove to Hyères, out of a sky blown clear by *mistral*, and furnished with enormous stars.

We had been given Queen Victoria's former drawing room at the Hotel Costabelle, a magnificent apartment full of crimson brocaded furniture, with a big balcony overlooking sea and garden.

We had agreed to spend our entire bank balances in equal shares, on these resplendent weeks. How we managed to spend so much money in so short a time I shall never know, but the amount of enjoyment we contrived to obtain was certainly greater than that usually found in so great an expenditure.

We knew what might lie at the end of it; but curiously enough we were far too happy to admit of fear. If grief can blot out the whole beauty of the world, so can happiness wipe out the whole of ugliness.

For three weeks, we were free to realize what we could make out of our

> *long and sure-set liking,*
> *This boundless will to please.*

We, who had had to learn so painfully and for so long how to live apart, had now only to learn how to live together.

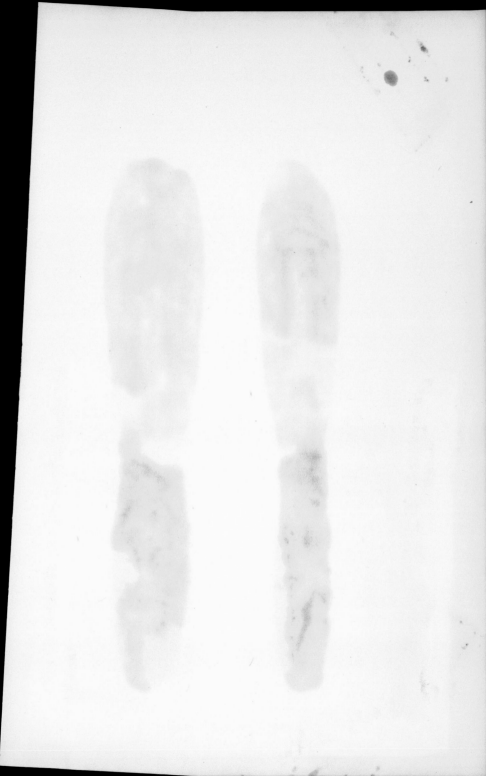